D1602445

A Crisis of Expectations

A Crisis of Expectations

UN Peacekeeping in the 1990s

EDITED BY

Ramesh Thakur
and Carlyle A. Thayer

WestviewPress
A Division of HarperCollins*Publishers*

Copyright © 1995 by Westview Press, Inc., A Division of HarperCollins Publishers, Inc.

Published in 1995 in the United States of America by Westview Press, Inc., 5500 Central Avenue, Boulder, Colorado 80301-2877, and in the United Kingdom by Westview Press, 12 Hid's Copse Road, Cumnor Hill, Oxford OX2 9JJ

Library of Congress Cataloging-in-Publication Data
Thakur, Ramesh Chandra, 1948–
   A crisis of expectations : UN peacekeeping in the 1990s / Ramesh
Thakur and Carlyle A. Thayer ; foreword by Gareth Evans.
      p.   cm.
   Includes index.
   ISBN 0-8133-8840-6
   1. United Nations—Armed Forces.   2. International police.
3. Peace.   I. Thayer, Carlyle A.   II. Title.
JX1981.P7T478   1995
341.5'84—dc20   95-19957
                                                                                  CIP

The paper used in this publication meets the requirements of the American National Standard for Permanence of Paper for Printed Library Materials Z39.48-1984.

10   9   8   7   6   5   4   3   2   1

Contents

Foreword

The horrors of Somalia, Bosnia and Rwanda have brought to the fore, in the starkest terms, the new challenges which the United Nations faces as it seeks to grapple with what is clearly one of its central aims, the promotion and protection of international peace and security. Images of Blue Helmets unable to prevent fighting, or confined to the role of onlookers in the face of horrific abuses, have become all too familiar in the international media. Such perceptions may be having a corrosive effect on public attitudes towards the United Nations, but they overlook the UN's recent positive achievements, such as the humanitarian benefits of these UN operations or its successes in Mozambique, Namibia, Cambodia and El Salvador.

A major tool of UN peace operations efforts for over forty years, peacekeeping is neither defined nor described in the UN Charter. But this has not prevented the UN's peacekeeping effort rightly winning credit over the years, not least with a Nobel Peace Prize in 1988, for the important role it has played in international efforts to restore peace. Nor has it prevented UN peacekeeping activities expanding in recent years from its more traditional roles (monitoring, supervising and verifying arrangements for cease-fires, troop withdrawals, or respect for buffer zones) to cover activities such as election monitoring and organisation, human rights protection, and assisting with civil administration functions during the transition to independence or democracy. These ambitious changes have not only led to peacekeeping operations with more complex mandates, and with make-ups and sizes of a much greater order than was the case in the past. They have also required more thorough and focused thinking by the international community about the nature and proper scope of peacekeeping—about how to match expectations with harsh realities.

A Crisis of Expectations: UN Peacekeeping in the 1990s represents a very useful and timely contribution to the burgeoning international literature in the field of peacekeeping. It seeks to address the various dimensions of the concept of peacekeeping, providing both case studies of the major UN peacekeeping operations and analyses of the various conceptual questions which the qualitative and quantitative changes that the practice of UN peacekeeping has, since the end of the Cold War, thrown up for consideration. As such, it is a very welcome addition to the ongoing international debate about the role and nature of UN peacekeeping in the 1990s.

Senator Gareth Evans
Minister for Foreign Affairs
Canberra

Acknowledgments

Ramesh Thakur would like to record his appreciation of the work done by his research assistant Christine Wilson of the Peace Research Centre, Australian National University. She proofread the manuscript and compiled the index with exemplary meticulousness. Carlyle A. Thayer would like to thank the International Institute for Strategic Studies (IISS) for financial support which enabled him to visit Cambodia in 1993. He would also like to acknowledge the assistance and support that he received from Captain D. M. Fitzerald, the Australian Deputy Attache to the Supreme National Council; Dr. William Maley of the Australian Defence Force Academy; Sue Aitken, formerly with the *Canberra Times;* Harish Mehta, Indochina correspondent for the *Business Times* (Singapore); and Dr. Frank Frost, Legislative Research Service, Parliament House, Canberra.

Ramesh Thakur
Carlyle A. Thayer

.

About the Editors and Contributors

Amitav Acharya is Associate Professor, Department of Political Science, York University, Toronto. He is also a Research Fellow at York's Centre for International and Strategic Studies. His research focuses on Southeast Asian politics, regional security and conflict management. His recent publications include *A New Regional Order in Southeast Asia: ASEAN in the Post-Cold War Era* (London: International Institute for Strategic Studies, 1993).

Mats R. Berdal is a graduate in International Relations from the London School of Economics and Oxford University where he completed his doctorate in 1992. He is presently a Research Fellow at the International Institute for Strategic Studies (IISS) in London specialising in the study of UN peacekeeping and, more generally, the problems of ethnic conflict and the use of force in international relations after the Cold War.

Kenneth Christie is a Lecturer in Politics at the University of Natal in South Africa. He is the author of *Political Protest in Northern Ireland: Continuity and Change* (Reading: Link Press, 1992) and *Problems in European Politics* (Chicago: Nelson-Hall, 1994).

Raúl González Díaz received his B.A. and M.A. degrees in International Relations from the American University in Washington, D.C., and will commence his Ph.D. studies in Political Science at the University of Massachusetts (Amherst) in Fall 1995.

Paul F. Diehl is Professor of Political Science at the University of Illinois at Urbana-Champaign. Among other works, he is the author of *International Peacekeeping* (Baltimore: Johns Hopkins University Press, 1993) and *Territorial Changes and International Conflict* (London: Routledge, 1992).

Gerald Hensley has been the New Zealand Secretary of Defence since 1991. He previously held positions as Coordinator, Domestic and External

Security, 1987–89; Head of the Prime Minister's Department, 1980–87; and High Commissioner in Singapore, 1976–80. He was a Fellow at the Center of International Affairs, Harvard University, 1989–90.

Alan James is Research Professor of International Relations at Keele University in the United Kingdom. Among other works he is the author of *Sovereign Statehood: The Basis of International Society* (London: Allen and Unwin, 1986), and *Peacekeeping in International Politics* (London: Macmillan, in association with the International Institute for Strategic Studies, 1990).

Robert C. Johansen is Director of Graduate Studies and Senior Fellow at the Joan B. Kroc Institute for International Peace Studies and Professor of Government at the University of Notre Dame. He is the author of *The National Interest and the Human Interest: An Analysis of U.S. Foreign Policy* (Princeton: Princeton University Press, 1980), *Toward an Alternative Security System* (New York: World Policy Institute), and co-editor of *The Constitutional Foundations of World Peace* (New York: State University of New York Press).

Susan R. Lamb was awarded Honours degrees in Political Studies and Law from the University of Otago in New Zealand. She is presently a Rhodes Scholar reading for a doctorate in public international law at Balliol College, Oxford.

Samuel M. Makinda is Head of the Politics Department at Murdoch University in Perth, Australia, and Associate Editor of the *Current Affairs Bulletin*. He has been a researcher at the University of Cambridge, the International Institute for Strategic Studies in London, and the Brookings Institution in Washington, D.C. His recent publications include *Seeking Peace From Chaos: Humanitarian Intervention in Somalia* (London & Boulder: Lynne Rienner, 1993) and *Security in the Horn of Africa* (London: Brassey's for the International Institute for Strategic Studies, 1992).

William Maley is Senior Lecturer in Politics, University College, University of New South Wales, Australia. He has co-authored *Regime Change in Afghanistan: Foreign Intervention and the Politics of Legitimacy* (Boulder: Westview, 1991) and co-edited *Russia in Search of Its Future* (Cambridge: Cambridge University Press, 1994). He was a registered International Observer at the 1993 Cambodian election.

Robert G. Patman is a Lecturer in International Relations at the University of Otago in New Zealand. He is the author of *The Soviet Union in the Horn of Africa: The Diplomacy of Intervention and Disengagement* (Cambridge: Cambridge University Press, 1990). He is presently engaged in research on the disarmament of warring parties as a complement to peacekeeping operations.

Andrei Raevsky is a Research Associate at the United Nations Institute for Disarmament Research (UNIDIR) in Geneva. He is the author of *Development of Russian National Security Policies: Military Reform* (New York and Geneva: UNIDIR, 1993) and co-author of *Russian Approaches to Peacekeeping Operations* (New York and Geneva: UNIDIR, 1994). He is presently the Primary Project Researcher for UNIDIR's project on "Disarmament and Conflict Resolution: The Disarmament of Warring Parties as an Integral Part of the Settlement of Conflicts."

Ramesh Thakur, Professor of International Relations and Director of Asian Studies at the University of Otago in New Zealand, is Head of the Peace Research Centre at the Australian National University in Canberra for 1995–96. Among other works he is the author of *Peacekeeping in Vietnam: Canada, India, Poland and the International Commission* (Edmonton: University of Alberta Press, 1984) and *International Peacekeeping in Lebanon: United Nations Authority and Multinational Force* (Boulder: Westview, 1987).

Carlyle A. Thayer is Associate Professor and Head of the Department of Politics at the Australian Defence Force Academy in Canberra. In May 1993 he was an International Observer for the UNTAC elections in Cambodia. Among other publications, he is the author of a forthcoming *Adelphi Paper* entitled "Indochina in Transition."

Larman C. Wilson is Professor of International Relations and Co-ordinator of the Western Hemisphere Program, School of International Service, The American University, Washington, D.C. The co-author of two books published in the 1970s, he is the author most recently of "The Organisation of American States and the Haitian Experience," in G. A. Fauriol, ed., *The Haitian Challenge: U.S. Policy Considerations* (Washington, D.C: Center for Strategic & International Studies, 1993); and "The United States and the OAS," in D. W. Dent, ed., *U.S.-Latin American Policymaking: A Reference Handbook* (Westport, CT: Greenwood, 1995).

Abbreviations

ACABQ	Advisory Committee on Administrative and Budgetary Questions
ADF	Australian Defence Force
ARF	ASEAN Regional Forum
ASEAN	Association of Southeast Asian Nations
ASG	Assistant Secretary-General
AWACS	Airborne Warning and Control System
BRA	Bougainville Revolutionary Army
CG	Contadora Group
CGDK	Coalition Government of Democratic Kampuchea
CIA	Central Intelligence Agency
CIAV	International Commission for Support and Verification
CIVPOL	Civilian police
CIVS	International Commission for Verification and Follow-up
CNN	Cable Network News
COPAZ	National Commission for the Consolidation of the Peace
CPP	Cambodian People's Party
CSCE	Conference on Security and Cooperation in Europe
CSSDCA	Conference on Security, Stability, Development and Cooperation in Africa
DAM	[UN] Department of Administration and Management
DHA	[UN] Department of Humanitarian Affairs
DK	Democratic Kampuchea
DPA	[UN] Department of Political Affairs
DPKO	[UN] Department of Peacekeeping Operations
ECOWAS	Economic Community of Western African States
EOSG	Executive Office of the Secretary-General
FDR	Democratic Revolutionary Front
FMLN	Farabundo Martí Front for National Liberation
FOD	[UN] Field Operations Division
FUNCINPEC	*Front Uni National Pour un Cambodie Indépendent, Neutre, Pacifique et Cooperatif*

GCC	Gulf Cooperation Council
HQ	Headquarters
ICJ	International Court of Justice
IISS	International Institute for Strategic Studies
IMF	International Monetary Fund
JDISS	Joint Deployable Intelligence Support System
JIM	Jakarta Informal Meeting
MINURSO	UN Mission for the Referendum in Western Sahara
MPLA	*Movimento Popular de Libertacao de Angola*
MRND	*Mouvement Républicain National pour le Development et la Democratie*
NACC	North Atlantic Cooperation Council
NATO	North Atlantic Treaty Organisation
NGO	Non-Governmental Organisation
NZDF	New Zealand Defence Force
OAS	Organisation of American States
OAU	Organisation of African Unity
OECS	Organisation of Eastern Caribbean States
ONUCA	United Nations Observer Group for Central America
ONUMOZ	UN Operation in Mozambique
ONUSAL	UN Observer Mission in El Salvador
P5	Five permanent members of the UN Security Council
PDC	Christian Democratic Party
PICC	Paris International Conference on Cambodia
PNG	Papua New Guinea
PRK	People's Republic of Kampuchea
ROC	Republic of Cyprus
ROE	Rules of Engagement
RPF	Rwanda Patriotic Front
SAARC	South Asian Association of Regional Cooperation
SADC	Southern African Development Community
SIPRI	Stockholm International Peace Research Institute
SNC	Supreme National Council
SOC	State of Cambodia
SWAPO	South West African People's Organisation
TAG	Technical Advisory Group
TNC	Transitional National Council
TRNC	Turkish Republic of Northern Cyprus
UNAMIR	UN Assistance Mission for Rwanda
UNAVEM	UN Angola Verification Mission
UNDOF	UN Disengagement Observer Force

UNDP	UN Development Programme
UNFICYP	UN Force in Cyprus
UNHCR	UN High Commissioner for Refugees
UNICEF	UN International Children's Emergency Fund
UNIDIR	UN Institute for Disarmament Research
UNIFIL	UN Interim Force in Lebanon
UNIKOM	UN Iraq–Kuwait Observer Mission
UNITA	*Uniao Nacional para a Independencia Total de Angola)*
UNITAF	Unified Task Force
UNMIH	UN Mission in Haiti
UNMOGIP	UN Military Observer Group in India and Pakistan
UNO	United Nations Organisation
UNOMIG	UN Observer Mission in Georgia
UNOMIL	UN Observer Mission in Liberia
UNOMUR	UN Observer Mission in Uganda–Rwanda
UNOSOM	UN Operation in Somalia
UNPA	UN Protected Area
UNPROFOR	UN Protection Force
USG	Under-Secretary-General
UNTAC	UN Transitional Authority in Cambodia
UNTAG	UN Transition Assistance Group
UNTSO	UN Truce Supervision Organisation
URNG	Guatemalan National Revolutionary Unit
WEU	Western European Union
WFP	World Food Programme

PART ONE

Introduction

1

UN Peacekeeping in the New World Disorder

Ramesh Thakur

In the 1990s, Cold War acrimony between the superpowers has been giving way to a new world order harmony. As the cohesiveness of the familiar power blocs declined, so the role of the United Nations gathered fresh momentum. Between 1948 and 1994, the United Nations launched 35 peacekeeping operations involving more than 700 000 personnel at a total cost of US $9bn. The phrase "New World Order" was used by Soviet President Mikhail Gorbachev in an address to the United Nations on 7 December 1988,[1] and given much wider international currency by President George Bush after the Iraqi invasion of Kuwait. The UN played a pivotal role in the Gulf War; will it occupy centre stage in the new order through expanded scope and greater numbers of peacekeeping forces?

Coercive Collective Security

Conflict among organised human groups is as old as human society itself. International organisation is an important means for arranging the functioning of the state-based international system more satisfactorily than had proved to be the case in conditions of international anarchy. The two major international organisations of the 20th century have been the League of Nations and the United Nations. Article 1.1 of the UN Charter declares the primary purpose of the organisation as being to maintain international peace and security. The Charter specifies two chief means to this end,

---

1. Mikhail Gorbachev, "Address to the UN General Assembly," *Soviet News* 6455 (14 December 1988), p. 459.

namely pacific settlement of disputes (chapter VI) and collective enforcement against threats to or breaches of the peace (chapter VII). The world has failed to realise a collective security system centred on the UN for three reasons: an intrinsic tension in the notion; the veto clause; and the Cold War.

Efforts to devise an operational collective security system in the League and the UN have been thwarted by a fundamental tension in the concept. Only the prospect of war between powerful states directly, or their involvement on rival sides in a quarrel between minor powers, can pose a challenge to the international order. War between lesser states may be deplorable and unhealthy for their nationals but cannot endanger *world* peace. Collective security understood as the maintenance of international peace and security is therefore superfluous in respect of small states. Equally, however, collective security is impossible to enforce against major powers. For any attempt to launch military measures against a great power would bring about the very calamity that the system is designed to avoid, namely a world war.

The United Nations sought to avoid the latter eventuality by making the great powers permanent members of the Security Council and giving them the ability to veto any action launched by the Council (Article 27.3). The practical effect of the clause is that the extensive decision-making competence of the Security Council, necessary for the successful operation of a collective security system, is severely curtailed by the equally extensive decision-blocking competence of the permanent members.

The veto clause thus effectively negates the collective security aspect of the UN. The reality of the Cold War, which registered profound, irreconcilable and transcendental differences between the two blocs, produced a frequent resort to the veto clause by whichever permanent member saw its or its clients' interests under threat from an assertive majority coalition. The closest that the UN has come to engaging in collective enforcement action was in Korea in 1950. Yet the collective security character of the UN action in Korea was heavily qualified: it was a temporary marriage of convenience between collective security and collective defence.[2]

With the end of the Cold War and cooperation among the five permanent members, the UN has been relieved of the disability of great-power disagreement. During the Gulf War (1990–91), the Security Council adopted resolutions by consensus and with urgency. The most important long-term significance of UN actions in the Gulf lay in the crossing of the conceptual Rubicon by authorising enforcement of sanctions and then military eviction

---

2. One of the best discussions of the difference between collective security (one for all and all for one) and collective defence (us against them) remains Arnold Wolfers, *Discord and Collaboration* (Baltimore: Johns Hopkins University Press, 1962), Ch. 12. See also Inis Claude, *Swords into Ploughshares* (New York: Random House, 1964), pp. 225–27.

of the aggressor by troops not even nominally under UN command. As in Korea in the 1950s, the advantage of the procedure was that it allowed the United Nations to approximate the achievement of collective security within a clear chain of command necessary for large-scale military operations. The cost was that the Gulf War, like the Korean War, became identified with American policy over which the organisation exercised little real control.

The new promptness and near-unanimity of the Security Council do not herald a sudden feasibility of collective security. The Third World states are unlikely to relinquish their control of the General Assembly and the UN agenda and return to the world of 1945. Far from buttressing the international *status quo*, they are intent on challenging it through the UN with new political and economic legitimising principles. To them, equity is as important as order; collective security elevates order above justice. China, India, Iran and others could coalesce into an "Asian bloc" to counter Western pressures on human rights. How relevant will be the concept of collective security if the fault lines of international conflict are going to develop along the ridges of the world's major civilisations?[3]

The will to design and construct a collective security system is strong in the immediate aftermath of a major war. Initially, leaders as well as people act in the consciousness that appeasement of aggressors is counter-productive. With the passage of time, they begin to believe that the existing peace should not be lightly risked, that the rigid requirements of collective security are risk-inviting rather than problem-solving. Negotiation and compromise rule the world, and peace and security do become divisible.[4] To be successful, collective security must rest on the certainty of response from the world community to an act of aggression anywhere by any power. In practice, the individual and collective responses will rarely be clear-cut. People and governments will differ on the timing in regard to initiating as well as terminating military action, the choice of means, and interpretations of the outcome. Collective security is a system designed to deter and defeat interstate aggression, as of Kuwait by Iraq. It fails to match the requirements of civil strife, which is the more common type of conflict to confront the UN. Collective security requires multilateralism; successful military operations require centralised command and control. That is, collective security is predicated on decisive leadership. In today's world, such leadership can come only from the United States. But the latter has given no indication that its global leadership role will be free of calculations of national interest.

---

3. See Samuel P. Huntington, "The Clash of Civilizations?," *Foreign Affairs* 72 (Summer 1993), pp. 22–49.

4. Inis Claude, "Collective Security After the Cold War," in Gary L. Guertner, ed., *Collective Security in Europe and Asia* (Carlisle, PA: U.S. Army War College, 1992), p. 14.

Consensual Peacekeeping

Once collective security was seen to be unattainable, states moved to guarantee national security by means of collective defence, and the international community groped towards damage-limitation techniques to avoid and contain conflicts. Peacekeeping as an institution evolved in the grey zone between pacific settlement and military enforcement. Collective security necessitates three elements that are in opposition to peacekeeping requirements: a definition and determination of aggression; identification of the guilty party; and a contribution of forces by the major powers. Dag Hammarskjöld's approach focused on noncoercive and facilitative activities rather than on repelling aggression through armed combat. The main goals of peacekeeping were to bring about and preserve a cessation of hostilities, promote international stability and support peaceful change outside the axis of great-power rivalry. For this reason, traditional peacekeeping operations were more akin to armed police work than standard combat. Success for the military means battlefield victory or surrender by the enemy. Peacekeeping forces had no military objectives: they were barred from active combat, located between rather than in opposition to hostile elements, and required to negotiate rather than fight.

The jump in the number of peacekeeping operations in the 1990s (Table 1.1) is testimony to the enhanced role of the United Nations in the new world order. In 1988, when the Nobel peace prize was awarded to UN peacekeeping, just over ten thousand persons from 35 countries were serving with seven operations, at an annual cost of $230m.[5] In June 1994, there were 17 UN peacekeeping operations at an annual cost of almost US $4bn for the total of more than 87 000 troops, police and civilian officers involved. To put this in perspective, by the late 1980s Americans were spending $3bn on dog food and another $2bn on cat food each year;[6] global defence expenditures in the 1980s averaged one trillion dollars per year.[7]

The range of activities which are only loosely covered by the aggregative term "peacekeeping" demonstrate the notable flexibility and responsiveness that has come to characterise UN operations. The force in Cyprus is almost a model traditional peacekeeping operation. But the nature of peacekeeping has been changing. The cardinal distinction between collective security and peacekeeping lay in their reliance upon force and consent respectively.

---

5. *UN Chronicle* 25 (December 1988), pp. 6–8.

6. *Economist* (London), 18 March 1989, p. 92.

7. Boutros Boutros-Ghali, *An Agenda for Peace: Preventive Diplomacy, Peacemaking and Peace-keeping* (New York: United Nations, 1992), para. 47.

Table 1.1: UN Peacekeeping Operations, May 1994

Force	Location	Starting date	Authorised size[a]	Annual cost ($m)	Fatalities
UNTSO	Middle East	6/1948	220	30	28
UNMOGIP	India/Pakistan	1/1949	39	8	6
UNFICYP	Cyprus	3/1964	1320	47	165
UNDOF	Golan Heights	6/1974	1035	35	35
UNIFIL	Lebanon	3/1978	5912	138	196
UNIKOM	Iraq-Kuwait	4/1991	3645	70	2
UNAVEM II	Angola	6/1991	203	25	3
ONUSAL	El Salvador	7/1991	1357	24	2
MINURSO	Western Sahara	9/1991	3000	40	3
UNPROFOR	Yugoslavia	3/1992	37204	1900	87
UNOSOM II	Somalia	4/1992	20000	1000	113
ONUMOZ	Mozambique	12/1992	5760	327	11
UNOMUR	Uganda-Rwanda	6/1993	97	0[b]	0
UNOMIG	Georgia	8/1993	55	5	0
UNOMIL	Liberia	9/1993	651	65	0
UNMIH	Haiti	9/1993	1637	100	0
UNAMIR	Rwanda	10/1993	5540	98	11
TOTAL			**87675**	**3912**	**662**

a. The total size includes the sum of military troops and support personnel, military observers, civilian police, international civilian staff and local staff. In some cases there are considerable variations between the authorised and deployed strengths of operations. For example, MINURSO's actual strength in May 1994 was 526 against the authorised total of 3000. The total number of peacekeepers (troops, military observers and civilian police) deployed on 30 June 1994 was 71 543. The annual costs, on the other hand, refer to costs of operations as actually deployed.

b. UNOMUR costs are included in the costs of UNAMIR.

Source: *United Nations Peace-keeping* (New York: UN Document PS/DPI/6/Rev.5, May 1994).

Traditional peacekeeping had seven distinguishing characteristics:

- Consent and Cooperation of Parties
- International Backing
- UN Command and Control
- Multinational Composition
- No Use of Force
- Military Neutrality
- Political Impartiality

Peacekeeping operations in the 1990s have expanded not just in numbers but also in the nature and scope of their missions. They have been required to undertake the following eight types of tasks:[8]

- Military
- Policing
- Human Rights monitoring and enforcement
- Information dissemination
- Observation, organisation and conduct of elections
- Rehabilitation
- Repatriation
- Administration

Peacemaking

The goal of peacekeeping units is not the creation of peace but the containment of war so that others can search for peace in stable conditions. The in-theatre stabilisation facilitated and supervised by peacekeeping forces is meant to be supplemented by an ongoing search for a diplomatic solution to the underlying conflict. UN multilateral diplomacy differs from traditional interstate diplomacy in some important respects.[9] Guided by Charter principles, it offsets the unfavourable position of the weaker party. It aims to establish a just peace as well as a stable balance of power. And it takes into account the interests of member-states as well as the disputants, thereby broadening the support base for any solutions reached. Australia's Foreign Minister Gareth Evans has drawn attention to the attractions of using UN channels and modalities for resolving disputes peacefully and to the abysmal imbalance in resources devoted to preventive diplomacy as opposed to band-aid solutions.[10] At times the major UN political organs have given the impression of being more interested in finger-pointing than problem-solving.

A noteworthy recent development has been the use of UN auspices for implementing multilateral agreements and supervising free and fair elections. The comprehensive operations in Namibia and Cambodia, as well as UN missions in Central America, Western Sahara and Somalia reflect a trend towards a more clearly political orientation of UN involvement in efforts at

---

8. See United Kingdom, House of Commons, Foreign Affairs Committee, *The Expanding Role of the United Nations and Its Implications for United Kingdom Policy,* Vol. 1 (London: HMSO, 23 June 1993), para. 35.

9. Javier Pérez de Cuéllar, "The Role of the UN Secretary-General," in Adam Roberts and Benedict Kingsbury, eds., *United Nations, Divided World: The UN's Role in International Relations* (Oxford: Clarendon, 1988), pp. 67–69.

10. Gareth Evans, *Cooperating for Peace: The Global Agenda for the 1990s and Beyond* (Sydney: Allen & Unwin, 1993), pp. 61–63.

tension-reduction and conflict-resolution. UN activities have thus begun to move beyond the conflict-localising characteristic of peacekeeping operations and towards a peacemaking role. This is especially so because, contrary to first impressions, the conduct of elections is not a one-off act but a multifaceted and ongoing process. Electoral legislation has to be drafted to the satisfaction of all contending parties; candidates and groups must be able to compete in conditions of rough equality; voters must be protected from pressure tactics and intimidation; individuals and factions must be socialised into a code of conduct appropriate to the election process; and the logistics of holding elections can be a major undertaking under conditions of inadequate communications and transportation.

In the past, UN involvement in such a political process would have been rejected for being an interference in the internal affairs of a country. Increasingly, the view has gained ground that the international standards and imprimatur of the UN is the most accepted means of an exercise of national sovereignty by a people. This was the case, for example, in Cambodia. The government installed by the army of a foreign power was never accorded international legitimacy, even though it had displaced an exceptionally odious regime. The most visible expression of Cambodia's national sovereignty was elections organised, supervised and conducted by the UN. The tension between peacekeeping and national sovereignty is analysed by Alan James who not only makes useful distinctions between jurisdictional, political and international sovereignty; but also between peace-restoring and peace-enforcement actions within "prickly peacekeeping."

UN assets and qualifications for peacemaking, discussed by Bill Maley, remain what they have always been: its authority and impartiality as a third party representing the entire international community. If a conflict is caused by ignorance or lack of understanding, it can be solved by making use of UN fact-finding modalities. If a conflict is perpetuated because of cognitive rigidity of the disputants, it can be solved by imaginative formulations presented by the UN from outside the conflict framework. If the conflict buttresses regime needs of unappetising leaders, its insidious effects can be countered by the spotlight of UN-led world public opinion. If conflict-resolution is delayed because of the political price that will have to be paid by governments, the UN can step in to provide a face-saving formula. And if a conflict is based on a genuine clash of interests, a UN interpository force can at least dampen tendencies for its eruption into full-fledged war.

Civil Wars

The United Nations was designed to cope with inter-state war. Founded on the principle of national sovereignty, it is ill-equipped to cope with civil conflict. Yet the disputes clamouring for the world body's attention are mainly domestic. Humanitarian, peacekeeping, electioneering and enforcement measures by the UN face distinctive problems when they have to be undertaken with regard to civil rather than international wars.[11] It is difficult to inject UN forces into active civil wars in which no government—if one exists—has invited them, the fighting forces are unwilling to cooperate with the UN forces, and there is little possibility of bringing pressure to bear on the several factions.[12]

Where peacekeeping is injected because of an internal authority vacuum in a collapsed state, a solution requires the establishment and maintenance of a stable and lasting government. Most civil conflicts have deep historical roots and are characterised by broad and mutual suspicions based on past traumatic experiences. Objective analyses and rational solutions are meaningless in such contexts.[13] In many parts of the world, the "state" is a Western juridical concept that bears little resemblance to the ground reality. Whose power and authority is going to be restored in such a country? Time is a better solution to historical conflicts. UN intervention in sectarian strife must accordingly acknowledge the prospect of an indefinite commitment. Yet there can be no assurance that a political order grafted on a host country by itinerant international forces will not crumble as the country reverts to pre-intervention tribalism. Nation-building is a formidable challenge even under non-combat conditions. It is all the more problematical in a post-conflict environment.

Most Third World countries would fear UN intervention in civil wars. Charles Krauthammer at least had the honesty to acknowledge that outside intervention to solve problems like those of Somalia is tantamount to colonialism.[14] A new colonialism will not be acceptable to the Third World majority in the United Nations. The elemental force of ethnonationalism is more likely to defeat UN efforts than be tamed by the world body: "despite the lure of riches and glory, the imperial powers lacked the will to sustain

---

11. See Alan James, "Internal Peace-keeping: A Dead End for the UN?," *Security Dialogue* 24 (December 1993), pp. 359–68; Adam Roberts, "The United Nations and International Security," *Survival* 35 (Summer 1993), pp. 9–11.

12. Brian Urquhart, "Who Can Police the World?," *New York Review of Books,* 12 May 1994, p. 29.

13. At a panel discussion held at the UN in April 1993, Charles William Maynes, the editor of *Foreign Policy,* used the analogy of the Los Angeles riots. There was no black or hispanic leader to go to for stopping the riots, and the people could not be threatened, bribed or persuaded to end the rioting. The two "terrible alternatives" were to allow the riot to burn out, as it did with the loss of 53 lives, or to impose martial law and risk the death of 53 or 153 lives; United Nations, *New Realities: Disarmament, Peace-building and Global Security* (New York: UNO, 1993), p. 338.

14. Charles Krauthammer, "The Immaculate Intervention," *Time,* 26 July 1993, p. 66.

[their] role; it is not clear why an international force should fare better, absent any specific national interest."[15]

To be effective in a peacekeeping role, the United Nations must negotiate with all significant sectarian leaders. But by negotiating with them, the UN endows them with a degree of legitimacy. In return, however, leaders of ill-disciplined and uncoordinated guerrilla groups may not be able or willing to honour the agreements made with the UN representatives. Compared to the relative stability of border conflicts, civil conflicts are characterised by political fluidity. The stakes are higher too: the entire territory, not just a border readjustment; and, possibly, life and death, not just victory or defeat in battle. In most civil wars today, the distinctions between combatants and civilians have been almost totally eroded. UN intervention necessitates measures to protect widely dispersed and highly vulnerable populations that are bitterly hostile towards one another. Not only are civil wars not fought by large armies; their weapons too are generally small arms not easily controlled or neutralised by bombings and arms embargoes. Unlike inter-state wars, there is no territorial *status quo ante* which can be restored after international intervention. Ceasefires "in-place" will risk legitimising ethnic cleansing by the militarily most powerful; efforts to delay a ceasefire until territorial gains have been forcibly reversed will drag the UN into the quagmire of an internal war.

Most importantly, UN intervention in internal conflicts raises the impossible political question of how a world body committed to maintaining the territorial integrity of its member-states will decide when to support and when to oppose the "legitimate" government against attempts at secession. If the use of force is an illegitimate method of changing international frontiers, then should it be proscribed with equal conviction as a method of changing the territorial *status quo* from within? It is easy to see that the use of force by the United Nations cannot be politically neutral insofar as the outcomes of civil conflicts are concerned. The challenge of peacekeeping in civil conflicts is analysed by Paul Diehl.

Peace-Enforcement

Should the UN use robust force to quell international disorder? Peace-making and peace-enforcement are not synonymous. The United Nations is indeed the appropriate channel for national reconciliation and the recons-titution of government and legitimate authority. The problem is that the organisation's peacemaking credentials are tarnished and its peacemaking

---

15. Paul D. Wolfowitz, "Clinton's First Year," *Foreign Affairs* 73 (January/February 1994), p. 38.

mission is imperilled when a peacekeeping operation is transformed into a peace-enforcement one. The conflict entangling UNOSOM in Mogadishu detracted attention from its humanitarian work elsewhere in Somalia towards ending famine, improving security and establishing local administrative, police and judicial structures.

The consensus on "traditional" peacekeeping was that peacekeepers should not have the obligation, the soldiers or the equipment to engage violators in hostilities. International peacekeeping forces expressed and facilitated the erstwhile belligerents' will to live in peace; they could not supervise peace in conditions of war. Turning them into a fighting force erodes international consensus on their function, encourages withdrawals by contributing contingents, converts them into a factional participant in the internal power struggle and turns them into targets of attack from rival internal factions. The transition from peacekeeping to peace-enforcement is discussed by Kenneth Christie.

In his *Agenda for Peace,* Boutros-Ghali defined peacekeeping as "the deployment of a United Nations presence in the field, *hitherto* with the consent of all the parties concerned."[16] By implication, then, he believed that future operations could be organised without the consent of all the parties. But the difficulties associated with the organisation, deployment and use of military force do not disappear simply because of UN authorisation. States are reluctant to transfer control over their national armed forces to the UN because of doubts over its managerial capacity for military operations,[17] scepticism about its institutional capacity to police the world wisely and effectively and the fear of creating a military monster that might one day turn against them. The inhibitions on the use of UN force include an inoperative Military Staff Committee, non-fulfilment of Articles 42 and 43 requiring national troop contingents to be placed at the disposal of the United Nations, and recurring suspicions of majority coalitions in the Council by important individual or groups of member-states.

Peacekeeping operations face the danger that their conception of the international interest can be so abstract as not to coincide with the interests of any group of UN members. Nations are unwilling to authorise and arm an international soldier unless assured that the soldier will fight their battle. In restricting the use of force by peacekeeping units to narrow self-defence, the UN tries to ensure that it is maintaining a neutral stance between the disputants, not serving the political interest of any faction in the conflict or at

---

16. Boutros-Ghali, *An Agenda for Peace,* para. 20. Emphasis added.
17. Major-General Lewis Mackenzie, the former Canadian head of UN forces in Sarajevo, made the memorable comment that a UN commander in the field should not get into trouble "after 5 p.m. in New York, or Saturday and Sunday. There is no one to answer the phone."

the UN, and not imposing the will of a UN majority upon any party. There may be sufficient international consensus for a peacekeeping force to be emplaced in a conflict zone. But the circle of consensus tends to be narrow rather than broad, its scope restricted rather than expansive, and its strength brittle rather than durable. States are divided by real differences of interests and perspectives. The rules of engagement of troop-contributing countries show a marked difference in the latitude of intervention.

The use of force also raises questions about the appropriate balance between an impossibly long chain of command and the operational flexibility of the field commanders in being able to respond quickly to swiftly changing circumstances in a dynamic environment. When faced with a collapsing peacekeeping operation, the difficulty for major troop contributors will be to withdraw with honour. Conversely, converting a peacekeeping mission into a peace-enforcement operation leaves the force hostage to an unpredictable future. The predicament of peacekeeping soldiers on the ground is that they are unable to move forward into an unwinnable battle, unable to stay put taking casualties for no purpose, and unable to withdraw without repercussions for national foreign policy credibility.

The result of dithering over the incompatibility of a peacekeeping mandate applied to conditions of civil war is to make eventual and inevitable withdrawal needlessly messier. There is unlikely to be a surgically clean decision after the initial outbreaks of violence to cut the losses and pull out. The vacillation also creates a double political crisis. In the field, troop-contributing countries end up being on bad terms with one another and with aid agencies. At home, their governments find themselves confronting worsening crises of public confidence. National public opinion is unlikely to support high-risk ventures in far-off lands for the sake of quarrelling foreigners. That is, "mission creep" leads to "peacekeeping fatigue." It is relatively easy for national governments to set out criteria for participation in peacekeeping operations. It is far more difficult to apply these when the crunch comes, as was shown when New Zealand agreed to contribute a 250-strong rifle company to Bosnia despite domestic controversy and unease.[18] The issues that concern a troop-contributing country like New Zealand are canvassed by Gerald Hensley.

Human Rights

The use of robust force by UN peacekeeping units also raises the vexed

---

18. See Robert Patman, "Gains for NZ in Troops Commitment," *Dominion* (Wellington), 9 June 1994, and Ramesh Thakur, "Why New Zealand Should Say No to Bosnia," *Dominion*, 27 May 1994.

issue of how the laws of war might be applied to military conduct by troops acting under UN authorisation. A slide into rationalisations of the use of force, as happened with the operation in Somalia,[19] will steadily undermine the authority of the United Nations as the body responsible for moderating the use of force in international relations.

The UN is also committed to setting, promoting and enforcing international human rights standards by state-governments. Typically, human rights abuses take place in the context of security operations by national police or military units. Muscular peacekeeping operations raise with particular cogency the question of the applicability of human rights instruments to actions in the name of the organisation itself. The United Nations and Amnesty International play complementary roles in human rights.[20] The proliferation of UN peacekeeping operations has turned Amnesty's attention to the accountability and transparency of their human rights record.[21] It argues that the time is overdue for the UN to build measures for human rights promotion and protection into its own peacekeeping activities. Troops serving in UN peacekeeping operations should be trained in those standards and understand their obligations. Their use of force must satisfy the long-established conditions of *necessity* with less harmful alternatives not being available, *proportionality* in respect to the threat faced and the goal sought, and *discrimination* between combatants and non-combatants.

In the recent past, a number of UN peacekeeping operations have also been criticised for lax standards of social morality. Among other things, blue-helmeted troops are alleged to have patronised a brothel containing captive Croat and Muslim women in Bosnia[22] and paid for sex with children in Mozambique.[23] If the UN is to maintain its human rights credibility, then soldiers committing abuses in its name must face investigation and prosecution by effective international machinery.

Reforms

UN operations are conducted essentially within the framework of a Charter signed half a century ago. The time is long overdue to consider substantial reforms that would realign the organisation with present-day realities. Of the major UN organs, the Council reflects the anticipated power

19. See, for example, Sam Kiley, "UN Gathers Men and Arms for 'Final Assault' on Aidid," *Times* (London), 17 August 1993.

20. See Ramesh Thakur, "Human Rights: Amnesty International and the United Nations," *Journal of Peace Research* 31 (May 1994).

21. Amnesty International (AI), *Peace-keeping and Human Rights* (London: AI, 1994).

22. *Press* (Christchurch), 4 November 1993.

23. *International Herald Tribune*, 26–27 February 1994.

realities of 1945, the Assembly is wordy, tedious and ineffective, and the Secretariat is demoralised and dogged by outdated personnel and management practices.[24]

The Security Council

The Security Council bears the chief responsibility for maintaining international peace and is the authorising body for peacekeeping operations. Its permanent membership needs addressing for four reasons. First, in terms of the logic of permanent membership: international stratification is never rigid, and states are upwardly and downwardly mobile. A static permanent membership of the Council will undermine the logic of the status, thereby diminish the authority of the organisation and breed resentment in the claimants to the ranks of the great powers. The Council is unrepresentative also in a second sense. A 51-member UN had an 11-member Security Council in 1945. Today, 184 member-states are represented by a mere 15 on the Council. A third possible principle is economic representation.[25] Fourth, it is unfortunate that the permanent membership is coterminous with the five nuclear-weapon powers. This feeds a perception that the possession of nuclear weapons confers the status of great power. If non-nuclear-weapon states like Germany and Japan could be admitted to the hallowed ranks of permanent membership of the Security Council, then the international community would effectively divorce the status of great power from the possession of nuclear weapons. Defenders of the *status quo* might respond that the Council is organised on the principles of responsibility and capacity, not representativeness. The principle of equitable geographical representation has sometimes been brought into disrepute by the manner and extent of its application. Yet the principle is essential to the philosophy of the organisation and adds to its legitimacy.

The world community may have to address the question of the unit of UN membership. One of the more interesting questions in coming years might be the balance of security maintenance responsibilities between regional organisations and the UN, as discussed by Amitav Acharya. Perhaps regional organisations could be given quotas for permanent membership of the Security Council. An alternative would be to create a third tier of permanent but veto-less Security Council membership for countries like Brazil, India and Nigeria. Or the prohibition on immediate re-

---

24. Peter Wilenski, "Reforming the United Nations for the Post-Cold War Era," in Mara Bustelo and Philip Alston, eds., *Whose New World Order?* (Sydney: Federation Press, 1991), pp. 123–24.

25. See Peter Wallensteen, "Representing the World: A Security Council for the 21st Century," *Security Dialogue* 25 (March 1994), pp. 65–67.

election could be lifted. Whatever formula is adopted, the challenge will be to combine the efficiency and representational arguments: membership of the Council must reflect current global political, economic and military power relationships; but not be so large as to make it an unwieldy executive body.

The Security Council also needs to reform its decision-making procedures. Much greater transparency needs to be brought into its deliberations. At present it operates very much in the mould of an old boys' club with a membership restricted to the five permanent members (P5). (In fact, the "steering committee" comprising France, the UK and the U.S. has effectively narrowed the P5 to the P3.) Habits of consultation and dialogue could be applied to the Security Council. Its president could hold more consultations with regional organisations; its individual members could liaise more systematically with their regional groups.[26] Alan James also points to the need for the Council to cultivate the General Assembly in order to allay fears of an emerging great-power directorate.

The Secretary-General

The discretionary authority vested in the Secretary-General by Article 99 of the Charter linked the chief executive of the UN constitutionally and symbolically to its central ideal. The failure of the principal political organs to function as originally envisaged placed a disproportionate burden on the shoulders of the Secretary-General, including oversight of peacekeeping operations. As a result the office became one with little power but considerable influence. The chief executive of the organisation came to symbolise as well as represent the United Nations. In turn this enhanced the importance of the qualities required of Secretaries-General: integrity, independence of mind and the ability and willingness to set the collective interest of the United Nations above the partisan interests of member-states. The Secretary-General is looked to to provide intellectual leadership, managerial ability, negotiating skill and, in an age of mass communications, the ability to establish a rapport with an international audience. He or she must know when to take the initiative in order to force an issue and when to maintain a tactful silence; when courage is required and when discretion is advised; and when commitment to the UN vision must be balanced by a sense of proportion and humour.

The process of selecting Secretaries-General has been haphazard and *ad hoc*. The General Assembly appoints a Secretary-General on the advice of

---

26. Jeffrey Martin and Bruno Pigott, *The Role and Composition of the Security Council.* Report of a Vantage Conference sponsored by the Stanley Foundation and the International Peace Academy (Muscatine, IA: Stanley Foundation, 1993), pp. 9–10.

the Security Council; "appointment" supposedly stresses the administrative, while "election" would have suggested a more clearly political role. The Council vote is subject to veto by a permanent member. This immediately changes the thrust from selecting someone who commands the widest following to someone who is least unacceptable to the major powers. Undue deference to the major powers by a Secretary-General is reinforced if the incumbent should be interested in re-election.[27] Even other governments would not generally wish a Secretary-General to oppose them publicly. As U.S. Ambassador Max Finger put it, member-states want of their Secretary-General "excellence within the parameters of political reality."[28]

Ordinary people might prefer excellence within the parameters of human reality. The Secretary-General is the chief symbol of the international interest, advocate of law and rights, general manager of the global agenda and a focal point in setting the direction of world affairs. Some of the built-in disadvantages of the office could be overcome by altering the term from five to seven years, making it non-renewable and systematising the practice of choosing a successor through a search group comprising a cross-section of Security Council members.[29] The procedure could also be exempted from the veto. Parochial and political calculations will always shape the choice of a Secretary-General, but should not dominate the process of selecting someone for the only truly representative office of the world.

Peacekeeping

In the absence of a clear Charter basis to peacekeeping, there is a temptation to characterise the Security Council's power to organise peacekeeping operations as inherent, implied, general or assumed. The most important codification of current practice would be to enact a new clause giving constitutional sanction to UN peacekeeping.[30] The advantages of UN peacekeeping are the organisation's accumulated experience and its proven structures for establishing and managing such operations. But there is room for improvement. Each peacekeeping venture has to be started from scratch and each faces a cash-flow problem. In 1994 the UN's peacekeeping arrears were in excess of $2bn. The financial insecurity afflicting the UN has been

---

27. This may have affected the Secretary-General's mediation in the dispute between France and New Zealand in 1986. See Ramesh Thakur, "A Dispute of Many Colours: France, New Zealand and the 'Rainbow Warrior' Affair," *World Today* 42 (December 1986), p. 211.

28. Quoted by Brian Urquhart and Erskine Childers, *A World in Need of Leadership: Tomorrow's United Nations* (Uppsala: Dag Hammarskjöld Foundation, 1990), p. 18.

29. *Ibid.*, pp. 29–33.

30. See Philippe Kirsch, "The Legal Basis of Peacekeeping," *Canadian Defence Quarterly* (September 1993), pp. 18–23.

almost as striking as the institutional innovation and political resilience of the organisation. Mats Berdal analyses the importance of adequate and reliable finances for strengthening the organisational capacity of the UN.

To rescue peacekeeping from "adhocracy," Boutros Boutros-Ghali has recommended that a revolving reserve fund of $50m should be established to finance the start-up costs of peacekeeping operations; the General Assembly could appropriate one-third of the estimated costs of the first year of operations immediately, with the balance to be appropriated upon approval of the budget.[31] Additionally, a reserve stock of basic peacekeeping equipment could be established under UN auspices. The Secretary-General also canvassed a number of other interesting ways by which more money might be raised. Upon reflection, however, the innovative ideas turn out to contain hidden dangers. Should there be a small tax on the international arms trade? This would give the UN a financial stake on an expanding arms trade. The Ogata–Volcker report too concluded that non-governmental sources of financing the UN were "neither practical nor desirable."[32] But the proposal to establish a unified peacekeeping budget, a single annual assessment to cover the recurrent costs of ongoing peacekeeping operations and separate line items for each peacekeeping operation[33] may be worth implementing. Figures provided by Australia's Foreign Minister[34] on contributions by different groups—the P5, industrialised states and developing countries—to peacekeeping costs compared with their military expenditures suggest that perhaps the developing countries should be asked to contribute a substantially higher proportion to the UN peacekeeping budget than their current assessed shares. The New Zealand Foreign Minister has noted that the peacekeeping contributions of some countries with extraordinary growth rates over five or ten years have stayed constant or even declined.[35]

In some notable instances, such as southern Lebanon in 1982, the presence of UN peacekeepers has proven no barrier to fresh hostilities. To enhance the credibility of UN peacekeeping operations, it may be necessary to introduce a category of a military deterrent force. The full conceptual continuum of UN military operations could range from peacekeeping through deterrent to compellent forces. Boutros-Ghali argues that "peace-enforcement units," to be deployed and to act under Security Council

---

31. Boutros-Ghali, *An Agenda for Peace*, para. 73.

32. Shijuro Ogata, Paul Volcker *et al.*, *Financing an Effective United Nations: A Report of the Independent Advisory Group on U.N. Financing* (New York: Ford Foundation, 1993), p. 28.

33. Evans, *Cooperating for Peace*, pp. 119–20.

34. *Ibid.*, p. 118.

35. Don McKinnon, "Address to the United Nations General Assembly," 27 September 1994, p. 5; copy of text supplied to the author by the Ministry of Foreign Affairs and Trade, Wellington.

authorisation and the command of the Secretary-General, are warranted as a provisional measure under Article 40 of the Charter.[36]

One means of enhancing the deterrent effect of UN peacekeeping forces would be to interpose them between known rivals in advance of hostilities breaking out. Boutros-Ghali suggested that preventive diplomacy could be complemented with "preventive deployment," that is the emplacement of peacekeeping missions in advance of conflicts erupting into violence. This could be done at the request of all parties in an internal conflict, or at the request of either party in an inter-state conflict.[37] Australia's Senator Evans has provided sensible criteria for future use of preventive deployment: clear objectives, clear mandates, high probability of objectives being met, and clear linkage to a broader conflict resolution process.[38]

While the use of UN troops in a trip-wire function brings forward the timing of their deployment into conflict situations, naval peacekeeping, as was suggested during the Iran–Iraq war, envisages the offshore deployment of an institution that has so far been confined to land operations. Additional roles, such as arms control verification and narcotics interdiction, could also see air units being brought under the umbrella of UN peacekeeping. While each innovation has its attractions, each also contains some limitations.

For example, only great powers have significant naval and air military capabilities. But great-power involvement in UN peacekeeping carries a greater risk that the performance of international duties will be jeopardised by calculations of national interests. A militarily and politically neutral international peacekeeping presence, underpinned by the authority of the United Nations, can help major powers keep clear of confused local conflicts. UN peacekeeping enables them to pursue a policy of area denial to adversaries without asserting a direct military presence.[39] By contrast, direct participation in the MNF in Beirut (1982–84) meant that American presence in the Middle East became as politically exposed as the marines were militarily exposed at Beirut airport.[40]

A recurring debate concerns the feasibility and merits of a standing or standby UN force.[41] A permanent UN force could have the advantages of

---

36. Boutros-Ghali, *An Agenda for Peace,* para. 44.

37. *Ibid.,* paras. 28–32.

38. Evans, *Cooperating for Peace,* p. 85.

39. See, for example, Andrei Kozyrev and Gennadi Gatilov, "The UN Peace-Making System: Problems and Prospects," *International Affairs* (Moscow) 1990/12, p. 81.

40. See Anthony McDermott and Kjell Skjelsbaek, eds., *The Multinational Force in Beirut, 1982–1984* (Miami: Florida International University Press, 1991).

41. See Lester B. Pearson, "Force for U. N.," *Foreign Affairs* 35 (April 1957), pp. 395–404 and Brian Urquhart, "For a UN Military Volunteer Force," *New York Review of Books,* 10 June 1993, pp. 3–4.

professional and specialised training, rapid reaction time, organisational efficiency and financial stability. But there are too many difficult issues that would need to be circumvented: of authority, structure, training, administration, logistics and financing.[42] Boutros-Ghali himself concluded subsequently that a standing force would be impractical and inappropriate, and asked instead for more extensive and systematic standby arrangements.[43] Several countries have been prepared to indicate the number and types of troops that can be made available for UN peacekeeping on a response-on-request basis, and the UN is compiling an appropriate database.

The Problem of the United States

In the new order, the United Nations and the United States will have to learn to coexist in a world in which there is only one superpower and only one general international organisation. One has power, the other has authority. Progress towards a world order based on justice and law requires that U.S. power be harnessed to UN authority. There is wisdom and virtue in imposing the international discipline and moderating influence of the UN upon the exercise of U.S. power. Conversely, there is danger in permitting American power calculations to be cloaked uncritically in the UN flag.

The United Nations is a political institution. Its decisions are the resultants not of judicial but political processes of calculations and reconciliations of national interests. Across Asia and Africa there is a gathering undercurrent of unease and trepidation that the UN, led by a U.S.-dominated Security Council, is being used as an instrument of Western interests. Huntington notes that "The West in effect is using international institutions, military power and economic resources to run the world in ways that will maintain Western predominance, protect Western interests and promote Western political and economic values."[44] Chandra Muzaffar, a former Amnesty International "prisoner of conscience," notes that Washington can now shape UN actions to U.S. national interests. Instead of being an impartial monitor of human rights, the UN has become "nothing more than an instrument of the U.S. and other Western powers."[45] Andrei Raevsky notes some significant discontinuities in the command and control of peacekeeping operations between the UN and its more powerful member-states.

---

42. Paul F. Diehl, *International Peacekeeping* (Baltimore: Johns Hopkins University Press, 1993), pp. 108–19.

43. Boutros Boutros-Ghali, "Empowering the United Nations," *Foreign Affairs* 71 (Winter 1992/1993), p. 93.

44. Huntington, "The Clash of Civilizations?," p. 40.

45. Chandra Muzaffar, *Human Rights and the New World Order* (Penang: Just World Trust, 1993), pp. 155–61.

Resort to UN multilateralism contains costs as well as benefits for the U.S. too. It could enmesh the U.S. in a myriad of complex and costly operations that have little to do with its national interest and entail a high risk of failure. Madeleine Albright, the U.S. ambassador to the United Nations, testified before a Congressional subcommittee on 5 May 1994 that UN peacekeeping is "a contributor, not the centerpiece of, our national strategy." The UN, in order to retain diplomatic credibility, has to remain impartial between belligerents. But impartiality may be less useful for military credibility. Consequently, UN peacekeeping "is not…a substitute for vigorous alliances and a strong national defense."[46]

Modifying the Gulf War precedent somewhat, there seems to be an emerging pattern of UN-authorised military action by a major power (as by the U.S. in Somalia and Haiti, the French in Rwanda and the Russians in Georgia), at the conclusion of which the UN takes over in a peacekeeping capacity. The danger of this is that major powers take military action only when and where their national interests are engaged. The UN by contrast is the custodian of the international interest. Should the majority of UN members be convinced of the subordination of UN principles to Western interests, they will withdraw support from the organisation. But if the UN refuses to advance Western interests, powerful circles in the Washington establishment would prune back diplomatic, material and financial support for the organisation. How to reconcile these cross-cutting pulls of different national interests with broader conceptions of international interests is discussed in the final chapter by Robert Johansen.

Conclusion

In the new world order, the United Nations must meet the challenge of a balance between the desirable and the possible. In Hammarskjöld's words, "the constant struggle to close the gap between aspiration and performance…makes the difference between civilization and chaos."[47] Echoing these words, Senator Evans describes peacekeeping as a means of "bridging the gap between the will to peace and the achievement of peace."[48] The greatest strength of the United Nations is that it is the only universal forum for international cooperation and management. It must continue to play a central role in establishing a normative order which strikes a balance be-

---

46. Madeleine K. Albright, "The Clinton Administration's Policy on Reforming Multilateral Peace Operations," *U.S. Department of State Dispatch* 5 (16 May 1994), p. 315.

47. Quoted in Brian Urquhart, *A Life in Peace and War* (London: Weidenfeld and Nicolson, 1987), p. 378.

48. Evans, *Cooperating for Peace*, p. 99.

tween the competing demands of equity and political reality.

International peacekeeping has proven to be remarkably resilient as a circuit-breaker in a spiralling cycle of violence. If a military solution proves illusory but peaceful settlement remains elusive, then peacekeeping forces are needed, wanted and a useful instrument of conflict management. But they risk being mistaken as an adequate substitute for conflict resolution at one end of the continuum, and collective security at the other. In the past, the United Nations has emphasised abortion to the neglect of prophylaxis. It needs to sharpen its skills at identifying potential conflicts before the fact so that parties to disputes can be brought together during the period of infancy: disputes are much harder to resolve when they have matured to fully grown conflicts. The UN also needs to become involved in post-conflict peace-building by identifying, supporting and deepening the structures for consolidating peace and enhancing people's sense of confidence and well-being.[49]

On the cautionary side, the UN will have to address the problem of overload.[50] During the Cold War, peacekeeping emerged as a substitute for unattainable collective security. After the Cold War, it can be used to supplement fitful collective security.[51] But it is not synonymous with collective security. Contrary to traditional peacekeeping, peace-enforcement does not work within a broad consensus of all the parties to a conflict, does prejudice the rights of at least one of the parties and moves beyond a minimalist to a muscular conception of self-defence. Where the UN suffered from a lack of credibility during the Cold War, it has been afflicted by a crisis of expectations since the end of the Cold War. The zeal to intervene everywhere will have to be tempered with caution about entering into entangling commitments. The UN's dilemma is that it must avoid deploying forces into situations where the risk of failure is high; yet not be so timid as to transform every difficulty into an alibi for inaction.

Withdrawal of UN peacekeeping machinery in the face of armed challenges can of course be cruel in human terms. But it is better in the long run for the organisation to withdraw with its reputation intact and capable of intervention elsewhere with the consent of all parties, than to turn into a factional participant, part of the problem instead of a solution, the object of armed reprisals and street demonstrations. Traditional peacekeeping lacked coercive or protective power but was also low-risk. The new burst of vigour multiplies the probability of casualties and failure and could stretch the conceptual fabric of UN peacekeeping beyond the point of viability.

---

49. This was recognised by Boutros-Ghali in his *Agenda for Peace*, paras. 55–59.
50. Roberts, "The United Nations and International Security," pp. 6–8.
51. Sverre Lodgaard, "In Defence of International Peace and Security: New Missions for the United Nations," *UNIDIR Newsletter* 24 (December 1993), p. 9.

PART TWO

Case Studies

2

Peacekeeping in the Middle East

Ramesh Thakur

The history of UN peacekeeping is a mirror to the record of the organisation's own evolution: the initial high hopes, the many frustrations on the ground, and the sometimes bitter disappointments in the end. Another thread that is common both to the United Nations and its peacekeeping ventures is the failure of states to make full use of the international machinery available to them for the avoidance of war and the peaceful resolution of conflicts. Nowhere is this truer than in the Middle East, which has been the setting for several UN and some non-UN peacekeeping operations. Some of these have been seminal in the evolution of the very institution of peacekeeping and the establishment of its defining characteristics. The UN Truce Supervision Organisation (UNTSO) was the first instance of UN peacekeeping observer mission. The first UN Emergency Force (UNEF I, 1956–67) was the prototype UN peacekeeping force which demonstrated both the utility and the limitations of traditional peacekeeping. The Middle East was also the setting in the 1980s for a displacement of UN peacekeeping by multilateral peacekeeping: the Multinational Force and Observers (MFO) in the Sinai (1982–present),[1] and the Multinational Force (MNF) in Beirut (1982–84).[2] And the Middle East was the context for the United Nations shaking off one of the last remaining relics of the Cold War period. On 16 December 1991, by a vote of 111 to 25 with 13 abstentions, the General Assembly revoked

---

1. For a study of the MFO, see Mala Tabory, *The Multinational Force and Observers in the Sinai* (Boulder: Westview, 1986).

2. For studies of the MNF, see Anthony McDermott and Kjell Skjelsbaek, eds., *The Multinational Force in Beirut 1982–1984* (Miami: Florida International University Press, 1991), and Ramesh Thakur, *International Peacekeeping in Lebanon: United Nations Authority and Multinational Force* (Boulder: Westview, 1987).

Resolution 3379 of 10 December 1975 equating Zionism with racism.[3]

Table 2.1: UN Peacekeeping Missions in the Middle East, 1994

Force	Date Established	Police	Troops	Observers	Total
UNTSO	June 1948	0	0	220	220
UNDOF	June 1974	0	1035	0	1035
UNIFIL	March 1978	0	5313	0	5313
UNIKOM	April 1991	0	896	251	1147

Source: *United Nations Peace-keeping* (New York: UN Document PS/DPI/6/Rev.5, May 1994).

In mid-1994, there were four UN peacekeeping missions still operational in the Middle East: UNTSO, the UN Disengagement Force (UNDOF), the UN Interim Force in Lebanon (UNIFIL) and the UN Iraq–Kuwait Observer Mission (UNIKOM) (see Table 2.1). (There is also a non-UN peacekeeping mission still in operation in the Middle East, namely the MFO in the Sinai.) To this list should be added a fifth operation, the UN Iran–Iraq Military Observer Group (UNIIMOG) which completed its task in February 1991.

Background, Mandates and Structures

In the case of all five operations under review in this chapter, at all times the forces were (and are) under the exclusive command of the United Nations. All were set up by enabling resolutions adopted by the Security Council in the wake of wars and function under its authority. The Secretary-General is responsible for the organisation, direction and conduct of each force, and he alone reports to the Security Council and keeps it fully informed about the force. Any matter which may affect the continued effective functioning of a force must be referred to the Security Council for its decision. Each force commander is appointed by the Secretary-General with the consent of the Security Council and responsible to him. The commander designates the chain of command for a force and has full authority with respect to all assignments of members of the force. Troop contingents are provided by selected member-states upon the request of the Secretary-General, in consultation with the Security Council, with the

---

3. This was only the second time in UN history that the organisation had rescinded one of its own edicts. The first occasion was in 1950, when the General Assembly repealed a four-year old resolution which had urged member-states to reduce links with Spain because of General Francisco Franco's support of Adolf Hitler during the Second World War.

consent of host governments, and bearing in mind the principle of equitable geographical-cum-political representation. The civilian administrative staff is provided by the Secretary-General from his existing UN staff.

UNTSO

The Arab–Israeli conflict has been one of the most prominent, intense and enduring conflicts since the Second World War. It has also claimed more UN time and attention than any other issue. The problem of Palestine, a territory being administered by Britain under a mandate from the League of Nations, was brought before the United Nations in early 1947. The General Assembly endorsed a partition plan for Palestine in November 1947, dividing the territory into an Arab and a Jewish state with Jerusalem to be placed under international status. The plan was rejected by the Palestinian Arabs (who made up about two-thirds of the territory's two million population at the time) and the Arab states. The Jews proclaimed the State of Israel on 14 May 1948 when Britain relinquished its mandate over Palestine, and the first Arab–Israeli war began on the following day as Arabs attacked the new state from all sides.

The UN Security Council called for a ceasefire and decided that the truce should be supervised by the UN Mediator for Palestine (Count Folke Bernadotte of Sweden) with the assistance of a group of military observers (Resolution 50 of 29 May 1948). A four-week truce came into effect on 11 June. The first batch of 36 UNTSO observers was deployed in Palestine and some of the Arab countries between 11 and 14 June. Their number was later increased to 93. An early dispute concerned the selection procedure of UNTSO military observers. Moscow argued that the matter should be decided by the UN Security Council and that Soviet observers should be included. The Council decided otherwise, and observers were initially drawn only from the three states members of the Truce Commission (Belgium, France and the United States). UNTSO Headquarters, located initially at Haifa, was transferred on 25 May 1949 to Government House in Jerusalem (the former seat of the British Mandatory Administration).[4] On the financial side, UNTSO has been funded since establishment from the regular UN budget. Its annual costs of around $30m are assessed as part of each biennial program budget of the organisation.

UNTSO observers remain under national army establishments, receiving their normal salaries but with a supplementary subsistence allowance from

---

4. Israeli forces occupied Government House on 5 June 1967 after fighting broke out in Jerusalem. But after repeated representations from the Secretary-General as well as the UNTSO Chief of Staff, Israel handed the House back to UNTSO on 22 August. See UN document S/7930/Add.29 (1967).

the UN. The original observers even wore national uniforms, but with a UN armband. The distinctive blue beret with the UN badge was not used until the establishment of UNEF I in November 1956. While on assignment with UNTSO, the observers take orders only from UN authorities.

UNDOF

The Yom Kippur War began with a surprise two-front attack on Israel by Egypt and Syria on 6 October 1973. Fighting ended after the ceasefire call by the Security Council in Resolution 338 (1973) of 22 October. UNEF II was set up by the Council as an interpository force between the Egyptian and Israeli armies in the Suez Canal area (Resolution 340 of 25 October 1973). Despite the end to fighting, tension remained high on the Israel–Syria border. UN military observers reported a number of incidents in and around the buffer zones under their supervision, including artillery and mortar exchanges and overflights by Israeli and Syrian aircraft. The security environment began to deteriorate from March 1974 onwards until the signing of a U.S.-brokered disengagement agreement on 31 May. This was not a peace agreement, but rather a step towards a just and durable peace on the basis of Resolution 338. It called for the establishment of an "area of separation" between the two armies, and two equal "areas of limitation" of armaments and forces on both sides of the area of separation. The detailed plans for disengagement were to be worked out by Israeli and Syrian officers in a Military Working Group within six days of the agreement.

UNDOF was established by the Security Council to underwrite that agreement (Resolution 350 of 31 May 1974). Its mandate was to maintain the ceasefire, supervise the disengagement of forces, and supervise the areas of separation and limitation. In carrying out its tasks, the force would comply with Syrian laws and not hamper the functioning of civil administration. It was financed from the Special Account established for UNEF II by General Assembly Resolution 28/3101 of 11 December 1973. Although UNEF II was terminated in July 1979, the special account remained open for UNDOF. Headquartered in Damascus and located on the Syrian side of the Golan Heights, UNDOF has had its mandate extended at regular six-monthly intervals. The Syrians, citing lack of progress in the settlement of the wider Middle East conflict, posed some objections to UNDOF's renewal in the first two years. The renewal has been more or less routine since November 1976.

The force was originally composed of Austrian and Peruvian infantry units, and Canadian and Polish logistic elements transferred from UNEF II. (UNTSO observers already deployed in the area assisted as well.) The Peruvian infantry unit was withdrawn in July 1975 and replaced by an

Iranian contingent, which in turn was withdrawn in March 1979 and replaced by a Finnish contingent. When Finland decided to withdraw its unit at the end of 1993, Poland's offer to replace the departing Finnish infantry battalion was accepted by the Security Council. In 1994 UNDOF was composed of infantry battalions from Austria and Poland of 461 and 357 personnel respectively, and a 215-strong Canadian logistic unit.[5]

UNIFIL

The frontier between Israel and Lebanon remained relatively quiet for more than twenty years after the armistice agreements of 1949. But from the 1970s onwards the Lebanon crisis has presented one of the gravest and most complex challenges to international order. The domestic political and military balance in Lebanon was dramatically altered with the influx of Palestinian fighters fleeing from Jordan after the "Black September" massacre of 1970. The unstable equilibrium established in Lebanon after the 1975–76 civil war saw the Palestine Liberation Organisation (PLO) become the *de facto* government on the northern borders of Israel.

A UN peacekeeping force was injected into southern Lebanon in order to stabilise the anarchic conditions there in the spring of 1978. Al Fatah, a Palestinian guerrilla group, claimed responsibility for a major terrorist raid on Israel on 11 March 1978 in which 34 Israelis, one American and nine guerrillas were killed. Two days later, Prime Minister Menachem Begin vowed in the Israeli Knesset to cut off the arm of evil. Israel invaded Lebanon on the night of 14 March and was in effective control of the entire region south of the Litani river, with the significant exception of the PLO stronghold of Tyre. The initial Israeli objective had been limited to establishing a 10km security belt along the border. When it became clear that the United Nations was about to emplace a peacekeeping force, Israel decided to move up to the Litani in order to ensure that the UN force would be located there rather than on Israel's border.[6]

The scale and method of Israel's invasion meant that it was more than mere retaliation for a terrorist raid. Lebanon lodged a formal complaint in the UN Security Council on 15 March. Security Council Resolution 425 of 19 March 1978 reaffirmed Lebanese territorial integrity, sovereignty and political independence; called for an immediate Israeli withdrawal from Lebanon; and proposed the immediate establishment of UNIFIL "for the

---

5. *United Nations Peacekeeping* (New York: UN Document PS/DPI/6/Rev.5, May 1994), p. 14.

6. Naomi Joy Weinberger, "Peacekeeping Options in Lebanon," *Middle East Journal* 37 (Summer 1983), pp. 342–43; M. Boerma, "The United Nations Interim Force in Lebanon," *Millennium: Journal of International Studies* 8 (Spring 1979), p. 53.

purpose of confirming the withdrawal of Israeli forces, restoring international peace and security and assisting the Government of Lebanon in
ensuring the return of its effective authority in the area." Significantly, the
mandating resolution failed to delineate either UNIFIL's precise area of
operation or its capacity to respond to any challenges to its functioning.[7]

On the same day the Security Council approved a report from Secretary-
General Kurt Waldheim[8] on the modalities of the new peacekeeping force
(Resolution 426 of 19 March 1978). UNIFIL was to execute a two-stage
operation: confirm Israeli withdrawal, and maintain an area of operation
agreed to by the parties. UNIFIL would supervise the ceasefire in the area
and patrol it in order to ensure its demilitarisation, control the movement of
people in it and prevent the entry of unauthorised personnel. The force
requirement was estimated at 4000 troops. (This was increased to 6000
within three months.)

UNIFIL was stitched together with units drawn from UNTSO and
Canadian, Iranian and Swedish personnel detached from UNDOF on the
Golan and UNEF II in the Sinai. Additional troops came from France,
Nepal and Norway. The extra 2000 troops in June were provided mainly by
Fiji, Iran and Ireland. On 12 April 1978, command of UNIFIL was
entrusted to UNTSO Chief of Staff Maj. Gen. Emmanuel S. Erskine of
Ghana. In mid-1994, in addition to 5313 troops, UNIFIL was assisted by
59 military observers from UNTSO's Observer Group Lebanon and about
540 local and international civilian staff.

UNIIMOG

Trying to take advantage of the turmoil in Iran following the
revolutionary overthrow of the Shah's regime, Iraq invaded the newly-
established Islamic republic on 22 September 1980. It was a costly blunder
(foreshadowing the even costlier miscalculation in the Iraqi invasion of
Kuwait a decade later), for the war of attrition raged for eight years before
both sides acknowledged the reality of a military stalemate. Acting under
Article 99 of the UN Charter, Waldheim brought the matter to the attention
of the Security Council on 23 September. Its first involvement in the war
came in Resolution 479 of 28 September 1980 calling for a settlement of the
dispute. By failing to identify Iraq as the aggressor, however, the Council
ensured that it would be ignored by Iran for the next several years.

The war turned increasingly horrific with the use of chemical weapons

---

7. The discussion of UNIFIL in this chapter draws heavily upon Ramesh Thakur,
"International Peacekeeping: The U. N. Interim Force in Lebanon," *Australian Outlook* 35
(August 1981), pp. 181–190.

8. UN document S/12611 (1978).

and missiles targeted at cities.[9] On 9 June 1984, Secretary-General Javier Pérez de Cuéllar appealed to both sides to refrain from deliberate attacks on civilian centres of population.[10] With both Iran and Iraq amenable to this, Pérez de Cuéllar informed the Security Council of his decision to deploy inspection teams to the region for the purposes of investigating alleged attacks on civilian areas. The truce in the "war of the cities" lasted for some nine months. One inspection team each, composed of three officers seconded from the military personnel of UNTSO and one official from the UN Secretariat, was installed in Baghdad and Tehran by the end of June. Their presence was to expedite the establishment of UNIIMOG in both capitals four years later.

The escalation of the Iran–Iraq war in 1986–87 had increasingly international repercussions, especially for shipping in the Persian Gulf. The next substantial UN involvement of any note was when the Security Council unanimously adopted Resolution 598 on 20 July 1987 calling for an immediate ceasefire; a discontinuation of all land, air and sea military actions; and a withdrawal of all forces to internationally recognised boundaries. The two warring parties were urged to cooperate with the UN Secretary-General in achieving a just and comprehensive settlement of all outstanding issues; all other states were called upon to exercise utmost restraint. Pérez de Cuéllar was also asked to dispatch a team of UN observers to verify, confirm and supervise the ceasefire and withdrawal.[11] However, it was not until 17 July 1988 that Iranian President S. Ali Khamenei wrote to Pérez de Cuéllar accepting Resolution 598. Iraq reaffirmed its agreement with the principles embodied in Resolution 598 on the following day.[12] Pérez de Cuéllar held nine and six meetings with the Iranian and Iraqi foreign ministers respectively between 26 July and 7 August aimed at bringing about implementation of Resolution 598.

Iran and Iraq finally agreed to a combined ceasefire and peace talks under UN auspices. The modalities of the ceasefire were worked out by a technical team headed by UNTSO Chief of Staff Lt. Gen. Martin Vadset of Norway which visited the region from 25 July to 2 August 1988. UNIIMOG was established by Security Council Resolution 619 of 9 August, adopted unanimously, to verify, confirm and supervise the cessation of hostilities and the withdrawal of all forces to internationally recognised boundaries. Comprising some 350 blue-helmeted and unarmed military observers drawn

---

9. The use of chemical weapons by Iraq was confirmed in UN documents S/20060 (20 July 1988) and S/20134 (19 August 1988); and by Iran in UN document S/20063 (25 July 1988).
10. UN document S/16611 (9 June 1984).
11. *UN Chronicle* 24 (November 1987), pp. 19–20.
12. UN documents S/20020 (17 July 1988) and S/20023 (18 July 1988).

from 26 countries, UNIIMOG was deployed along the 1200km border several days before the ceasefire came into effect on 20 August. It had two headquarters—in Baghdad and Tehran. The Force Commander was Maj. Gen. Slavko Jovic of Yugoslavia.

On 7 August 1988, Pérez de Cuéllar submitted a report outlining his proposals for the composition, mandate and operating principles of UNIIMOG.[13] He recommended that the Group be set up in accordance with the guidelines that had been applied to peacekeeping forces set up since 1973. The costs of the Group were to be considered as expenses of the United Nations to be borne by member-states in accordance with Article 17.2 of the Charter. The principle was implemented in General Assembly Resolution 42/233 (17 August 1988) which approved $35.7m for the first three months of UNIIMOG operations. Of this, $20.6m was to come from the five permanent members of the Security Council; $14.1m from the other industrialised member-states; and the balance from the developing-country member-states.[14]

UNIKOM

UNIKOM is the one peacekeeping operation in the Middle East established after the end of the Cold War. Flushed with success in the new model of cooperation between the UN Security Council and a multinational military coalition which had driven Iraq out of Kuwait, the international community acted through the United Nations to set up an observer mission on the disputed border in the Gulf. UNIKOM was established under Resolution 689 of the Security Council, adopted unanimously on 9 April 1991. It was to consist eventually of 1440 military personnel. Its military contingent comprised armed and unarmed personnel; it was not authorised to take physical action to prevent the entry of military personnel or equipment into the demilitarised zone (DMZ), any use of force being restricted to self-defence only; and it was not authorised to assume responsibilities within the competence of the host governments, such as the maintenance of law and order or the civilian administration of the DMZ. In other words, even though UNIKOM was created after the end of the Cold War and in the wake of successful multinational military action, its operating principles were very much derived from traditional peacekeeping.

UNIKOM's concept of operations is based on a combination of patrol and observation bases, ground and air patrols, investigation teams, and liaison with the parties at all levels. Its tasks were to monitor the 200 km-

---

13. UN document S/20093 (1988).
14. *UN Chronicle* 25 (December 1988), p. 21.

long DMZ extending 10 km into Iraq and 5 km into Kuwait based on borders established under a 1963 agreement, and also the 40 km Khar Abdullah waterway between the two countries. In order to check that no military personnel or equipment were within the DMZ, UNIKOM was to monitor the withdrawal of any armed forces in the zone; operate observation posts on the main roads, as well as at selected locations in the DMZ; monitor traffic; conduct land and air patrols in the DMZ; and carry out investigations as appropriate. In addition, UNIKOM was expected to deter boundary violations and observe any hostile or potentially hostile actions. The modalities for UNIKOM were to be renewed every six months by the Security Council.

Achievements

UNTSO

UNTSO was set up to supervise the original truce of 1948. When the initial truce expired on 9 July, Israel accepted but the Arabs rejected the Mediator's proposal for an extension. When fighting broke out again, the Security Council *ordered* a ceasefire, with the clear threat of applying chapter VII enforcement measures in the event of non-compliance (Resolution 54 of 15 July 1948). The truce came into effect on 18 July and held. The size of UNTSO was increased to 572 observers and auxiliary technical personnel.[15]

Israel became a UN member on 11 May 1949. UNTSO's functions were transformed with the conclusion of four General Armistice Agreements in 1949 between Israel and its four neighbours (Egypt, Jordan, Lebanon and Syria). Its main task was changed to supervising the implementation of these four agreements (Security Council Resolution 73 of 11 August 1949). In consequence, UNTSO has to manage relations with five host countries. The office of the Mediator was terminated and UNTSO became an autonomous operation under the command of its own Chief of Staff. Its size was reduced to between 30 and 120 observers, depending on the circumstances prevailing at any given time.

UNTSO established two ceasefire observation operations after the 1967 war, one in the Suez Canal area and the second in the Israel–Syria sector. (A third such operation was established in southern Lebanon in 1972.) UNTSO played quite a crucial role in the modalities of ending the 1967 war. Fighting began on 5 June. The Security Council adopted three resolutions (233 on 6

---

15. *The Blue Helmets: A Review of United Nations Peace-keeping,* 2nd ed. (New York: United Nations, 1990), p. 19.

June, 234 on 7 June and 235 on 9 June) calling for a ceasefire. UNTSO
Chief of Staff Lt. Gen. Odd Bull of Norway, acting on instructions from the
Secretary-General, contacted Israeli and Syrian authorities on 10 June and
worked out the modalities of the ceasefire. UNTSO officers were deployed
along the front lines on 11 June to observe the ceasefire and to demarcate the
ceasefire lines in the following days. General Bull's arrangements were endorsed by the Security Council in Resolution 236 on 11 June 1967, which
called for full cooperation with UNTSO in implementing the ceasefire.

The rapid deployment of experienced UN observers drawn from UNTSO
has been invaluable in the starting-up phase of a number of peacekeeping
operations, including UNEF I in 1956 and the UN Observation Group in
Lebanon (UNOGIL) in 1958. UNTSO observers were seconded to new
peacekeeping operations in the region as they were established in order to
help them get started: UNEF II in the Sinai in 1973, UNDOF on the Golan
Heights in 1974, and UNIFIL in southern Lebanon in 1978. A group of
UNTSO officers were constituted as Observer Group Beirut in August 1982
in the aftermath of the Israeli drive to Beirut in the 1982 war. UNTSO
personnel have been attached to peacekeeping operations outside the Middle
East theatre as well: the UN Operation in the Congo (ONUC) in 1960, the
UN Yemen Observation Mission (UNYOM) in 1963, the UN Good Offices
Mission in Afghanistan and Pakistan (UNGOMAP) and UNIIMOG in
1988, UNIKOM in 1991, and the UN Protection Force (UNPROFOR) in
ex-Yugoslavia and the UN Operation in Mozambique (ONUMOZ) in 1992.
Moreover, UNTSO observers participated in a technical mission to Angola
in 1987, and its Chief of Staff led the preliminary fact-finding mission to
gather technical information for the Paris Conference on Cambodia in 1989.

In 1994, UNTSO's 220 military observers were drawn from 19 countries, including China, France, Russia and the United States from among the
permanent members of the Security Council, as well as Switzerland as a
non-UN member-state.[16] UNTSO observers assigned to UNDOF operate
eleven observation posts in the area of separation on the Golan Heights.
They also conduct fortnightly inspections of demilitarised areas as per the
1974 disengagement agreement. A separate UNTSO detachment serves in
Syria and performs support functions for the group of observers deployed
on the Golan. Similarly, UNTSO observers have been assigned to assist
UNIFIL in southern Lebanon.[17] And finally, UNTSO retains a presence in

---

16. *United Nations Peacekeeping,* p. 5.

17. Service with Observer Group Lebanon is apparently a highly sought-after posting for
UNTSO observers; Anthony Webster, "The Peacekeepers: Experiences of Australian
Personnel," in Hugh Smith, ed., *Australia and Peacekeeping* (Canberra: Australian Defence
Studies Centre, Australian Defence Force Academy, 1990), p. 62. This despite the fact that the
United Nations itself describes southern Lebanon as "the most hazardous assignment for

the Egypt–Israel sector. Headquartered in Ismailia, Observer Group Egypt operates outposts in the Sinai and conducts patrols in the peninsula. UNTSO also maintains offices in Amman, Beirut and the Gaza.

UNTSO has acquired quasi-permanent status because of the widespread belief that it is needed and it works, not as a panacea, but as a long-lived expedient. By the presence of its military observers in demilitarised and buffer zones, "a deterrent [is] provided to every incident being magnified into a justification for disproportionate riposte."[18] It is responsible for helping all parties and many individuals in the region. In addition it is the source relied upon for all UN operations in the Middle East. And it can provide the kernel of personnel needed in a hurry when a new peacekeeping operation is set up anywhere in the world. The cumulative total cost for all these activities from inception in 1948 until the end of 1989 was a mere $310.5m.[19] Considering the range of tasks performed for the number of operations over a forty-year period, UNTSO must be one of the most cost-effective conflict management tools ever devised.

UNDOF

UNDOF was set up on 31 May 1974; advance parties had arrived in the area of operation on 3 June and the strength was raised to 1218 (close to the then authorised level of 1250) within two weeks. Most observers are agreed that, occasional irritations notwithstanding (such as restrictions on the movement of inspection teams), UNDOF has generally performed its tasks effectively and with the cooperation of the two parties. A difficulty arose in that Poland had no diplomatic relations with Israel. The latter therefore restricted the movement of Polish officers with UNDOF on the Israeli side of the area of separation. The problem was resolved with the establishment of diplomatic relations after the collapse of the communist regime in Poland.

The disengagement operation was conducted in four phases between 14 and 27 June 1974. In the first three phases (14, 18 and 19 June), Israeli forces handed over designated areas to UNDOF; Syrian forces then began deploying in these areas while UNDOF established new buffer zones further west of the evacuated area. In the fourth phase (24–25 June), Israeli forces evacuated the area of separation. UNDOF units were then deployed in the area, followed by the establishment of Syrian civilian administration. On 26 June, UNDOF inspected the areas of limitation in the 10 km zone on each

---

UNTSO observers"; *The Blue Helmets,* p. 39.

18. Anthony Verrier, *International Peacekeeping: United Nations Forces in a Troubled World* (Harmondsworth: Penguin, 1981), p. 4.

19. *The Blue Helmets,* p. 41.

side of the area of separation, followed by inspections of the 20 km and 25 km zones on the next day. With the disengagement operation having been completed, UNDOF turned its attention to demarcating the lines bounding the area of separation. With Israeli and Syrian assistance and cooperation, the task was completed in early July 1974.

As the disengagement was completed and the area of separation delimited, UNDOF set up checkpoints and observation posts within the area. These are manned on a 24 hour basis. In addition, UNDOF conducts foot and mobile patrols by day and night. Two base camps were also established, one on each side of the area of separation. From time to time, temporary outposts are set up and additional patrols undertaken in the discharge of specific tasks. In the area of limitation, UNDOF conducts fortnightly inspections of armaments and force levels to ensure that they are within the specified thresholds. The force's unit commanders maintain liaison with the parties at the local level through designated liaison officers; UNDOF Headquarters maintains close liaison with the two host authorities through senior military representatives.

UNDOF's presence and activities have contributed to the maintenance of quiet on the Israel–Syria border. The last major incident occurred in November 1977 when two Iranian soldiers were wounded by Israeli gunfire. One of the most impressive achievements of UNDOF, as of many other peace-keeping operations, is the performance of humanitarian tasks and the instilling of confidence in the local civilian populace. For example, UNDOF has sometimes been called upon to provide medical treatment to the local population. The civilian population of the area of separation has doubled in the twenty years of UNDOF operations.[20] The force's good offices have been used occasionally for arranging the transfer of released prisoners and the bodies of war dead. On 28 June 1984, for example, UNDOF helped the Red Cross with the exchange of 297 prisoners-of-war, 16 civilians and the remains of 77 persons.[21] UNDOF also assists the Red Cross with exchange of parcels and personal effects across the area of separation.

UNIFIL

Bearing in mind that UNIFIL is still deployed in southern Lebanon, the words "Interim" in its title and "immediate" in its mandate have done little to enhance the prestige of traditional UN peacekeeping. Much as the UN "Safe Areas" in Bosnia became known as "UNsafe Areas" in 1994, so in 1982 Prime Minister Menachem Begin dismissed UNIFIL as the UN "Insecurity

---

20. *United Nations Peacekeeping,* p. 13.
21. *The Blue Helmets,* p. 108.

Force" in Lebanon.[22] The United Nations was originally reluctant to agree to the UNIFIL proposal. General Ensio Siilasvuo, Chief Coordinator of UN Peacekeeping Missions in the Middle East at the time,[23] argued against it. UN officials, fearing that a long-term commitment would drag the UN peacekeeping force into the Lebanon quagmire, inserted the word "Interim" in order to underscore the UN understanding that the force was a short-term expedient.[24] As Brian Urquhart later conceded, UNIFIL was confronted with continual controversies and difficulties because political calculations were allowed to override an inadequate and unrealistic mandate.[25]

The first UNIFIL contingents arrived in the war zone on 23 March 1978 and tried to take up positions between the Israeli and Palestinian lines. The Palestinian and Christian militia forces rejected UNIFIL's mandate, and Israeli and PLO soldiers demurred from cooperating fully with the UN force. In the end, Tyre was excluded from UNIFIL's area of operation because the PLO had never lost control of the pocket, and armed PLO elements that had held their positions during the Israeli occupation were even permitted to remain within UNIFIL's zone of deployment. As a result of all this, UNIFIL offered no assurance to Israelis that there were no armed Palestinians within its area prepared to launch raids on Israel; it could not prohibit either Israel from exercising the right of an occupying power to conduct military operations within the UNIFIL area of operation, nor the inhabitants of the area from exercising legal rights of resistance against a foreign occupying power;[26] and its battalions were physically separated across a geographically dislocated area of operation under the control of Christian militias backed, armed and trained by Israel. As Israel evacuated its troops from north of the border, it turned over control of the enclave to its proxy Christian militias rather than to UNIFIL.

It took General Erskine just six months to acknowledge that he had no choice but to compromise with the Christian militias.[27] Pragmatic accommodation of ground realities is an important explanation of UNIFIL's success as a long-lived expedient. Thus UNIFIL adopted a compromise on the dilemma of controlling violent incidents while respecting the right of

---

22. Quoted in Madeleine G. Kalb, "The UN's Embattled Peacekeeper," *New York Times Magazine,* 19 December 1982. p. 59.

23. The post was discontinued in 1979.

24. Alan James, "Painful Peacekeeping: The United Nations in Lebanon 1978–1982," *International Journal* 38 (Autumn 1983), p. 618.

25. Brian Urquhart, "Peacekeeping: A View from the Operational Center," in H. Wiseman, ed., *Peacekeeping: Appraisals and Proposals* (New York: Pergamon, 1983), p. 164.

26. For the Secretary-General's appreciation of the dilemma, see UN document S/17093 (27 February 1985).

27. *Times* (London), 20 November 1978.

armed resistance against a foreign occupying force: it would not interfere in clashes between the PLO and Christian militias unless the security of its own personnel or innocent noncombatants was endangered.

Not surprisingly, the parties to the conflict made every effort to use UNIFIL for their own purposes. The Palestinians believed that since the force had been set up in response to an Israeli invasion, it should, consistent with its mandate to confirm *Israeli* withdrawal, contain Israeli expansionism. The Israelis believed that UNIFIL should concentrate on keeping PLO terrorists out of the area and leave the Christians alone. The lack of full cooperation from the parties was aided and abetted by their superpower patrons. Both Moscow and Washington were prepared to veto Security Council efforts to exert effective pressure on the Arabs or Israelis respectively.

UNIFIL was merely an acceptable political cost rather than a difficult military obstacle to the larger Israeli invasion of Lebanon on 6 June 1982. The Force Commander was given 28 minutes' notice of the invasion and informed that the Israeli army did not expect to encounter any physical difficulty from UNIFIL troops. Israeli forces drove through UNIFIL lines in under one hour. In the next few days, Israeli and Christian militia troops forced entry into UNIFIL installations, destroyed its checkpoints and placed restrictions on the movement of its personnel.[28] There would have been little point to armed resistance of Israeli advances. UN analysts concluded that Israel would use and exaggerate every incident to try to show to the world that the UN force was incapable of guaranteeing a safe northern border. Consequently, UNIFIL was instructed from New York to try to "avoid clashes and situations where safety of our soldiers may be imperilled."[29] By maintaining a low profile, UNIFIL was at least able to undertake considerable humanitarian work behind Israeli front lines.

In fact UNIFIL remained behind Israeli lines in its entirety for three years. Even after partial withdrawal in 1985, Israel retained control of a crucial area in southern Lebanon both directly and through its proxy the South Lebanon Army. Between them, as of mid-1994 the two maintained 72 military positions within UNIFIL's area of operation. Unable to implement its mandate to confirm Israeli withdrawal, UNIFIL makes every effort to prevent its area of operation from being used for hostile activities and to protect civilians living in the area. Both tasks are based on a network of positions which are operational 24 hours a day. The network consists of:

- 45 checkpoints for controlling movement on the main roads in

28. See *UN Chronicle* 19 (October 1982), pp. 3–11.
29. Robert Fisk, "Israel Wages War of Nerves on UN Force," *Times,* 7 February 1983.

UNIFIL's area;

- 95 observation posts for observing movement on and off the roads;
- 29 checkpoints/observation posts which combine the functions of control and observation; and
- 5 observation posts plus 5 mobile teams in the area under Israeli control which are maintained by unarmed military observers seconded from UNTSO but who are under the operational control of UNIFIL's commander.

Each position is entrusted with the responsibility for preventing hostilities from being undertaken from its surrounding area. It does so by maintaining a watch and through foot and mobile patrols. The network of fixed positions and mobile patrols is extremely valuable to UNIFIL in its humanitarian tasks as well.

The events of 1982 proved beyond doubt that UNIFIL is best described as a war-dampening rather than a peacekeeping force. Its mandated task has proven beyond reach, yet its presence has remained indispensable. Of the original three-part mandate, the two requiring confirmation of Israeli withdrawal and re-establishment of Lebanese government sovereignty remain as elusive as ever. Even so, the presence of UNIFIL has acted as a deterrent and physical obstacle to the transformation of southern Lebanon into Israeli-occupied territory or its possible annexation as Israel's "North Bank." UNIFIL has also provided Israel with a reasonable security buffer against hostile infiltration through southern Lebanon. Israeli attitudes underwent a gradual transformation from initial suspicion of UNIFIL to grudging recognition of its positive contribution to national security goals. Were it not for UNIFIL, for example, Israel would have been compelled to intervene directly on behalf of Christian militias subjected to heavy and repeated attacks from the PLO.[30]

The third goal, of restoring peace and normalcy to southern Lebanon, has been substantially achieved. UNIFIL broke the cycle of Palestinian commando operations against Israel from southern Lebanon and Israeli reprisals against Palestinian bases there. Both sets of hostilities decreased in frequency and intensity. As well, UNIFIL has helped to rebuild a functioning infrastructure of local government above and beyond the call of duty as spelt out in its formal mandate. Development work and humanitarian assistance—providing emergency relief to refugees, supplying water and electricity, escorting farmers, dispensing medical aid,[31] constructing sewage systems,

---

30. Weinberger, "Peacekeeping Options in Lebanon," p. 346.

31. On average, UNIFIL medical centres and mobile teams have provided care to 2800 patients per month; *United Nations Peacekeeping*, p. 16.

helping with the burial of the dead and so on—are quasi-governmental functions that have elicited commensurate trust and loyalty from the local people towards the United Nations and its peacekeeping force. The population in UNIFIL's area of operation increased from around 10 000 in 1978 to over 400 000 a decade later. One reason for this was that the inhabitants of the area enjoyed a greater measure of peace, security, freedom and economic activity than was to be had elsewhere in Lebanon. And they knew it: a Druze sheikh said that "UNIFIL is our government," a Sunni *Mouktar* (village elder) observed that "UNIFIL is part of our family now and families should never separate."[32]

UNIIMOG

The Chief Military Observer of UNIIMOG and his senior staff, known as the Command Group, spent alternate weeks at each of the two headquarters in Baghdad and Tehran. In the field the observers were deployed in four sectors on the Iranian side and three on the Iraqi. Each sector controlled a number of team sites which were located as close to the 1400 km of ceasefire lines as possible. Teams of two or more military observers conducted mobile land, air and water patrols. Their primary task was to check compliance with the ceasefire, both by their own observations and by investigating complaints. They negotiated a return to the *status quo* wherever possible, or else referred the matter to sector headquarters to be taken up with liaison authorities. The military observers also engaged in a number of humanitarian and confidence-building measures, for example facilitating the exchange of war dead found on the battlefield.[33]

UNIIMOG observers conducted their operations against the backdrop of diplomatic activity aimed at achieving a lasting settlement to the conflict. The first round of talks between Iran and Iraq began at the Palais des Nations in Geneva on 25 August 1988. They involved direct negotiations between the Iranian and Iraqi foreign ministers, as well as between Pérez de Cuéllar and each of the two foreign ministers separately. Throughout the talks, the Secretary-General reported that the continued existence of UNIIMOG was essential for further progress, and the Security Council kept renewing its mandate at six-monthly intervals in accordance with his wish. In his report on UNIIMOG in September 1989, Pérez de Cuéllar concluded with some observations on how to proceed further with the peace talks.[34] On 27

---

32. Quoted in Marianne Heiberg, "Observations on UN Peacekeeping in Lebanon" (Oslo: Norwegian Institute of International Affairs, NUPI notat no. 305, 1984), p. 24.
33. This paragraph draws upon private discussions held with Australian and New Zealand officers who served with UNIIMOG.
34. UN document S/20862 (22 September 1989).

February 1990, the Security Council expressed full support for his efforts to hold under his auspices "appropriately structured direct talks" between Iran and Iraq, with a specific agenda proposed to the parties by him.[35] Foreign Ministers Ali-Akbar Velayati of Iran and Tariq Aziz of Iraq had a combined meeting with Pérez de Cuéllar in Geneva on 3 July 1990: the first occasion on which all three men had come together for a face-to-face meeting.

The talks proved fruitful. Iraq began its troop withdrawal on 17 August 1990, and the withdrawal of forces across both sides of the border was almost completed in just four days. UNIIMOG monitored the withdrawal, as also the repatriation of prisoners-of-war held by each side. A general calm descended on the region while UNIIMOG recorded the new positions occupied on both sides of the international border. In a report submitted in September,[36] Pérez de Cuéllar argued that this would help UNIIMOG to monitor the ceasefire in the post-withdrawal period. He described the troop withdrawal as a welcome development and a major step towards the full implementation of Resolution 598. In the meantime, UNIIMOG would continue to verify, confirm and supervise the remaining stages of the withdrawal; help the parties resolve any local tensions that might arise; and assist the parties in establishing an area of separation. These tasks could be carried out by only 60 percent of the existing number of military observers.

With the pace of conflict resolution having quickened appreciably, the Security Council unanimously renewed UNIIMOG's mandate for another two months (Resolution 671 of 27 September 1990). And on 28 November, the Council extended the mandate for one final term until 31 January 1991 (Resolution 676). By 25 February 1991, the strength of UNIIMOG had fallen to 114 observers. The Secretary-General recommended that its mandate should be allowed to expire because of the successful conclusion of its major tasks.[37] In consultations held on 27 February 1991, the members of the Security Council accepted his recommendation.[38]

UNIKOM

Set up by Security Council Resolution 689 on 9 April 1991, UNIKOM was fully deployed by 6 May. It monitored the withdrawal of armed forces still deployed in its assigned zone. Upon the completion of the withdrawal, the DMZ established by Security Council Resolution 687 (1991) came into effect on 9 May. UNIKOM initially included five infantry companies drawn from the UN Force in Cyprus (UNFICYP) and UNIFIL. These were with-

35. *UN Chronicle* 27 (June 1990), p. 21.
36. UN document S/21803 (21 September 1990).
37. UN document S/22263 (26 February 1991).
38. *UN Chronicle* 28 (June 1991), p. 18.

drawn by the end of June 1991. In fulfilment of its mandate to observe and monitor, UNIKOM divided the DMZ into three sectors. Each has a headquarters and six observation posts or patrol bases. Observers patrol their assigned sectors from these and visit temporary observation points set up in areas of particular activity or where paths enter the DMZ.

UNIKOM has also maintained contact and provided technical support to other UN missions working in Iraq and Kuwait, for example the Boundary Demarcation Commission.[39] Moreover, UNIKOM provides movement control in respect of all UN aircraft operating in the area. And finally, UNIKOM provided assistance with the relocation of Iraqi citizens from Kuwait to Iraq, a task that was completed in February 1994.

From inception in May 1991 until January 1993, UNIKOM noted three types of minor violations: ground incursions by pockets of soldiers; overflights by military aircraft; and the carrying of weapons other than side-arms by police officers.[40] A series of Iraqi provocations tested UNIKOM's (and the UN's) resolve. For example, on 8 January 1993 Iraq banned UN flights in its airspace. On 10 January, Secretary-General Boutros Boutros-Ghali reported that a party of about 200 Iraqis forced its way into six ammunition bunkers on Kuwaiti territory, brushing aside UNIKOM protests.[41] On 11 January the UN Security Council condemned Iraqi incursions into Kuwait and requested the Secretary-General to consider restoring UNIKOM to its full strength, and also the need for rapid reinforcement as a means of enhancing its effectiveness. This was followed by air raids against Iraqi targets by U.S. and British bombers on 13 January. On the 16th, Iraq agreed to permit UN flights into Iraq on a "case-by-case" basis,[42] and on the 19th, Boutros-Ghali reported that Iraq had withdrawn, under UNIKOM supervision, the six police posts located on Kuwaiti territory.[43]

In his response to the Security Council's request of 11 January 1993, on 18 January the Secretary-General reminded it that UNIKOM had neither the authority nor the means to enforce Council decisions. It was adequately performing the observation functions required of it in its original mandate. If the Security Council wished to change its mandate to require a forceful response to minor challenges, then it would require a capacity to take physical

---

39. The Iraq-Kuwait Boundary Demarcation Commission was established in May 1991 with a mandate to demarcate the boundary between the two countries as set out in the Agreed Minutes of 1963. The Commission approved the geographic coordinates of the boundary and the area's map at a final session in New York on 17–20 May 1993. This was the first instance of the UN drawing a border between two member-states.

40. *United Nations Peacekeeping,* p. 19.

41. UN document S/25085 (1993).

42. UN document S/25111 (1993).

43. UN document S/25085/Add.1 (1993).

action. Specifically, unarmed observers would need to be replaced by infantry battalions, giving UNIKOM a total strength of more than 3600 personnel. Even this would be dependent on Iraq and Kuwait cooperating with the restructuring of UNIKOM. The Secretary-General's report was approved by the Security Council on 5 February 1993 (Resolution 806). In effect the Council authorised an enlarged and militarised UN presence in the region. The Secretary-General was requested to execute a phased deployment of the strengthening of the Mission. In fulfilment of this, a mechanised infantry battalion from Bangladesh was deployed in the northern sector of the DMZ in January 1994.

Problems

Problems faced by UN units over the years include impaired military efficiency because of the political requirement of representative heterogeneity in force composition; inadequate security because of the emphasis on negotiation and a restrictive interpretation of self-defence; risks of involvement in domestic power struggles when confronted with an authority vacuum in the host country; financial hiccups; non-cooperation from major powers or local belligerents; reluctance on the part of lesser powers to contribute contingents; and erosion of credibility as conflicts appear no nearer to solution after years of peacekeeping. All of these can be illustrated by the different peacekeeping operations in the Middle East.

Major Steve Meekin of the Australian Army comments that the maintenance of a balance among troop-contributing countries might have been designed "to ensure that incompetence was shared around the mission."[44] The UN peacekeeping experience can be hostage to incompetent administration: "a bloated and sluggish organisation with a huge international bureaucracy." UNIIMOG Headquarters was slow to make decisions at higher levels, incapable of providing clear direction to observers in the field, and "weak and vacillating in its relations" with the host governments. With the exception of the Australian, Indian and New Zealand units, most contingents were ill-equipped to meet the challenges of UNIIMOG: they lacked "basic military skills" and suffered from "poor physical fitness and a general lack of interest in the mission."[45]

In retrospect, Lebanon is probably one of the earlier examples of plurally

---

44. Steve Meekin, "The Peacekeepers: Experiences of Australian Personnel," in Smith, ed., *Australia and Peacekeeping*, p. 66.

45. *Ibid.*, p. 68. Some (but not all) of these harsh judgments might reflect a middle-level soldier's inability to grasp the intricacies of international politics involved in any UN peacekeeping operation.

segmented and failed states that have posed almost insuperable obstacles to international peace and security. UNIFIL was being asked really not to re-establish authority but to create it by taking over many tasks of civil administration. And the lack of governmental authority meant that UNIFIL's relations with local armed elements and foreign occupiers were correspondingly more complicated. Through all this, the UN force has had to be seen to be impartial.

The four UN operations still functioning in the Middle East cost a little over $270m per year between them (see Table 1.1 above). The amount outstanding to their combined accounts was almost exactly the cost of one full year's operation for the four missions—$261m ($21m for UNDOF, $216m for UNIFIL and $24m for UNIKOM).[46] In the case of UNIIMOG, two years after deployment, $24.4m, equivalent to 14 percent of the sums levied on member-states, was still outstanding.[47] The impact of financial problems bedevilling UN missions varies from one troop-contributing country to another. It is particularly severe on the small and poor countries like Fiji, which at times has had to divert funds from its social services budget (water supply, health, schools and roads) to cope with delays in reimbursement for soldiers deployed in UN peacekeeping operations.[48]

By an odd coincidence, the numerical figure for the number of peacekeepers to have died by 1 May 1994 while serving with these four operations is the same as the cumulative total of outstanding dues: 261 (see Table 1.1 above). The technology available to UN peacekeepers can fail to keep pace with the rapid strides made by national armies, with consequential adverse repercussions for their safety and their ability to discharge their functions efficiently. As a senior British journalist noted, "UNDOF is always chronically short of equipment, and what it has is usually obsolete or obsolescent. The UNMOs [UN Military Observers} on the Golan have First World War binoculars; the Israelis and Syrians have radar."[49]

UNIFIL is unusual among traditional UN peacekeeping operations for having to operate without an agreement among the parties to the conflict regulating the implementation of the UN force's mandate. For example, UNEF II and UNDOF, the two operations immediately preceding UNIFIL, were established *after* the signing of agreements between Egypt and Israel,

---

46. Figures taken from *United Nations Peacekeeping*, pp. 14, 17 and 21. This is still a considerable improvement from the position four years earlier. As of mid-1990, the amount still owing to UNDOF was $30m, and to UNIFIL $318m (equivalent to two years of its budget); *The Blue Helmets*, pp. 105 and 152.

47. *The Blue Helmets*, p. 333.

48. See Ramesh Thakur, "Ministate and Macrocooperation: Fiji's Peacekeeping Debut in Lebanon," *Review of International Studies* 10 (October 1984), pp. 269–284.

49. Verrier, *International Peacekeeping*, p. 116.

and Israel and Syria. True, UNIFIL had the consent and full support of the Government of Lebanon: but Lebanon was not a party to—although it was a victim of—the conflict which necessitated the establishment of UNIFIL. And, again departing from the UNEF II and UNDOF precedents, all relevant local and interested (and mutually antagonistic) great-power parties were not fully involved in the negotiating process. This ensured that UNIFIL never had the type and level of support in the Security Council that was forthcoming to the other two operations. Hence in turn the debilitating effects on its operational effectiveness.

Because UNIKOM was established in the aftermath of the Gulf War, the international community has demonstrated sufficient will to respond robustly to any challenges emanating from Iraq. For example, in adopting Resolution 806 (1993) in response to continual Iraqi challenges, the Security Council effectively transformed UNIKOM from an unarmed observer contingent into an armed force capable of preventing small-scale violations of the DMZ. Another index of the broad international base of support for the Mission is the fact that in April 1994, 33 countries provided the total of 251 military observers serving with UNIKOM.[50]

To Leave or Not to Leave

Analysts have long recognised, and UN hands have often averred, that peacekeeping missions can serve their purpose only if accompanied by serious and persistent efforts to find solutions to the conflicts which require the injection of peacekeeping forces in the first place. Yet this is a pre-requisite to successful peacekeeping that is honoured more in the breach. As early as June 1979, for example, Waldheim warned that UNIFIL could be withdrawn if certain conditions were not met, namely the establishment of an adequate security zone around force headquarters at Naqoura; a cessation of harassment from *de facto* forces (meaning the Christian militia in southern Lebanon); a change to a more cooperative stance by Israel; and cooperation from the PLO. The Security Council took these points on board when extending UNIFIL's mandate for another six months (Resolution 450 of 14 June 1979). It is doubtful if any, let alone all, of these conditions were met. But UNIFIL has not been withdrawn.

The situation confronting UNIFIL has often been said to be unacceptable by UN officials, including more than one Secretary-General. Why then does the United Nations continue to put up with it?[51] Indeed whatever effect

---

50. *United Nations Peacekeeping*, p. 21.
51. An excellent discussion of the arguments for and against the termination of UNIFIL is provided by Bjørn Skogmo, *UNIFIL: International Peacekeeping in Lebanon, 1978–1988* (Boulder: Lynne Rienner, 1989), pp. 253–65.

threats of withdrawal might have in inducing recalcitrant parties to cooperate in other places and at other times has been put at risk by not carrying the threat through in Lebanon. It is always better to avoid making non-deliverable threats, for it is the credibility of the body issuing the threats that is put on the line. As was to be shown in Bosnia more cruelly in the 1990s, the United Nations is yet to learn this lesson. This is all the more regrettable because, other than a resort to military force (with all its inherent risks and uncertainties), the threat of withdrawing a functioning peacekeeping operation is the only tool available to the UN to pressure parties into cooperating with its peacekeeping forces.

Another flow-on cost to the United Nations of indefinite commitment even when the mandate is manifestly not being fulfilled is that potential contributors will be reluctant to agree to a commitment of personnel in the first place. Promises of peacekeeping missions being interim and conditional measures will simply not be persuasive. The lucidity of analyses offered by Secretaries-General as explanations for non-attainability of mandates needs to be backed by the requisite political will to terminate non-performing missions and devote all attention and resources to the better-performing ones.

The dilemma confronting the United Nations was recognised in an unusually frank report by Secretary-General Pérez de Cuéllar in 1985.[52] The situation in southern Lebanon, he said, was dangerous and unsatisfactory. A prolonged Israeli presence in its so-called security zone there could lead to spiralling violence. Conditions for the fulfilment of UNIFIL's mandate were neither extant nor attainable in the foreseeable future. The situation was contrary to Security Council directives and of concern to UNIFIL contingents as well as UN member-states. On the other hand, there was the prospect of an escalating cycle of violence if UNIFIL was withdrawn. In returning to the subject in an interim report two months later,[53] Pérez de Cuéllar observed that should violence follow any UNIFIL withdrawal, blame for it would be put on the United Nations and the concept of UN peacekeeping would be correspondingly weakened. This is why the organisation could not shirk its duty and abandon Lebanon to a cruel fate.

There is another important argument, namely denying to an aggressor nation the political fruits of military success. Israel is in a position to frustrate efforts by UNIFIL to fulfil its mandate. The United Nations is in a position to deny to Israel the ability to translate military dominance into more enduring political control. UNIFIL is a symbol of the international community's determination not to concede political victory to the party that has been

---

52. UN document S/17577 (10 October 1985).
53. UN document S/17684 (16 December 1985).

the most obstructionist towards UNIFIL.[54] Conversely, a withdrawal of UNIFIL would signal UN willingness to let aggressors get away with open defiance of Security Council directives.

In the final analysis, despite the many frustrations and provocations, UNIFIL's mandate is renewed regularly because of its contribution to stability in the region and because of the sense of protection and reassurance that it provides to the local population. The political and financial price of staying the course in a less than satisfactory situation has not so far exceeded the political and military cost of the alternatives: mission termination or peace-enforcement.

There is a silver lining to the problems of UN peacekeeping. The experience can be professionally useful for contributing national military forces even when war breaks out in the theatre of operations. For example, an Australian Army captain serving in the Middle East in 1982–83 remarked on the opportunity, provided by the Israeli invasion of Lebanon, to witness first-hand large-scale mobilisation and mechanised operations.[55]

Lessons

In his annual report in 1984, Secretary-General Javier Pérez de Cuéllar noted that "Peace-keeping is an expression of international political consensus and will. If that consensus or will is weak, uncertain, divided or indecisive, peace-keeping operations will be correspondingly weakened."[56] All the peacekeeping operations discussed in this chapter confirm the validity of the diagnosis offered over a decade ago. For example, when the international political consensus and will came together in respect of the Iran–Iraq war in the 1980s, a UN peacekeeping mission was emplaced and complemented with appropriately structured peacemaking activities under UN auspices. These proved successful to the point where UNIIMOG was terminated for having completed its tasks within three years: a rare enough event for the lessons to receive close scrutiny and be filed in the institutional memory bank of the United Nations.

Even great power concert today needs the legitimising approbation of the UN for optimum effectiveness in regulating international behaviour. As an editorial in the *New York Times* put it after the Iran–Iraq ceasefire, "When the great powers start to see a common interest in resolving conflicts, they

---

54. The United Nations expresses this argument in the following words: UNIFIL's continuance is "a symbol of the international community's commitment to the sovereignty, independence and territorial integrity of Lebanon"; *The Blue Helmets*, p. 152.

55. Webster, "The Peacekeepers," pp. 62–63.

56. Javier Pérez de Cuéllar, *Report of the Secretary-General on the Work of the Organization 1984* (New York: United Nations, 1984), p. 8.

find this unwieldy international forum [the United Nations] indispensable"
—not just helpful or useful, but indispensable.[57]
The successes achieved by peacekeeping forces in the Middle East are
due in no small measure to working within the parameters of traditional
peacekeeping, including (with the exception of UNIKOM) a refusal to cross
the line from consensual peacekeeping to coercive peace-enforcement. As
unarmed military observers, UNTSO officers, for example, operate with the
consent of the parties. That is, they are totally dependent on the cooperation
of the parties in carrying out their functions. They have neither the power to
prevent a truce violation nor the means to enforce any decisions. The theory
is that their very presence is a deterrent to unwanted truce violations. The
chain of complaint for failure to resolve violations on the spot runs from
observers in the field to supervisors, the UN Mediator, the Secretary-
General and ultimately the Security Council.

UN peacekeeping forces can neither deter hostilities (in the conventional
sense of the word) nor defend their positions against sustained attack from a
source prepared to pay the political price. All they can do is exact such a
price, and hope that that prospect will be sufficient to reduce the chances of
hostilities being initiated against them. In November 1973, for example,
peacekeepers at a UNEF II observation post were molested by Israeli
soldiers. The Finnish battalion commander collected about 90 UN personnel
(mostly cooks and drivers rather than soldiers) and formed them into a
square, officers to the front. The Israelis first threatened the UN "force"
with bulldozers, and then confronted them with tanks. The blue-helmeted
commander ordered his men to sit down and said to the Israelis: "You open
fire and it will be on weaponless UN soldiers in contradiction of promises
made by your politicians and in the presence of the world's press." The
decidedly Gandhian tactic worked and the Israelis retreated.[58]

Of all the peacekeeping missions established since the new burst of
vigour in 1988, UNIIMOG conformed the most closely to the traditional
concept of peacekeeping. UN military observers were deployed to monitor a
ceasefire between belligerent states parties while diplomatic initiatives were
pursued to achieve a comprehensive settlement. Tensions during the period
of UNIIMOG's existence both highlighted the need for it and testified to its
usefulness as a confidence-building and tension-defusing mechanism. Yet
for the effective performance of its mandate, UNIIMOG was throughout

57. "A Revived U.N. Needs U.S. Cash," *New York Times*, 22 July 1988. The same was said
of the setting up of UNEF II in 1973; Indar Jit Rikhye, Michael Harbottle and Bjørn Egge, *The
Thin Blue Line: International Peacekeeping and Its Future* (New Haven: Yale University Press,
1974), p. 315.
58. Verrier, *International Peacekeeping*, p. 109.

totally dependent on the cooperation of the two parties, the contribution of troops from UN member-states and the financial security essential for all peacekeeping missions.

The Middle East operations also demonstrate the distinctive discipline imposed on UN peacekeeping soldiers as well. In early 1979, the Iranian Kurdish battalion serving with UNDOF was located just inside Israeli-held territory on the Golan Heights. After a series of harassments from the Israelis, and with no effective assistance forthcoming from the United Nations in New York, Force Commander Maj. Gen. Hannes Philipp ordered the Kurdish battalion to be relocated to Damascus. During the shift, the soldiers were subjected to intense abuse from the Israelis. The Kurds refused to retaliate, although the battalion commander commented later, "I would like to talk to these gentlemen without my blue beret on."[59]

Israeli challenges to UN peacekeeping forces were often rooted in perceptions of UN partiality to Arab votes in the General Assembly and a guaranteed defeat of any anti-Arab resolution in the Security Council. Israeli determination and ability to ensure its own security is a fact of Middle East life. One significant consequence of this is their refusal to countenance UN peacekeeping forces on Israeli territory. The pattern was set with UNEF I, which was not permitted to be relocated in Israel even when expelled by Egypt in 1967 as the curtain-raiser to the six-day war. But a significant result of Israeli refusal to accept UN forces on its soil is that UN peacekeeping forces can be misperceived as containing Arab armies rather than acting as a buffer between the Arab and Israeli armies. The impression was reinforced with the expulsion of UNEF I.

Paradoxically, and contrary to popular beliefs about that sorry episode, the benefits of UN peacekeeping to Israeli security of the 1967 UNEF I expulsion were to be proven in 1973. There was no existing UN force that had to be cleared out of the way before Egypt and Syria commenced hostilities in the Yom Kippur War. Their initial battlefield successes were due mainly to the element of surprise; the Arab successes began to be reversed as the Israeli forces mobilised rapidly and fully. The prior presence of a UN peacekeeping force like UNEF I would have made the element of surprise correspondingly more difficult for the two Arab armies to achieve.

Conclusion

Tensions and conflicts in the Middle East have spanned the entire period of UN existence. The Middle East region has been the setting for many firsts in UN peacekeeping. UNTSO was the first UN *peacekeeping*

---

59. *Ibid.*, p. 117.

observer mission ever. UNEF I was the first *peacekeeping force* to be established and the first to be expelled by a host government. UNEF II was the first to include a Soviet bloc contributor (Poland)[60] and the first to be disbanded after the successful conclusion of a peace treaty. In 1982 UNIFIL became the first to operate in territory under foreign occupation.

The region was especially instructive in analysing the potential and limitations of the United Nations in regional conflicts during the Cold War where local antagonisms intersected with the U.S.–Soviet rivalry. Since the 1980s, conflicts outside the Arab–Israeli axis have demanded more of the UN's attention. The region was the setting for a successful, UN-authorised multinational military coalition against an aggressor nation in 1990–91 in the first test of the organisation after the end of the Cold War. Nevertheless there is yet to be an instance of "expanded" or "second-generation" UN peacekeeping in the Middle East. It has been observed even of the one non-UN force still deployed in the region, namely the MFO in the Sinai, that "the UN can take pride in the fact that the Sinai force has been entirely organised on the basis of UN experience in peacekeeping."[61]

The future of southern Lebanon will in the end be decided by a number of external variables over which UNIFIL has no influence: the shifting balance of military and political power between the several Lebanese sects; changes of policy and government in Israel; the state of relations between Israel and Syria; the salience of and broader approach to the Middle East by the U.S. administration of the day; the state of relations between the five permanent members of the UN Security Council; and, most importantly, the fate of the eternal search for peace in the Middle East.

Israel and the PLO signed a path-breaking Declaration of Principles on Palestinian Interim Self-Government Arrangements in Washington on 13 September 1993. This was followed by the Cairo Agreement on Palestinian self-rule in Gaza and Jericho on 4 May 1994. The "good news" implication of these historic agreements is that decades of traditional peacekeeping can be followed by peace accords. The "bad news" implication is that a peace agreement does not necessarily lead to a winding down of peacekeeping missions in the area. The mandates of UNDOF and UNIFIL keep being renewed monotonously at six-monthly intervals. Should Lebanon and Syria be brought within the fold of peace treaties, the possibility of peacekeeping mandates being altered to suit the new environment will be higher than of a total termination of peacekeeping operations in the Middle East.

---

60. Rikhye *et al.*, *The Thin Blue Line*, p. 335.
61. Indar Jit Rikhye, *The Theory and Practice of Peacekeeping* (London: C. Hurst, 1984), p. 73.

3

The UN Force in Cyprus

Alan James

The world is getting tired of the Cyprus problem, and extending its fatigue to the UN Force in Cyprus (UNFICYP) which for 30 years has been helping to keep the island calm. Increasingly, Cypriots are seen as the indulgent inhabitants of an emotional hothouse, spurning opportunities for a settlement and so tying up valuable peacekeeping resources. Such irresponsible behaviour, it is being implied, can no longer be tolerated. Cypriots must, in the idiom of the day, "get their act together." Indeed they will be pressed to do so. Moreover, they must realise that if they fail to sort out their problem, the already-much-diminished UNFICYP may be yet further diminished or even removed altogether.

In this chapter it will be suggested that the world's response to the admittedly aggravating situation may reflect a reversal of proper priorities. Possibly the pressure for the re-establishment of a single political entity in Cyprus should be eased, not intensified; and if it is to undergo further change, UNFICYP should perhaps not be reduced but expanded.

One State, Two Communities

Cyprus came to birth as a sovereign state in 1960. It was endowed with a constitution replete with checks and balances, aimed at reconciling the political interests and anxieties of the Greek-Cypriot majority of about half a million and the Turkish-Cypriot minority of about one-fifth of that figure. Unhappily, it failed to work. The colonial control valve having been replaced by one of a different design, this volatile polity boiled over. Fighting broke out at the end of 1963, causing great worry in the West at the possibility of intervention by Turkey and Greece, and hence of conflict between two Nato allies in a strategically sensitive area. As a temporary measure, British troops maintained calm. But with a haste which hardly befitted the country's role as a formal Guarantor of the Cypriot Constitution (but which was otherwise entirely explicable), Britain handed this troublesome problem on to a UN peacekeeping force.

The fighting resulted in a marked geographical consolidation of the two Cypriot communities. But Cyprus was still discernibly a single, ethnically mixed, state. In this context UNFICYP made what was arguably an essential contribution to the maintenance of the local and probably the wider peace. For, notwithstanding the general wish to avoid further fighting, this would have been exceedingly hard to achieve had a neutral intermediary force not been stationed at inflammable points of contact and confrontation throughout the island.[1]

Territorial Division

In 1974, however, a complex series of events resulted in the invasion of Cyprus by Turkey and the consequential territorial division of the state into two ethnically unified areas. The mainland Turks (in the shape of a substantial military presence) and the Turkish-Cypriots now controlled the northern third of the island which in 1983 proclaimed itself as an independent entity: the Turkish Republic of Northern Cyprus (TRNC). It has made appearances at various Islamic fora, but has been formally recognised only by Turkey and so lives in uncomfortable diplomatic isolation. But, for as long as it remains bolstered by Turkey, the TRNC has no real security worries. The Greek-Cypriot administration, on the other hand, has found universal acceptance (save by Turkey) for its loud and frequent announcements that it is the only legitimate government in the territory which in 1960 was constituted as the Republic of Cyprus (ROC). It impatiently awaits the re-establishment of a single rule (under the ultimate control, naturally, of the majority community) over the whole of the Cypriot inheritance. However, because of the ROC's military inferiority to those in the north, it can itself do little directly to advance the coming of that much-desired day.

UNFICYP sits between these two distrustful communities. It is in effective but not formal charge of an indistinctly demarcated buffer zone which extends across the island for a distance of about 180km. In width it varies between 20 metres and seven kilometres and covers about three percent of the island. The task of the force is to conduct some humanitarian and economic activities, but chiefly to do what it can to maintain the military

---

1. A detailed argument to this effect is presented in Alan James, *The Politics of Peacekeeping* (London: Chatto and Windus, 1969), pp. 328–33.

status quo and prevent a recurrence of fighting. In this cause it keeps the buffer zone under surveillance from about 150 observation posts (only 20 of which, in mid-1994, were constantly manned), patrols the zone on foot and in vehicles, watches over it from the air and also keeps an eye on its seaward extensions. This it does with just 1184 military personnel and 34 civilian police (as of 7 June 1994). The military elements come mainly from Argentina, Austria and the United Kingdom.[2]

International Dissatisfaction

These numbers represent a reduction of almost fifty percent since December 1990 when the force was 2132 strong[3]—a figure which, except for UNFICYP's initial composition in 1964 and an increase which followed the events of 1974, was close to its average size. Thus, although there have not been changes either in UNFICYP's mandate or in the situation on the ground, and notwithstanding earlier very thorough investigations into possible economies,[4] UNFICYP has been cut by about half. This is indicative of the degree of dissatisfaction which the situation in Cyprus has attracted. Undoubtedly it stems in part from the ending of the Cold War. The West no longer has to worry about the advantages that might accrue to the Soviet Union (or, now, Russia) from an intra-Nato conflict in the area which was seen as the alliance's "soft underbelly." But there are two deeper reasons for the discontent.

UNFICYP's Financing

At the time when UNFICYP was established, the UN was heading for a crisis over the financing of peacekeeping. The organisation had accumulated considerable debts, chiefly because of the refusal of the Soviet Union and France to pay sums which had been lawfully assessed for peacekeeping. And these refusals were taking the malefactors, particularly the Soviets, close to the point at which they would become liable, under Article 19 of the UN Charter, to lose their votes in the General Assembly. The repercussions of such a deprivation would possibly be considerable, even to the point of imperilling the whole UN. It was no time to be contemplating major

---

2. UN Document S/1994/680 (7 June 1994), paras. 2–11. The Argentineans arrived in 1993, creating—given memories of the Falklands/Malvinas War eleven years earlier—an interesting juxtaposition. It was reported that the British troops had been warned, in a play on words which one does not always associate with the military, that "we will be castrated if there is any argy-bargy"; *Times* (London), 27 September 1993.

3. UN Document S/26777 (22 November 1993), para. 93.

4. In particular, see the report of an enquiry made in 1980: UN Document S/14275 (1 December 1980).

additions to the members' peacekeeping bills.

Accordingly, UNFICYP's financing was fudged. The money was to be raised "in a manner to be agreed upon"[5] by the states contributing contingents and by Cyprus. The possibility of voluntary contributions was also mentioned—which were soon very necessary but not very forthcoming. As of the end of 1990, only 77 states—about half the UN's then membership—had contributed to the costs, and no fewer than 26 states had not contributed since 1980.[6] The result has been that, despite the contributors meeting most of their own costs, the UN has been about 10 years in arrears in reimbursing the balance.

Unsurprisingly, this caused dissatisfaction. The withdrawal by Finland of its battalion in 1977 may have been connected with financial reasons; Sweden's similar action in 1988 was, at least in part, certainly so motivated;[7] Austria and Canada have complained bitterly about the situation;[8] and Denmark made it known that withdrawal on financial grounds was being considered.[9] Subsequently the Danes and the Canadians withdrew (except for token elements) in 1992 and 1993 respectively, and the remaining two battalions (from Austria and Britain) underwent cuts. Thus, by the end of 1992 the Secretary-General was pointing out that "largely for financial reasons...the viability of [UNFICYP's] present operational concept is in doubt."[10]

As long ago as 1986 the Secretary-General's predecessor had begun to urge that UNFICYP's net costs should be assessed on all member-states in the usual peacekeeping way, but certain permanent members of the Security Council showed no inclination at all to go down this particular road. Finally, however—and after a hiccup involving the only veto of recent years[11]—the requisite resolution (831 of 27 May 1993) was adopted. This did not mean that UNFICYP was out of the financial wood: at the end of 1993 the UN's reimbursement of claims covered the six-month period ending in December 1981.[12] But this development removed a sizeable irritant which had accompanied UNFICYP's functioning and a major obstacle to its continuation.

---

5. Security Council Resolution 186 of 4 March 1964, para. 6.
6. UN Document S/21982 (7 December 1990), Appendix I.
7. These two suppositions reflect private conversations.
8. UN Document S/PV.3022 (12 December 1991).
9. UN Document S/21982 (7 December 1990), para. 52.
10. UN Document S/24917 (1 December 1992), para. 44.
11. See UN Document S/PV.3211 (11 May 1993). The veto was cast by the Soviet Union in respect of a draft resolution proposed by Britain. Unless this was a spur-of-the-moment decision (an unlikely event), it would seem that British diplomacy had slipped.
12. UN Document S/26777 (22 November 1993), para. 52.

Political Context

However, it is not just the financial problem which has upset member-states, not least the contributors. They have also got very dissatisfied with the political stalemate which has existed in Cyprus throughout UNFICYP's life, and been especially marked since the division of the island in 1974. It has been reported that Sweden's withdrawal of its battalion was "owing to the lack of political progress,"[13] although that may not be the whole story. Denmark withdrew its troops partly because they were "more needed elsewhere."[14] Canada—the doyen of peacekeeping—complained, in a primarily but not exclusively financial context, that its "presence in Cyprus cannot be taken for granted indefinitely,"[15] and subsequently withdrew its battalion.

A political solution has not been lost through want of trying. The UN has been working away at the problem ever since UNFICYP's establishment, but to no avail.[16] Success has sometimes seemed tantalisingly near, but one or other of the parties has then balked. A former high-ranking UN official has referred to one such series of talks as "the most frustrating negotiations in my experience."[17] More generally, he has professed to knowing of no problem "more bedeviled by mean-spiritedness and lack of mutual confidence, nor of a problem where all concerned would so obviously gain from a reasonable settlement."[18] In a similar vein, an unofficial Canadian commentator has written of the "petty and relatively meaningless animosities" of the parties standing in the way of "a solution which will ensure the creation of a peaceful and secure island."[19]

Undoubtedly, this frustration has also been experienced by the remaining contributors to UNFICYP. "Several" of them, it was reported in 1993 in the carefully chosen words of a UN report, have expressed the view that UNFICYP "in its present form was not contributing to progress in resolving the underlying political issues." They wanted to send a "political message"[20] to the parties by reducing UNFICYP to an observer mission. That is, if the

---

13. Nancy Crawshaw, "A New President for Cyprus," *World Today* 44 (May 1988), p. 76.

14. The words of the Danish defence chief, *Kibris. Northern Cyprus Monthly* 1 (December 1992), p. 4.

15. UN Document S/PV.3022 (12 December 1991), pp. 14–15.

16. For an examination of the UN's mediation efforts over most of this period, see Farid Mirbagheri, "International Peacemaking in Cyprus between 1964 and 1968," unpublished Ph.D. dissertation, Keele University, 1993.

17. Brian Urquhart, *A Life in Peace and War* (London: Weidenfeld and Nicolson, 1987), p. 259.

18. *Ibid.*, p. 198.

19. Editorial matter in *Peacekeeping and International Relations* 21 (November/December 1992), p. 8.

20. UN Document S/25492 (30 March 1993), para. 15.

parties will not settle, they should more or less be left to stew in their own juice! The United States has weighed in, weightily, in the same sense. Speaking in the Cyprus context, its representative has said that the Security Council should "no longer [be] prepared to accept open-ended peace-keeping commitments which are not linked to the resolution of disputes."[21]

This approach was endorsed in 1992 by the present UN Secretary-General only months after his assumption of office. He urged a "critical look" at long-lived operations such as UNFICYP:

> If a Force has for 28 years maintained conditions in which a peaceful settlement to a dispute can be negotiated but negotiations have not succeeded, it has to be asked whether that Force has a priority claim on the scarce resources that member States can make available to the Organization's peace-keeping activities.[22]

Later he developed the point by saying that "It is often asked whether UNFICYP is not part of the problem in Cyprus, rather than part of the solution."[23]

The UNFICYP Card

Threatening to withdraw UNFICYP is, however, not the most convincing of strategies, for three interlocked reasons. Firstly, as with any unrepeatable sanction, the sanctioning body would have to be quite sure that this was what it really wanted. The UN, being a collectivity of states with varying interests and opinions on the matter, might have difficulty in coming to such a clearcut view. In theory it would be possible to take a less drastic course—reducing UNFICYP to an observer mission backed by a small infantry element, or just to an observer mission. But the first of these possibilities would be no less costly than the present force;[24] and either of them could result in the UN getting the worst of both worlds: an inadequate sanction and an ineffective peacekeeping device.

This leads to the second reason—that this particular sanction would be an especially hazardous one. The UN Secretariat has, year in and year out, expressed the view that the peacekeeping requirements of the Cyprus situation demand nothing less than a force. Thus the conclusions of the Secretariat Survey Team appointed in 1980[25] were echoed by a Review Team appointed a decade later. The latter drew attention to the fact that:

---

21. UN Document S/PV.3211 (11 May 1993), p. 10.
22. UN Document S/23780 (3 April 1992), para. 33.
23. UN Document S/26777 (22 November 1993), para. 101.
24. See UN Document S/25492 (30 March 1993), Annex.
25. See UN Document S/14275 (1 December 1980).

...there is still no formal agreement between UNFICYP and the two sides on the complete delineation of the ceasefire lines and on the use and control of the buffer zone. The parties persist in their attempts to establish their own version of the ceasefire line. In certain areas, the two sides remain dangerously close to each other. This can easily fuel incidents and tensions, which can be controlled only by UNFICYP's continuous presence throughout the buffer zone and, if necessary, the rapid deployment of troops between the two sides. The buffer zone contains five populated villages (four Greek Cypriot villages and one mixed Greek Cypriot/Turkish Cypriot village) and a variety of civilian activities are undertaken there by members of both communities. Furthermore, there are frequent civilian demonstrations close to the ceasefire line on the Greek Cypriot side, with attendant risks of unauthorized breaches of the buffer zone....

[Thus] the maintenance of the *status quo* and the prevention of a recurrence of fighting are not self-sustaining.... The relative calm that prevails between the ceasefire lines is the result of UNFICYP's presence and efforts. The Team has no doubt that, given the prevailing conditions, an active presence by UNFICYP is necessary if its mandate is to be fulfilled.[26]

Of course, it would be possible to say that if the parties kept their troops under tight discipline and their civilians under close watch (perhaps moving some of them and abandoning agriculture in the buffer zone), the need for a peacekeeping body would be that much less. Removing or reducing it could provide the necessary spur for these policies. However, it remains that on any calculation Cyprus would be a more dangerous place without a peacekeeping force strung out between the exceedingly distrustful parties. To take the ultimate step of termination would be a curious choice for an organisation premised on the value of peace.

Furthermore—and this is the third reason why the United Nations might not wish to withdraw UNFICYP—such a decision would seem to make little political sense. In the nature of the situation, any settlement involving the restitution of a single state (and all discussion is based on that assumption) is likely, as between the two parties, to be most painful for the TRNC. Although its president has emphasised that "There can be no agreement without concessions,"[27] it is as certain as anything can be that it would have to give up more territory than it could easily agree to, as well as complete self-government. Thus, when in 1992 the UN Secretary-General presented his ideas on "territorial adjustments"[28] in the context of two federated states, his approach was described by the TRNC Prime Minister as an "ultimatum"[29] and the accompanying map was called, in Turkish-

---

26. UN Document S/21982 (7 December 1990), paras. 30–31.
27. *Kibris. Northern Cyprus Monthly* 46 (July 1993).
28. UN Document S/24472 (21 August 1992), para. 6.
29. *Kibris. Northern Cyprus Monthly* 1 (July 1992), p. 1.

Cypriot circles, a "non-map."[30] The talks made little progress. It is the TRNC therefore on which the greater pressure will probably need to be applied. But as things stand at present it is the TRNC which, having military superiority, can afford to be the more relaxed about the possibility of UNFICYP's departure.

By contrast, the ROC would feel much more exposed in UNFICYP's absence. Should tension then rise and fighting break out, as is very possible, the ROC might be quite unable to turn its widespread diplomatic support into the needed military reinforcements. And even if Greece could be persuaded to intervene in its favour, that state is much less impressive as an armed ally than Turkey. Threatening to remove UNFICYP could therefore have a powerful effect on the ROC. But it is the ROC which is in any event likely to be more amenable to a settlement. It must be emphasised that in Cyprus political amenability of any degree is not a commodity in noticeably abundant supply. But it remains that for the ROC almost any conceivable settlement would have more political and security gains than losses. It is, after all, the Greek-Cypriots who are bound to be in the main driving seat of a reunited state. They, therefore, hardly need such an astringent inducement to settle as UNFICYP's threatened removal.

Doubtless it was worry on this score which has, on the one hand, produced an attempt at scare-mongering by the ROC, and on the other a sweetener. The first was exemplified by a warning from its president that UNFICYP's withdrawal could lead to a Greco–Turkish war.[31] The second took the form of an offer to pay "on a continuing basis" one-third of UNFICYP's annual cost—providing the force was maintained on the basis of infantry units.[32] (Greece also offered to increase its voluntary annual contribution.[33]) Clearly, maintaining an effective UNFICYP is, from the ROC's point of view, a major priority.

Given the ROC's assiduous diplomacy, a fair amount of international support can probably be mobilised for this view. Its membership in both the Non-Aligned Movement and the Commonwealth helps considerably in this regard. (The ROC's position was doubtless graphically presented at the Commonwealth Heads of Government Meeting which it hosted in October 1993.) Moreover, so far at least the ROC has been able to rely on Britain— UNFICYP's bedrock contributor—to endorse its policy on UNFICYP. The question mark over Britain's continued Security Council seat must be a slight worry to the ROC in this respect. But on the other hand Britain has

---

30. *Ibid.* See also *New Cyprus* 7 (June–July 1992), p. 1.
31. See *Cyprus Bulletin* 30 (18 December 1992), p. 1.
32. UN Document S/25647 (26 April 1993).
33. UN Document S/25912 (9 June 1993), para. 41.

removed one possible source of domestic criticism of its continued partici-pation in UNFICYP by calling on the UN to meet its costs.[34] Therefore, in the light of UNFICYP's present, surely bare-bones, shape, and the more satisfactory financial footing on which it now operates, it seems on balance unlikely that threats to withdraw or recast the force will be implemented. Where, however, does that leave the search for a settlement?

Confidence-Building Measures—and Then?

Accepting the existence of "a deep crisis of confidence" between the two sides, the Secretary-General decided in 1993 to approach an overall settle-ment indirectly through the adoption of "confidence-building measures."[35] With the Security Council's backing he embarked on a series of talks which came to focus on the possibility of agreements regarding Varosha and Nicosia International Airport.

Varosha is a modern suburb of the ancient city of Famagusta in eastern Cyprus. Since 1974 part of it, lying between the UN buffer zone and the Turkish-Cypriot held area, has been fenced off and become derelict—in striking contrast to its former role as a thriving (largely Greek-Cypriot owned) holiday resort. The UN has proposed that it be placed under its administration[36] and used for bicommunal contact and commerce. Nicosia airport, also lying between the two sides (and under UNFICYP protection), has since 1974 become derelict too.[37] The proposal here is that it be opened under UN administration for the use of the two communities.[38] The Secretary-General has gone to great pains to explain how these measures could not fail to be of considerable advantage to both sides.[39]

However, after intensive discussions he reported that "an already familiar scenario" presented itself—"the absence of agreement due essentially to a lack of political will on the Turkish Cypriot side."[40] Later, however, he was able to announce "considerable progress" with the Turkish-Cypriots. But, in what is another not altogether unfamiliar scenario, the Greek-Cypriots now

---

34. UN Document S/26777 (22 November 1993), para. 58.

35. UN Document S/26026 (1 July 1993), para 2.

36. The idea is not new. An agreement over Varosha has long been canvassed as the best starting point for a step-by-step settlement and in 1984 the Turkish Cypriots agreed in principle to its being placed under an interim UN administration; see *Times*, 3 April 1984.

37. At that time it was the scene of a notable incident involving UNFICYP. See Francis Henn, "The Nicosia Airport Incident of 1974: A Peacekeeping Gamble," *International Peacekeeping* 1 (Spring 1994), pp. 80–98.

38. For both proposals, see UN Document, S/26026 (1 July 1993).

39. See, for example, UN Documents S/26026 (1 July 1993), paras. 47 and 48, and S/1994/629 (30 May 1994), paras. 48 and 49.

40. UN Document S/1994/629 (30 May 1994), para. 53.

discovered a "difficulty" in "accepting [the] manner of proceeding" proposed by the Secretary-General (the other side was also unhappy about it). Thus, despite "a very substantial measure of agreement," progress, it was claimed, was being held up by a lack of agreement "on how to record the clarifications that have emerged from recent discussions."[41]

It is certainly conceivable that the parties will come to accept some version of the proposed confidence-building measures. But it cannot be assumed that this would have the hoped-for ameliorating effect on their attitudes, particularly that of the TRNC, to an overall settlement. Were the TRNC to be abandoned by Turkey, both diplomatically and militarily, the picture would undergo a dramatic change. At one point a report circulated of the TRNC being "under intense pressure from Ankara." But the credibility of the report was somewhat tarnished by its statement that in consequence the TRNC had "all but agreed"[42] to a new dividing line which would give them, in the context of a federal solution, 29 percent of Cyprus as compared to the 37 percent they have held since 1974. For the TRNC had in principle agreed to 29 percent a number of years earlier.[43] And in the event the particular territorial disposition which was being proposed, and which elicited the report, was far from one which secured agreement.

It does seem that although Turkey finds the TRNC something of an international incubus, not least in respect of its wish to join the European Union (of which Greece is a member, and wields a veto on new applications), it would be almost politically impossible in the present situation for Turkey to cut all links with the territory which is not just its creation but which has received its ostentatious protection for two decades. The underlying strength of the link is illustrated by the outcome of a recent attempt by Turkey's Prime Minister, responding to American and British pressure, to persuade the TRNC to accept the UN's proposed confidence-building measures: it was reported to have caused "opposition uproar."[44] Of course, nothing is impossible in politics. But at least in the context of a continued Cypriot stalemate, it is improbable that the TRNC will lose Turkish support.

As Turkey is hugely better placed than any other source to twist the TRNC's arm, but is itself in a reasonable position to resist most third-party pressure, there would seem to be little future in trying to advance a settlement through greater external toughness. Yet this is what the UN now seems to be contemplating. For the Security Council has recently asked the Secretary-General "to begin consultations with members of the Council,

---

41. UN Document S/1994/785 (1 July 1994), pp. 4 and 5.
42. *Independent* (London), 13 August 1992.
43. Cf. *Times*, 31 July 1992 and UN Document S/24472 (21 August 1992), para. 20.
44. *Times*, 31 May 1994.

with the Guarantor Powers [Britain, Greece and Turkey], and with the two leaders in Cyprus with a view to undertaking a fundamental and far-reaching reflection on ways of approaching the Cyprus problem in a manner which will yield results" (Resolution 939 of 29 July 1994). It may be, however, that "results" in the shape of a settlement are barely compatible with the approach which has now been followed without success for thirty years. That raises the question whether the UN's approach should itself be reconsidered. It would mean thinking the hitherto unthinkable.

What Sort of Settlement?

The problem in Cyprus reflects the deep suspicion which each community has of the other. This chiefly comes to notice in relation to the sense of insecurity felt by the minority group, the Turkish-Cypriots—an insecurity which has been described as "justified by history."[45] Thus, at least some years ago, on entering the TRNC at the crossing point in central Nicosia, one was invited by a notice to visit the nearby "Museum of Barbarism," which illustrated acts of that kind done to the Turkish-Cypriots by the other Cypriot community. At the crossing point itself there was, in 1993

...a photographic display put up by the Turkish Cypriots depicting the bloody sectarian violence before 1974 and paying tribute to the 30,000 troops from mainland Turkey stationed in the north since. "No more massacres, no more mass graves since 1974," the sign says. "Thanks to Turkey, thanks to the Turkish army, thanks to our fighters."[46]

But there is insecurity on the other side too. It is less obvious these days, but there are keen folk memories of Turkish atrocities against Greeks when the Turks were top dogs—chiefly during the three centuries of Islamic Ottoman rule prior to Britain taking over the island in 1878. This sort of consciousness is also fuelled in a more general way by the long-standing strain and rivalry in relations between Greece and Turkey in the eastern Mediterranean. Very specifically, and contemporaneously, the animosity is brought to life by the fighting between Islamic and Greek Orthodox groups in Bosnia–Herzegovina. On a wider canvas it is the Greeks who are in a minority. In that context more than 2000 years of Greek civilisation counts for little.

Given the deep suspicion and distrust to which this historical record gives rise, the appropriateness of trying to recreate a single state to encompass both communities may be questioned. Back in the early 1960s the initial scheme lasted for little more than three years. Tomorrow's federation

---

45. Leading article in *Times,* 30 May 1989.
46. *Independent,* 28 October 1993.

would be much looser than the earlier arrangement, and it must be noted that the Greek-Cypriots have gone so far as to accept the idea that their co-community should enjoy a defined territory and run its own internal affairs. But the Greek-Cypriots are bound to want a relatively strong centre—at the least one which will probably be too strong for the Turkish-Cypriots. Even if signatures could be secured for such a plan, it would surely also have to be approved by referenda in both communities, which would be an additional hurdle—doubtless of some magnitude. And even if it were sur-mounted, the nagging thought remains: how long would it last? A political association between erstwhile adversaries holds promise only if there seems to be an underlying reconciliation. In Cyprus—where a very large ethnic fault-line is located—such a reconciliation is hard to perceive.

Considered just in isolation, therefore, the outlook for a Cypriot federation is not that bright. Placed in the perspective of the fissiparous proclivities shown by federations in recent years, it becomes decidedly gloomy. There could therefore be something to be said for focusing instead on the fact that here are two ethnic groups divided by a comfortingly solid political line. In the contemporary world, that might be seen as a mercy.

Such an approach would have been broadly acceptable to virtually all outsiders at any time prior to the last 50 years. The TRNC could have been incorporated into Turkey, or protected by Turkey as its sovereign puppet or (to use a somewhat less discommoding terminology) satellite—which is what it currently is. Half a century ago, however, the illegitimacy of acquiring territory by the use of force was established in law by the UN Charter, and has since been elevated to one of the most basic orthodoxies of the international society—indeed, probably the most basic. Here lies the source of the TRNC's problem. Attempts to counter it by appealing to the idea of self-determination have made no headway. For, notwithstanding that principle's high position in the international pantheon, its citation is un-heeded in situations which involve the involuntary loss by a sovereign state of some of its metropolitan territory.[47]

Only, therefore, if the ROC should renounce its claim to all the northern part of the island of Cyprus and recognise the (doubtless territorially adjusted) TRNC does the latter have a chance of international recognition as a legitimate state. This is certainly one theoretical route to an overall settlement. An outsider might suggest that there is much to be said for it. Economically, the ROC has prospered in recent years and no longer needs

---

47. When becoming the sovereign state of Bangladesh in 1971, the former East Pakistan benefited from its geographical separation from West Pakistan (where the Government of Pakistan was located) inasmuch as this encouraged the idea that it was not truly a part of Pakistan's metropolitan territory.

the once valuable north. (Indeed, a federation could have quite substantial economic costs for the south.) A reconciliation with the TRNC could also reduce the ROC's military budget (Cyprus is, on both sides, quite densely militarised), not to mention its anxiety about its territorial security. In a broader context, too, recognition of the TRNC could make the ROC feel more secure, for such a move could help to detach the TRNC, in both political and military terms, from the much feared Turkey.

But such a course would require a truly heroic act of renunciation on the part of the ROC. Again it must be remembered that the most surprising things happen in politics. But even on the most remotely realistic calculation, an act of this magnitude is not within the ROC's present political reach—and is unlikely to be contemplated until another generation has assumed office, and perhaps not even then. Acceptance of territorial truncation flies in the face of the main political and legal developments of the twentieth century.

Notwithstanding, therefore, all the setbacks it has encountered, the search for a settlement involving the re-creation of a single state will assuredly continue. Most modern politicians seem unable to bear the thought that a problem may have to be laid aside, at least for a while, as insoluble. (Perhaps they feel it threatens their *raison d'être*.) They must "press forward" and "be positive." Nor would the UN's bureaucrats be happy with inaction. And those many academics with an itch to contribute to policy and peace also push on in the same direction.

The suggestion may, however, be ventured that the virtues of a timetable and an agenda of a relatively relaxed and unambitious kind should not be forgotten. The idea that time is running inexorably out so that an early agreement is vital is often met in this case (as in others), yet for those without an axe to grind it is a curiously unpolitical approach. In an apparently well embedded stalemate, a low-key, step-by-step strategy would seem to be suggested. Renewed and less frenetic attention could be paid to the variety of possible confidence-building measures. The ROC might not like the lack of urgency, but it could be reminded that as between the TRNC and itself, its position is much the more favourable. For the TRNC, the ongoing prospect of being tied to Turkey's apron strings as a weak and unrecognised state must, in the small hours of the night, look rather bleak.

UNFICYP's Role

This, however, implies the continuation of the present distrustful confrontation. In that context, and on the assumption that a resort to arms is undesirable, UNFICYP has a most important role. The UN Secretariat's arguments about its value are thought to be convincing. Currently therefore the question is whether the UN believes that maintaining peace in Cyprus is more important than punishing the parties for their involvement in a dispute which both quite genuinely find intractable. And if it does, there is a further question as to whether the UN may have gone too far in cutting down the size of the force, the capacity of which "to react to incidents (on average 90 per month) to prevent them from escalating"[48] has, it is claimed, already been adversely affected. This, too, carries conviction.

Accordingly, despite all the pressures which UN peacekeeping and its contributor-states are now under, there is a case for some expansion of UNFICYP. With many states now supplying peacekeepers for the first time, the Cyprus force could even be looked on as a kind of training ground for traditional peacekeeping—which, especially when conducted at borders, is perhaps more fruitful than peacekeeping of a prickly kind.[49]

Additionally, it should be borne in mind that a settlement in Cyprus—of any sort—is unlikely to dispense with the need for peacekeepers. The coming into force of a federal agreement, for example, will not magically remove all tension. Both sides may want the continued presence of an impartial intermediary force—and if the Greek-Cypriots should want it less than now (due to the withdrawal of Turkish forces), the Turkish-Cypriots are likely to want it more. The point is no less applicable to an agreement which represented a formal parting of the ways. And in either case it is possible that the Security Council might wish to toughen the legal basis for the force by making it clear that it was not removable at the whim of one side only.

It is indeed an unfortunate fact of life that some disputes, such as the one in Cyprus, resist settlement. But fact of life it is. If, in the meanwhile, the world wishes (as it proclaims) to avoid armed accidents, then peacekeeping may be needed over a long period. The case of Cyprus illuminates this point too. Impatience at the extraordinary length of this particular peacekeeping enterprise has understandably crept in. But there is no call for pique. UNFICYP has contributed most valuably to the maintenance of calm in Cyprus and is required still. The world should not begrudge that need.

---

48. UN Document S/26777 (22 November 1993), para. 93.
49. See the writer's other chapter in this volume ("Peacekeeping, Peace-Enforcement and National Sovereignty") for a discussion of the nature of prickly peacekeeping.

4

The UN Protection Force in Former Yugoslavia

Susan R. Lamb

UN peacekeeping operations in the 1980s and early 1990s registered several successes, which bred the belief that the UN offered, if not a new world order, a new capacity to deal with disorder.[1] The Balkans conflict provided the particular setting for an early test of Security Council reaction in a post-Cold War world. Yet the UN Protection Force in Yugoslavia (UNPROFOR), established in 1992 and covering Croatia, Bosnia and the former Yugoslav Republic of Macedonia, has also been a sobering reminder of the limits of the UN's authority. Resource and organisational limitations, the number of problems crying out for attention and the intractability of so many of them highlight the difficulties that lie ahead in the attempt by the United Nations to adapt to new conditions. This chapter traces the background to the establishment of UNPROFOR, describes the nature of this response, the mixed fortunes of UNPROFOR and finally draws some lessons from its experiences for UN peacekeeping in general.

Background

Yugoslavia has deep and long-standing ethnic and religious cleavages, giving rise to a variety of historical antagonisms. In 1991, these ancient ethnic animosities, inflamed by modern political movements, exploded into civil war.[2]

---

1. D. Smith, "Just War, Clausewitz and Sarajevo," *Journal of Peace Research* 31 (May 1994), p. 136.
2. For greater detail and a variety of perspectives on the origins of the Balkan conflict, see

Fighting first broke out in former Yugoslavia when, after Croatia and Slovenia proclaimed their independence on 25 June 1991, the Yugoslav army went into action against Slovenia. However, Slovenian resistance was fierce and the West condemned the federal army's intervention and mounted several mediating missions.[3] Hostilities were quickly ended and, after only a brief fight with federal troops, Slovenia won independence in June 1991.

The next stage of the crisis was the escalation of the conflict into Croatia. After a series of ceasefires broke down, the European Community (EC) sought to facilitate a diplomatic settlement of the dispute. The EC members, however, were divided as to the appropriate response. Germany favoured the recognition of Croatia and Slovenia, on the basis that war between neighbouring states is easier to end than an internal dispute; that is, it could then intervene to protect Croatia, at Croatia's request. Most EC members initially resisted recognition, in the belief that it would make Serbia even more obdurate and leave its other neighbours exposed.[4] On 15 January 1992, however, Slovenia and Croatia were recognised by the EC.[5]

With Germany's and, shortly afterwards, the EC's collective decision to disregard UN Secretary-General Javier Pérez de Cuéllar's warning that "any early, selective recognition would widen the present conflict and fuel an explosive situation especially in Bosnia–Herzegovina," the stage was set for a particularly brutal phase of the evolving Yugoslav conflict: war in the multiethnic patchwork of Bosnia.[6] By the late summer of 1992, the humanitarian consequences of the war, brought about by the destruction of villages and the displacement of civilian communities on a scale not seen since the Second World War, seemed to demand that action be taken.[7] It was against this backdrop that UNPROFOR was established.

Noel Malcolm, *Bosnia: A Short History* (London: Macmillan, 1994); Mark Almond, *Europe's Backyard War: The War in the Balkans* (London: Heinemann, 1994); Misha Glenny, *The Fall of Yugoslavia: The Third Balkan War* (London: Penguin, 1993); Dusko Doder, "Yugoslavia: New War, Old Hatreds," *Foreign Policy* 91 (Summer 1993), pp. 3–23; and William Pfaff, "Invitation to War," *Foreign Affairs* 72 (Summer 1993) pp. 97–109.

3. *Economist* (London), 6 July 1991, p. 51.

4. Germany had recognised Croatia on 23 December 1991; *Economist*, 18 January 1992, p. 41. For an account of the EC response to the Yugoslav conflict, see Jonathan Eyal, *Europe and Yugoslavia: Lessons from a Failure* (London: Whitehall Paper Series, 1993).

5. For an account of the complexities, in international law, surrounding the recognition of the former Yugoslav republics, see Marc Weller, "The International Response to the Dissolution of the Socialist Federal Republic of Yugoslavia," *American Journal of International Law* 86 (July 1992), pp. 569–607.

6. Mats Berdal, "United Nations Peacekeeping in the Former Yugoslavia," in D. Daniel and B. Hayes, eds., *Beyond Traditional Peacekeeping* (London: Macmillan, forthcoming).

7. *Report of the Secretary-General Pursuant to Security Council Resolution 752 (1992)*, II.

Negotiations Leading to the Establishment of UNPROFOR

The manifest failure of European institutions to arrest the violent turn that the disintegration of the Yugoslav Federation took in the summer and autumn of 1991 led the UN to assume a more prominent role in finding a solution to the conflict. Amidst growing signs of divisions within Europe over the handling of the crisis, the UN was viewed as a body whose credibility was "uncontaminated by national biases, historical memories or proximity to the epicentre of the conflict."[8] In late 1991, the UN began to consider whether the circumstances were appropriate for the dispatch of a peacekeeping force, and the Security Council asked the UN's special envoy Cyrus Vance to report to it about the practicalities of peacekeeping.[9]

The controversy surrounding sending peacekeepers in without a firm ceasefire led some to conclude that the choice of peacekeeping as a mode of international intervention in former Yugoslavia was inappropriate from the outset.[10] Indeed, there was initially considerable uncertainty as to whether conditions in Bosnia and Croatia were suitable for the dispatch of peace-keeping forces. The stumbling block was the doubt that existed over the likelihood of the parties instituting an effective ceasefire and then co-operating with the representatives of the world body. The uneasy nature of the peace seemed to clash with the common-sense principle that peace-keepers should not be sent where there is no peace to keep, and there were those within the UN itself who argued in early 1992 that the UN should stay out of the developing conflict. In their view, to seek to establish a UN operation dedicated to ancillary relief (the provision of humanitarian aid) without a ceasefire in place is futile.[11] Moreover, and although the Serbs formally accepted the UN plan, not all politicians and soldiers on each side saw an advantage in peace.[12]

There were, nonetheless, pressures for UN involvement that both the Secretariat and the member-states found difficult to resist. For instance, with the deteriorating human rights situation and manifest intransigence of some of the parties to the conflict, it was seen as a moral imperative for previous

8. Berdal, "United Nations Peacekeeping in Former Yugoslavia."
9. *Economist,* 30 November 1991, p. 49.
10. "Everything about the situation in the former Yugoslavia has made it unsuitable for peacekeeping, and appropriate for enforcement action"; Rosalyn Higgins, "The New United Nations and Former Yugoslavia," *International Affairs* 69 (July 1993), p. 470. See also Michael Dewar, "Intervention in Bosnia: The Case Against," *World Today* 49 (February 1993), pp. 32–34. For a contrary view, see Jane M. O. Sharp, "Intervention in Bosnia: The Case For," *World Today* 49 (February 1993), pp. 29–31.
11. Higgins, "The New United Nations and Former Yugoslavia," p. 469.
12. *Economist,* 22 February 1992, p. 15.

UN action to be effectively followed up.[13] Additionally, and even though all sides in the civil war may not have agreed unequivocally to the UN ceasefire plan, UN Secretary-General Boutros Boutros-Ghali and his special envoy Cyrus Vance still believed there to be a real chance for peace, given the high degree of war-weariness and domestic dissent within Serbia and Croatia themselves.[14] Additionally, the sending of peacekeepers was seen as a means of consolidating the initial Croatian ceasefire (even if it was tenuous) and of deterring the resumption of violence, although it was recognised that the eventual resolution of the dispute required the willingness of the parties to negotiate for a lasting settlement.

Thus the pressure for involvement was (for good humanitarian reasons) irresistible. With the concurrence of the Security Council, the Secretary-General dispatched 50 military liaison officers to Yugoslavia in January 1992.[15] By the end of January, the Croatian ceasefire appeared to be holding and in early February, there were talks that led to the deployment of an approximately 14 000-strong UN peacekeeping force to replace the Serb-led Yugoslav army in the three enclaves that it had seized in Croatia.[16] On 15 February, the Secretary-General recommended the establishment of UNPROFOR, which was endorsed by the Security Council in Resolution 743 (21 February 1992). Later, the UN's peacekeeping work was extended into Bosnia–Herzegovina and Macedonia.

Mandate, Structure and History of UNPROFOR

Sanctions imposed by the United Nations against the constituent republics of former Yugoslavia since 1991 have been essentially in two parts: an arms embargo on all of the former Yugoslav republics (which has been controversial from the outset because of its potentially discriminatory burden on Bosnian Muslims) and economic sanctions of successively increasing stringency against Serbia and Montenegro.[17]

UNPROFOR was established by Resolution 743 "to create conditions of peace and security required for the negotiation of an overall settlement of the Yugoslav crisis." It was to be deployed in three UN Protected Areas (UNPAs): Eastern Slavonia, Western Slavonia and Krajina. The mandate of UNPROFOR had four main aspects. The first was to consolidate the cease-

---

13. A. Rosas, "Towards Some International Law and Order," *Journal of Peace Research* 31 (May 1994), p. 129.
14. *Economist,* 22 February 1992, p. 15.
15. *United Nations Peacekeeping* (UN Document PS/DPI/6/Rev.5, May 1994), p. 56.
16. *Economist,* 18 January 1992, p. 41.
17. Security Council Resolutions 713 (25 September 1991), 757 (30 May 1992), 787 (16 November 1992) and 820 (17 April 1993).

fire throughout the UNPAs. Second, all armed forces, paramilitary and irregular forces within the UNPAs were to be disbanded, demobilised or demilitarised. Third, unarmed UN civilian police monitors would oversee the activities of local police forces and ensure that basic human rights within the UNPAs were protected, especially against ethnic cleansing. Fourth, the force was to assist humanitarian agencies in returning such displaced persons who wished to return to their homes in the UNPAs.[18] In June 1992, the Security Council enlarged UNPROFOR's mandate to include monitoring of the "pink zones" of Croatia, that is, Serb-controlled areas adjacent to the UNPAs.[19]

As for size, as of 30 April 1994 the total strength of UNPROFOR was 34 555 and included military personnel, civilian police and international civilian staff drawn from 35 countries.[20]

The question as to who is to comprise UN forces has traditionally been a stumbling block. The need for impartiality led to the general practice of not using troops from certain countries. In particular, the UN avoided using troop contingents from the permanent members of the UN Security Council and from neighbouring powers. In the particular setting of Yugoslavia, these issues have underscored the importance, in an operational environment where consent is far from absolute, of maintaining impartiality with respect to the local parties. Equally important is the need to develop an awareness of the sensitivities, both cultural and political, which are unique to the area of deployment. The deployment of certain contingents within UNPROFOR have tended to work against these principles. The Russian battalion, for instance, was foolishly deployed to the sector in Croatia adjacent to Serbia proper with whom Russia was thought locally to be sympathetic.[21]

However, departures from the ordinary peacekeeping practice of not sending troops from states with interests in the region involved was exacerbated in the case of UNPROFOR by severe troop shortages. This has been caused, in part, by the dramatic increase in the number of large-scale peacekeeping operations in the 1990s. The demand overload has created an acute need for new troop-contributing countries, which suggests, in turn, that the UN may have to accept help from wherever it is offered. In addition, this has inevitably meant that troops actually deployed have varying degrees of familiarity with the principles and procedures of peacekeeping. The uneven troop quality, lack of agreed staff procedures and standard operating procedures concerning activities such as communications and logistics have

---

18. UN Document S/23592, 15 February 1992, para. 18.
19. *United Nations Peacekeeping* (UN Document PS/DPI/6/Rev.5, May 1994), p. 57.
20. *Ibid.*, pp. 171–75.
21. Berdal, "United Nations Peacekeeping in Former Yugoslavia."

70   Susan R. Lamb

frequently complicated the smooth functioning of the force.[22]
In Bosnia, the focus of UN operations became explicitly humanitarian. In
the summer of 1992, the UN commenced the delivery of humanitarian relief
into the Bosnian capital, Sarajevo, and UNPROFOR's mandate was
extended into Bosnia. Peacekeeping forces were given the primary task of
supporting "efforts by the UNHCR [UN High Commissioner for Refugees]
to deliver humanitarian relief throughout Bosnia and Herzegovina, and in
particular to provide protection, at UNHCR's request, where and when
UNHCR considered such protection necessary" (Security Council Resolution 758, 8 June 1992). The Council, acting under chapter VII of the
Charter, called on member-states to "take all measures necessary" either
nationally or through regional organisations to facilitate, in coordination
with the UN, the delivery of humanitarian aid (Resolution 770, 13 August
1992). In early 1993, the Council renewed UNPROFOR's mandate to
"ensure the security of UNPROFOR" and "its freedom of movement for all
its missions" (Resolution 807, 19 February 1993).
    Chapter VII was similarly invoked in relation to safe areas, authorising
enforcement of the "no fly zone" in Bosnia–Herzegovina. On 9 February
1994, NATO issued a threat of military action against heavy weaponry in
and around Sarajevo. The legal basis for this was Security Council Resolution 836 (1993) which gives member-states, acting nationally or through
regional organisations, the right to take "under the authority of the Security
Council and UNPROFOR, all necessary measures, through the use of air
power, in and around the safe areas in the Republic of Bosnia and
Herzegovina."[23]
    UNPROFOR is, however, only partly a chapter VII peace-enforcement
operation, and is mandated to use armed force only on a limited basis.
Chapter VII mandates were assigned to certain aspects of UNPROFOR to
ensure, particularly in Bosnia–Herzegovina, the safe delivery of humanitarian aid, the security and freedom of movement of personnel, the protection of safe areas and, as mentioned above, the enforcement of the "no fly
zone" in Bosnia–Herzegovina.[24] However, it has never been given limitless
enforcement powers.
    A further significant development was UNPROFOR's preventive deploy-
ment in Macedonia, which involved the positioning of forces on the Macedonian side of the republic's border with Albania and the Federal Republic

---

22. Adam Roberts, "The Crisis in UN Peacekeeping," *Survival* 36 (Autumn 1994), p. 116.
    23. This action is in turn linked to a ban on military flights in the airspace of Bosnia–
Herzegovina, established by Security Council Resolution 781 (9 October 1992).
    24. Security Council Resolutions 770 (13 August 1992), 807 (19 February 1993), 824 (6
May 1993), 836 (4 June 1993), 844 (18 June 1993) and 816 (31 March 1993).

of Yugoslavia (Serbia and Montenegro). Preventive deployment is a new concept for the UN that was given prominence by the Secretary-General's advocacy in *An Agenda for Peace* and used for the first time in Macedonia. The essence of this strategy is that it is a preventive military response, involving the positioning of troops, military observers and related personnel on one or both sides of a border between entities that are in dispute (or where there is an emerging threat of conflict), with the primary object of deterring the escalation of that situation into armed conflict.

In the case of Macedonia, there was a concern (in the context of the deteriorating situation in former Yugoslavia generally, and its own continuing dispute with Greece) that if the neighbouring Kosovo area of Serbia were to erupt in a conflict between the Serbs and Albanian Muslims, Macedonia—with a quarter of its own population Albanian—could be rapidly drawn into a conflict, with other powers possibly also becoming involved.[25] Macedonia thus presented a clear "emerging threat" situation. In December 1992, the Security Council authorised the deployment of a small force of 700, plus military observers and civil police, to monitor Macedonia's borders and report developments which could signify a threat to its territory. This was augmented in July 1993 by a further 300 troops. The operation in Macedonia has a mandate to monitor developments in the border areas which "could undermine confidence and stability in Macedonia or threaten its security" (Security Council Resolution 795, 11 December 1992).

The forces deployed in Macedonia are clearly too small on their own to handle any actual armed conflict that might erupt in the area. The "deterrent" instead consists in the fact that the Security Council has demonstrated its interest in the situation; all the relevant parties are under close international scrutiny; and there is at least an implied willingness to take further action if there is any resort to violence. The force signals a commitment on the part of the international community to ensure that the conflict in Bosnia does not spread southwards. Its credibility as a deterrent will depend on the weight that potential transgressors give to international opinion and their assessment of the likelihood of a strong Security Council reaction.[26]

Successes and Failures

With the exception of Macedonia, the UN forces in former Yugoslavia have had to contend with continual harassment from the warring factions,

---

25. For background to the Macedonian issue, see James Pettifer, "The New Macedonian Question," *International Affairs* 68 (July 1992), pp. 475–85.

26. Gareth Evans, *Cooperating for Peace: The Global Agenda for the 1990s and Beyond* (Sydney: Allen & Unwin, 1993), pp. 81–82.

and the armed conflict in Bosnia continues virtually unabated. UNPROFOR has not been without its achievements. In almost any situation short of all-out war, the presence of UN peacekeepers is likely to have some impact on the local scene. Opportunities arise for ameliorative activity and the parties are generally not disposed to disregard totally the representatives of the world body.[27]

In Croatia, one early achievement was persuading both sides to withdraw their heavy artillery and tanks to a distance of 30km from the line of confrontation, thus eliminating breaches of the ceasefire through the use of these weapons. Furthermore, much of this weaponry was handed over for safekeeping to the UN and, as agreed, the Yugoslav and Croatian army units withdrew from the UNPAs.[28] More generally, Western Slavonia seems to have been relatively calm. The UN Civil Police are said to have received much local confidence, notwithstanding the fact that theirs is only a monitoring role.[29] There also seemed to have been some improvement in the local security situation in many parts of the UNPAs over the two months straddling Christmas 1992.

UNPROFOR also had some success outside the UNPAs. The Yugoslav National Army had initially been reluctant to withdraw from the Dubrovnik area of Croatia because of the strategic importance of the nearby peninsula and Gulf of Kotor, the only significant harbour available to Serbia and Montenegro. Eventually, however, agreement was reached that the peninsula should be demilitarised and heavy weapons removed from the neighbouring areas of Croatia and Montenegro. UNPROFOR was to monitor the implementation of this agreement, and the necessary extension of its mandate was granted by the Security Council.[30] Elsewhere in Croatia, the UN was able to assist with the defusing of tension over the Peruca High Dam to the southeast of Knin by persuading all concerned that it should become an UNPROFOR responsibility.[31]

In Bosnia, the NATO threat of military action under Resolution 836 led, initially at least, to the withdrawal or transfer to UN control of most of the heavy weaponry involved, and breaches of the "no fly zone" significantly decreased following the adoption of Resolution 816.[32] In addition, military

27. Alan James, "The UN in Croatia: An Exercise in Futility?," *World Today* 49 (May 1993), p. 94.
28. UN Document A/24353, 27 July 1992, paras. 3–6.
29. UN Document S/24848, 24 November 1992, para. 15.
30. UN Document S/24600, 28 September 1992, para. 24 and Security Council Resolution 779 (6 October 1992).
31. During a recurrence of fighting in early 1993, however, the dam was damaged. *Times* (London), 29 January, 30 January and 1 February 1993.
32. Evans, *Cooperating for Peace*, p. 150.

capabilities and technical expertise in areas of communications and logistics have undoubtedly been of critical importance in supporting the humanitarian operation. In particular, through effective cooperation UNPROFOR has enabled the UNHCR to maintain the Sarajevo airlift (the largest such airlift in the history of humanitarian operations), repair basic infrastructure and ensure access to roads which would otherwise have been impassable because of mines. UNPROFOR's engineering units, though clearly of too limited a capacity given the nature of the tasks in Bosnia, have also been able to do essential repair work on roads and bridges.[33]

UNPROFOR's problems, however, far outweigh its achievements. Some of the former stem from difficulties regarding the boundaries of the UNPAs. The UNPAs, as designated in the original UN plan, did not cover all the Croatian territory which was under Serb control. Croatia refused to allow any extension of the protected areas into the so-called "pink zones."[34] However, it is the situation within the UNPAs which has caused the UN the most anguish, for the Serbs have resolutely obstructed the execution of UNPROFOR's central mandate—the demilitarisation plan. No sooner had the force been deployed than the Secretary-General was noting that the withdrawal of the Yugoslav National Army was accompanied by the "parallel emergence of strengthened police and military organisations."[35] In July 1992 UNPROFOR tried to take a tough line on this matter, blockading groups of Serb police in two separate areas. But in each case, the situation deteriorated rapidly and, to avoid bloodshed, it was decided to suspend the use of force.[36] A short while later an attempt to disarm Serbian irregulars resulted in UN troops being surrounded and in further threatening moves.

Such measures led to the so-called "police" becoming increasingly hostile towards UNPROFOR personnel. As the Serb forces numbered some 16 000 armed men, equipped with armored personnel carriers, mortars, machine guns and other arms prohibited under the peacekeeping plan, it is not surprising that the UN force has since avoided forceful initiatives. Nor is it surprising that violations of the ceasefire have occurred frequently.

More significantly, UNPROFOR has been unable to protect the local population. Early on, success in checking mass expulsions was reported. But lesser instances of intimidation were rife, indicative of a concerted effort to change the areas' ethnic composition. Daily reports were received of

---

33. Berdal, "United Nations Peacekeeping in Former Yugoslavia."
34. As a fallback position it was agreed that the UN might monitor the situation in the Zones and that in this connection a Joint Commission should be set up. UN Document S/24353, 27 July 1992, para. 10.
35. UN Document S/24353, 27 July 1992, para. 7.
36. UN Document S/24600, 28 September 1992, para. 5.

murders, the burning and demolition of houses, the destruction of churches, armed robberies and assaults, all of which crimes were usually aimed at members of national minorities.[37] Given this situation, virtually no progress has been made with that part of UNPROFOR's mandate which refers to the return to their homes of displaced persons.[38]

Explanations for Successes and Failures

UNPROFOR has been dogged by resource constraints, logistical problems, difficulties of command and control, ambiguous mandates, the tenuous nature of local consent and the sheer intractability of local conflicts.

Mismatch Between Objectives and Resources

The continuing brutality of the war, especially in Bosnia–Herzegovina, has generated constant pressure for further action, including a progressive enlargement of earlier mandates. Yet, as Berdal notes, the manpower, logistical and financial resources required to match the aspirations contained in the rapidly changing mandates have been far more difficult to obtain.[39]

Perhaps the clearest expression of this tendency is seen in the number of resolutions declaring and subsequently authorising UNPROFOR to "act in self-defence to deter attacks" against six so-called "UN safe areas" in Bosnia (Sarajevo, Tuzla, Zepa, Gorazde, Bihac and Srebrenica). In support of this decision, Resolution 844 (18 June 1993) authorised the deployment of 7600 troops, the "minimal light option" recommended by the Secretary-General to ensure a modicum of safety in the identified enclaves (even though the Force Commander had initially estimated that to "obtain deterrence through strength," some 34 000 troops would have to have been deployed). By February 1994, only some 3500 troops had actually been deployed, most of them in Sarajevo and Tuzla, while in Zepa a UN advance party consisted of 10 soldiers only. While the deployment of even limited troops to the safe areas has been beneficial in terms of halting incursions by ground troops, it has "done rather less to reduce the intensity of indirect fire against several of the towns supposedly safe from Serbian aggression."[40]

The mismatch between commitments and resources has also been evident in the financing of UNPROFOR. As of 30 April 1994, contributions outstanding to its special account were about $686m.[41] Such resource limi-

37. UN Document S/24848, 24 November 1992, para. 15.
38. James, "The UN in Croatia," p. 95.
39. Berdal, "United Nations Peacekeeping in Former Yugoslavia."
40. *Ibid.*
41. *United Nations Peacekeeping* (UN Document PS/DPI/6/Rev.5, May 1994), p. 84.

tations act as a considerable, though perennial, constraint on UN activity.

Multiple and Undeliverable Mandates

Some UNPROFOR mandates have proven impossible given the available resources, others mandates have appeared to be unrealistic *per se*. On many occasions it has seemed as if the UN was saddling itself with a series of tasks which were beyond the reach of any peacekeeping mission, even one as large as UNPROFOR. For instance, there was arguably no realistic prospect that all parties to the conflict would allow themselves to be demilitarised and thus, as a practical matter, the portion of UNPROFOR's mandate pertaining to demilitarisation was a non-starter.[42]

Other resolutions have clearly been, if not undeliverable, of little more than symbolic significance even though their actual implementation has entailed considerable activity on the part of the contributing powers. The decision to establish a "no fly zone" in the airspace over Bosnia–Herzegovina on 9 October 1992, and the subsequent decision to "enforce" it was a clear example of a resolution which had little direct impact on the war itself, and even less on the political efforts aimed at resolving the conflict.

Security Council mandates, by their very nature, will continue to embody political compromises reflecting the competing interests of member-states. As such they are unlikely ever to satisfy a ground commander's wish for an unambiguous mission statement. Still, the excessive proliferation of mandates in UNPROFOR has created problems of its own by the gulf between the Security Council resolutions and the means available to put them into effect. Over time this has "undermined the effectiveness of UNPROFOR and has reduced the in-theatre credibility of the UN."[43]

Lack of Consent on the Ground

The chapter VII basis of UNPROFOR illustrated that the issue of consent was in practice complex and nuanced. Consent proved difficult to attain in former Yugoslavia due to the multitude of parties involved and disputes about their status.[44] Indeed, the cooperation from all parties deemed essential for the implementation of the UN peace plan has never been forthcoming, and this has made it increasingly difficult for UNPROFOR to fulfil its mandate of meeting pressing humanitarian needs and protecting threatened civilian populations. For instance, Serbian irregular and paramilitary elements refused from the outset to allow UN control at the inter-

---

42. James, "The UN in Croatia," p. 93.
43. Berdal, "United Nations Peacekeeping in Former Yugoslavia."
44. Roberts, "Crisis in UN Peacekeeping," pp. 98–100.

national borders. The situation in the UNPAs deteriorated after the deployment of UN forces who were unable to prevent forced expulsions, ethnic persecutions and other atrocities against civilian populations. This in turn undermined UN credibility. In January 1993, Croatian forces launched a coordinated attack on Serb positions in the UNPAs and "pink zones," overrunning UN positions and blatantly violating the agreed ceasefire.[45] The attack further heightened tensions and mutual suspicions and ruled out the implementation of other aspects of the peace plan, such as the return of refugees and displaced persons to their villages.

Continuing non-cooperation by the local Serbs and consistent violations of the ceasefire by Croatian authorities mean that the "conditions of peace and security" required for the pursuit of a negotiated solution and the fulfilment of other humanitarian tasks have never been established. In this regard Bosnia highlights the difficulty of making peacekeeping work *vis-à-vis* armed groups outside the direct control of recognised political authorities with whom the UN can conclude the necessary political and practical agreements.[46] Instead, UNPROFOR is merely overseeing an uneasy and fragile truce in an unresolved Serb–Croat conflict.

Deficiencies in Planning, Implementation and Logistics

In general, UN troops often depend for their effectiveness and survival on an infrastructure that is increasingly not up to the task.[47] The lack of a contingency planning mechanism and the resulting inability of UN planners in New York to anticipate logistical requirements accounts in part for the difficulties encountered in UNPROFOR. In particular, the absence of a proper planning capability that could coordinate logistics activity and direct the initial logistics flow into the mission area slowed down the deployment.

Additionally, UNPROFOR has never been able to set up an integrated logistics system and has therefore been unable to sustain forces in the field efficiently. Given the endemic lack of operational readiness in the UN field support system, the size of the deployment meant that UNPROFOR had to rely heavily on the logistical capabilities of individual units. An important factor contributing to the delays has been the UN procurement system. A further problem throughout has been the lack of delegation of financial authority from New York to the field and the inability to conduct long and medium-term budget planning because of short mandate periods. Added to

45. *United Nations Peacekeeping* (UN Document PS/DPI/6/Rev.5, May 1994), pp. 57–58.
46. Marrack Goulding, "The Evolution of United Nations Peace Keeping," *International Affairs* 69 (July 1993), p. 459.
47. J. Ruggie, "Wandering in the Void: Charting the UN's New Strategic Role," *Foreign Affairs* 72 (November/December 1993), p. 26.

this, specific rules governing the processing of requests enormously complicate and delay the process of resupply to contingents in the field.

Three additional factors have also adversely influenced the logistical
situation in former Yugoslavia.[48] The first of these has been the difficulty of
obtaining logistic and engineering units from member-states. A second has
been the acute lack of spare parts, maintenance facilities and stocks of
peacekeeping equipment, all of which are needed to enhance UNPROFOR's
operational efficiency. Finally, rapid changes in UNPROFOR's mandate
have further contributed to the unsatisfactory logistical arrangements under
which peacekeeping forces have laboured in former Yugoslavia.

Command, Control and Communications

UNPROFOR has been beset with problems of command, control and
communications which have contributed to a sub-optimal performance.[49]
Shortage of sophisticated communications and intelligence equipment,
incompatibilities in the equipment brought by various contingents and highly
unfavourable terrain have all reduced the effectiveness of in-field communications.[50] The destruction of civilian telecommunications networks and
interference by local parties have further exacerbated these problems.

The UN in former Yugoslavia has sought to develop *ad hoc* systems of
command and control, containing important elements from both troop-
contributing countries and UN headquarters.[51] This has often created a
problematic relationship between the UN and national commands. The
general lack of a clearly defined chain of command within the mission is
highly unsatisfactory.[52] There are several aspects to this problem. In the
first place, the multi-component nature of UNPROFOR and the involvement
of numerous civilian agencies working, often uncomfortably, alongside the
military units have undermined the unity and integrity of command. The fact
that UNPROFOR's military observers have not been under the control of
the Force Commander has complicated matters further.

Another important factor has been the tendency of contributing nations
not to cede full command authority to the Force Commander. All the
principal troop contributors in former Yugoslavia, including Britain, France,
Spain and the Nordic countries, have on occasion either refused, or imposed

---

48. See Berdal, "United Nations Peacekeeping in former Yugoslavia."
49. *Ibid.*
50. Ruggie, "Wandering in the Void," p. 30.
51. Adam Roberts, "The United Nations and International Security," *Survival* 35 (Summer 1993), p. 18.
52. John Mackinlay, "Improving Multi-Functional Forces," *Survival* 36 (Autumn 1994), pp. 160–61.

their own conditions on, orders issued by the Force Commander. While this practice is hardly unique in the history of peacekeeping, its effects in the unique circumstances of Yugoslavia have made the exercise of full operational control by the Force Commander impossible. A further complicating factor in former Yugoslavia has been the failure to spell out clearly the relationship between those involved in the negotiating process in Geneva, those directing operations at headquarters in New York and the Special Representative and Force Commander in the theatre.[53]

Further difficult questions of divided command and control are raised in Yugoslavia by the extensive involvement of regional organisations. Though alleviating resource constraints at a time when the UN is notoriously overstretched, the involvement of regional organisations also allows for vacillation and inter-institutional squabbling. Institutional separation can give rise to the possibility of bureaucratic wrangling and the emergence of responsibility vacuums. Similarly, complex problems of coordination have arisen within UNPROFOR due to its mix of military and civilian functions.[54] The military–civilian interface in Bosnia, whereby the UNHCR has acted as the "lead agency," has highlighted the need for strengthened coordination and planning between the military and humanitarian components of the mission. In this regard, Berdal suggests that "agreement on delineating tasks and responsibilities must be made in the UN Secretariat as well as in-theatre."[55]

The Basic Intractability of the Dispute

A further explanation for the mixed fortunes of UNPROFOR is to be found in the inherently difficult nature of the issues being tackled and the intransigence of the parties to the conflict. For instance the Serbs do not appear likely to surrender their arms, allow the UN to control their enclaves or permit the return of displaced persons. Nor is the displacement of the Bosnian Muslims an incidental by-product of the war but the Serbs' very objective. In similar terms, Croatia is not going to agree that the enclaves may secede and will actively pursue efforts to establish its authority over them. Thus tension between the warring factions in former Yugoslavia is likely to continue for the foreseeable future. Given this reality, the UN has little appetite to launch the kind of military intervention required to reverse Serb gains or to seek to impose its original plan.[56] But equally it will be very reluctant simply to walk away from the problem.

This raises a very large question about the appropriateness of the UN's

---

53. Berdal, "United Nations Peacekeeping in Former Yugoslavia."
54. Mackinlay, "Improving Multi-Functional Forces," pp. 167–68.
55. Berdal, "United Nations Peacekeeping in Former Yugoslavia."
56. David Gompert, "How to Defeat Serbia," *Foreign Affairs* 73 (July/August 1994), p. 30.

present peacekeeping arrangements, and indeed, what the goal of intervention actually is. Is it to defend Bosnia against Serb aggression; to intercede in the civil war in Bosnia; or to create a situation in which Bosnian territory cannot be defined by Serbian intransigence? While a degree of pragmatism and a constant re-evaluation and reassessment of means and objectives is desirable, the problem in former Yugoslavia is that the adjustments made to peacekeeping operations have sometimes been more political or diplomatic than of a practical kind enabling the peacekeeping force to meet its goals more effectively.

Lessons

There can be little doubt that the military requirements of UN peacekeeping have changed dramatically in recent years and that this has necessitated a reassessment of operational techniques developed before 1988. Indeed, the experience of UNPROFOR has exposed the obsolescence of traditional methods of organisation and management, many of which are now clearly undermining the effectiveness of troops and civilians deployed in the field. Existing structures in New York have found it increasingly difficult to plan, command and control the greatly increased peacekeeping activities in recent years.[57] Moreover, UNPROFOR has also shown that in the context of intrastate, ethnic and communal conflict, greater attention must be given to force protection, tactical mobility, adequate communications and intelligence support. Above all, it has shown that, at the tactical level, a peacekeeping force may have to accept only partial or sporadic consent from warring parties and anticipate casualties: as of 30 April 1994, UNPROFOR had sustained 87 fatalities.[58]

The UN involvement in former Yugoslavia has occurred in tandem with an ongoing academic and professional military debate about the doctrinal implications of more "powerful" or "muscular" peacekeeping. The debate has centred on attempts to conceptualise an area of military activity between classical peacekeeping, more complex field operations and outright enforcement. In this regard, influential work has already been done on developing a concept of "second generation multinational operations" in which the critical assumption has been that an outside force should not necessarily rely on, promote or be guided by the need for consent. According to this view, a peacekeeping force that is properly equipped and underpinned by the appropriate operational concepts and rules of engagement may engage in

---

57. Goulding, "Evolution of United Nations Peace Keeping," p. 460.
58. *United Nations Peacekeeping* (UN Document PS/DPI/6/Rev.5, May 1994), p. 84.

various intermediary acts, categories or "levels" of enforcement.[59]

In 1992 and 1993, UNPROFOR was given some specific chapter VII enforcement authority to assist in the delivery of humanitarian relief and the protection of safe areas in Bosnia–Herzegovina.[60] Hence UNPROFOR also builds upon the nascent practice of peace-enforcement in support of humanitarian objectives. As the concept of using force to support efforts to provide humanitarian relief is very much an expansion of the traditional peace-keeping role, attitudes to it are still evolving. There has long been broad agreement on the right of peoples to receive humanitarian assistance.[61] What has not previously been accepted, however, is that there is any basis for that assistance being forcibly rendered, in reliance on the security provisions of the UN Charter.[62] Yet, even with UNPROFOR, there is no evidence of meticulous attention having been paid to the threshold criteria for intervention. Both the resultant conceptual confusion and operational difficulties in the field underscore the importance of attempting to define clearer criteria for humanitarian-motivated peace-enforcement operations in the future. Additionally, and in order to escape the charge of double standards, clearer means to determine which of the world's numerous troublespots should attract UN attention, and for what reasons, must be articulated.[63]

On the other hand, the UN involvement in former Yugoslavia does not indicate that the essential characteristics of traditional peacekeeping should be lightly abandoned. Consent will never be absolute and should not equate with universal approval of every action taken by a peacekeeping mission in-field. For this would be tantamount to giving any renegade faction the capacity to forestall any UN initiative.[64] However, it is the conscious promotion of consent, through operational techniques such as minimum

---

59. Ruggie, "Wandering in the Void," pp. 26–31; John Mackinlay and Jarat Chopra, *A Draft Concept of Second Generation Multinational Operations* (Providence, RI: Thomas J. Watson Jr. Institute for International Studies, Brown University, 1993), pp. 4–5. Other writers are nevertheless more sceptical of such "middle ground" theories; see Charles Dobbie, "A Concept for Post-Cold War Peacekeeping," *Survival* 36 (Autumn 1994), pp. 121–48; Roberts, "Crisis in UN Peacekeeping," pp. 93–120.

60. Evans, *Cooperating for Peace,* pp. 154–55.

61. For an excellent summary of the legal considerations surrounding humanitarian intervention, see David M. Kresock, "Ethnic Cleansing in the Balkans: The Legal Foundations of Foreign Intervention," *Cornell International Law Journal* 27 (Winter 1994) pp. 203–39.

62. This debate was set running by the Security Council's "Operation Provide Comfort" decision in 1991 in the aftermath of the Gulf War, which determined that Iraq's repression of the Kurds threatened "international peace and security in the region" and demanded "that Iraq end this repression" and "allow immediate access by international humanitarian organisations to all those in need of assistance in all parts of Iraq and make available all necessary facilities for their operations." Evans, *Cooperating for Peace,* p. 153.

63. Goulding, "Evolution of United Nations Peace Keeping," pp. 461–62.

64. Dobbie, "A Concept for Post-Cold War Peacekeeping," p. 124.

force, civil affairs programmes and constant liaison and negotiation, which distinguishes peacekeeping from enforcement. In practice, as UNPROFOR has amply demonstrated, contemporary peacekeeping operations are likely to represent a continual struggle to preserve and sustain whatever consensual framework might exist. But the very existence of such a framework means that force may not be used without fatally undermining the perception of impartiality which remains essential to preserving the UN image as a disinterested third party. Moreover, the downgrading of consent serves only to increase the vulnerability of lightly-armed UN forces in the field.[65]

Many of the principles and procedures for managing and supporting field operations which have crystallised in the course of years of UN experience were always going to be badly suited to cope with the demands imposed by UNPROFOR's multifaceted mission and complex operational environment. While attempts have been made to remedy the principal areas of weakness, the pressure of events, and the difficulties of instituting and pursuing UN reform, have continued to create problems in the execution of policy. In addition, the fragmented structure in New York and the diffusion of responsibilities among departments, divisions and offices, have made it very difficult to provide unified direction and effective support in the field.[66] Thus the UNPROFOR experience highlights the need for a machinery that is capable of contingency planning and overall field support.

In broader terms, the UN involvement in former Yugoslavia also demonstrates that the peacemaking or negotiating process, which precedes or accompanies that of peacekeeping, must be closely coordinated with peacekeeping, so that each can be fully relevant to the actual situation on the ground. The "requirement for closer linkage between the ongoing political process and the activities of those charged with implementing UN resolutions applies to New York, as well as to the tactical level where peacekeepers are continually confronted with the challenge of building trust in communities torn by ethnic strife."[67]

However, the difficult operational experience of UNPROFOR has to a large extent been shaped by factors extraneous to the UN system itself. Given that UNPROFOR has from the outset based its activities on the assumption of cooperation and consent from the parties, the lack of such cooperation has limited its ability to accomplish the original objectives. Similarly, the fact that different military contingents maintain contacts and take their orders from national capitals has immensely complicated the Force Commander's task of securing unity of command within the mission.

---

65. Roberts, "Crisis in UN Peacekeeping," p. 102.
66. See the chapter by Mats Berdal later in this volume.
67. Berdal, "United Nations Peacekeeping in Former Yugoslavia."

Taken together, these features suggest that even if political will had been present, the UN is patently not equipped to conduct large-scale enforcement operations. The "delegation of such action to a group of states, possibly a regional organisation or a 'coalition of the willing' acting under the legitimising authority of the UN, should therefore be explored more carefully."[68] Yet the extent to which UN responsibilities can be transferred to regional organisations may be limited. Potential problems in devolving responsibility to regional organisations may include constraints in resources and decision-making capacity, perceived partiality and limited membership and objectives.[69]

One perennial difficulty besetting the UN involvement in former Yugoslavia has been that in most cases, intervention occurred only after the outbreak of violence, by which time positions were more entrenched and the conflict correspondingly more intractable. Hence, a further important lesson to be derived from the tragedy which the collapse of Yugoslavia produced, is that in politically fragile and ethnically torn communities where the prospect of civil strife is present, an early international response to forestall a violent turn of events is essential. Accordingly, calls within the UN system for emphasis on more proactive types of action such as early-warning measures and preventive deployment should be heeded.[70]

In terms of future preventive deployments and early-response measures, a cautionary note is nevertheless required. Careful consideration must be given to the effect of such deployments on the perceived impartiality of a UN force. By deploying only on one side of a disputed border, the impression that the UN is taking sides in the conflict may destabilise a peacekeeping environment rather than increase confidence overall. For the same reason, the choice of troop-contributing countries, equipment and operational concepts for a preventive force deployment must be made with a view to the impact locally on all parties to a conflict.

Most fundamentally, the Yugoslav conflict demonstrates that if a peacekeeping operation becomes merely a substitute for addressing the root cause of ethnic and communal violence and is not closely linked to an ongoing political process aimed at conflict resolution, it may prolong the war itself. In this regard, the decision to establish and protect "safe areas" in eastern Bosnia illustrates the problem. Under the circumstances, it was a short-term and necessary decision to alleviate a rapidly deteriorating humanitarian situation. However, in the absence of political settlement and with only a half-hearted commitment to provide the resources required for the implemen-

---

68. *Ibid.*
69. Roberts, "The United Nations and International Security," pp. 5, 8.
70. Roberts, "Crisis in UN Peacekeeping," p. 102.

tation of the mandate, the "safe areas" have become little "more than large refugee camps surrounded by enemy forces under increasingly precarious conditions."[71] The practicability of individual mandates must therefore be looked at more carefully, as otherwise there is a real danger of the peace-keeping mission becoming mired in, and indeed becoming a permanent feature of, the conflict itself. Thus the UN experience in Bosnia shows that armed protection can certainly not be a substitute for negotiations and the need continuously to transmit and promote consent among the parties on the ground. Where troop-contributing countries are not prepared to contemplate a long-term engagement with a particular conflict (and most are not), there is a need for a signposted exit, and a willingness to withdraw a peacekeeping force in the event of a failure to accomplish core objectives.[72]

These considerations, however, merely highlight a broader and more important issue:

> Humanitarian action.... cannot serve as an indefinite cover for the lack of a coherent and long-term policy towards a conflict. When the conflict continues unabated and no political progress is made, humanitarian operations, aid and access are manipulated and politicised by the warring factions for their own purposes, not with a view to reaching a political solution but rather to promote and sustain their own war effort.[73]

Hence it may be necessary, but not sufficient, to say that the UN role in a crisis is essentially humanitarian. There is always a need for tough analysis of the broader questions raised by UN involvement in a conflict, the problems that created the need for aid and the policies for tackling them.[74]

Conclusion

The Yugoslav problem represents within the UN a microcosm of all the problems that this body faces today: what to do about peacekeeping, if and when to turn to enforcement, where decisions should be taken, how human rights abuses should be dealt with, and who will pay.[75]

The parameters and political framework of limited UN involvement laid down by the Security Council for the Yugoslav conflict have been aimed at alleviating the excesses and brutalities of ethnic warfare, as well as urging and assisting the parties themselves to reach a broader political settlement. Numerous chapter VII resolutions notwithstanding, there has been no political will in the Security Council for sanctioning coercive military

---

71. Berdal, "United Nations Peacekeeping in Former Yugoslavia."
72. Evans, *Cooperating for Peace,* pp. 112–13.
73. Berdal, "United Nations Peacekeeping in Former Yugoslavia."
74. Roberts, "Crisis in UN Peacekeeping," p. 98.
75. Higgins, "The New United Nations and Former Yugoslavia," p. 465.

involvement. This is due, first, to the unpalatable prospect of an open-ended commitment not underpinned by any compelling political or national interest that could sustain public support in troop-contributing states.[76] Second, and at a deeper level, the issues of self-determination, humanitarian intervention and state succession raised by the conflict in former Yugoslavia are extremely complex.[77] There is no consensus among member-states of the Security Council, let alone the UN as a whole, as to how tensions generated by the espousal of competing, even mutually exclusive, principles raised by this conflict should be reconciled.[78]

In short, the familiar dilemma has re-emerged as to whether it is ever possible to enforce peace.[79] Indeed the concept of peace-enforcement has recently been described as an oxymoron.[80] Even if there exists sufficient NATO or UN force to achieve short-term military objectives (whatever they might be), success in terms of sustainable political objectives (whatever they might be) appears far less likely in the absence of a genuine commitment on the part of all combatants to establish and maintain peace.

In these terms, UNPROFOR demonstrates the limits to the capacities of modern-day UN implements for peacekeeping and peace-enforcement. Visions of a Balkan quagmire, with high casualty rates and significant economic costs, have served to define the limits of involvement. As a test case for the "new humanitarianism," former Yugoslavia has shown that where national self-interest is not involved, few governments will be prepared to pay the potentially high price in blood and resources that may be entailed through dispassionate engagement in the relief of suffering.[81]

---

76. Berdal, "United Nations Peacekeeping in Former Yugoslavia."
77. See Marc Weller, "The International Response to the Dissolution of the Socialist Federal Republic of Yugoslavia," *American Journal of International Law* 86 (July 1992), pp. 569–607; Kresock, "Ethnic Cleansing in the Balkans"; Higgins, "The New United Nations and Former Yugoslavia."
78. Berdal, "United Nations Peacekeeping in Former Yugoslavia."
79. Smith, "Just War, Clausewitz and Sarajevo," p. 141.
80. Ramesh Thakur, "From Peacekeeping to Peace-Enforcement: The UN Operation in Somalia," *Journal of Modern African Studies* 32 (September 1994), p. 409.
81. "Peacekeeping, War, Humanitarian Action, and Human Rights—the Former Yugoslavia," Annex to Statement by Cedric Thornberry, Conference at Princeton University, 22 October 1993, pp. 4–5.

5

The UN Operation in Somalia

Robert G. Patman

At the time of writing, the UN seemed poised to end its controversial two-year "humanitarian" intervention in Somalia. In 1992, constant civil war and drought had combined to produce a catastrophic famine killing an estimated 300 000 Somalis.[1] Unable to break the cycle of starvation and disorder through the deployment of 500 lightly-armed Pakistani peacekeepers in September 1992, the UN Security Council opted for drastic action in December 1992. The peace-enforcement mandate was substantially widened on 26 March 1993 by Security Council Resolution 814 which gave the UN Operation in Somalia (UNOSOM) extensive powers to uphold law and order.

But the UN operation did not live up to expectations. Instead of presiding over the political reconstruction of Somalia, UNOSOM II became involved in a bloody confrontation with the most formidable of the Somali warlords, General Mohamed Farah Aideed. The precipitating event was the murder of 24 Pakistani peacekeepers during a weapons inspection visit in South Mogadishu on 5 June 1993. By early October President Bill Clinton, under siege from Congress over the growing U.S. casualty list, effectively ended the UN's experiment in peace-enforcement by announcing the withdrawal of all U.S. troops within six months. Obliged to revert to traditional peace-keeping methods, the remaining UN force has since been marginalised as Somalia largely slipped back to pre-intervention levels of clan-fighting, banditry and attacks on foreign aid workers and peacekeepers. Because of the absence of any progress towards national reconciliation, the U.S. ended its official presence in Mogadishu in mid-September and the UN seemed

---

1. "Editorial: No Time for Celebration," *Somalia News Update* (SNU) [electronic mail] 3 (27 August 1994).

likely to follow suit.[2] Having spent around $1.8bn on an operation that has cost the lives of more than 100 peacekeepers, it now seems clear that the continued presence of UNOSOM in southern Somalia perpetuates the tendency towards violent conflict. By contrast, the most stable region of Somalia, the northwest, has been virtually starved of UN resources since it declared itself independent in 1991.

The task of this chapter is to analyse the impact of the UN mission in Somalia. To this end, we will consider the origins of the Somali crisis, the failure of preventive diplomacy, the UN strategy of peace-enforcement, the UN retreat to traditional peacekeeping and some of the lessons of the UN experience in Somalia. The basic argument that emerges is that while the UN intervention in Somalia was not wrong in principle, it was flawed in both design and execution.

Origins of the Somali Crisis

Strategically located in the Horn of Africa, Somalia was one of the most spectacular examples of state disintegration following the end of the Cold War order. The roots of this political cataclysm were local as well as international in character. From the time of Somalia's independence in July 1960, the persistence of clan loyalties frustrated the efforts of the central government to build an enduring post-colonial Somali nationalism based on allegiance to the state. In the 1960s, Western-style democracy failed to bridge the tribal divisions within the country.[3] In October 1969, General Mohammed Siad Barre seized power in a military coup. Thereafter, regional rivalries in the Horn intersected with the Cold War to produce fluid and shifting alliances.[4] Internally, armed opposition to Siad's corrupt and brutal dictatorship gradually escalated. The turning point came in June 1988 when the Somali government launched a genocidal military campaign against the Somali National Movement (SNM), a rebel group drawn from the Isaaq clan in the northwest of the country. Hargeisa, the second-largest Somali city, was reduced to rubble and around 400 000 Isaaq Somalis fled to refugee camps in Ethiopia and Djibouti.

While the Bush administration initially responded to the civil war by shipping arms to the Siad regime, the end of the Cold War made it increasingly difficult for Washington to ignore the excesses of the Siad

2. *Guardian Weekly*, 25 September 1994.
3. Ioan Lewis, "The Politics of the 1969 Somali Coup," *Journal of Modern African Studies* 10 (October 1972), pp. 397–400.
4. See Robert G. Patman, *The Soviet Union in the Horn of Africa: the diplomacy of intervention and disengagement* (Cambridge: Cambridge University Press, 1990) p. 143.

dictatorship. In 1989, the U.S. Congress, citing well-documented human rights violations in northern Somalia, forced the administration to suspend its military and economic aid programme in Somalia.[5]

Meanwhile, other armed clan-based rebel groups emerged in southern and central Somalia. By 1990, the Siad regime, bereft of virtually all foreign aid, exercised only limited control over the regions surrounding Mogadishu and some other major southern towns. Because of the civil war, the Somali state had, in institutional, political and economic terms, already fallen apart before the United Somali Congress (USC) delivered the final *coup de grâce* in January 1991. This long-awaited event, however, failed to halt the process of disintegration. The leaders of the triumphant USC, which drew its support from the Hawiye clans, became absorbed in a power struggle almost as soon as they had driven Siad from Mogadishu. The USC military commander General Aideed, who played a key role in defeating Siad,[6] refused to accept Ali Mahdi Mohamed as interim president of a new USC government. The struggle also had a tribal dimension. Ali Mahdi's support base was in the Hawiye subclan, Abgal, while Aideed's backing derived from another Hawiye subclan, Habar Gidir.

Mogadishu turned into a bloodbath as the two heavily-armed USC factions slugged it out for control of the Somali capital. Between November 1991 and February 1992, 14 000 people are estimated to have been killed and 27 000 wounded in what often seemed to be indiscriminate artillery and automatic weapons fire.[7] But the fighting was not confined to Mogadishu. Siad's retreating troops adopted a scorched-earth policy as they moved through Somalia's farmland belt, in the Juba valley area, towards the region south of Mogadishu belonging to Siad's own clan, the Marehan, or associated clan, the Darod. The troops slaughtered livestock, plundered crops and massacred local cultivators. On top of this, there was fierce fighting with and between forces under General Aideed and Ali Mahdi. Devastation and starvation spread throughout southern Somalia.[8]

Beneath these relatively organised factional wars, looting, random killing and banditry was carried out by gangs of Qat-chewing, armed teenagers, known as *mooryaan*. At the same time, drought, a cyclical problem in Somalia, magnified the impact of the man-made damage to the country. Famine spread rapidly throughout Somalia. By 1992, the UN estimated a

---

5. Theodore Dagne, "The Horn of Africa: A Trip Report," *CRS Report for Congress*, 91-823F, 15 November 1991, p. 15.

6. John Drysdale, *Whatever Happened to Somalia?* (London: Haan Associates, 1994), pp. 27–28.

7. *Africa Watch*, "No Mercy in Mogadishu," cited in *Guardian*, 27 March 1992.

8. Jonathan Stevenson, "Hope Restored in Somalia?," *Foreign Policy* No 91 (Summer 1993), p. 143.

death toll of 300 000 from starvation, while 400 000 Somalis sought refuge in Kenya and another 300 000 did the same in Ethiopia.[9] Meanwhile in the northwest, the victorious SNM insurgents, confronted with the chaos in the south, declared unilateral independence from Somalia in May 1991. While the "Republic of Somaliland" failed to achieve any international recognition, it did attain a measure of stability and embarked upon a process of political reconciliation.[10]

UN Failure to Engage in Preventive Diplomacy

Despite the plight of Somalia in 1990–91, the UN was very slow to respond. In part, this was a reflection of the attitude of the permanent members of the Security Council, especially the United States. Senior officials in the administration resisted recommendations to put Somalia on the UN Security Council agenda until January 1992. According to a State Department official, Washington initially viewed Somalia as just another humanitarian crisis in Africa.[11] Besides, the Bush administration was preoccupied with the Persian Gulf conflict, the disintegration of the USSR and the unravelling of Yugoslavia. In the words of T. Frank Crigler, former ambassador to Somalia, America "turned out the lights, closed the door and forgot about the place."[12]

In addition, the UN found it difficult to operate in an environment where there had been a total collapse of the structure of central government. The UN Secretariat in New York was alerted to the gravity of the Somali situation some months before the fall of the Siad regime.[13] Nevertheless, the UN and its specialised agencies (UNICEF, UNHCR and WHO) withdrew their staff from Mogadishu for security reasons. This absence was, in the words of one UN insider, the organisation's "greatest failure" after the Cold War.[14] As an upshot, the UN provided no assistance in 1991 and showed little sign of understanding the depth of the catastrophe until late 1991 when Mogadishu became a killing field. Meanwhile, with the Arab League and the Organisation of African Unity (OAU) largely ignoring the Somali political

9. Ioan Lewis, *Making History in Somalia: Humanitarian Intervention in a Stateless Society,* Discussion Paper 6, Centre for the Study of Global Governance (London: September 1993), p. 3; Ken Menkaus and Terrence Lyons, "What are the Lessons to be Learned from Somalia?" *CSIS Africa Notes* No 144 (January 1993), p. 3.

10. Rakiya Omaar, "Somaliland: One Thorn Bush at a Time," *Current History* 93 (May 1994), p. 232.

11. Ambassador David Shinn, Director for East African Affairs, Department of State, interview with author, Washington DC, 24 January 1994.

12. Cited in Daniel Volman, "Africa and the New World Order," *Journal of Modern African Studies* 31 (March 1993), p. 7.

13. Drysdale, *Whatever Happened to Somalia?,* p. 24.

14. *Observer,* 2 August 1992.

crisis, it was left to a handful of non-governmental organisations (NGOs) such as the International Red Cross and Save the Children Fund to give humanitarian aid in appalling conditions. These organisations found it necessary to employ Somali guards to protect their houses, offices, stores and hospitals.

According to Mohamed Sahnoun, the Security General's Special Envoy to Somalia (April–October 1992), the UN missed three opportunities to prevent the catastrophic collapse of the Somali state before 1992.[15] The first chance came in 1988 when the UN failed to put pressure on the Siad government to halt the savage repression against the Isaaq population in northern Somalia and to mediate between Siad's regime and the SNM movement. A second opportunity came in May 1990 with the publication of a manifesto in Mogadishu, signed by a coalition of over 100 Somali politicians, intellectuals and businessmen, calling for a national reconciliation conference and democratic elections; the UN failed to support the Manifesto Group. The third opening came shortly after Siad fled the presidential palace. Instead of evacuating its staff, Sahnoun maintained that the UN should have worked on the ground to promote a dialogue between the contending factions.

Limitations of Traditional Peacekeeping

One year after the Siad government fell, the UN Security Council finally addressed the issue of the Somali conflict. In January 1992, Security Council Resolution 733 called on the new UN Secretary-General Boutros-Ghali to mediate in the civil war and impose an arms embargo on Somalia. The latter was largely meaningless given the vast leftover stocks of superpower weaponry inside the country and ethnically porous frontiers with Kenya and Ethiopia that facilitated a thriving local arms trade.[16] But on the mediation front, Under-Secretary-General for Political Affairs James Jonah was dispatched to Mogadishu during January to try and persuade the major factions to negotiate an immediate ceasefire.

At this point, a problem arose which was to haunt UN diplomacy in Somalia thereafter. The UN Secretariat, presumably unaware of the political nuances of the Ali Mahdi–Aideed conflict, "accepted by default Mahdi's status as interim-President."[17] While such recognition provided a formal link between the UN and a country without a government, it compromised

---

15. Mohamed Sahnoun, "Preventing Conflict: The Case of Somalia," *Secretary's Open Forum*, Washington DC, 12 January 1994.

16. Lewis, "Making History in Somalia," p. 14.

17. Drysdale, *Whatever Happened to Somalia?*, pp. 39–40.

the UN's impartiality in Aideed's eyes and he rejected Jonah's mission. It was not until early March that the UN managed to broker a shaky ceasefire, but only after the UN gave Aideed fresh reassurances on its impartiality.[18]

The reduction in hostilities in Somalia highlighted the growing problem of the looting of humanitarian aid, often by those charged with protecting food convoys. Thus, while food aid was subject to such racketeering it was actually contributing to the very conflict that had caused the famine in the first place.[19] In a bid to overcome this problem, the UN Security Council passed Resolution 751 on 24 April 1992 which authorised a UN Operation in Somalia (UNOSOM I) under the overall direction of Sahnoun, the Secretary-General's special envoy to Somalia. The resolution approved the deployment of 50 UN observers to monitor the ceasefire and the deployment of 500 Pakistani UN troops to provide security in and around the focal point of the relief effort, Mogadishu, in consultation with "the parties in Mogadishu."[20] Appointed in April, Sahnoun quickly made a favourable impression by seeking to implement Resolution 751 through pursuing a "bottom up" strategy in Somalia. While working hard to establish good relations with major warlords like Aideed and Ali Mahdi, Sahnoun also bypassed them by cultivating the support of clan elders, a traditional source of authority in Somali society, for a sustained grassroots reconciliation effort along the lines initiated in northern Somalia.[21] The strategy was analogous to plucking the feathers of a bird until the bird could no longer fly.[22]

But the warlords, particularly Aideed, were in no mood to passively accept the plucking of their feathers. It took two months just to persuade Mahdi and Aideed to accept the deployment of the 50 UN observers. At the same time, the UN itself complicated these negotiations. In mid-June 1992, a Russian Antonov plane with UN markings delivered military hardware and newly printed Somali currency to Ali Mahdi's airfield in north Mogadishu. The UN had no ready explanation for this highly disruptive blunder which prompted an already suspicious Aideed to accuse the UN of favouring his arch-rival.[23]

Tortuous negotiations also preceded the deployment of the UN security force. Again Mahdi accepted with alacrity while Aideed appeared to drag his feet. The protracted discussions reflected Aideed's concern that the intro-

---

18. *Ibid.*
19. Lewis, "Making History in Somalia," p. 9; Menkhaus and Lyons, "Lessons to be Learned from Somalia," pp. 3–4.
20. Drysdale, *Whatever Happened to Somalia?*, p. 42.
21. Ioan Lewis, "Misunderstanding the Somali Crisis," *Anthropology Today* 9 (August 1993), p. 2.
22. Sahnoun, "Preventing Conflict."
23. Stevenson, "Hope Restored in Somalia?," p. 145.

duction of peacekeeping troops would not only erode his competitive position with Ali Mahdi in Mogadishu—his faction exercised control over the lucrative Mogadishu harbour and airport facilities—but also affect his political base elsewhere in Somalia. Eventually, on 12 August, four months after Resolution 751, Aideed and his SNA allies signed an agreement with Sahnoun for the deployment of the 500 peacekeepers. As part of the agreement, Sahnoun stated that any increase in the number of UN troops would require the consent of Aideed's SNA leadership.[24]

Nonetheless, despite the desperate humanitarian situation in Somalia, it took yet another month before the first group of Pakistani peacekeepers arrived in mid-September. Complications in UN decision-making due to the unprecedented use of peacekeepers in a humanitarian role[25] and also the apparent reluctance of the White House to raise the profile in an election year contributed to this. Whatever the reasons, the delay meant that no UN troops had arrived when on 28 August the Security Council authorised a further deployment of 3500 troops across four operation zones in Somalia (Resolution 775). This decision was made without consulting the UNOSOM delegation in Mogadishu, the governments of neighbouring countries or the militia leaders and tribal elders as had been done before. Yet the additional deployment was once again contingent on the consent of the local war-lords.[26] The response from Aideed was wholly negative. Convinced that the UN announcement contravened his August agreement with Sahnoun, Aideed threatened to send UN troops home in bodybags. The security environment in Somalia rapidly deteriorated.

While all of the Pakistani peacekeepers had arrived by late September 1992, the force's terms of reference, based on traditional notions of what constituted peacekeeping, proved to be totally inadequate to the Somali challenge. There was no durable ceasefire to preserve and cooperation with the warring parties was either non-existent or unreliable and inconsistent. Far from fulfilling their mission to secure the airport, seaport and the lines of communication in and around Mogadishu, the lightly-armed Pakistanis struggled to protect themselves from repeated militia attacks and were pinned down in their barracks near Mogadishu airport for the first two months after arrival.

This debacle intensified pressure on the UN "to do something" about famine-stricken Somalia. In July 1992 the international media took up the story, beaming horrific TV pictures of starving Somalis to the U.S. and

24. Drysdale, *Whatever Happened to Somalia*, p. 53.
25. Elisabeth Lindenmayer, UN Department of Peacekeeping Operations (DPKO), interview with author, New York, 27 January 1994.
26. Samuel M. Makinda, *Seeking Peace from Chaos: Humanitarian Intervention in Somalia*, (Boulder: Lynne Rienner for the International Peace Academy, 1993), p. 63.

other countries. These extremely powerful but misleading media images reinforced Boutros-Ghali's own desire for quicker results. During the UN debate on Bosnia in July 1992, the Secretary-General rebuked the Western countries for paying more attention to the "rich man's war" in the former Yugoslavia than to the Somalian tragedy.[27] The timing of Boutros-Ghali's intervention came shortly after the publication of his report *An Agenda for Peace*. This envisaged a more active role for the post-Cold War UN in new areas such as peacemaking and peace-building in countries "torn by civil war and strife."[28]

Meanwhile, stung by domestic criticism, President George Bush launched a spectacular airlift of food aid to Somalia in August 1992. However, this initiative was soon overshadowed by the basic problem of looting. Some relief agencies claimed that something like 50 percent of all humanitarian aid delivered was being stolen by gunmen linked to the war-lords.[29] In September, food ships were shelled and turned away at the Mogadishu port, and UN officials were assaulted at Kismayo. A frustrated Sahnoun criticised the UN for its bureaucratic inertia and pleaded for more time from New York to secure Aideed's consent for the deployment of the 3500 peacekeepers. But the UN leadership was getting "very impatient" with Sahnoun's meagre results. From New York's standpoint, there were few signs that he was on the verge of a diplomatic breakthrough.[30] Indeed, a suspicion existed within the UN Secretariat that Sahnoun was misreading the Somali situation. With thousands of Somalis dying from hunger each week and warlords like Aideed effectively exercising a veto on UN action, the organisation perceived it faced a crisis of credibility. On 27 October, Sahnoun was forced to resign. He was replaced by Ismat Kittani, an Iraqi diplomat, who soon reached the conclusion that Aideed would never agree to a substantial UN peacekeeping presence.[31]

The Strategy of Limited Peace-Enforcement

Unable to reverse the trend of starvation and disorder in Somalia, Boutros-Ghali concluded in November 1992 that the UN's policy in Somalia had become "untenable."[32] He believed there was little alternative but to adopt more forceful measures to protect humanitarian operations.

---

27. *Otago Daily Times* (Dunedin), 29 July 1992.
28. Boutros-Ghali, cited in Thomas J. Callahan, "Some Observations on Somalia's Past and Future," *CSIS Africa Notes* No 158 (March 1994), p. 3.
29. *Guardian*, 27 November 1992; *Observer*, 11 October 1992.
30. Lindenmayer, interview with author, 27 January 1994.
31. *Ibid.*
32. Cited in Menkhaus and Lyons, "Lessons to be Learned from Somalia," p. 4.

President Bush agreed. In a surprising departure from previous U.S. policy, on 25 November he proposed that U.S. troops should lead a UN operation in Somalia. After some negotiations over the command structure of the operation, Boutros-Ghali accepted the U.S. offer. It was unanimously endorsed on 3 December by the Security Council. Resolution 794 asserted that the Somali situation constituted a threat to international peace and authorised the U.S.-led Unified Task Force (UNITAF) to all use "all necessary means to establish as soon as possible a secure environment for humanitarian relief operations."[33] This landmark decision was the first time that the Security Council sanctioned an enforcement action under chapter VII of the UN Charter in a theoretically sovereign state.

UNOSOM I and UNITAF coexisted but were independent of each other in Somalia. Boutros-Ghali would have preferred a humanitarian enforcement operation in Somalia under UN command and control. But he recognised that the UN lacked the financial and logistical capacity to carry out a rapid military intervention. Thus, UNITAF represented a convergence rather than an identity of interests between the U.S. and the UN.

UNITAF forces entered Somalia on 9 December 1992. Approximately 40 percent of Somalia, mainly the central and southern regions, fell under the mandate of UNITAF which at its peak comprised 37 000 troops from 25 countries, including 26 000 from the U.S.[34] From the outset, Washington saw UNITAF as a limited enforcement operation. Its humanitarian mission was simply "to open the supply routes, to get the food moving and to prepare the way for a UN peacekeeping force to keep it moving."[35] Bush spoke about getting out of Somalia by 20 January 1993. While President-elect Bill Clinton expressed scepticism on this withdrawal timetable, he shared Bush's view that the U.S. should not stay any longer than was absolutely necessary.

So why did the U.S. choose to intervene in Somalia? Defense Secretary Dick Cheney listed four reasons for U.S. participation in UNITAF.[36] First, there was a clear humanitarian justification for such a mission. Second, the Pentagon believed it was "militarily doable." Third, UNITAF was not an open-ended commitment. And fourth, U.S. casualties were not expected to

---

33. Peter V. Jakobsen, "The Four 'Ws' of UN Collective Military Peace Enforcement in the New World Order: Why, When, What, (by and against) Whom?" paper prepared for Workshop 10: Military Security and its Controversial Dimensions, at the Second European Peace Research Conference in Budapest, 12–14 November, 1993, p. 12.

34. Walter S. Clarke, "Testing the World's Resolve in Somalia," *Parameters* 23 (Winter 1993–94), p. 43.

35. President George Bush, cited in "Substantial American Force Ordered to Somalia," U.S. Information Agency (USIA), *East Asia/Pacific Wireless File,* 4 December 1992, p. 2.

36. Defense Secretary Dick Cheney and General Colin Powell, "U.S. Mission to Somalia is Necessary and Clear," USIA, *East Asia/Pacific Wireless File,* 4 December 1992, p. 12.

be high.

In humanitarian terms, UNITAF made a positive difference to Somali society. The overwhelming foreign military presence encountered little resistance and quickly broke the stronghold that rival militias had over supply routes. Most of the needy areas such as Bardera in the southwest started to receive food. The looting of relief supplies and the protection rackets operated by some merchants practically stopped. As a result, something like 250 000 people had their lives saved.[37] Improved security also facilitated some significant improvements to Somalia's shattered infrastructure. UNITAF repaired more than 1800km of roads, restored two airfields and revamped 14 water wells.[38] In the short term, UNITAF helped to establish a secure environment for humanitarian supplies in areas under its jurisdiction. But there was an operational ambiguity about UNITAF's humanitarian focus. The Bush administration felt obliged to deny it would "dictate political outcomes" and said it respected Somalia's "sovereignty and independence."[39] This early failure to recognise that Somalia was always more than a simple humanitarian operation deprived UNITAF of any coherent strategy and promoted conditions leading to confrontation.

First, on the political front, UNITAF broke its own guidelines by quickly establishing a working relationship with the main warlords. Many Somalis expected the warlords to be arrested by UNITAF.[40] Although the UN-led intervention initially put the warlords on the back foot, Robert Oakley, chief of the U.S. Liaison Office in Mogadishu, publicly embraced Ali Mahdi and General Aideed after they signed a U.S.-brokered ceasefire on 11 December 1992.[41] With this gesture, the warlords gained a spurious legitimacy as political leaders. Moreover, Oakley's embrace de-emphasised the "bottom up" strategy of Sahnoun (and pursued in a token fashion by his successor Kittani) and thereby reduced the freedom of action of UNOSOM I in searching for a political solution. In January 1993, the Secretary-General opened a peace conference of the Somali factions in Addis Ababa. These talks culminated in a peace accord signed by 15 of Somalia's factions at a UN conference on national reconciliation in March 1993. But it was clear that the warlords were shaping the political process. Under pressure to put together a Somali government as soon as possible, the UN provided a guaranteed

37. Shinn, interview with author, 24 January 1994.
38. Clarke, "Testing the World's Resolve in Somalia," p. 48.
39. Cited in "Substantial American Force Ordered to Somalia," p. 4.
40. Daniel Campagnon, "The Lack of Consideration for Internal Political Dynamics in the International Intervention in Somalia," paper presented at International Colloquium on Integration and Regionalism, Talence, Bourdeaux, 27–30 April 1994, p. 19.
41. Alex de Waal interviewed on *The World Today*, BBC World Service Radio, 14 August 1993.

seat to each warlord in a Transitional National Council (TNC) that was to guide the country over two years towards elections. The agreement was not signed by the self-proclaimed "Somaliland Republic" which was offended by the UN's characterisation of the TNC as "a repository of Somali sovereignty."[42]

Second, on the security front, the impact of UNITAF was largely cosmetic. Heavy weapons and military trucks disappeared from the streets. Some were hidden while others were simply moved into the interior beyond UNITAF's reach. As it became clear that the militias had no intention of surrendering their weapons, Bush and Boutros-Ghali clashed publicly over what constituted "a secure environment" in Somalia. Bush maintained that troops would be used only to disable or disarm weaponry threatening food and medical supplies to famine zones, while Boutros-Ghali argued that before withdrawing, UNITAF should ensure that the heavy weapons of the organised factions had been "neutralised and brought under international control."[43] A State Department official conceded subsequently that it was probably a mistake for UNITAF to have left the heavy weaponry of the warlords untouched in the north and south of the country.[44] Evidently, this was a tactical move to avoid direct conflict with the powerful Somali factions in the early stages of the intervention. Certainly, there was confusion over UNITAF's stance on disarmament. The French who had started to apply what they thought was UNITAF's policy, systematically confiscating weapons found in vehicles, were rebuked by the U.S. military for exceeding the mandate of the operation.[45] As for the warlords, the Addis Ababa peace agreement of 27 March 1993 committed the parties to "complete" disarmament within 90 days. But no timetable was agreed for implementing this. So UNITAF passed the problem of disarmament more or less intact to its successor UNOSOM II.

Taken together, UNITAF's lack of a clear political agenda and the failure to eliminate the heavy weaponry of the warring Somali factions greatly reduced the likelihood that UNOSOM II could avoid a challenge from the warlords. In fact, the uneasy calm which had been the initial reaction to the U.S.-led intervention soon began to fade. In February 1993, after Aideed accused the U.S. of supporting Siad Barre's son-in-law General Siad Hersi Morgan, Mogadishu was gripped by three days of anti-UNITAF demonstrations and armed disturbances. The charge was prompted by the fact that General Morgan boldly seized part of Kismayo from Colonel Omar Jess, an

42. Lewis, "Making History in Somalia," p. 12.
43. Makinda, *Humanitarian Intervention in Somalia*, p. 71.
44. Shinn, interview with author, 24 January 1994.
45. Colonel M. Couton, UN DPKO, interview with author, New York, 28 January 1994.

ally of Aideed's, without encountering resistance from UNITAF forces. The U.S. strongly denied complicity, but relations between Washington and Aideed were clearly on the slide.

The Strategy of Permissive Peace-Enforcement

On 4 May 1993, UNITAF was formally replaced by UNOSOM II. Security Council Resolution 814 of 26 March authorised the transition. In effect, it widened the scope of peace-enforcement powers from the establishment of a secure environment solely for the protection of humanitarian relief activities to the "consolidation, expansion and maintenance of a secure environment throughout Somalia."[46] Under the new mandate, UNOSOM II had three key functions: to maintain a ceasefire, ensure the delivery of humanitarian aid and create conditions conducive to a political settlement *inter alia* through a programme of disarmament. Thus, the new UNOSOM II force, which consisted of 20 000 troops and 8000 logistical support from 33 different countries, was supposed to do what UNITAF had been unable to do with 17 000 troops more: disarm the warlord militias and take charge of the remaining 60 percent of Somalia's territory. While this unprecedented UN peacekeeping operation owed a lot to the ideas of Boutros-Ghali, the whole operation had a significant U.S. dimension. For the first time, the U.S. placed around 5000 of its troops under direct UN command, but it was a command structure dominated by U.S. or U.S.-nominated personnel.

Almost immediately, the hastily-assembled and ill-prepared UNOSOM II force was overstretched. It also had a shortage of quality military equipment such as armoured personnel carriers (APCs).[47] These developments occurred amid growing tension between the UN and Aideed who, despite a pledge to disarm, was busy moving new weaponry into Mogadishu. At the same time, Aideed publicly challenged the expanded mandate of UNOSOM II through a series of hostile radio broadcasts and an attempt to manipulate the new UNOSOM authorities into backing an Aideed-sponsored peace conference in May. It seemed almost inevitable that the resolve of the new UN force would be subjected to a more severe test.[48] That happened on 5 June 1993 when 24 Pakistani peacekeepers were brutally killed during pre-arranged weapons verification inspection visits to some of Aideed's ammunition stores in south Mogadishu. (The Addis Ababa agreement of 27 March 1993 stipulated that arms would be kept in stock, under the care of the

---

46. *U.S. Department of State (US DoS) Dispatch* 4 (12 April 1993), pp. 240–43.
47. Colonel Couton, interview with author, 28 January 1994.
48. A confidential source in the State Department's Bureau of Intelligence said that the attack on the Pakistani peacekeepers was "not a surprise."

factions, in places listed by UNOSOM until they could be handed over to the future Somali army or be destroyed.) The incident occurred near Aideed's radio station which some of his militia apparently thought the UN was about to seize. According to a report presented to the UN Security Council by a committee investigating the events of 5 June, Aideed believed that the UN was involved in a concerted campaign to politically marginalise him.[49] That cannot be ruled out, but there were other motivations connected with his Habar Gidir subclan constituency that prompted this premeditated ambush.

In any event, the 5 June incident triggered a vicious cycle of escalating violence. From the UN perspective, an important principle was at issue— that UN peacekeepers simply could not be killed with impunity. If UNOSOM pursued a passive policy after such an outrage, it was believed that the Pakistani troops would be withdrawn by their government, Aideed's opponents would resort to violence to counter him and the entire mission would be jeopardised.[50] As a result, the UN launched a manhunt for Aideed and unleashed a series of military strikes on buildings controlled by Aideed supporters in south Mogadishu. Ironically, UN reprisals melted internal opposition to Aideed within his Habar Gidir clan and his chairmanship of the USC was extended for 6 months while he was evading arrest.[51]

The tough line taken by UN Special Envoy Jonathan Howe provoked serious strains within UNOSOM II. Italy, one of the former colonial powers in Somalia, condemned the anti-Aideed stance. For its part, the UN leadership asked Italy to remove the commander of its peacekeeping contingent in Somalia, General Bruno Loi, for refusing to obey orders from the UN military commander.[52] There was also tension between Nigeria and Italy following an incident in which seven Nigerian peacekeepers were killed in South Mogadishu because the Italians had refused to open fire to assist the Nigerians. Concurrently, 26 international aid agencies in a joint message to the Secretary-General said that the UN's military tactics were actually hindering the distribution of humanitarian aid.[53]

By September 1993, the spiralling violence in Mogadishu prompted the U.S. Senate to demand that President Clinton explain his policy in Somalia to Congress by 15 October. Shortly before the deadline, 18 U.S. servicemen were killed in a savage battle with Aideed's militiamen. U.S. domestic support for the Somali operation collapsed. Once again, media coverage had a significant impact. Televised images of chanting Somalis dragging a U.S.

---

49. *International Herald Tribune,* 1 April 1994.
50. Ken Menkhaus, "Getting Out Vs Getting Through: US and UN Policies in Somalia," *Middle East Policy* 3:1 (1994), p. 157.
51. Drysdale, *Whatever Happened to Somalia?,* p. 199.
52. *Guardian,* 17 July 1993.
53. *Ibid.,* 16 August 1993.

soldier's body through the streets and pictures of a distressed helicopter pilot held hostage caused domestic disquiet. Clinton swiftly responded by announcing that all troops would be withdrawn from Somalia within six months. The hunt for General Aideed was abandoned. At a stroke, Washington had effectively ended Boutros-Ghali's peace-enforcement strategy.

Did UNOSOM II provoke the June attack on the Pakistani peacekeepers? The evidence is ambiguous. While there was general unhappiness among senior UNOSOM officials over Aideed's blatant attempts to upstage both UNOSOM and his political rivals shortly before the confrontation,[54] Admiral Howe was acting within his mandate when he decided to conduct an inspection of Aideed's five weapons storage sites on 5 June 1993, one of which was in the compound of Radio Mogadishu. Some believe that the UNOSOM weapons inspection visit was a deliberate provocation, the real purpose of which was to take over Aideed's radio, a source of hostile anti-UN propaganda.[55] But an equally plausible case can be made that Aideed had a personal stake in a showdown with the UN. He understood that UNOSOM II's programme of disarmament and political reconstruction would gradually erode his power base.[56] Moreover, with the international intervention of December 1992, Aideed's clan had lost control of the lucrative port and airport facilities and faced the prospect of a political settlement that would force them to return properties seized from the Abgal clan during the civil war of 1991–92. As political leader of the Habar Gidir clan, Aideed could not remain indifferent to these concerns.[57]

What is clear, however, is that UNOSOM II's response to the incident of 5 June 1993 was less than effective. While the attack did not come as a complete surprise to the UNOSOM II leadership, the implementation of peace-enforcement encountered two key problems. In the first place, it was bedevilled by chain of command problems. It was not so much joint decision-making, but the absence of joint decision-making that impeded the efficiency of UNOSOM II.[58] During the critical period from March to September, "the most influential policy advisers surrounding Admiral Howe were American State Department officials."[59] Top UN officials were

---

54. Drysdale, *Whatever Happened to Somalia?*, p. 168.
55. *Ibid.*, p. 182. Intriguingly, a UN source said Aideed correctly anticipated that his radio station was a target.
56. Menkhaus, "Getting Out Vs Getting Through," p. 156.
57. Callahan, "Observations on Somalia's Past and Future," p. 6.
58. Lindenmayer, interview with author, 27 January 1994; General Couton, interview with author, 28 January 1994. The same point was also made by Gerard van Bohemen, Deputy Permanent Representative, New Zealand Mission to the United Nations, interview with author, New York, 28 January 1994.
59. Menkhaus, "Getting Out Vs Getting Through," p. 155.

frequently bypassed and were privately frustrated at what they saw as an American show, particularly in the military sphere where the U.S. operated under a separate command and refused to discuss military tactics with other peacekeeping countries.[60] To make matters worse, a number of national contingents within UNOSOM's force believed that the American military's use of helicopter gunships and high-tech firepower in a suburban environment was disproportionate, inaccurate and politically counter-productive.[61] U.S. unilateralism in what was supposed to be a multilateral military operation strained the unity of purpose within UNOSOM and led to some very public squabbling inside its ranks.

In addition, Admiral Howe failed to exercise sufficient leadership over his military commanders during the campaign to arrest Aideed. By late July 1993, after four or five futile attempts to capture him, it was rather obvious that UNOSOM forces were unlikely to do so.[62] That Howe persisted in this disastrous direction illuminated two important factors. First, UNOSOM found it very difficult to obtain good intelligence in Mogadishu. According to John Drysdale, in a clan-based society like Somalia, the "use of an agent outside his clan territory renders him suspect" while the use of "an agent from within his own clan risks disinformation."[63] Faulty intelligence certainly constrained the operational effectiveness of peace-enforcement. Second, the UNOSOM leadership markedly underestimated the "staying power" of General Aideed. Despite Aideed's military background and the fact that many of his followers were battle-hardened fighters of the civil war years, several U.S. officials expressed surprise that the Somali leader did not flee towards the Kenyan border when the fighting escalated.[64]

The Marginalisation of UNOSOM II

The UN's current strategy in Somalia has been in place since late October 1993 when the UN Secretary-General said it was "no longer possible to impose peace" in that country.[65] The return to traditional peacekeeping was codified in a revised UN Security Council mandate for UNOSOM II,

---

60. *International Herald Tribune,* 1 April 1994; General Couton, interview with author, 28 January 1994.

61. General Couton, interview with author, 28 January 1994; Drysdale, *Whatever Happened to Somalia,* p. 197.

62. Ambassador David Shinn, interview with author, 24 January 1994.

63. Drysdale, *Whatever Happened to Somalia,* p. 209; confidential source, State Department's Bureau of Intelligence, 25 January 1994.

64. Confidential sources. It was interesting that Colonel Mike Dallas, Commander of the American Quick Reaction Force, commented after a confrontation with Somali gunmen on 10 September 1993: "Their willingness to stand and fight surprised me." Cited in Drysdale, *Whatever Happened to Somalia,* p. 210.

65. Boutros-Ghali, cited on *World News,* BBC World Service Radio, 28 October 1993.

adopted on 4 February 1994. This explicitly precluded UNOSOM forces from intervening in inter-clan conflicts.[66] Under the revised mandate, the main task of a slimmed down UNOSOM force, drawn largely from Asian and African countries, was to protect Somalia's principal ports and airports and provide security for the main transport arteries for moving humanitarian supplies. The resolution stressed the need to find a political settlement by implementing the March 1993 peace accord.

It soon became apparent there was an inherent tension between the constraints of traditional peacekeeping and the role as a political mediator in stateless Somalia. Quite apart from the fact that UNOSOM's confrontation with Aideed had compromised such a role in his view, the UN had to operate in a fast-deteriorating security environment which it no longer had the authority to attempt to moderate. On 18 November 1993, the way was cleared for Aideed's political comeback when the Security Council decided to "suspend arrest actions against those responsible" for the June killing of 24 Pakistani soldiers.[67] In early December, the U.S. flew Aideed to UN-sponsored informal talks at Addis Ababa with Ali Mahdi's group. The talks ended in deadlock. Then, on 25 March 1994, as American troops were completing their withdrawal from Somalia, the UN announced with considerable fanfare that Aideed and Ali Mahdi had signed a new ceasefire and agreed on a date for a national reconciliation conference. But the planned conference was postponed repeatedly as inter-clan fighting steadily escalated in Mogadishu and beyond.[68] Encamped in heavily fortified compounds and unable to respond except in self-defence, the UNOSOM force found itself powerless to deter such fighting.

With UNOSOM reduced to something of a spectator, several key functions of the mission have been seriously eroded. For one thing, the UN peacekeepers have been unable to halt a dramatic upsurge in banditry. A humiliating example of theft occurred in April 1994 when someone sneaked into UNOSOM's headquarters and walked off with nearly $4m.[69] And because of the very real threat of kidnapping and attacks, a number of NGOs and UN agencies suspended their humanitarian operations. In July 1994, two agencies with an unbroken record in Somalia—Save the Children and the International Red Cross—were forced to retreat to Nairobi. Several agencies, including the World Food Programme and Oxfam, have publicly criticised the level of security provided by UNOSOM for relief operations in

---

66. Menkhaus, "Getting Out Vs Getting Through," p. 147.
67. *Africa Research Bulletin (ARB)*, November 1993, p.11242.
68. Michael Maren, "The UN Provides Somalis the Incentive to Fight," *SNU* 3 (11 July 1994).
69. "The Rise and Fall of a SRSG," *SNU* 3 (18 May 1994).

Mogadishu.[70] Certainly, UN peacekeepers remain targets for Somali gunmen: 5 Nepalese and 7 Indians were killed in May and August 1994 respectively.

Thus it now seems clear that the large and costly UNOSOM presence in southern Somalia is out of all proportion to the marginal influence the operation has in the country. Despite desperate efforts in the last 12 months to cobble together a government through the warlords, UNOSOM has failed to advance the goal of national reconciliation. More worryingly, the presence of UNOSOM may have actually become an obstacle to effective Somali peacemaking. First, the UN inadvertently provides some of the incentives for the warlords to keep fighting by bringing the Somalis the very spoils they seek to control. In the most fiercely contested areas of the country such as Mogadishu, the UN presence "means jobs, contracts and money to the supporters of the different factions."[71] Second, while UNOSOM's cultivation of the warlords was born out of weakness, it had some unfortunate political consequences. Since early 1994, UNOSOM has extended large sums to various individuals linked to the militias, including those opposed to the elected government of Ibrahim Egal in the virtually autonomous and largely stable Somaliland Republic.[72] The big question now facing the Security Council is whether or not Somalia would be better off without UNOSOM. The United States, which terminated its diplomatic presence in Mogadishu in September 1994, believes it would.[73] The UN Security Council eventually agreed: Resolution 953 of 31 October 1994 called for a secure and orderly withdrawal of UNOSOM II by 31 March 1995.

Lessons

The UN operation in Somalia has been a bitter disappointment to those in the international community who saw it as a model for dealing with the disorder and conflicts of the post-Cold War world.[74] While famine no longer stalks the land, the enmities that caused the Somalian disaster still do. Having failed to bring a durable peace to the country, UNOSOM has been relegated to the sidelines as southern Somalia slips back into chaos.

---

70. *Guardian,* 4 August 1994.
71. Michael Maren, "The UN Provides Somalis the Incentive to Fight," *SNU* 3 (11 July 1994).
72. "UNOSOM and the Price for Peace," *SNU* 3 (14 September 1994).
73. *Guardian Weekly,* 25 September 1994.
74. Edward J. Perkins, former U.S. Ambassador to the UN, "Fact Sheet: Somalia—Operation Restore Hope," *US DoS Dispatch* 3 (21 December 1992), p. 898; Ambassador Herman J. Cohen, former U.S. Assistant Secretary of State for Africa Affairs, in "An Exit Interview with Hank Cohen," *CSIS Africa Notes* No. 147 (April 1993), p. 2.

For some observers, this outcome was fairly predictable. According to this perspective, the UN made a fundamental error when it abandoned diplomacy and the principles of traditional peacekeeping to intervene unilaterally in Somalia's civil war. By embracing a peace-enforcement strategy, it is argued that the UN turned its back on the cumulative experience of peacekeeping acquired during the Cold War era. In the process, the UN compromised one of its main assets, namely political impartiality, by becoming embroiled in a confrontation with General Aideed.[75] This not only led to the death of about 6000 Somalis in Mogadishu but actually complicated the task of humanitarian relief in the country.

Certainly, the UN's unhappy experience in Somalia underlines the wisdom of the old maxim that prevention is better than cure. The UN's negligence towards Somalia in 1991 was almost criminal. Having failed to prevent the Somali tragedy, the UN soon discovered when it got involved that a traditional peacekeeping operation was totally inappropriate for the extraordinarily complex situation in Somalia.[76] UNOSOM I forces were not deployed when needed because obtaining the permission of warlords took either too long or was not possible. This presented the UN with a stark challenge. Could the UN preserve any credibility if it continued to allow Somali warlords to exercise a veto on international assistance to sections of the Somali population dying from starvation? In the age of CNN and the global communications revolution, it was virtually impossible for the UN to ignore this challenge. Thus, while the risks of the UN's peace-enforcement strategy were considerable from the outset, the human costs of persisting with conventional diplomacy and peacekeeping were even greater.

So if UN intervention was right in principle, why did it go wrong in practice? The UNITAF/UNOSOM II operation contained four basic flaws. First, the UN was dependent on the vagaries of member governments. It did not have the military capacity to carry out peace-enforcement in Somalia in 1992–93. Thus Boutros-Ghali had to turn to the U.S. for military and logistical assistance. And, as noted, early American decisions concerning disarmament and the *de facto* recognition of the Somali warlords as legitimate leaders had profound repercussions for the viability of UNOSOM II. Member-states who contributed to UNITAF or UNOSOM II did so on an *ad hoc* basis and were subject ultimately to their own government's views, views which changed, especially in the event of UN casualties.[77]

Second, there was a basic mismatch between the UN's desire for a

---

75. Ramesh Thakur, "From Peacekeeping to Peace Enforcement: The UN Operation in Somalia," *Journal of Modern African Studies* 32 (September 1994), pp. 387–410.

76. Makinda, *Humanitarian Intervention in Somalia,* p. 86.

77. Terence O'Brien, former New Zealand Permanent Representative to the UN Security Council, interviewed on *Insight,* New Zealand National Radio, 10 July 1994.

political quick fix and the long-term support necessary for reconstituting a desperately divided Somalia. Don McKinnon, the New Zealand Foreign Minister, said the job of helping to make Somalia self-governing again would probably take between five and ten years.[78] But the UN was not in a position to wait for results. Immediately after the launch of UNITAF in January 1993, Boutros-Ghali convened a national reconciliation conference. Many analysts—in particular the Somali group at the Life and Peace Institute at Uppsala—judged that such a meeting was premature for it simply helped to strengthen the position of the warlords before peaceful regional leaders had a chance to emerge in the political space created by the intervention.[79]

Third, the U.S./UN administrators made a colossal organisational error in centralising the operation in south Mogadishu.[80] From a logistical point of view, the decision was understandable. The location contained the country's major port and airport as well as the large walled U.S. embassy compound. But the concentration of UNOSOM activities in one place—one controlled by General Aideed—became a trap once hostilities broke out. The politically astute Mohamed Sahnoun had anticipated this problem shortly before his resignation and had proposed to decentralise the UN operation into five regions so as to make it "less dependent on the conditions prevailing in Mogadishu."[81]

Fourth, the general lack of relevant expertise amongst UNOSOM staff undermined the quality of its performance. With some rare exceptions, UNOSOM has been staffed at all levels by expatriates with little knowledge of Somalia and with no briefing programme to enable them to understand the local culture or Somalia's clan-based politics.[82] Such ignorance generated a number of blunders. These included UNOSOM's persistent failure to recognise the critical importance of radio broadcasting in shaping Somali public opinion in what is predominantly an oral culture[83] and Admiral Jonathan Howe's ethnocentric decision to offer a reward for General Aideed's arrest.

Despite these intrinsic flaws in design, the UN mission was not doomed from the start. The fact the operation malfunctioned was also due to the way policy was executed. An internal report in April 1994 by an inquiry commission of the UN found that the UN and the U.S. pursued a misguided policy in Somalia and should share the blame with General Aideed for the

---

78. Don McKinnon, New Zealand Foreign Minister, "New Zealand and the UN Security Council," address to Otago University, 26 October 1993.
79. Compagnon, "Internal Intervention in Somalia," p. 22.
80. Menkhaus, "Getting Out Vs Getting Through," p. 155.
81. Sahnoun, "Preventing Conflict."
82. Ioan Lewis, "White-Washing the UN's Failures in Somalia," *SNU* 3 (27 August 1994).
83. Lewis, "Misunderstanding the Somali Crisis," p. 2.

descent into violence after June 1993.[84]

In the final analysis, however, while the UN "humanitarian" intervention in Somalia was poorly conceived and mistake-ridden, it failed ultimately because of the truculent and myopic leadership of a dozen or so Somali warlords. Having started a civil war which ravaged the country and the lives of so many of its people, these power-hungry faction leaders spurned the opportunity to make peace under UN auspices.

Nevertheless, the UN operation in Somalia remains important because it highlights the dilemma of peacekeeping in the 1990s. The conditions that led to the use of peace-enforcement in Somalia—civil war in a failed state—are set to reappear elsewhere. In the emerging post-Cold War world, there are many more Somalias, especially in Africa, where debt, drought, disease and civil strife are widespread. In these circumstances, the challenge for the UN may be to develop a concept that goes beyond traditional peacekeeping while falling short of out-and-out peace-enforcement.

---

84. *ARB,* April 1994, p. 11415.

6

UN Peacekeeping in Africa

Samuel M. Makinda

In a BBC interview in late 1993, a former Special Representative of the UN Secretary-General to Angola said that some of the permanent members of the Security Council were reluctant to support a greater UN involvement in Angola because they felt that they had done enough for Africa through the UN Operation in Somalia (UNOSOM).[1] Although Africa is a huge continent with more than 50 countries, much of the outside world tends to see it as one unit. In dealing with African states, therefore, it is necessary to emphasise the huge political, economic, ethnic and demographic differences among them. Moreover, because of these important differences, African leaders often react to the outside world in varied ways. For example, Nigeria's economic needs are not any closer to Uganda's than they are to Poland's; Rwanda's social and political problems might be similar to Bosnia-Herzegovina's rather than to Algeria's.

However, because of their recent colonial past and their place in the international division of labour, African states sometimes experience similar economic, political and social problems. This means that an analyst explaining, for example, the economic, scientific and political marginality of African societies needs to strike a balance between the uniqueness of each African state's problems and aspirations, and the common experiences of all of them. One of the common experiences of African states is that in the post-Cold War era, they have been ignored by the industrialised nations. It is partly because of this Western indifference to the needs of African states that

---

1. For a discussion of the UN operation in Somalia see Samuel M. Makinda, *Seeking Peace From Chaos: Humanitarian Intervention in Somalia* (Boulder: Lynne Rienner for the International Peace Academy, 1993).

the majority of their conflicts in recent years have gone out of control.[2]
Indeed, between 1989 and 1994, the UN had to send peacekeeping
operations to six African countries: Angola, Mozambique, Namibia,
Rwanda, Somalia and Western Sahara. There are two other serious conflicts
in which the UN has not intervened: Liberia and southern Sudan. Liberia
has been engulfed in civil war since 1989, and the peacekeeping operation
there was assembled by the Economic Community of Western African
States (ECOWAS). ECOWAS organised a five-nation peacekeeping force
code-named ECOMOG. However, by 1994 the 4000-strong ECOMOG had
become a combatant rather than a peacekeeper.

In dealing with disputes on the African continent, the UN has usually
sought the cooperation of the Organisation of African Unity (OAU). For
example, the OAU was consulted prior to the dispatching of UN peacekeeping operations to Angola, Mozambique, Namibia, Rwanda, Somalia
and Western Sahara. However, the OAU's role in some of these conflicts
has been abysmal. This is largely because the OAU lacks the finance and
infrastructure to assemble a peacekeeping force; its member-states are in
desperate economic conditions; and it lacks the expertise and resources
needed for peacemaking and peace-building.[3]

The purpose of this chapter is to analyse UN peacekeeping operations in
Africa in the 1990s. Rather than explain each operation separately, this
chapter looks at their common experiences, focusing on Angola, Namibia
and Rwanda, which could be described as Lusophone, Anglophone and
Francophone respectively. The problems of these three countries emanated
from completely different sources. For example, Namibia's problems have
to be understood in the context of a transition from colonialism to independence; the Angolan situation represents difficulties left behind by superpower rivalry during the Cold War; and Rwanda's circumstances represent
the breakdown in law and order due to dictatorial rule, corruption and
politically-motivated ethnic conflict.

Background

The first UN peacekeeping operation in Africa was deployed in the
Congo (now Zaire) from 1960 to 1964; it was on a visit in connection with
this operation that the UN Secretary-General, Dag Hammarskjöld, died in

---

2. For a discussion of African conflicts see Raymond W. Copson, *Africa's Wars and Prospects for Peace* (New York: M. E. Sharpe, 1994).

3. The concepts of peacemaking and peace-building are used here in the sense in which they are defined by Australian Foreign Minister Gareth Evans in *Cooperating for Peace: The Global Agenda for the 1990s and Beyond* (Sydney: Allen & Unwin, 1993), pp. 39–98.

an air crash.[4] While there was no UN military intervention in African conflicts from the mid-1960s to the late 1980s, there have been six UN operations between 1989 and 1994. Why has it been necessary for frequent UN interventions in African countries in the 1990s?

The reasons have to do with factors in the international system as well as within African states. The tumultuous changes in the international political system following the end of the Cold War, the rejection of communism in Eastern Europe and the disintegration of the former Soviet Union, have affected African states profoundly. These changes have been accompanied by severe economic problems in much of Africa, the insistence by the International Monetary Fund (IMF) and the World Bank that African states undertake political and economic reforms, and the indifference of Western nations to the plight of African states.[5] It is these external factors, coupled with weak state institutions, authoritarian rule and misguided macro-economic policies in some African states, that have accounted for the frequency and intensity of conflicts in Africa since the beginning of the 1990s.

Indeed, the reasons for the UN interventions in Angola, Mozambique, Namibia, Rwanda, Somalia and Western Sahara range from the delicate transition to independence as was the case in Namibia, through long-running civil wars as was the case in Angola and Mozambique, to the breakdown of state institutions as was the case in Somalia. However, there have been common themes in most of these conflicts, which include severe economic problems that have sometimes been exacerbated by poor planning, gross mismanagement and corruption. These states have also had dictatorial or authoritarian governments which have weakened or destroyed public institutions, such as the judiciary, political parties, the military and the civil service. In other words, most states had political and economic systems that lacked accountability.

For example, Namibia's security problems were precipitated by colonial rule through which South Africa, the colonial power, denied basic civil and political rights to Namibians. South Africa's rule in Namibia was established under the League of Nations mandate in 1919, following the defeat of the former colonial power, Germany, in the First World War. From the 1960s, the UN passed several resolutions requiring South Africa to facilitate Namibia's move to independence and withdraw from there. In fact, in 1966, the International Court of Justice ruled that Pretoria's occupation of Namibia was illegal, but South Africa ignored its verdict.

---

4. For an analysis of the politics and nature of peacekeeping during this early period see Indar Jit Rikhye, *The Theory and Practice of Peacekeeping* (London: C. Hurst, 1984).

5. For a discussion of some of these issues see Carol Lancaster, "Democratisation in Sub-Saharan Africa," *Survival* 35 (Autumn 1993), pp. 38–50.

The strongest internal challenge to South Africa's rule in Namibia came from the South West African People's Organisation (SWAPO), a liberation movement which was established in 1960. For more than two decades, SWAPO waged a guerrilla war against the South African forces. SWAPO was subsequently recognised by the OAU and the UN as the legitimate representative of the Namibian people. Its legitimacy was also acknowledged by the Contact Group of Western nations, comprising the UK, the USA, France, Canada and Germany. The Contact Group was established in 1977 to try to persuade South Africa to withdraw from Namibia. The Contact Group's proposals on Namibia's independence, like those of the OAU, were incorporated in Security Council Resolution 435 of September 1978, which authorised the UN to assume legal responsibility for Namibia's transition to independence.[6]

In efforts to circumvent external pressure, the South African government appointed an Administrator-General for Namibia with full powers in 1977. Through the Administrator-General, Pretoria sought to facilitate an internal settlement that would have marginalised SWAPO, but its plans fell apart.

Following Angola's independence from Portugal in 1975, SWAPO moved its operation bases there. Because Angola's ruling party, the MPLA *(Movimento Popular de Libertacao de Angola),* received military support from the Soviet Union and Cuba from the mid-1970s, Angola came to be used as a fighting ground for the USA, China, South Africa and the USSR. It was for this reason that in the 1980s the United States under President Ronald Reagan linked Namibia's transition to independence to the withdrawal of Cuban troops from Angola. It was largely because of the internationalisation of the Angolan conflict that the peace accords of 22 December 1988 which paved the way for Namibia's independence were negotiated by Angola, Cuba and South Africa, with the U.S. and the USSR as observers. SWAPO was not a party to these negotiations, and this fact contributed to the misunderstandings, suspicions and uncertainty that accompanied Namibia's move to independence on 21 March 1990.

Although the 22 December 1988 tripartite peace agreement was crucial to Namibia's move to independence in 1990, its significance lay in facilitating South Africa's implementation of Security Council Resolution 435. The peace accord reiterated much of what was in Resolution 435, calling for a ceasefire and for free elections under UN supervision followed by a South African troop withdrawal and national independence. According to the agreement, the all-powerful, South African-appointed Administrator-

---

6. For an analysis of Namibia's road to independence see Robert S. Jaster, *The 1988 Peace Accords and the Future of South-west Africa* (London: International Institute for Strategic Studies [IISS], Adelphi Paper No. 253, 1990).

General was to administer Namibia during the transition period. However, there was no provision for the sharing of power between the Administrator-General and the UN representative. It was under these conditions that the UN Secretary-General's Special Representative, Martti Ahtisaari, arrived in Windhoek with a small staff on 31 March 1989 to oversee the transition to independence. However, the transition began with uncertainty and moved through a period of growing suspicions and armed violence before culminating in a move towards national reconciliation.

While the UN stepped into Namibia to resolve a conflict between the colonial power and a nationalist movement, in Angola the UN went in to try to help rival nationalist movements reach an accommodation. In one way, the situation in Angola was a classic civil war resulting from a combination of several factors, including personal ambitions and ideological and ethnic differences. In another way, Angola was a classic example of colonial irresponsibility: the colonial power departed quickly without adequate arrangements for a peaceful transition to nationalist rule. If Angola's transition to independence had been similar to Namibia's, it is probable the rivalry between the ruling MPLA and UNITA (*Uniao Nacional para a Independencia Total de Angola*) would have taken different dimensions.[7]

The Angolan civil war dates back to the country's independence in November 1975. The three main liberation movements, the MPLA, UNITA and the FNLA (*Frente Nacional de Libertacao de Angola*) were bitterly divided over power-sharing. As the independence date approached, each group sought weapons and allies to wage war against the others. It was these factors that, in part, accounted for the Soviet, U.S., Chinese, Cuban and South African involvement in the Angolan civil war in the mid-1970s. As the best-organised and most disciplined movement, the MPLA took Luanda, the capital, and declared itself the government and was supported by the USSR and Cuba. UNITA, which had few international connections at the time, was supported by China and South Africa. The FNLA, which had well developed links with the CIA through its bases in Zaire, was aided by the United States. Despite Congressional efforts to prevent American involvement in Angola, the CIA was a major player.[8] By the early 1980s, the FNLA had virtually disintegrated, leaving the ruling MPLA and UNITA as the main protagonists.

UNITA's hopes of destabilising the MPLA government were rekindled

---

7. For analyses of the Angolan civil war see John Marcum, *The Angolan Revolution, Vol. 2: Exile Politics and Guerrilla Warfare* (Cambridge, MA: MIT Press, 1978); and Arthur Jay Klinghoffer, *The Angolan War: A Study in Soviet Policy in the Third World* (Boulder: Westview, 1980).

8. See John Stockwell, *In Search of Enemies: A CIA Story* (New York: W. W. Norton, 1978). Stockwell was head of the CIA Angola Task Force.

by the Reagan administration's keen interest in reducing the Soviet and Cuban presence in much of the Third World. Washington not only gave support to UNITA in the 1980s, but it also endorsed South Africa's insistence that Namibia's independence and the Cuban withdrawal from Angola were linked. By the late 1980s, Soviet President Mikhail Gorbachev, who had started to reassess Soviet involvement in Third World conflicts, put pressure on Cuba to withdraw its forces from Angola. However, the most decisive factor in the Angolan (and Namibian) peace process was the victory of the MPLA and Cuban forces over the UNITA and South African forces at the battle of Cuito Cuanavale which lasted from March to May 1988. It was these developments that drove Angola, Cuba and South Africa to sign the December 1988 accords calling for the implementation of Resolution 435 on Namibia, the removal of South African troops from southern Angola and the phased withdrawal of an estimated 50 000 Cuban troops from Angola.

Notwithstanding the removal of the foreign military presence in Angola, it was not until two and a half years later, in May 1991, that the MPLA and UNITA signed the peace agreement at Bicesse, Portugal, ending a 16-year civil war. While the Bicesse agreement provided for the transition to a popularly elected government, it did not sufficiently take account of the deep hatred and suspicions between UNITA and MPLA leaders.[9] Moreover, the accord was implemented while the MPLA was still in power, alongside the Joint Political and Military Commission, comprising UNITA, the MPLA and representatives from the United States, the Soviet Union and Portugal. After the conclusion of the Bicesse accord, the Security Council authorised the establishment of the UN Angola Verification Mission (UNAVEM II), consisting of a small group of military observers, police monitors and election supervisors.

Like the conflict in Angola, the problem in Rwanda also stemmed partly from the colonial past and personal ambitions. However, unlike Angola, the Rwandan conflict had much more to do with the misguided policies of the post-independence leaders, dictatorial rule and ethnic competition between the majority Hutus and minority Tutsis. The Belgian colonial policies favoured the Tutsis and helped buttress their feudal system. Indeed, Belgium's policy of divide-and-rule succeeded in keeping Hutus and Tutsis apart by creating a layered society in which Belgians were at the top, followed by Tutsis, with Hutus at the bottom. The Hutus and Tutsis speak the same language and have similar customs, but during the colonial period,[10]

---

9. For an analysis of the problems of establishing democracy in Angola see Keith Somerville, "The Failure of Democratic Reform in Angola and Zaire," *Survival* 35 (Autumn 1993), pp. 50–77.

10. Rwanda and Burundi were part of German East Africa from the 1890s until the end of

Belgian authorities used wealth to differentiate Hutus from Tutsis: anyone who had more than ten head of cattle was considered a Tutsi, and virtually all poor people were regarded as Hutus. What this basically suggests is that there are few, if any, "ethnic" differences between Tutsis and Hutus. However, the two ethnic groups have had unequal access to political and economic power at different times. The Rwandan tragedy, therefore, should also be seen in terms of this unequal access to political and economic power.

Prior to Rwanda's independence in 1962, and especially between 1959 and 1961, the Belgian colonial authorities switched their support to the Hutus, who rebelled against the Tutsis. The Tutsi monarch was deposed and forced into exile with his supporters in 1962. The situation that erupted in early 1994 was partly due to the efforts by the children of the exiled Tutsis who wanted to return to Rwanda and share power with the Hutus.

Following the outbreak of mass killings in Rwanda in April 1994, most press reports explained the situation in terms of ethnic differences between the Hutus and Tutsis. However, this explanation does not take account of the differences between northern and southern Hutus which has resulted in many Hutus killing each other. The civil war certainly drove Hutus and Tutsis further apart, but it also exacerbated the hatred between northern and southern Hutu politicians, which was traditionally centred around two rival politicians: former President Juvenal Habyarimana, a northern Hutu, who was killed in a plane crash on 6 April 1994; and Habyarimana's predecessor, Gregoire Kayibanda, a southern Hutu, Rwanda's first president from 1962 to 1973 when he was ousted from power by Habyarimana.

Since the mid-1970s, the Rwandan army's officer corps has come from the northern Hutus. Non-northern officers were often given posts where they did not command troops. In contrast, in the 1960s Kayibanda had concentrated political power among the southerners. However, following Habyarimana's military coup in 1973, political power came to be wielded predominantly by the northern Hutu. For this reason, it could be argued that the fighting has been as much between the northern and southern Hutu as between the Hutus and Tutsis.

The tragedy also arose from the revolt by both Hutus and Tutsis against Habyarimana's dictatorial rule. It was caused by a yearning for democracy and demands for justice and human rights. Habyarimana's supporters manipulated ethnicity to cover up their human rights violations. The majority of Hutus who had been denied justice were persuaded to accept their

World War I. After Germany had lost the war, German East Africa was divided into Tanganyika (now Tanzania), ruled by Great Britain, and Rwanda-Urundi (now Rwanda and Burundi), ruled by Belgium.

oppressors as saviours and to see Tutsis as enemies who should be extermi-
nated.[11]

The two main protagonists in Rwanda from 1990 were the MRND
(*Mouvement Républicain National pour le Development et la Democratie*)
the ruling party dominated by the northern Hutus, and the Tutsi-dominated
Rwanda Patriotic Front (RPF), which was established in Uganda in 1987.
The RPF invaded Rwanda in October 1990 with a view to taking power, but
it was repulsed by the Rwandan army with support from Belgium, France
and Zaire. Following the RPF incursion, the Habyarimana regime made
attempts to reform the political system and agreed to negotiate with the RPF.
The two sides signed a wide-ranging agreement in Arusha, Tanzania, on 4
August 1993. It was after the conclusion of this accord that the Security
Council passed Resolution 872 in October 1993 authorising the establishment of the UN Assistance Mission to Rwanda (UNAMIR) to monitor its
implementation.

The UN operation in Rwanda, like those in Angola and Namibia before
it, were designed to help the peace process in these countries. But, how
were they structured and what kind of mandates were they given?

Structure and Mandate of UN Operations

As UN Secretary-General Boutros Boutros-Ghali has argued, peacekeeping operations are a UN invention.[12] The UN Charter does not make
any reference to peacekeeping operations.[13] Because of the resulting need
for improvisation, every peacekeeping operation assumes its own structure
and mandate, which are generally influenced by: the nature of the conflict to
be resolved; the availability of resources; the interests of the permanent
members of the Security Council; and the interests of the participating
nations. It is also these factors that ultimately determine the success or
failure of any peacekeeping operation.

While "traditional" peacekeeping forces carry small arms and can fire
them only in self-defence, peace-enforcement forces usually have a much
wider mandate.[14] Apart from Somalia, where the mandate of the UN

11. For a discussion of some of these issues see David Dorward, "Rwanda and Burundi: The
Politics of Ethnicity and the Psychology of Victimisation," *Current Affairs Bulletin* 71
(June/July 1994), pp. 31–38.
12. Boutros Boutros-Ghali, *An Agenda for Peace* (New York: UN, 1992), para. 28.
13. For analyses of the evolution of UN peacekeeping operations see William J. Durch, ed.,
The Evolution of UN Peacekeeping: Case Studies and Comparative Analyses (New York: St.
Martin's Press, 1993).
14. For discussions of peacekeeping operations in general see Mats R. Berdal, *Whither UN
Peacekeeping?* (London: IISS, Adelphi Paper No. 281, 1993); F. T. Liu, *United Nations
Peacekeeping and the Non-Use of Force* (Boulder: Lynne Rienner for the International Peace

operation changed from a mere interposition force to one with enforcement powers, the operations in other African countries did not have much power beyond the traditional role of an observation or interposition force. The structures and mandates of UN operations in Angola, Namibia and Rwanda were different, reflecting the unique circumstances of each state, the interests of the permanent members of the Security Council at the time of passing the resolutions authorising them, and the processes and negotiations that preceded the deployment. For instance, in Rwanda, diplomatic negotiations between the Rwandan government and the guerrilla forces of the RPF took place in Arusha in 1992–93. The principal brokers were the neighbouring states, especially Tanzania, Uganda, Burundi and Zaire. Although Belgium and France dispatched troops to Rwanda to help the Habyarimana government in late 1990, there was little direct extra-regional involvement in the negotiations.

The parties eventually signed an agreement on 4 August 1993, calling for a ceasefire, the establishment of a transitional government and the return of refugees. It was on the basis of the Arusha agreement that the UN Security Council authorised the establishment of UNAMIR for an initial period of six months. Its mandate was quite limited: to contribute to the security of Kigali, Rwanda's capital; monitor the observance of the ceasefire agreement; monitor the repatriation of refugees; and "monitor the security situation during the final period of the transitional government's mandate, leading up to the elections" (Resolution 872, 5 October 1993).

The Security Council extended UNAMIR's mandate to 29 July 1994 "with a six-week review provision on the understanding that progress would be made in establishing the transitional institutions provided for under the Arusha Peace Agreement" (Resolution 909, 5 April 1994). However, on 6 April 1994 President Habyarimana was killed in a plane crash and, in the face of the rapid deterioration of security in the country, the Security Council adjusted the mandate of UNAMIR and reduced its size to 270 troops. Ironically, the Security Council authorised this reduction in the size of UNAMIR by the same Resolution 912 (21 April 1994) which claimed that the UN was appalled "at the ensuing large-scale violence… which resulted in the death of thousands of innocent civilians, including women and children…including those who sought refuge with UNAMIR."

A month later, and following the worldwide condemnation of the deaths in Rwanda, the Security Council authorised the expansion of UNAMIR to 5500 troops and expanded its mandate to contribute to the security and

Academy, 1992); and Brian Urquhart, "The United Nations: From Peacekeeping to Collective Security?" (London: IISS, Adelphi Paper No. 265, 1992).

protection of civilians at risk as well as providing security and support for humanitarian relief operations (Resolution 918, 17 May 1994). Although several countries, most of them African, pledged troops, they attached many conditions, and by the end of June 1994 the 5500 troops had not been raised.

In late June 1994, the Security Council passed Resolution 929 authorising the deployment of French troops under chapter VII of the UN Charter for a two-month period. The Security Council had determined that "the magnitude of the humanitarian crisis in Rwanda" constituted "a threat to peace and security in the region" and gave the French contingent the authority to use "all necessary means to achieve the humanitarian objectives." "Operation Turquoise" was withdrawn at the end of August 1994 and replaced by an expanded UNAMIR. Yet by the end of September 1994 UNAMIR had still not reached its full strength of 5500 troops.

Unlike Rwanda, where the UN operation was deployed soon after the resolution authorising it had been passed, Namibia had to wait for eleven years before the relevant Security Council resolutions were implemented. Resolution 431 (27 July 1978) called for the "appointment of [the Secretary General's] Special Representative for Namibia in order to ensure the early independence of Namibia through free elections under the supervision of and control of the United Nations." Resolution 435 (29 September 1978) called for the establishment of "a United Nations Transition Assistance Group" (UNTAG) in order to assist the Special Representative to carry out the mandate of Resolution 435.

It was not until 1989 that these resolutions were implemented. Through Resolutions 629 and 632 of 1989, the Security Council confirmed 1 April 1989 as the date on which implementation of Resolution 435 was to begin. This was also the date on which UNTAG was deployed. Resolution 632 (16 February 1989) also stated that Resolution 435 would be implemented "in its original and definitive form to ensure conditions in Namibia which will allow the Namibian people to participate freely and without intimidation in the electoral process." The UNTAG force of 4650 troops was deployed along the Namibia–Angola border to monitor the ceasefire. UNTAG had the mandate to monitor the ceasefire and the elections that preceded independence in early 1990. UNTAG commander General Prem Chand of India arrived in Windhoek on 26 February 1989. Ten days earlier the Security Council had voted unanimously to adopt Resolution 632 approving the reduction of UNTAG troops from 7500 to 4650.

The Namibian settlement had a positive effect on the peace process in Angola. As has already been indicated, negotiations for the Angolan peace settlement took place following the end of the Cold War and the subsequent decline of regional and international intervention in the country's civil war. In the wake of the December 1988 tripartite agreement between Angola, Cuba and South Africa, the Security Council established the first UN Angola Verification Mission (UNAVEM I), whose task was to verify the phased and total withdrawal of Cuban troops from Angola. In the meantime, between 1989 and May 1991, Portugal, supported by the USSR and the USA, was involved in mediating the conflict between UNITA and the MPLA. The Bicesse agreement of May 1991 between UNITA and the MPLA needed international supervision to be successfully implemented. It was for this reason that the Security Council adopted Resolution 696 (30 May 1991) authorising the deployment of the second UN mission in Angola for a period of 17 months. UNAVEM II comprised 350 military observers, 90 police monitors and 400 election observers, and operated under the direct control of the Secretary-General's Special Representative Margaret Anstee.

The small UNAVEM II contingent had a demanding but limited mandate which included overseeing the confinement of 124 000 MPLA troops and 23 000–70 000 UNITA guerrillas in assembly points. It was deployed at 46 points and also required to monitor the disarming and demobilisation of UNITA and MPLA forces. The 400 election supervisors had to monitor the elections throughout a country which had never had a free election before. In an effort to deal with increased problems and uncertainties, and following recommendations by the Joint Military and Political Commission, a new Monitoring Task Group was created on 11 January 1992 to strengthen the implementation of the peace accord. The Task Group included members from the MPLA, UNITA and UNAVEM. The ceasefire held tenuously up to election time, and the elections of 29–30 September 1992 were regarded by the UN and international observers as "free and fair" overall.

Problems of the UN Operations

As already stated, the success or failure of a peacekeeping operation has to be assessed in terms of its mandate and resources and the problems on the ground. Some operations have been given very limited mandates in very complex situations and the results have been abysmal. Other operations have been given broad mandates but without the resources to carry them out. Problems have also resulted from the linguistic differences and lack of co-operation among the participating nations and different levels of training of the soldiers.

UN operations in Namibia, Angola and Rwanda faced numerous difficulties. While some of these hurdles could have been anticipated, others were extremely hard to predict.

The Namibian operation was successful overall, but it had to endure serious problems on the way. Most of these difficulties stemmed from suspicions and violence between the main protagonists, namely the South African forces and SWAPO guerrillas. The ceasefire in Namibia was due to begin on 1 April 1989. By this time, South African forces were to be restricted to their bases, SWAPO guerrillas confined to their camps north of the 16th parallel in Angola and a UN force of 7500 troops deployed along the Namibia–Angola border to monitor the ceasefire.

However, in mid-January 1989, the first hitch occurred when the UN Security Council decided to cut the UN military force from 7500 to 4650 troops as an economy measure. African and other Third World states protested vigorously, arguing that it would open the way for South Africa to manipulate the elections. This problem led to a threat to withhold funding for the entire peacekeeping operation. However, as some analysts have pointed out, it was temporarily defused in mid-February 1989 "by a face-saving agreement to carry 7500 troops on the books while deploying only 4650 in Namibia."[15] Nonetheless, the dispute delayed the dispatch of the UN forces and, by the time of the ceasefire, only 1000 UNTAG troops had arrived and none of them had been deployed to their monitoring posts.

The Namibian situation was full of uncertainties. For instance, three months prior to the ceasefire, the country was very calm. However, on 31 March 1989, just hours before the ceasefire, Namibia witnessed the bloodiest violence since the start of guerrilla fighting 23 years previously. This violence resulted from a clash between about 1500 SWAPO guerrillas who were trying to slip into Namibia before the ceasefire and South African mechanised police units. During the fighting, South Africa threatened to repudiate the settlement and unleash its troops from their bases. Indeed, the biggest problem in Namibia was suspicion between South Africa and SWAPO, and it was this suspicion that occasionally erupted in violence.[16]

Another problem which the Namibian operation experienced was the relationship between the UN Secretary-General's Special Representative and the Administrator-General. The former had only an observation role without authority to overrule the latter, who had the power to make and implement laws. This meant that whenever the Special Representative found certain government actions unacceptable, his only weapon was publicity.

The problems of UNAVEM II resulted partly from the fact that the small force had been given an impossible task. The operation was also frustrated by the deep hatred and suspicions between the MPLA and UNITA. The leaders of both political parties were governed by the fear and expectation

---

15. See *Strategic Survey 1989–1990* (London: IISS, 1990), p. 75.
16. For details see Jaster, *The 1988 Peace Accords,* especially pp. 33–71.

that whichever won the election of 29–30 September 1992 would use government power to crush its opponent.

Indeed, one of UNAVEM II's hurdles was that it did not have the resources to monitor effectively the demobilisation of UNITA and MPLA forces. Jonas Savimbi of UNITA had kept a significant number of troops from the demobilisation exercise in case he lost, or in case the MPLA lost and refused to step down. He did not give accurate information about the size of his forces, concealing thousands of guerrillas and their weapons in remote areas. Moreover, demobilisation was very slow and by election time it had not been completed. By the end of September 1992, only 45 percent of government troops had been demobilised, while only 24 percent of the assembled UNITA fighters had given up their weapons. By the end of the election exercise, the UNITA guerrilla army was still intact and the MPLA had thousands of troops that had been transferred into the paramilitary police. It could be argued that had UNAVEM II had the resources to disarm and monitor the demobilisation of forces on both sides, the result would have been different.

As had been expected, the MPLA won the majority of seats at national and provincial level, to give it an absolute majority in the National Assembly. The MPLA leader, Jose Eduardo dos Santos, obtained 49.6 percent of the presidential vote, just short of the 50 percent needed to avoid a second round, while Savimbi of UNITA obtained 40.1 percent. However, the announcement of election results on 17 October 1992 was merely a signal for more fighting. UNAVEM II was scheduled to be wound up by 30 November 1992. But the fighting intensified following UNITA's claim that there had been widespread electoral fraud. Throughout the election campaign, Savimbi had said he would not lose a free election and that any election that resulted in his defeat would have been rigged.

UNAVEM II was not the only UN operation in Africa with enormous difficulties. UNAMIR in Rwanda also faced insurmountable problems. Some of its difficulties stemmed from its wavering mandate, the Security Council's uncertainty about how to deal with the Rwandan conflict and suspicions by the RPF that the UN operation was partisan. The mandate which the operation was given in October 1993 was altered in April 1994 and again in May. During this period the Security Council either did not know how to deal most effectively with the situation in Rwanda or was not interested in doing much about it. Moreover, the mandate of the first UNAMIR forces did not include the power to protect civilians. This made Rwandans lose confidence in the ability of the UN to protect them.

Suspicions on the part of the RPF were strengthened by the fact that France and Belgium, which had sent in troops to help Habyarimana between

1990 and 1993, agreed to participate in a supposedly neutral UNAMIR. This partly contributed to the failure of both parties to observe the ceasefire agreement. In addition, the UNAMIR forces could not be deployed for some months because of procrastination on the part of Habyarimana's government. Members of the Rwandan Presidential Guard, trained and armed by the French, were unwilling to comply with the Arusha agreement.

Conclusion: Successes, Failures and Lessons

The varied problems encountered by UN operations in Angola, Namibia and Rwanda ensured that their results were mixed. These results, in turn, provide important lessons for Africa, the UN and the international community in general.

As already indicated, UNTAG in Namibia was more successful than other UN operations in Africa. This was largely because the Namibian situation was a straightforward decolonisation process and one of the main protagonists, South Africa, had no alternative but to leave the territory. However, UNTAG's role would have been far easier had the UN Secretary-General's Special Representative been given more power. In other words, some of UNTAG's problems stemmed from its limited mandate and the lack of adequate resources.

Similarly, UNAVEM II was successful in organising and monitoring the elections of September 1992 in Angola. However, poor planning, limited resources and the inability to anticipate problems meant that the operation could not achieve the effective demobilisation of all forces. UNITA kept back a significant number of forces while the MPLA merely transferred troops from the army to the "civilian" police. Whereas the complications in Angola were partly due to the deep hatred between UNITA and MPLA leaders, the UN also failed to put in place arrangements which would have reduced the protagonists' ability and willingness to resume fighting soon after the elections. Shortly after UNITA had launched a new military offensive in November 1992, Under-Secretary-General for Peacekeeping Operations Marrack Goulding was dispatched to Luanda in an effort to resolve the crisis and restore peace. He reiterated the UN position that any solution to the conflict would have to be linked to the mandatory acceptance of the election results and full adherence to the Bicesse agreement. However, the fighting had not stopped by late 1994.

Unlike UNAVEM II and UNTAG, UNAMIR in Rwanda had no success. The first phase of UNAMIR from November 1993 was short-lived, and the operation's mandate was adjusted in April 1994 before it had had any impact on the security situation in the country. By April 1994, the transitional government had not been established, refugees had not been repatriated and the date for the multiparty elections had not been set. The second UNAMIR which was deployed from July/August 1994 had a wider mandate, but in the light of the developments in the previous four months, it was too late.

The frequency, problems and experiences of UN operations in Africa in the 1990s call for increased African participation and involvement in Security Council debates. Moreover, Secretary-General Boutros-Ghali's complaint in mid-1992 that the Security Council had given less attention to the breakdown of security in Somalia because it was an African problem indirectly implies the need for reviewing permanent membership of the Security Council. Indeed, it is reasonable to infer that had there been an African state with permanent membership of the Security Council, the UN operations discussed above would have been given more resources and greater attention. Thus the case for an African permanent member of the Security Council should be seen not only in terms of geography, but also in terms of the frequency of Security Council decisions on African conflicts.

Another important lesson from the experiences of these UN operations is that threats to international peace and security in Africa do not always emanate from external military sources. They are increasingly caused by forces within states, namely the breakdown in state institutions, a lack of social cohesion, ethnic rivalry, economic misery, the denial of human rights and authoritarian governments. While military operations have been useful in establishing law and order in some situations, it is mainly through the elimination of these non-military factors that African states will enjoy peace and security.

Finally, the magnitude of the Rwandan tragedy highlights the need to design strategies for rapid intervention to prevent conflicts from deteriorating. This also means a readiness to reinterpret state sovereignty.[17] Moreover, in situations of imminent danger, the Security Council can authorise intervention under chapter VII of the UN Charter, thus avoiding the prohibition in Article 2.7 against interference in the domestic affairs of sovereign states. The Rwandan problem was detected early, but the Security Council had no political will to intervene and prevent massacres.

---

17. These issues have been canvassed on several occasions by Gareth Evans. See, for instance, his *Cooperating for Peace,* especially Chs. 3–6.

7

The UN Transitional Authority in Cambodia

Carlyle A. Thayer

In December 1978 Vietnamese military forces, accompanied by Cambodian exiles, invaded and occupied Cambodia. Vietnam quickly installed a sympathetic government in power in Phnom Penh, the People's Republic of Kampuchea (PRK). The former incumbent, Democratic Kampuchea (DK), was forced to withdraw to sanctuaries in the frontier region along the Thai border.

Vietnam's actions provoked an immediate regional outcry. Members of the Association of Southeast Asian Nations (ASEAN) condemned the use of force and called on parties to the conflict to cease fighting and for all "foreign forces" to withdraw. China responded by launching a limited duration punitive attack on Vietnam's northern border provinces. These events are collectively known as the Third Indochina War, a conflict which lasted for over a decade until its resolution in October 1991.

For most of this period the role of the United Nations was marginal. Action by the Security Council was stymied by the Soviet Union which essentially vetoed any anti-Vietnamese proposals. The situation in the General Assembly was different. Efforts to unseat Democratic Kampuchea were easily defeated by a coalition of states led by ASEAN. The General Assembly also adopted an annual resolution on Cambodia which kept up the political pressure on Vietnam to withdraw its military forces and reach a negotiated settlement.[1]

---

1. For a detailed discussion see Ramses Amer, *The United Nations and Foreign Military Interventions: A Comparative Study of the Application of the Charter* (Uppsala: Uppsala University, Department of Peace and Conflict Research, Report no. 33, 1992).

A UN role in settling the conflict in Cambodia only became possible in the late 1980s with the ending of the Cold War and increased cooperation among the five permanent members of the UN Security Council (P5). This resulted in "new vitality and credibility" for the United Nations and an enhanced role in the settlement of the conflict in Cambodia.[2] As a result the United Nations Transitional Authority in Cambodia (UNTAC) was established and the United Nations became responsible for its largest and most complex peacekeeping operation (to that date).[3] According to Yasushi Akashi, the person who headed UNTAC as the Secretary-General's Special Representative:

> To a larger extent than in previous operations in UN history, UNTAC thus combines within itself elements of peacekeeping, peace-making, economic and social maintenance and nation-building. UNTAC has been given the responsibility to help create a new nation after a prolonged war that lasted over 20 years. The UN has had some experience in administering colonial territories, but Cambodia provides a new model of multi-faceted UN activity in an independent state.[4]

This chapter examines the role of the United Nations Transitional Authority in Cambodia in its peacekeeping and peace-building missions. It begins by examining the historical background to conflict in Cambodia. It then discusses the establishment of UNTAC, its mandate, structure and operations. Next it assesses UNTAC's successes and failures before considering some of the lessons learned from this experience.

Background

The Cambodian conflict is a complex multilayered one. As Australian Foreign Minister Gareth Evans observed:

> After the Middle East, the Cambodian conflict was possibly the most complex single diplomatic problem in the world to try and resolve, involving as it did not only four competing political factions within the country itself, but just about all the significant countries of the region and the major powers as well, each of whom had a direct relationship with one or other of the internal players.[5]

---

2. Gareth Evans, "The Comprehensive Political Settlement to the Cambodian Conflict: An Exercise in Cooperating for Peace," in H. Smith, ed., *International Peacekeeping: Building on the Cambodian Experience* (Canberra: Australian Defence Force Academy, Australian Defence Studies Centre, 1994), p. 9.

3. UN Secretary-General Boutros Boutros-Ghali, quoted in "UN Peacekeeping: The 'Second Generation'," *UN Chronicle* 30 (September 1993), p. 32. UNPROFOR in the former Yugoslavia is now the UN's largest peacekeeping mission.

4. Yasushi Akashi, "To Build a New Country: The Task of the UN Transitional Authority in Cambodia," *Harvard International Review* 15 (Winter 1993/94), p. 68.

5. Gareth Evans, "The Comprehensive Political Settlement to the Cambodian Conflict: An

At the core of this conflict lie historical animosities between the Khmer and Vietnamese people and the weakness of the Cambodian state. At the next layer is added traditional rivalry between Thailand and Vietnam. At its outer layer, the Cambodian conflict became a kind of proxy war between China and the Soviet Union. In 1977 Democratic Kampuchea initiated a border war against Vietnam. As the conflict grew in scope and intensity, China sided with the former. Vietnam signed a treaty with the Soviet Union and then invaded Cambodia. This prompted China to retaliate by attacking northern Vietnam in February–March 1979. The Soviet Union responded by offering further military aid to Vietnam. Thus what began as a subregional dispute between "brother enemies" became a major regional conflict if not a proxy war between Cold War adversaries.

China, in collusion with Thailand, backed the Khmer Rouge. Other anti-Vietnamese Cambodian resistance groups also emerged, of which only two became important: the Khmer People's National Liberation Front and forces loyal to Prince Norodom Sihanouk. Each of these groups represented the three main steams of post-independence Cambodian politics: monarchists (supporters of Sihanouk), republicans (supporters of Son Sann) and communists (Khmer Rouge led by Pol Pot). The non-communist resistance groups received backing from ASEAN, the United States, France and, to a lesser extent, Britain. In July 1992 these groups formed the Coalition Government of Democratic Kampuchea (CGDK) and represented the Cambodian state in the United Nations.

Negotiations Leading to the Establishment of UNTAC

The United Nations became involved in the search for a political settlement of the Cambodian conflict immediately following Vietnam's invasion.[6] In 1979 the General Assembly requested the Secretary-General to use his good offices to seek a peaceful settlement and to coordinate relief assistance to Cambodians affected by the fighting. The General Assembly also called for the convening of an International Conference on Kampuchea. The conference was held at UN headquarters in New York in July 1981

Exercise in Cooperating for Peace," Address by Senator the Hon. Gareth Evans QC, Minister for Foreign Affairs, to the Peace Keeping Seminar at the Australian Defence Force Academy, Canberra, 2 May 1994, *News Release,* p. 1.

6. This section relies on "Background Note on the Negotiating Process," in *Agreements on A Comprehensive Political Settlement of the Cambodia Conflict, Paris, 23 October 1991* (New York: United Nations Department of Public Information, January 1992), pp. ii–viii; and Michael Doyle, "UNTAC—Sources of Success and Failure," in Smith, ed., *International Peacekeeping,* pp. 80–84.

but failed to achieve concrete results. However, the Secretary-General kept the UN's role alive by requesting his Special Representative for Humanitarian Affairs in Southeast Asia, Rafeeuddin Ahmed, to involve himself in discussions with the parties concerned. The Secretary-General kept the Cambodian conflict before the United Nations in regular reports to the General Assembly.

Prospects for peace improved greatly after the accession to power of Mikhail Gorbachev as Secretary-General of the Communist Party of the Soviet Union.[7] The Indochinese states came under pressure from Moscow to take positive steps to resolve the Cambodian conflict through national reconciliation.[8] In July 1987 the foreign ministers of Indonesia and Vietnam met in Ho Chi Minh City and issued a joint communique which called for a dialogue between the Cambodian protagonists.[9] In December that year Norodom Sihanouk and the PRK's Hun Sen met in France for the first time to initiate the process of dialogue. They met again in January 1988.

Thereafter the momentum towards peace picked up considerably. The four Cambodian parties held their first meeting in July 1988 at informal talks hosted by Indonesia and dubbed the Jakarta Informal Meeting (JIM-1). A second informal meeting (JIM-2) was held in February 1989. This followed Vietnam's announcement in January that it would withdraw all its forces from Cambodia by September that year if a political settlement were reached. In April Vietnam dropped all preconditions on the withdrawal of its forces by September 1989.

Further informal talks were held in Paris in July after which the first Paris International Conference on Cambodia (PICC) was convened (30 July–30 August 1989) at the initiative of France. The PICC was attended by the four Cambodian parties and eighteen interested countries and was co-chaired by France and Indonesia. It considered a number of working documents presented by the Secretary-General which dealt with such matters as the monitored withdrawal of Vietnamese forces, a ceasefire, cessation of external support, the formation of a transitional administration, elections, repatriation of refugees and displaced persons, and assistance in rehabili-

7. Carlyle A. Thayer, "Kampuchea: Soviet Initiatives and Regional Responses," in Ramesh Thakur and Carlyle A. Thayer, eds., *The Soviet Union as an Asian Pacific Power: Implications of Gorbachev's 1986 Vladivostok Initiative* (Boulder: Westview, 1987), pp. 171–200.

8. Carlyle A. Thayer, "Prospects for Peace in Kampuchea: Soviet Initiatives and Indochinese Responses," *Indonesian Quarterly* 17 (2nd Quarter 1989), pp. 157–72. Vietnam's decision to withdraw from Cambodia was part of a larger reform process which entailed a strategic readjustment of Vietnam's defence doctrine; for a discussion, see Carlyle A. Thayer, "The Vietnam People's Army Under Doi Moi," *Pacific Strategic Paper* no. 7 (1994), pp. 14–19.

9. For background on discussions between ASEAN and Vietnam see Carlyle A. Thayer, "ASEAN and Indochina: The Dialogue," in Alison Broinowski, ed., *ASEAN Into the 1990s* (London: Macmillan, 1990), pp. 138–61.

tation and reconstruction under the supervision of an "international control mechanism." Differences between the PRK and the other Cambodian parties over the composition of the "transitional administration" led to the suspension of the conference. Vietnam withdrew all its formed military units in September on schedule but without the presence of international monitors.

It was at this moment of deadlock that on 24 November 1989 Australia proposed that the United Nations be directly involved in the civil administration of Cambodia during the transitional period. This proposal was designed to "sidestep the power-sharing issue which had bedevilled the Paris Conference, and constrain the role of the Khmer Rouge in the transitional arrangements."[10] The Australian proposal soon became an Australian initiative as the head of its Department of Foreign Affairs and Trade, Michael Costello, embarked on an exhaustive series of discussions involving "30 major meetings with key players in 13 countries over 21 days straddling the December 1989–January 1990 period."[11]

Australia's proposal now formed the basis for discussion by the P5. In late 1989, the United States proposed to the Soviet Union that they join with the other permanent members of the Security Council in a series of consultations on Cambodia. The first meeting was held in Paris from 15 to 16 January 1990 and worked out a set of principles to guide future discussions, including an enhanced UN role in the transition period. This meeting marked the commencement of a two-track approach to the settlement of the Cambodian conflict. One track involved the P5, the other involved the PICC co-chairmen.

Following the P5 discussions, Indonesia's Foreign Minister Ali Alatas convened an informal regional meeting on Cambodia in late February involving the four Cambodian parties, ASEAN, Vietnam, Laos and Australia (as a resource delegation). It was at this meeting that Australia tabled a series of working papers covering in detail elements of a comprehensive political settlement.[12] This meeting, which came close to endorsing a statement of principles to govern an enhanced UN role in a settlement, foundered on PRK insistence that the formal conference record should include a reference to preventing the recurrence of genocide. A subsequent

---

10. Gareth Evans, "The Cambodian Conflict: Settlement Efforts Prior to November 1989," Ministerial Statement, *Senate Hansard*, 6 December 1990, p. 5160. Senator Evans has noted that the specific idea of a neutral UN interim administration arose from discussions he had with U.S. Congressman Stephen Solarz in New York in October 1989.

11. *Ibid.*, p. 5161.

12. These were subsequently published with a red cover and became known collectively as the "Red Book"; see Commonwealth of Australia, *Cambodia: An Australian Peace Proposal: Working Papers Prepared for the Informal Meeting on Cambodia, Jakarta, 26–28 February 1990* (Canberra: Australian Government Publishing Service, 1990).

meeting of the Cambodian parties was held in Tokyo in June. Although DK delegates were physically present, they refused to attend the working sessions.

As discussions proceeded, the Secretary-General established a task force in the UN Secretariat to facilitate contingency planning for a UN peace-keeping role in Cambodia. The UN Secretariat worked closely with the PICC co-chairmen and the P5. As a result of these and other diplomatic discussions, the P5 were able to announce at their sixth meeting in August 1990 agreement on a framework for a comprehensive political settlement.

France and Indonesia, the co-chairmen of the first PICC, then convened another informal meeting of the Cambodian parties in Jakarta in September. This meeting agreed to accept the P5 framework document in its entirety as the basis for a settlement of the conflict, including its recommendation that the Cambodian parties form a Supreme National Council (SNC) "as the unique legitimate body and source of authority in Cambodia throughout a transitional period."[13] On 20 September the UN Security Council endorsed the P5 framework document in Resolution 668; the General Assembly did likewise in Resolution 45/3 (15 October).

It was now left to translate the framework document into a detailed negotiating text. In November, the PICC co-chairmen hosted a meeting of a working group composed of the PICC's three working committees,[14] the other four permanent members of the Security Council and a representative of the UN Secretary-General. This meeting considered a full draft nego-tiating text submitted by Australia. The Jakarta working group meeting also authorised the PICC co-chairmen to complete the drafting of the negotiating text. This was done at a meeting between the co-chairmen and represen-tatives of the UN Secretary-General and the P5 in Paris from 23–26 November.

On 26 November it was announced that agreement had been reached on a draft settlement text. This document was presented to the Supreme National Council the following month. Agreement was reached on most but not all points. In particular, the Phnom Penh authorities (now styled the State of Cambodia or SOC) expressed reservations about their vulnerability after the demobilisation of military forces and the implications of a UN role for

---

13. The SNC comprised twelve members, six from the State of Cambodia and two each from the three other parties, including the Khmer Rouge or Party of Democratic Kampuchea. Norodom Sihanouk was later made chairman.

14. The first committee dealt with military matters and was chaired by representatives from Canada and India; the second committee was concerned with the question of international guarantees and was chaired by representatives from Malaysia and Laos; the third committee, charged with the responsibiilty for the repatriation of refugees and displaced persons and the reconstruction of Cambodia, was chaired by representatives from Japan and Australia.

Cambodia's sovereignty. Other details needed to be worked out, including the question of interim enforcement of the ceasefire and arms cessation agreements.

These were discussed at a series of SNC meetings held in Jakarta (4–6 June), Pattaya, Thailand (24–26 June), Beijing, (17–18 July), and Pattaya (26–29 August); meetings between the SNC, PICC co-chairman Indonesia and P5 representatives in Pattaya (29–30 August) and New York (20–21 September); and a final meeting between the SNC and the PICC co-chairmen and Rafeeuddin Ahmed. This meeting considered the revised draft of the November 1990 P5 text.

On 30 September 1991 the UN Secretary-General issued a report to the Security Council recommending the establishment of a United Nations Advance Mission in Cambodia (UNAMIC) to assist the Cambodian parties in maintaining a ceasefire which had been declared by the SNC following its June 1991 meeting in Pattaya. The Security Council approved the report and agreed to the formation of UNAMIC immediately after the signing of a comprehensive political settlement (Resolution 717 of 16 October). On 21 October the Paris International Conference on Cambodia was reconvened. On 23 October it adopted the Agreement on a Comprehensive Political Settlement of the Cambodia Conflict (with five annexes),[15] Agreement Concerning the Sovereignty, Independence, Territorial Integrity and Inviolability, Neutrality and National Unity of Cambodia, a Declaration on the Rehabilitation and Reconstruction of Cambodia, and a Final Act. The adoption of these documents marked the start of the transition process in Cambodia.[16] The documents of the Paris Conference on Cambodia were approved by the Security Council in Resolution 718 of 31 October 1991 which also requested the Secretary-General to draw up a detailed implementation plan.[17] This was approved by the Security Council on 28 February 1992.

Mandate, Structure and History of UNTAC

UNTAC's mandate, when compared with the mandates of all previous UN peacekeeping missions, was unprecedented in scope. It went far be-

---

15. Hereafter referred to as the Paris peace agreements.

16. The transitional period was to end "when the constituent assembly elected through free and fair elections, organized and certified by the United Nations, has approved the constitution and transformed itself into a legislative assembly, and thereafter a new government has been created"; Article 1 of the *Agreement on A Comprehensive Political Settlement of the Cambodia Conflict.*

17. *Report of the Secretary-General on Cambodia,* 19 February 1992, (New York: United Nations Department of Public Information, May 1992).

yond the traditional interposition of force between belligerents who had agreed to cease hostilities. UNTAC was in effect given supreme authority to exercise control over all aspects of the comprehensive political settlement of the Cambodian conflict including civil administration, military functions, elections and human rights.

On the one hand, Article 3 of the Agreement on a Comprehensive Political Settlement of the Cambodia Conflict defined the Supreme National Council as "the unique legitimate body and source of authority in which, throughout the transitional period, the sovereignty, independence and unity of Cambodia are enshrined." On the other hand, Article 6 declared that "The SNC hereby delegates to the United Nations all powers necessary to ensure the implementation of this Agreement." Further, in order to ensure a neutral political environment for the conduct of free elections, "administrative agencies, bodies and offices which could directly influence the outcome of the election will be placed under direct United Nations supervision or control." This specifically included foreign affairs, national defence, finance, public security and information.

UNTAC's mandate was spelled out in Annex 1 to the comprehensive agreement under five headings: general, civil administration, military functions, elections, and human rights. Four additional annexes provided further details on the military aspects, elections, repatriation of Cambodian refugees and displaced persons, and the principles for a new constitution.

The general section of Annex 1 reiterated UNTAC's unprecedented mandate: "UNTAC will exercise the powers necessary to ensure the implementation of this Agreement, including those relating to the organisation and conduct of free and fair elections and the relevant aspects of the administration of Cambodia." The Secretary-General's Special Representative was given the power of veto over any action by the Supreme National Council which he found at variance with the comprehensive agreement. If the SNC became deadlocked in its deliberations and its president—Norodom Sihanouk—unable to act, "his power of decision will transfer to the Secretary-General's Special Representative" (Annex 1, section A.c).

Section B of the annex reiterated the main points of Article 6, namely, UNTAC would exercise "direct control" over "all administrative agencies, bodies and offices" acting in the five fields mentioned above in order to ensure their strict neutrality. The Secretary-General's Special Representative was given the authority to issue binding directives on all Cambodian parties. In addition, the Secretary-General's Special Representative, in consultation with the SNC, "will determine which other administrative agencies, bodies and offices could directly influence the outcome of the elections" and exercise "direct supervision or control" if necessary. These agencies, bodies and offices were obligated to comply with UNTAC directives. The powers of the Secretary-General's Special Representative extended to deciding which administrative agencies could continue to function during the transition period to ensure normal day-to-day life in Cambodia, such as civil police. The Secretary-General's Special Representative had the power to install UNTAC personnel in any administrative agency to ensure control. UN personnel were to have unrestricted access "to all administrative operations and information." The Secretary-General's Special Representative could also reassign or remove from office any person found to be obstructing the peace agreements. Finally, UNTAC was empowered to undertake investigations of complaints and allegations regarding actions by the existing administrative structures in Cambodia which were inconsistent with the Paris peace agreement. Such investigations could be in consultation with the SNC or on UNTAC's own initiative.

UNTAC's military mandate was equally comprehensive. In addition to supervising, monitoring and verifying the withdrawal of all foreign forces (and their weapons and equipment) and matters related to maintaining a ceasefire, UNTAC was charged with supervising the regroupment, cantonment, demobilisation and arms control (weapons security) of opposing forces. Other duties included monitoring the cessation of outside military assistance, liaison with neighbouring countries, locating and confiscating caches of weapons and military supplies, mine clearing, running mine awareness and clearance programs, and assisting in the release of prisoners-of-war and civilian internees.

Annex 2 set out further details regarding the withdrawal of foreign forces and the implementation of a ceasefire and related matters. This included a two-phase ceasefire in which the United Nations would assume direct responsibility for supervision, monitoring and verification only at the commencement of the second phase. Each Cambodian party was obligated to provide information to UNTAC on the size, organisation and precise disposition of their military and police forces, whether in or outside of Cambodia. The Cambodian parties were also required to provide comprehensive lists of arms, ammunition, and equipment as well as detailed records of the locations of minefields. Each party was also obligated to nominate a military official as its representative to the Mixed Military Working Group, which was responsible for liaison and for resolving any problems arising from the observance of the ceasefire.

During phase two of the ceasefire, each Cambodian party was to assign units to cantonment areas and proceed under UNTAC direction with the demobilisation of at least 70 percent of total military strength. This process was to be completed prior to the end of the voter registration process. The remaining military forces (30 percent) were slated for either complete de-mobilisation "before or shortly after the elections" or for incorporation into a new national army. UNTAC was given responsibility for assisting the re-integration of demobilised soldiers into civilian life. Finally, UNTAC's military component was given the additional responsibility of providing assistance in the repatriation of Cambodian refugees and displaced persons.

UNTAC's electoral mandate was unprecedented. UNTAC was given complete responsibility for the organisation and conduct of elections including drafting an electoral law, voter registration, registration of political parties, voter education, "overall direction of polling and the vote count," investigation of complaints and corrective action, and "determining whether or not the election was free and fair and, if so, certification of persons duly elected." Annex 1 (Section D.3.a) specified that UNTAC would consult with the Supreme National Council and establish "a system of laws, procedures and administrative measures necessary for the holding of a free and fair election in Cambodia, including the adoption of an electoral law and a code of conduct regulating participation in the election in a manner consistent with respect for human rights and prohibiting coercion or financial inducement in order to influence voter preference." UNTAC's powers also included ensuring fair access to the media for all approved political parties; the design of a system of monitoring of voter registration, campaigning and balloting by the Cambodian parties; facilitation of arrangements for international observation of electoral procedures; and the institution of a system of safeguards to prevent electoral fraud. Finally, UNTAC was given a nine-month period, starting with the commencement of voter registration, in which to conduct the elections.

The final aspect of UNTAC's mandate mentioned in Annex 1 related to human rights. UNTAC was charged with general human rights oversight during the transitional period, the investigation of human rights complaints and corrective action if necessary, and the development and implementation of a human rights awareness education program. In order to carry out these functions, UNTAC had the right to suspend or abrogate any existing law which was in conflict with the Paris peace agreements. Finally, UNTAC's mandate included responsibility for the repatriation of Cambodian refugees and displaced persons (Annex 4).

Structure

Overall responsibility for the implementation of the Paris agreements in Cambodia was placed in the hands of the Secretary-General's Special Representative Yasushi Akashi. The Special Representative exercised his control functions through a structure consisting of a small headquarters staff located in Phnom Penh[18] and seven independent components, six civilian and one military. Each of these elements is discussed in turn.

The human rights component was charged with responsibility during the transitional period for fostering an environment in which respect for human rights and fundamental freedoms was ensured. This component operated in three areas: human rights education program, human rights oversight, and investigation of human rights abuses.

The civil administration component was responsible for ensuring a neutral political environment in which free and fair elections could be held. It was to exercise direct control over existing administrative structures in five major areas (foreign affairs, national defence, finance, public security and information) and to exercise scrutiny over other administrative structures which could influence the outcome of the election. The component included an office for training and an office for complaints and investigation. Both the human rights and civil administration components operated from Phnom Penh, in the 21 provincial and municipal centres and from the 200 districts into which Cambodia was divided.

The electoral component was entrusted with the organisation and conduct of free and fair elections. It was headed by a Chief Electoral Officer. Its structure included three divisions and one unit: Training, Education and Communications Division, Operations and Computers Division, Administration Division, Complaints Compliance and Enforcement Division, and an Advanced Electoral Planning Unit. An Electoral Advisory Committee was appointed by the Special Representative to prevent electoral irregularities. The Electoral Component also operated at central, provincial and district level.

The military component was headed by Force Commander Lt. Gen. John Sanderson. It consisted of a headquarters group, sector headquarters, a Military Observer Group, twelve infantry battalions, an engineering element, air support group, signals and medical units, military policy, a logistics battalion and a naval element.

The civilian police (CIVPOL) component consisted of unarmed civilian police monitors who were responsible for supervising and exercising control over the local civilian police of the Cambodian parties to ensure that law and order was maintained impartially, and that human rights and fundamental freedoms were respected. Police were stationed at central, provincial and district levels.

The repatriation component was charged with the resettlement of 370 000 Cambodian refugees and displaced persons from Thai border camps back to

---

18. This comprised executive management; a coordination and liaison team; human rights, politics, legal and economic advisers; an information service and support staff.

Cambodia. Its responsibilities included movement, immediate assistance and reintegration. The UN High Commissioner for Refugees (UNHCR) was designated as the lead agency and provided the director of this component. The rehabilitation component was headed by a coordinator and a headquarters staff of seven who oversaw the planning of a program involving food security, health, housing, training, education, transport and infrastructure and public utilities. The coordinator was also responsible for raising funds and other resources from donor countries. In May 1992 a joint SNC/UNTAC Technical Advisory Committee on Rehabilitation was formed.

History

As was noted above, immediately following the signing of the Cambodian peace agreements, the United Nations authorised an advance mission, UNAMIC. It became operational on 9 November 1991 and comprised civil and military liaison staff, a mine awareness unit and logistics and support personnel. On 8 January 1992 UNAMIC's mandate was expanded to include mine-clearance training for Cambodians and the start of a mine-clearance program. Also noted above, on 28 February 1992 the Security Council approved the establishment of UNTAC in Resolution 745. UNTAC was given a mandate lasting eighteen months. UNTAC comprised 15 900 military, 3600 civilian police and 750 international civilian administrators from 34 countries. (An additional 1400 civilians were scheduled to join later to assist in the elections along with 56 000 locally recruited Cambodian staff.) UNTAC became operational on 15 March when the Secretary-General's Special Representative and UNTAC Force Commander arrived in Phnom Penh. At that time it absorbed UNAMIC. The total cost of UNTAC's operations was roughly $2.8 billion.

Resettlement began almost immediately, even before UNTAC'S military units were deployed. The first convoy of refugees and displaced persons left Thai border camps on 30 March 1992 and the last in April of the following year. On 9 May 1992 the UNTAC Force Commander declared that phase two of the ceasefire would start on 13 June. Voter registration commenced on 5 October 1992 and was completed four months later. The electoral campaign lasted from 7 April to 19 May 1993.

National elections to select deputies to a Constituent Assembly were held from 23 to 28 May and the results were declared on 11 June 1993. The pro-Sihanouk political party FUNCINPEC[19] garnered 45 percent of the vote,

---

19. *Front Uni National Pour un Cambodie Independent, Neutre, Pacifique et Cooperatif* or National United Front for an Independent, Neutral, Peaceful and Cooperative Cambodia.

while the incumbent Cambodian People's Party (CPP) received only 38 percent. No single party won the two-thirds majority needed to approve a new constitution, and as a consequence a three-party coalition government was formed.[20] The Constituent Assembly adopted a constitution in September which proclaimed Cambodia a monarchy. With this act, UNTAC's mandate came to an end. The last military forces withdrew in November. The peace agreements made provision for a small residual presence in the form of a Human Rights Centre. UN agencies, such as the UN Development Programme (UNDP), continued their operations to assist in reconstruction.

Successes and Failures

In the words of Senator Gareth Evans, UNTAC's operation was a "flawed, or qualified success."[21] If a ledger were drawn up listing the achievements and shortcomings of UNTAC's mission, the positive side would include repatriation/resettlement and the electoral process. On the deficit side, listing failures and shortcomings, we would find civil administration and civil police, the military mandate, and human rights. Somewhere in the middle, indicating mixed results, would fall reconstruction.

According to Jarat Chopra, "The results of repatriation, if not resettlement, were the most positive of any of the seven UNTAC components."[22] Nearly 370 000 displaced persons were returned to Cambodia in a program which guaranteed them freedom of choice of resettlement. This massive logistics exercise was conducted in an extended time frame which permitted the registration of all those eligible to participate in the election. This was one of the major objectives of the repatriation program and it was achieved.

UNTAC was charged with conducting a "free and fair" election in a neutral political environment. In the end, for reasons discussed below, it was only possible to conduct an election in which "acceptable minimum standards" were met.[23] The entire electoral process was a technically proficient exercise in all respects, from the registration of voters and political parties, issuance of cards, determination of candidate lists, approval of party platforms, central record keeping, and voter education, to the conduct of the ballot, counting and certification of the results. In the view of one participant with prior experience in Namibia, "Cambodia will be the primary reference

20. The third party was the Buddhist Liberal Democratic Party.
21. Evans, "Comprehensive Political Settlement to the Cambodian Conflict," p. 12.
22. Jarat Chopra, *United Nations Authority in Cambodia* (Providence: Brown University, The Thomas J. Watson Institute for International Studies, Occasional Paper no. 15, 1994), p. 64. Problems in repatriation are also discussed by the author.
23. United Nations Security Council, *Fourth Progress Report of the Secretary-General on the United Nations Transitional Authority in Cambodia*, S/25719 (3 May 1993).

model for elections organised and conducted by the UN for some time to come." [24]

The UNTAC elections must be counted a success because of the response of the Cambodian people. Despite threats by the Khmer Rouge to disrupt the elections or otherwise dissuade people from voting, nearly 90 percent of those eligible cast their votes. They did so with enthusiasm and dignity. UNTAC's success was evident from the very first day when large crowds of voters turned up to cast their ballots.

UNTAC's success lies not just in the technical competence of the electoral process but in the fact that the Cambodian people were convinced that they were taking part in an historically important process in which the secret ballot would be guaranteed. An incumbent government, with all the advantages of having been in power for fourteen years, failed to gain a majority of the votes despite its resort to political intimidation and outright violence. Two-thirds of the ballots cast went to the other political parties. The successful conduct of the election was the *sine qua non* of the comprehensive political settlement. The government which emerged from the 1993 elections is now universally recognised as a member of the international community. As a result, sovereignty was restored to the state of Cambodia. This achievement led Ledgerwood to conclude that the elections were UNTAC's "greatest accomplishment, the biggest gamble."[25] Yasushi Akashi concluded that "UNTAC has been able to accomplish an essential and historic task of aiding Cambodia in its rebirth as an independent nation, based on democracy, pluralism, human rights and the spirit of reconciliation."[26]

The above comments by the Secretary-General's Special Representative, the person in charge of implementing UNTAC's mission, elides UNTAC's shortcomings and UNTAC's failure to carry out its mandate in other fields. It is arguable whether UNTAC's failure to exert control over civil administration was greater than its failure to obtain a ceasefire, canton, demobilise and disarm the military forces of the contending factions.

UNTAC never obtained a complete ceasefire, though the arrival of its military forces did lead to a general lowering of the levels of violence experienced previously. A major offensive by the Cambodian People's Armed Forces (SOC's troops) against the Khmer Rouge in January 1993 went unchecked and directly contributed to the refusal of the Khmer Rouge

24. Michael Maley, "Reflections on the Electoral Process in Cambodia," in Smith, ed., *International Peacekeeping: Building on the Cambodian Experience*, p. 45.

25. Judy L. Ledgerwood, "UN Peacekeeping Missions: The Lessons from Cambodia," *Asia Pacific Issues* 11 (March 1994).

26. Yasushi Akashi, "The Challenge of Peacekeeping in Cambodia," *International Peacekeeping* 1 (Summer 1994), p. 215.

to take part in phase two of the ceasefire.[27] Troops belonging to the other factions, particularly those under the direction of the CPP, left the cantonment areas to go on "agricultural leave." Some weapons which had been secured by UNTAC were returned. In short, all factions retained their arms and military forces at the time of the election when the peace agreements called for them to be cantoned, disarmed and demobilised.

UNTAC never attempted to exert effective direct control over the five key areas (not ministries) of national defence, information, public security, finance and information. Indeed, because UNTAC had no access to territory controlled by the Khmer Rouge, it concentrated its efforts on only one of the four parties—the State of Cambodia. In this respect it lost impartiality. Not only that, the SOC easily evaded UN controls and in the words of one writer, "administered around UNTAC."[28] The UN's failure in this area was another contributory factor in the Khmer Rouge decision not to participate in the peace process.[29] It also emboldened SOC officials and CPP functionaries to ignore aspects of the peace settlement which they found unpalatable. For example, the SOC continued to broadcast commentary on the radio which violated UNTAC guidelines.

The failure of civil administration to accomplish its mandate was matched by the CIVPOL. They monitored but did not control the activities of the SOC police. They proved completely ineffectual in the face of blatant acts of violence and political intimidation conducted against supporters of FUNCINPEC by SOC police and military personnel.

The Supreme National Council adopted key international human rights covenants. However, in reality UNTAC was completely helpless in enforcing human rights or taking corrective action. It was hampered not only by the lack of a functioning judiciary but by the refusal of SOC-appointed judges to hear matters brought before them by UNTAC. When UNTAC finally drafted appropriate laws and set up an Office of Special Prosecutor, it was, in one writer's view "too little too late."[30] While numerous investigations were carried out to identify the perpetrators of human rights abuses or violators of UNTAC's code of contact, none was

---

27. D. M. FitzGerald, "The Cambodian Military Factions and their Role in the Election," unpublished manuscript, 1994. The author was Australia's Deputy Defence Representative to the Supreme National Council.

28. Michael Doyle, "UNTAC—Sources of Success and Failure," p. 89.

29. Damien Healy, "The United Nations Transitional Authority in Cambodia—Some Fundamental Lessons," Master of Defence Studies sub-thesis, University College, Australian Defence Force Academy, Canberra, October 1994. Lt. Col. Healy served as aide to the UNTAC Force Commander.

30. Mark Plunkett, "The Establishment of the Rule of Law in Post-Conflict Peacekeeping," in Smith, ed., *International Peacekeeping: Building on the Cambodian Experience*, p. 71.

ever brought to trial or removed from office.

UNTAC's failures and shortcomings to carry out its mandate in the areas of military control, civil administration, civilian police and human rights meant that there was no neutral political environment in which to conduct elections.

Explanations for Successes and Failures

The implementation of the Paris peace agreements on Cambodia and the UN's mandate worked best when the Cambodian parties either agreed with the proposed action or were unable directly to influence the outcome. For example, the repatriation process was almost entirely in UN hands and its implementation was not dependent on the compliance of the Cambodian parties. In this one area, the Khmer Rouge cooperated with UNTAC out of self-interest.

Three of the Cambodian parties favoured elections, while the Khmer Rouge was too weak to disrupt them entirely. The technical integrity of the electoral process was guaranteed by the UN's presence. When the UN failed to obtain a ceasefire and carry out "related matters" (cantonment, disarmament and demobilisation) it made a virtue of necessity. To ensure the success of the elections, UNTAC drew up a coordinated security plan which involved cooperation with the armed units of the Cambodian parties. They were deployed as the outer security screen between the Khmer Rouge and the UNTAC polling stations.

A final explanation for UNTAC's successes was the support it received from members of the international community, including the P5 and the United Nations Core Group.

There are several interrelated explanations for UNTAC's shortcomings and failures. First, the Paris peace agreements were the result of a complex negotiating process involving political compromise and unstated understandings. The agreement often fell silent on contentious matters. For example, throughout the long, drawn-out negotiation process the Khmer Rouge resisted all references to genocide and enforcement measures which might render them liable for punishment. While the word genocide was dropped and human rights written into the agreement, an enforcement mechanism was left out. To take another example, reconstruction during the transition period was seen by the Khmer Rouge and other Cambodian parties and their external backers as a process which would benefit the incumbent government, the SOC. It was downgraded in priority and given scant resources. Comparatively little attention was given to the resettlement of internally displaced Cambodian or demobilised troops for the same reasons.

The UN was ill-equipped and badly structured to handle efficiently an operation the size and scope of UNTAC. It had never been involved in civilian administration before as part of a peacekeeping mandate, and no clear doctrine was developed as to or how this very important responsibility was to be carried out. The UN selection procedures with respect to civilian police resulted in the recruitment of individuals who came from security guards, paramilitary, military police, border guards, anti-terrorist units or even redesignated units. That is, CIVPOL was not staffed with personnel with community policing experience. They were posted as individuals and not as national units. Many could not speak the official international languages, English and French, or more scandalously, could not even drive a motor vehicle. Standard operating procedures, for example stress on the geographical and political balance of nations contributing military units, resulted in the dispatch of troops to Cambodia who inadequately prepared and trained for their peacekeeping tasks.

Another major failure was the inability of the United Nations and its Secretariat to adequately engage in contingency and long-term planning. This was evident at the start when, according to Jarat Chopra, the United Nations was "taken by surprise" that a settlement of the Cambodian conflict was reached. UNAMIC was designed as an "afterthought" and was dispatched to Cambodia with inadequate resources.[31]

Several writers have noted that once a peace agreement is signed it has the effect of creating a new set of political dynamics in which the United Nations becomes involved.[32] Each party attempts to manipulate the agreements. Doyle calls this effect an "obsolescing bargain."[33] The failure of the United Nations to deploy quickly resulted in the failure to establish a pattern of compliance with its authority. The entire UN operation in Cambodia almost broke down prior to the start of formal UNTAC operations. According to one insider, it was a "near thing."[34] Another analyst has written that there were two UNTACs, "UNTAC 1" was designed to institutionalise the UN's authority and control and when this failed, "UNTAC 2" was reduced to ensuring that elections were held.[35]

During UNTAC 2 the United Nations failed to assert its authority across a broad number of areas covered by its mandate. The UN went "softly" on continued Thai support for the Khmer Rouge. This resulted in the rearming

---

31. Chopra, *United Nations Authority in Cambodia*, p. 29.
32. John Sanderson, "UNTAC: Successes and Failures," in Smith, ed., *International Peacekeeping: Building on the Cambodian Experience*, p. 18.
33. Doyle, "UNTAC—Sources of Success and Failure," pp. 96–97.
34. Healy, "The United Nations Transitional Authority in Cambodia."
35. Chopra, *United Nations Authority in Cambodia*, p. 35.

and re-equipping of Khmer Rouge military forces at a critical stage.[36] Also, it meant that UN attempts to apply economic sanctions on the Khmer Rouge (banning the export of timber and embargoing petroleum) to pressure them into compliance were completely ineffectual.

Other UN planning failures included the late hiring of directors of the various components. Akashi was appointed in January 1992, five months after the main outlines of a peace agreement had been negotiated. The director of civilian administration was not appointed until March 1992. Many component directors came into their jobs not only late but without an intimate knowledge of the process which had resulted in a peace settlement in the first place.[37]

There were also structural and administrative reasons to explain UNTAC's shortcomings and failures. Each component operated independently of the other. Success, when it was achieved, was attained by an informal alliance involving the military and electoral components. Both benefited by the dispatch to Cambodia of survey teams and advance units. Success in repatriation also resulted from advance planning, and the establishment of a UNHCR office in Phnom Penh as early as 1990.

Lessons

A number of "lessons learned" arise from the UN's involvement in Cambodia. It is evident that if the United Nations is to be involved in complex multidimensional "nation-building" and "peacemaking" enterprises in the future, it will have to conduct a thoroughgoing reform of UN headquarters in order to enable that body to engage in long-term strategic planning for such operations. There must be a complete shift in doctrine and conceptualisation from past values and procedures which guided more traditional peacekeeping operations. Additionally, the United Nations must alter its recruitment and selection patterns both for senior personnel and for national contributions. The former need the skills and expertise, for example, to exercise effective financial control over state administration. The latter need to be trained to a "UN standard."

The UN bureaucracy needs to become involved earlier in long-term

36. FitzGerald, "The Cambodian Military Factions and their Role in the Election."

37. Rafeeuddin Ahmed was the obvious choice as the Secretary-General's Special Representative. He reportedly indicated he did not want the job. Akashi was appointed because of his bureaucratic seniority. UNTAC's electoral success has overshadowed its shortcomings and failures and led to Akashi's appointment with UNPROFOR. Former UNTAC officials are reluctant to offer public criticism of his excessively cautious leadership style which had a direct bearing on the failure of UNTAC to assert its authority. Author's interviews in Phnom Penh, May 1993.

planning so that it can rapidly deploy its forces and establish the UN's authority and patterns of compliance at the outset. This is not a sequential exercise in which the military arrives first and establishes security, but an operation requiring the parallel deployment of several components whose functions are integrated. This is particularly the case with respect to relations between the military and civilian police. The United Nations needs to address the problem of liaison and information flow between headquarters in New York and senior officials in the field.

The UN must seriously address what role it wishes to play in the maintenance or re-establishment of law and order. It has been argued that it should develop a Criminal (or Justice) Charter which can be taken "off the shelf" and applied to countries where the United Nations intervenes. This legal package should include provisions for a special prosecutor and the powers for the United Nations to arrest, prosecute and detain violators.

The Cambodia case indicates a need for the United Nations to consider seriously establishing its own independent media network in countries where it intends to operate. The success of Radio UNTAC, initially opposed by UN bureaucrats, merits careful study, along with the other information and public awareness programs conducted in Cambodia.

Finally, the United Nations needs to consider what sort of post-electoral responsibilities should be written into its initial mandate. According to UNTAC's Force Commander, the United Nations lost the political initiative in Cambodia in the immediate post-election period when its mandate was unclear.

Conclusion

According to Michael Doyle,

The Paris Agreement launched the UN into a new and startlingly comprehensive role. The unique quality of the Paris Agreement lies in the fact that the settlement process concerned what the UN Secretary-General Boutros Boutros-Ghali refers to in his *Agenda for Peace* as "peace-building" in addition to peacemaking and peacekeeping. The international community charged the UN—for the first time in its history—with the political and economic restructuring of a member of the UN, as part of the building of peace in which the parties would then (it was planned) institutionalise their reconciliation.[38]

UNTAC succeeded in restoring sovereignty to Cambodia, ending outside interference by Vietnam and China, and relegating a regional flashpoint to the status of an internal conflict. Although the process of reconstruction has begun, it is not yet clear two years after the UNTAC-sponsored "free and

---

38. Doyle, "UNTAC—Sources of Success and Failure," pp. 84–85.

fair" elections that the Cambodian state has been politically and economically restructured along democratic lines.[39] Elections may have "opened up" the political process in Cambodia but they did not fundamentally alter the nature of political power in that country. According to one writer, "The UN's failure to solidify the rule of law through 'control' of the factions and to demobilize the factional armies may come back to haunt its electoral success."[40] The UNTAC experience should give pause to the United Nations before it embarks on another complex nation-building and peacemaking exercise.

39. William Shawcross, *Cambodia's New Deal* (Washington, D.C.: Carnegie Endowment for International Peace, Contemporary Issues Paper no. 1, 1994).
40. Doyle, "UNTAC—Sources of Success and Failure," p. 96.

8

UN Peacekeeping in Central America

Larman C. Wilson and Raúl González Díaz

The Central American peace process began in the early 1980s while the Cold War was still in effect and was precipitated by the increasingly tense confrontation between the Reagan administration and the Sandinista government of Nicaragua.[1] This confrontation resulted in a Latin American initiative to form the Contadora Group, which was outside the UN-affiliated regional organisation, the Organisation of American States (OAS), in order to head off an anticipated military intervention by the U.S.

The Latin American initiative and resultant multilateral negotiating mechanisms eventually prevailed over and gained the support of the U.S. These initiatives were aided greatly by bilateral Soviet-U.S. cooperation under the Gorbachev and Bush administrations, which laid the basis for the UN becoming an active part of the peace process, for the first time in collaboration with the OAS. This resulted in an end to the Nicaraguan civil war by disarming the U.S.-supported Contras and observing free elections in February 1990. The successful model of joint OAS–UN action developed for Nicaragua was altered in applying the peace process to the civil war in El Salvador in 1991 in that it became one of exclusive UN involvement.

The UN was successful in bringing about an accord, one signed at the end of 1992 between the Farabundo Martí Front for National Liberation (FMLN) and the government. In both cases, and for the first time in inter-American conflicts, the UN Security Council approved the creation of peacemaking forces in Central America: the UN Observer Group for Central America (ONUCA) in 1989 and the UN Observer Group for El Salvador (ONUSAL) in 1991. The same UN peace process model was also success-

---

1. This chapter is a shortened and revised version of a paper presented at the 34th Annual Convention of the International Studies Association in Acapulco, Mexico, 23–27 March 1993.

ful in overseeing the negotiation of a series of agreements in 1994, pending a final accord, which were signed by the Guatemalan National Revolutionary Unit (URNG) and the government.

From Contadora to Esquipulas

The mounting instability and conflict in Central America resulted from the coming to power of the Sandinista government in Nicaragua and its support of the FMLN, and the Reagan administration's response. The Sandinistas took over after leading a popular insurrection against General Anastasio Somoza, who fled the country in July 1979. Once the Sandinistas were in power, Nicaragua became a conduit for Cuban aid and a supporter of the FMLN in its armed efforts to bring down the Salvadorian government.

Taking office in 1981, the Reagan administration focused on the Nicaraguan government and the FMLN in El Salvador, which it considered to be linked, and developed a policy to subvert and overthrow the former while helping the government of El Salvador defeat the latter. The means for dealing with Nicaragua began with covert actions in the formation of the Contras in 1983, Nicaraguan exiles operating mainly out of Honduras, and the mining of the harbours in 1984. These actions were followed by open and mounting economic and military aid to the Contras and to the government of El Salvador.

The initial response to the increasing strife in Central America was the formation of the Contadora Group (CG) by Colombia, Mexico, Panama and Venezuela in January 1983. This group, formed outside the framework of the OAS and opposed by the U.S., attempted to lay a basis for resolving the strife in the region. A 21-point "Document of Objectives" was approved by the foreign ministers of the CG and Central American countries in September 1983.[2] In November, the CG produced four draft treaties on U.S. relations with Honduras and El Salvador, which were rejected by the U.S.

A CG-prepared draft treaty, drawn up the next year, also was rejected by the U.S. The opposition by the U.S. led to the suspension of the CG's efforts in late 1984. However, the process was revived and the efforts broadened and strengthened with the formation of the Support Group by Argentina, Brazil, Peru and Uruguay in July 1985.

The confrontation between the FMLN and the Salvadorian government acquired a new dimension with the victory of José Napoleón Duarte, candidate of the Christian Democratic Party (PDC), in the May 1984 presidential runoff. His victory over Roberto D'Aubuisson of the far right

---

2. Bruce Bagley, "The Failure of Diplomacy," in Bruce Bagley, ed., *Contadora and the Diplomacy of Peace in Central America* (Boulder: Westview, 1987), pp. 186–87.

Nationalist Republican Alliance (ARENA) made him the first popularly elected civilian president in more than fifty years.

Duarte demonstrated his willingness to move away from the Reagan administration's strategy of a total military victory when he invited the FMLN to hold talks with the government in October 1984. These talks were held in the Salvadorian town of La Palma and were attended by Duarte, representatives of the armed forces and of the FMLN and the Democratic Revolutionary Front (FDR), a coalition of leftist politicians which had entered into an alliance with the FMLN. The La Palma meeting's only real achievement was the tacit acceptance by both sides that a military victory in the civil war was impossible and that only a political settlement would put an end to the impasse. Although both sides continued periodically to issue proposals for negotiations, neither showed a willingness to compromise.[3]

In 1986, an effort was made to revive the Contadora process through a meeting of the Contadora Group, the Support Group and the Central American countries in Guatemala. In May, the Contadora and Support Groups met again in an effort to draw up a new draft treaty. In December 1986, the foreign ministers of the CG and the Support Group met in Rio de Janeiro with the Secretaries-General of the OAS and UN and established the Rio Group. As its first task, the Rio Group visited all Central American countries in an effort to revive the stalled negotiations. These efforts, however, were transcended by a bold initiative taken by the Central American presidents themselves.

Attempting to renew the peace process, President Oscar Arias of Costa Rica presented his peace plan at a meeting of Central American presidents in February 1987. The 10-point plan called for a ceasefire with the insurgent groups, whose military aid was to be suspended. Moreover, the plan called for the granting of amnesty to the insurgents and the initiation of a democratisation process, including supervised elections. The Central American presidents signed the plan, known as Esquipulas II or the Guatemala Agreement, on 7 August 1987. The Rio Group announced its approval of the agreement in mid-August.

Impact of Esquipulas

The signing of the Esquipulas II Agreement provided the Salvadorian government with a new instrument for negotiating an end to the civil war and Duarte promptly called for a meeting with the FRD–FMLN to be held

---

3. Terry Lynn Karl, "After La Palma: The Prospects for Democratization in El Salvador," in Marvin Gettelman, *et al.*, eds., *El Salvador: Central America in the New Cold War* (New York: Grove Press, 1986), p. 395; Terry Lynn Karl, "El Salvador: Negotiated Revolution," *Foreign Affairs* 71 (Spring 1992), p. 150.

on 15 September. The Esquipulas II Agreement, in fact, paralleled to a large extent the position of the Salvadorian government because it called for a ceasefire, amnesty, demobilisation of the insurgents and national elections with the current government remaining in power. On the other hand, the agreement called for international verification of the peace process, a position that was certain to be opposed by the far right and by large segments of the officer corps as a breach of national sovereignty. The FDR–FMLN reacted to the Esquipulas II Agreement by announcing that it did not consider itself bound to the agreement and argued that the agreement was tailored to the specific circumstances of the Nicaraguan conflict and thus was inapplicable to El Salvador. Duarte's attachment to the Esquipulas II Agreement cooled considerably during late 1987–early 1988 due in large part to the actions of the original International Commission for Verification and Follow-up (CIVS). The CIVS was a carry-over from the Contadora Peace Plan and was composed of the foreign ministers of the five Central American countries, the Contadora countries, the Contadora Support Group and representatives of the Secretaries-General of the OAS and the UN. Its mission had been left purposely vague by the Esquipulas II Agreement in order to avoid the kind of wrangling over details that had derailed the Contadora process. This vagueness allowed the CIVS the opportunity to monitor various aspects of the Central American governments' performance, while responding directly to the Central American presidents.

The CIVS presented its first report during the summit of Central American presidents held in Alajuela, Costa Rica on 15–16 January 1988. It caused a bitter reaction among the presidents of Guatemala, El Salvador and Honduras who complained that the report was inordinately harsh on their governments while holding Nicaragua to a lower standard. For the Central American presidents, with the exception of Nicaragua's Daniel Ortega, the CIVS report was a reflection of the commission's control by non-Central American nations (a complaint already voiced over the original Contadora process[4]), and they transferred the duties of the CIVS to the Executive Commission composed of their foreign ministers. Ortega also announced certain concessions at this summit meeting, declaring a political amnesty and the willingness to meet face-to-face with the Contras.

Sapoá Accord

Despite continued tensions between the U.S. and Nicaragua, negotiations began in the town of Sapoá, Nicaragua, between the government and the

---

4. Susan Kaufman Purcell, "Demystifying Contadora," in Bagley, ed., *Contadora and the Diplomacy of Peace in Central America*, p. 171.

Contras. Both sides agreed to allow two "official observers" during the negotiations: Cardinal Miguel Obando y Bravo, Head of the Roman Catholic Church in Nicaragua and OAS Secretary-General Baena Soares. After protracted on-and-off discussions, agreement was reached and the Sapoá Accord was signed on 23 March 1988, providing for a 60-day ceasefire to be monitored by the two observers.

On 7 April the Executive Commission met in Guatemala and announced the establishment of a Technical Advisory Group (TAG) which inherited the verification duties of the CIVS and ultimately was composed of representatives from Canada, West Germany, Spain, Venezuela and the Secretaries-General of the OAS and the UN.[5] TAG was to report to the Executive Commission.

While the FMLN continued to demand a "power sharing" formula as part of any peace agreement, the celebration of fair elections in 1984 and 1985 coupled with the signing of the Esquipulas II Agreement began to entice members of the FDR towards a return to the political arena. In 1987–88, several leaders of the FDR returned to El Salvador after years of exile and founded a new coalition of leftist politicians named Democratic Convergence (CD). The CD did not take part in the legislative elections of March 1988 in response to FMLN pressure to remain uninvolved in a system which the insurgent group officially considered to be a farce. The 1988 elections reversed the Christian Democratic majority forged in the National Assembly and gave ARENA half the seats in the assembly.

The 1989 presidential election took a startling turn on 23 January when the FMLN announced its willingness to recognise the electoral process and participate in the election if it was rescheduled from March to September.[6] While this proposal was initially received with enthusiasm, ultimately nothing came of it. First of all, the FMLN did not commit itself to a permanent ceasefire. Instead, it announced its willingness to suspend operations for a period of a few days surrounding the elections. This was perceived by many government officials as an unacceptable no-lose situation for the FMLN which would be given a chance to win the presidency legally while also retaining the capability to continue the armed struggle in case their political bid failed. The election was held as scheduled and was won by Alfredo Cristiani, ARENA's candidate, who obtained 54 percent of the vote as opposed to 36 percent obtained by the PDC.

In his inaugural address on 1 June 1989, Cristiani announced that he would revitalise the peace negotiations with the FMLN. Holding true to his

---

5. Jack Child, *The Central American Peace Process, 1983–1991: Sheathing Swords, Building Confidence* (Boulder: Lynne Rienner, 1992), pp. 55–56.

6. José Z. García, "Tragedy in El Salvador," *Current History* 89 (January 1990), p. 9.

inaugural pledge, Cristiani assembled a team of negotiators that had the duty of organising a meeting with the FMLN as soon as possible. Despite continued violence by both sides, talks began on 7 September in Mexico City on an FMLN proposal that would have established a ceasefire on 15 November with a full end to hostilities by January 1990. Surprisingly, both sides seemed to agree on the necessity for international observers to monitor any ceasefire and the human rights situation. The talks, however, produced no significant compromise except for an agreement to meet in San José in October; both sides invited representatives of the OAS and the UN to partici- pate as observers in the talks. These talks proved equally fruitless except for an agreement to continue talks in Caracas.

On 11 November 1989 the FMLN launched a massive urban offensive against San Salvador that caught the armed forces completely off guard. The guerilla offensive was a carefully planned operation designed to silence the Cristiani government's reports that the FMLN was finished, thus improving the insurgency's position at the negotiating table. Besides the bombing of San Salvador's neighbourhoods by the air force, the most dramatic event of the offensive was the murder of six Jesuit priests and their two servants on the campus of the José Simeón Cañas University of Central America in San Salvador by individuals wearing armed forces uniforms.

The UN in Nicaragua: ONUVEN and ONUCA

Although the implementation of the Esquipulas II Agreement had suffered a setback with the controversy over the CIVS, the Central American foreign ministers managed to revive the process at the inaugura- tion of Carlos Salinas de Gortari as President of Mexico in December 1988. There, the five Central American nations drafted an agreement calling for a contingent of UN peacekeeping forces in the region and the refurbishing of the verification mechanism. The five Central American presidents met again in Costa del Sol, El Salvador, from 12 to 14 February 1989. At this meeting the five presidents agreed to call for the establishment of a UN observer group to verify the repatriation of the Nicaraguan Contras. Linked to the repatriation process, the Nicaraguan government agreed to hold elections in February 1990 and also agreed to OAS and UN observers who would verify the integrity of the elections. The presidents agreed further on the establishment of small mobile UN observer teams to monitor the im- plementation of the process in each country, and of a larger force to monitor the Salvadorian–Honduran border for any possible transfer of weapons from the Sandinista government to the FMLN.

In March, the Nicaraguan Foreign Minister sent a letter to the UN

Secretary General requesting the creation of an international observer group. This action led to the establishment of the UN Observer Group for the Verification of Elections in Nicaragua (ONUVEN). This was an unprecedented role for the UN because it was its first peace operation in Latin America.

The five Central American presidents met once again in Tela, Honduras on 5–7 August 1989. This was the first summit meeting attended by Cristiani as President of El Salvador. In this crucial summit meeting, the five presidents agreed on the demobilisation and repatriation of the Contras by late 1989, coupled with the holding of elections in Nicaragua in February 1990 as previously agreed in Costa del Sol. In order to verify the peace process in Nicaragua the presidents called on both the OAS and the UN to establish an International Commission for Support and Verification (CIAV). The CIAV was to be in charge of overseeing the Contra repatriation and resettlement processes. (The UN half of the CIAV disappeared in January 1991 and CIAV became an OAS operation).

The five presidents also called upon the UN to establish a UN Observer Group in Central America (ONUCA). ONUCA was to be in charge of monitoring both the Nicaraguan–Honduran and the Salvadorian–Honduran borders. ONUCA was formally established by the Security Council on 7 November 1989 after the unanimous approval of Resolution 644. The original contingent was set at 260 military observers along with 200 aircraft and naval support personnel and a UN staff of around 104.[7] The mission was headed by Spanish General Agustín Quesada Gómez.

One of the thorniest issues discussed at Tela was the possibility of linking the demobilisation-repatriation of the Contras with a similar process taking place with the FMLN. While this linkage was pushed by Cristiani, reflecting a position previously expressed by both the U.S. and the Duarte governments, it was opposed by Ortega. At the end, the five presidents agreed to issue a statement separate from the proposals on Nicaragua in which they called for meaningful negotiations between the FMLN and the government leading to a ceasefire and the voluntary disarmament and reintegration of the FMLN back into society. The call for voluntary disarmament represented another difference from the Nicaraguan situation where Honduras was pushing for forced demobilisation of the Contras if they refused to lay down their weapons voluntarily.[8]

A surprising development was that the Soviet Union became a party to the peace process. It was involved multilaterally via the UN Security Council and bilaterally via the arms reduction and disarmament negotiations

---

7. *UN Observer Group in Central America: Report to the Secretary-General,* UN Document S/21194 (16 March 1990), p. 3.

8. Child, *Central American Peace Process,* pp. 63, 71.

with the U.S. During the Cold War it was always U.S. policy to rely on the OAS to resolve inter-American disputes and to keep the UN—and thus the Soviet Union—from becoming involved in the hemisphere. However, a new era of U.S.–Soviet relations resulted from the *glasnost* policy of Mikhail Gorbachev and the ending of the Cold War. Soviet curtailment of arms shipments to Nicaragua and pressure on Cuba and Nicaragua to reduce their aid to the FMLN was significant in the success of the peace process. Moreover, the Soviet Union voted in favour of the Security Council resolutions creating and expanding the mandate of ONUCA.

Throughout late 1989 and early 1990, ONUVEN documented a series of threats and harassment by Sandinista elements against the National Opposition Union, the main opposition force in the electoral process. Nonetheless, Violeta Chamorro, the Union's candidate, won the presidential elections held in February 1990 with almost 55 percent of the vote. The elections, monitored by 200 ONUVEN observers as well as a contingent from the OAS, were declared fair. Shortly thereafter, President-elect Chamorro called for the immediate demobilisation of the Contras and outgoing President Ortega announced a ceasefire.[9] Chamorro was inaugurated on 25 April. On 27 March 1990 the Security Council approved the expansion of ONUCA's role to include the demobilisation of irregular forces. A battalion of Venezuelan paratroopers was charged with the mission of verifying the disarmament of the Contras. By October 1990 ONUCA included 254 military observers from Brazil, Canada, Colombia, Ecuador, India, Ireland, Spain, Sweden and Venezuela, plus a naval squadron from Argentina and an air unit from Canada.[10]

The UN in El Salvador: ONUSAL

In December 1989, FMLN leaders met secretly in Montreal with Alvaro de Soto, Assistant Secretary-General of the UN who on 1 September had been appointed Personal Representative for the Central American Peace Process by UN Secretary-General Javier Pérez de Cuéllar from Peru. The FMLN informed de Soto of its willingness to return to the negotiating table and that as a gesture of goodwill it would suspend acts of sabotage against public transportation and private businesses. After being approached by the UN, Cristiani announced his willingness to resume negotiations, but he also stated that there would not be any changes in the 1983 constitution,

---

9. The best source with statistics about demobilisation in both Honduras and Nicaragua (along with the weapons turned in) is *United States Observer Group in Central America: Report to the Secretary-General*, UN Document S/21909 (26 October 1990). See appendices.

10. *Ibid.*, p. 9.

especially in Article 248. This article, drafted as a safeguard against the enactment of any law contrary to the interests of the right wing, stipulated that any amendment to the constitution had to be approved by two consecutive National Assemblies.[11] On 12 January 1990 Pérez de Cuéllar officially announced that he had accepted a role as intermediary in the peace negotiations.

On 4 April 1990 the government and the FMLN met in Geneva under the auspices of the UN in talks attended by the Secretary-General. There, the government and the FMLN signed an agreement setting a general agenda for the conduct of negotiations, which included a pledge to embark on a continuous negotiation process. The uninterrupted character of the talks was a key point in de Soto's strategy to forge a peace agreement. By keeping the two sides involved in direct negotiations, he hoped to build an atmosphere of trust while maintaining the momentum of the discussions. Finally, it was agreed that negotiations would continue the following month in Caracas.

The two sides met at Caracas on 16 May 1990 as agreed and approved a more detailed agenda and a schedule of dates for the settlement of the conflict. This agenda divided the negotiating process into two parts. First, negotiations would be held on the issues of political and institutional reforms. Once these were settled both sides would negotiate the terms of a ceasefire and conditions for the demobilisation of the insurgents. This represented a departure from the longstanding government position that a ceasefire was to precede any concrete talks on political or legal reforms.

Following de Soto's strategy of keeping the two sides negotiating, it was agreed that the next round of talks would take place the following month in Mexico City. Once the agenda was settled and the representatives turned to the issues of actual reforms, the negotiations stalled and ended in deadlock due to the government's refusal to consider reforming the structure of the armed forces; but both sides agreed to continue talks the following month in San José.

After realising that the issue of military reform loomed as a huge stumbling block with the potential to derail the process, de Soto attempted to sidestep it by steering the negotiations toward other issues. His success in this endeavour was no small feat, for the FMLN had insisted that no other issues were to be discussed until the reform of the armed forces was settled. Focusing on the issue of human rights, the negotiating parties agreed upon a formal document listing specific basic human rights to be respected by both sides. This formal document, which became known as the San José Agreement on Human Rights, called for the establishment of a UN observer mission with the duty of monitoring human rights violations in El Salvador.

---

11. Karl, "After La Palma," p. 157.

The San José Agreement proved to be extremely important because it established the framework and the mandate for the creation of ONUSAL.

With the signing of the San José Agreement, both negotiating parties and the UN intermediary abandoned any illusions of achieving an end to the conflict in a single negotiating session. Instead they adopted a "piecemeal" approach that consisted of reaching agreements on specific issues and then consolidating them into a final peace accord. Even this approach, however, did not prove immune to deadlock as the next series of talks proved. The negotiating sessions in August and September (also held in San José) proved to be completely fruitless. In fact, they threatened to paralyse the process as the FMLN hardened its position and demanded the complete elimination of the Salvadorian armed forces.

An important milestone was reached at the Mexico City meeting held in October 1990. There the negotiating parties agreed to upgrade de Soto's role from intermediary to mediator. This allowed the UN to formulate proposals, thereby assuming a more active role in the talks. This agreement proved crucial in speeding up the peace process once a softening of the two sides' positions took place in late September 1991.

On 10 March 1991 elections for the National Assembly were held throughout the country. While the FMLN did not hamper the voting, the armed forces and ARENA partisans were accused of intimidation and fixing electoral lists. International indignation about the electoral process translated into pressure on the Cristiani government to ease its position on the issue of constitutional reform. Since the government remained adamantly opposed to eliminating Article 248, this meant that any other constitutional amendment would have to be voted on before 30 April (when the lame-duck National Assembly concluded its term). Otherwise no amendment could be implemented until after the next legislative elections to be held in 1994. Since the FMLN was not willing to demobilise first and hope that a sympathetic legislature would approve the constitutional changes three years later, a failure to pass a package of amendments before 30 April would effectively put an end to the negotiations.

Under sharp international scrutiny and after three weeks of intense discussions, the negotiating parties reached a consensus on the constitutional articles to be amended. This consensus became known as the Mexico Agreement. Signed on 27 April 1991, the agreement divided the constitutional reforms into three categories: armed forces, judicial system and electoral system.[12] First of all, the constitution was to be amended to spell out in clearer terms the subordination of the armed forces to the civilian

---

12. ONUSAL, *Fact Sheet 4.* This UN report provides a copy of the agreement itself as well as a list with the specific alterations to the constitution.

government institutions. Amendments were also to be enacted in order to separate the three police forces from the military chain of command and to consolidate them into a single National Civil Police. The intelligence services too were to be separated from the military command and set up under the direct control of the president.

On the issue of judicial reform, the agreement called for the establishment of a National Counsel for the Defence of Human Rights and changed the voting procedure for the election of the Attorney-General and the Chief State Counsel. On the issue of electoral reform, an amendment provided for replacing the Central Electoral Board with a new Supreme Electoral Tribunal as the overseer of the electoral process. Moreover, legal political parties were authorised to monitor the process of compiling the voting lists.

The Mexico Agreement also called for the establishment of a Truth Commission. To be composed of three individuals appointed by the UN Secretary-General, the commission was given the mandate to investigate the most flagrant acts of brutality committed by both sides in the conflict since 1980. Acting on the basis of the Mexico Agreement, on 29 April the National Assembly voted to amend 24 articles of the constitution.

The peace process was strengthened even further on 20 May 1991 when the Security Council approved Resolution 693 which established the UN Observer Mission in El Salvador. ONUSAL represented a departure from the standard UN observer operation because it was created before the opposing sides had agreed upon and implemented a ceasefire. Its mission was twofold. First, it would be in charge of verifying that both the government and the FMLN were complying with the San José Agreement. Once a ceasefire was implemented, ONUSAL would also carry out peacekeeping duties.

ONUSAL was given an initial mandate period of one year at an estimated cost of $32m. The initial group was to be composed of 113 members, including 43 police and military officers, but the UN planners envisioned an eventual expansion to 90 civilians and 66 police officers.[13] The number of military personnel would remain at the same level—15. While ONUSAL was not formally created until May, in March the Secretary-General sent an advance group to El Salvador with the duty of exploring conditions in the country. ONUSAL formally began operations on 26 July.

With an agreement reached on almost all other issues, the negotiating parties were forced to deal again with the issue of reductions in the size of the armed forces and the purge of officers involved in human rights violations. This led to another deadlock in the negotiations, one which lasted until the September meeting held in New York. Realising that both sides

---

13. Child, *Central American Peace Process*, p. 135; *UN Chronicle* 28 (September 1991), p. 23.

were simply holding to their positions without presenting any new ideas to end the impasse, the Secretary-General summoned both President Cristiani and the five *commandantes* of the FMLN to attend the September negotiations as heads of their respective delegations. There, Pérez de Cuéllar and de Soto took full advantage of their official roles as mediators to propose a plan designed by the UN to settle finally all outstanding issues.

The plan called for the establishment of an Ad Hoc Commission that would evaluate the record of the Salvadorian officer corps and would have the authority to recommend the discharge of those individuals found to have violated human rights. The commission would be composed of three Salvadorians of recognised integrity and two representatives of the armed forces. The latter would serve as observers only. The plan also called for the admission of FMLN members into the new integrated police force. This process was to occur in exchange for the FMLN dropping its demands for either joining the armed forces or eliminating the whole military establishment.

The plan also established the National Commission for the Consolidation of the Peace (COPAZ) to be made up of ten members: two appointed by the government, two by the FMLN and the remaining ones by those parties with members in the National Assembly.[14] The Roman Catholic church and ONUSAL would serve in COPAZ as observers. COPAZ was given the duty of supervising both the implementation of the agreements between the negotiating parties and the implementation of an eventual ceasefire. Finally, the plan called for a reduction in the size of the armed forces. This plan, known as the New York Agreement, was signed by both sides on 25 September 1991.

After the signing, only one issue remained to be settled, namely the size of reductions in the armed forces. Recognising that this was the last obstacle to a peaceful resolution of the brutal civil war, all political groups exerted pressure on the military to accept substantial reductions in its personnel. In a surprising development, a dying D'Aubuisson and the most Leninist FMLN leaders found themselves on the same side in supporting the peace process and trying to keep under control the forces they had created with their demagoguery. The Bush administration also exerted pressure on the Salvadorian armed forces, threatening to cut off all military aid. Finally, the military relented and agreed to a 50 percent personnel reduction.[15]

Once this issue was settled, the talks moved with astounding swiftness toward the procedures for a ceasefire and FMLN reintegration into society. On 14 November, the FMLN declared a unilateral truce as a gesture of goodwill. Cristiani reacted by stating that the government would take re-

---

14. *UN Chronicle* 28 (December 1991), p. 31.
15. *El Nuevo Día* (San Juan, Puerto Rico), 2 July 1993.

ciprocal measures. On 16 December, the FMLN and the government began what would be their last round of negotiations in New York. It was agreed that a ceasefire would begin on 1 February 1992, with the demobilisation of the FMLN to be completed by October of the same year. Also in December, the Secretary-General appointed Belisario Betancur (former President of Colombia), Reinaldo Figueredo (former Venezuelan Foreign Minister) and Thomas Buergenthal (a U.S. citizen and judge on the Inter-American Court of Human Rights) as the three members of the Commission on the Truth.

Although a few minor procedural points remained to be settled, both sides agreed to sign the document, officially known as the Act of New York, on 31 December in recognition of the vital role played by Pérez de Cuéllar, whose term expired with the New Year. It was agreed that if the outstanding points were not settled by 10 January, the UN would have the authority to make the final decision on them.

Implementation of the Agreements

The final peace treaty was formally signed on 16 January 1992 in Mexico City. The same day the Security Council voted to terminate the mandate of ONUCA as of the next day. Thus ONUSAL became the sole UN peacekeeping force in charge of overseeing the implementation of the peace process. On 14 January, the Security Council approved Resolution 729 which expanded ONUSAL's mandate as well as its personnel and budget in order to cope with the peacekeeping duties it would assume after 1 February. After the expansion, ONUSAL would consist of a military division in charge of monitoring the ceasefire and a police division in charge of monitoring the maintenance of public order during the crucial interim period in which the Salvadorian police force would make a transition from military to civilian control. (These two divisions were to join the already-established human rights division). The military division would be composed of troops from Brazil, Canada, Colombia, Ecuador, India, Ireland, Norway, Spain, Sweden and Venezuela.[16] This force was placed under the command of Brig. Gen. Víctor Suanzes Pardo of Spain. The police division was to be staffed by 630 officers under the command of Homero Vaz Bresque of Uruguay.

The biggest obstacles to the implementation of the peace agreement were posed by the government's handling of the mandated cuts in the police and the armed forces, its reaction to the report presented by the commission in charge of purifying the officer corps and the FMLN's response to these actions. The peace agreements clearly stated that among the three police

---

16. *UN Chronicle* 29 (June 1992), p. 31.

forces, two of them (the Treasury Police and the National Guard) were to be completely eliminated. Their former members then would be assigned to regular armed forces units where they would be subjected to the troop reductions.

The government also was supposed to start the formation of the new National Civil Police whose members were to be drawn from the general population (60 percent), the FMLN (20 percent) and the National Police (20 percent).[17] While elements from the National Police were recruited into the new force, the government delayed recruiting FMLN members and civilians. The government also violated the agreements in terms of the personnel reductions in the armed forces. The armed forces presented statistics listing their total strength at about 63 000. Both the FMLN and ONUSAL disputed these statistics, arguing that the armed forces actually had a total strength of 40 000 men.

In retaliation for the government's violations of the agreement, the FMLN suspended its demobilisation process which was supposed to occur in five stages: 20 percent of the total insurgent forces were to turn in their weapons at each stage. The first demobilisation stage, which was supposed to take place in April, was suspended due to the government's failure to abolish the Treasury Police and the National Guard. The FMLN finally demobilised the first 20 percent of its forces on 30 June, a week after the government agreed to abolish both police forces. On that occasion ONUSAL warned that violations of the agreement by one side were not to be used by the other as an excuse to engage in its own violations. The warning went unheeded, however, for the FMLN retaliated against each government violation by suspending its demobilisation process.

The FMLN's refusal to demobilise its first contingent in April meant that the agreement's timetable had to be reworked. The new agreement reached after UN mediation stipulated that the FMLN was to demobilise another 20 percent of its forces on the last day of each month, with the last 20 percent being demobilised on 31 October. The FMLN, however, refused to demobilise on 31 July as scheduled, arguing that the government had not kept its promise of providing economic aid and social programs to the demobilised insurgents. The new deadlock in the implementation process was broken after a new schedule for both sides was arranged by a UN mediation team. The new schedule called for the FMLN demobilisation to take place in four stages between 21 September and 31 October. The government, on the other hand, pledged to initiate training for the members

17. Linda Garrett, "Toward Demilitarization: The Salvadoran Armed Forces in Transition," paper presented at the 17th International Congress of the Latin American Students Association, Los Angeles, 24–27 September 1992, p. 6.

of the new civilian police, implement the socioeconomic programmes to aid the ex-FMLN combatants in their transition to civilian life and create a special temporary police corps (composed of elements of ONUSAL, the National Police and cadets of the National Civil Police) to patrol the areas formerly controlled by the FMLN. These reforms were to take place on 1 September. Meanwhile, the FMLN applied for recognition as a legal political party before the new Supreme Electoral Tribunal on 5 September .

While the FMLN carried out the second 20 percent demobilisation on 21 September, it suspended the process shortly after, again pointing out that the government was dragging its feet on its scheduled reforms. As the 31 October deadline approached and the FMLN remained steadfast in its refusal to demobilise until the government fulfilled its part of the agreement, there was a fear that the ceasefire would fall apart and the conflict be resumed. On 23 October, the UN proposed shifting the demobilisation deadline to 15 December. The government, however, opposed any rescheduling. On 26 October, the FMLN accepted the new UN-proposed timetable for the demobilisation of the remaining 60 percent of its forces. Two days later, and after again being subjected to intense pressure by UN officials, Cristiani accepted the rescheduling for FMLN demobilisation, but announced the suspension of the armed forces' reduction schedule until after the FMLN finished its demobilisation. The third 20 percent group of insurgents was demobilised on 31 October.

While attention was being devoted to the issue of FMLN demobilisation, another possible crisis loomed on the horizon—the purging of military officers accused of atrocities, which was scheduled to take place on 22 November. The Ad Hoc Commission in charge of revising the record of the officer corps handed in its report on 24 September. While the report was supposed to remain secret, leaks soon revealed the names of most of the officers whose dismissal was recommended. Among these was the defence minister, René Emilio Ponce.

Cristiani accepted the commission's report and promised to implement its suggestions, an action that led the most far right elements of the party to complain bitterly that Cristiani was selling the country to the foreigners and communists. Indeed, the pressure on the Cristiani government by high-ranking officers and far right civilians was so intense that the president was forced to ask the UN for a postponement of the purges until August 1993, when most of the officers listed were slated to retire.

This request was rejected by both the FMLN and the UN, as was another timetable postponement until May 1993. Conscious, however, of the tremendous pressure that the armed forces were exerting on Cristiani and not wanting to push him into a situation where he would be forced to reject the purges altogether, the UN allowed a postponement until December. According to the new schedule, the high-ranking officers mentioned in the commission's report were to be dismissed on 31 December. In total, the commission's report recommended the dismissal of 76 officers and the transfer of 26.[18]

The FMLN carried out its last two demobilisation stages as scheduled on 30 November and 15 December. That same day, in a moving ceremony held in San Salvador, the civil war was officially declared over.

Purification of the Armed Forces

Although the civil war was officially ended and the FMLN had demobilised all of its forces, two issues still remained unresolved as the new year began: the implementation of the purges and the report by the Commission on the Truth. Although the Cristiani administration had agreed on a timetable that would have led to the dismissal of some of El Salvador's higher ranking officers on 31 December, the day came and went without any mention of the issue by the defence ministry.

On 4 January 1993, Cristiani tried to erase the image of impotence *vis-à-vis* the military establishment by presenting the UN with the final secret list of officers to be dismissed. It was revealed, however, that the list did not include the highest echelon of officers that the commission had slated for purging. Cristiani's show of strength was weakened even further on 12 January when it became publicly known that the list presented to the UN contained only 23 of the 76 officers whose purge had been advised.[19] It was also revealed that Ponce and seven other top echelon officers were not to retire at mid-year as popularly believed, but were to remain in their posts until the last day of the Cristiani administration. Of the remaining 45 officers, 38 were to be separated from their posts, but would continue on the armed forces payroll in order to be eligible for a full pension. The remaining seven would remain on active service, but were to be sent abroad.

Although facing both international and domestic criticism for his decision to spare Ponce and the other officers, Cristiani probably felt obliged to Ponce because the latter had kept the officer corps under tight control when the peace agreements were implemented. Ponce also had been careful not to criticise Cristiani while criticising the commission's suggestions, a difference most other officers to be purged did not make. Finally, facing continued pressure from the UN and the FMLN, Cristiani agreed to purge all officers whose dismissal had been recommended by the Ad Hoc Com-

---

18. *UN Chronicle* 30 (June 1993), p. 26.
19. *Washington Post*, 12 January 1993.

mission over a six-month period. In a concession to Cristiani, the UN agreed to consider administrative leave without pay as an acceptable measure to accomplish the purges.[20] The process ended on 1 July, with the retirement of Ponce and three other high-level officers.

The Commission on the Truth's report, released on 15 March, indeed mentioned Ponce as one of five officers who planned the assassination of the Jesuit priests on November 1989. Moreover, the report named the late D'Aubuisson as the mastermind behind Archbishop Romero's murder and revealed that a former defence minister had attempted to cover up the murder of four U.S. churchwomen in 1980. The report also held the five *commandantes* of the FMLN responsible for the murder of conservative ideologues, of at least eleven town mayors and of six unarmed U.S. servicemen. Furthermore, the commission recommended that all individuals revealed as human rights violators should be banned from public office for a period of ten years and forbidden from ever holding any military or security position. Moreover, the commission was highly critical of the judicial system and called for the dismissal of all Supreme Court members.[21]

On 20 March, the ARENA-dominated National Assembly hastily approved an amnesty covering all politically related atrocities from 1980 to 1990. The amnesty was approved by Cristiani and was officially implemented on 31 March.

In May 1993, the Security Council approved the expansion of ONUSAL's mandate to include overseeing voter registration and the fairness of the 1994 elections. The last months of the year saw an increase in the level of political violence as high-level members of both the FMLN and ARENA were brutally murdered. This situation led the UN to establish a Joint Group for the Investigation of Illegally Armed Groups, formed by two representatives from the government, the Counsel for the Defence of Human Rights and the head of ONUSAL's Human Rights Division.[22]

On 20 March 1994, 900 UN election observers monitored the Salvadorian elections which were deemed "acceptable."[23] While no widespread fraud was observed, the electoral process was rife with inefficiency. The UN drafted a list of improvements to be enacted for the second round (none of the presidential candidates obtained the required 50 percent of the vote) to be held on 24 April. Armando Calderón Sol of ARENA emerged

---

20. *UN Chronicle* 30 (June 1993), p. 27; *El Nuevo Dia*, 3 April 1993.

21. For a more detailed summary of the commission's recommendations see U.S. Congress, House of Representatives, Committee on Foreign Affairs, Subcommittee on Western Hemisphere Affairs, *The Peace Process in El Salvador*, 16 and 23 March 1993 (Washington D.C.: U.S. Government Printing Office, 1993), pp. 113–20.

22. *El Nuevo Dia*, 5 June 1994.

23. *UN Chronicle* 31 (June 1994), p. 18.

victorious in the second round with 68.2 percent of the vote, defeating Rubén Zamora of the FMLN–CD coalition.

Conclusion

This chapter has examined the development and nature of the Central American peace process, its success in bringing about the demobilisation of the Contras and a peaceful transfer of power in Nicaragua in 1990; the end of the civil war and the demobilisation of the FMLN in El Salvador; and agreements between the government and the URNG in Guatemala in 1994 on the way to a final settlement. It was the first UN involvement in the demobilisation of an irregular force (the Contras by ONUCA, the FMLN by ONUSAL). And it was a special joint OAS–UN collaboration in Nicaragua.

While the Arias plan resulted in the revival of the Contadora process and contributed to the 1988 Sapoá accord and to Esquipulas II, when applied to El Salvador the model became an exclusive UN operation. Similarly the UN became the sole actor in the Guatemalan process. The Contadora and the Arias peace plans began outside the OAS. In fact, the regional organisation did not get involved in a major way until Arias had unveiled his proposal.

The transition from a joint OAS–UN role to a solely UN operation was the result of a number of factors. First, the Central American presidents and Mexico opposed an OAS peacekeeping role because they believed it was beyond the capabilities of the OAS. Moreover, such an operation would be dominated by the U.S. Second, the U.S. lacked confidence in the ability of the OAS to play such a role effectively. Third, the use of armed soldiers for ensuring demobilisation and security required approval by the UN Security Council. Finally, the U.S. preferred a UN role for financial reasons: its share for peacekeeping would be 28 percent in the UN, whereas it would be more than 50 percent in the OAS.

A number of new actors and practices emerged as a result of the process: Contadora, the Rio Group, the Central American Summits, CIAV, CIVS, ONUVEN, ONUCA, ONUSAL and the cooperation between the two Secretaries-General. Another important change was that Soviet–U.S. co-operation became important in the peace process, for the former restrained its clients in aiding Nicaragua and the FMLN. This, in turn, provided the U.S. with enough confidence to allow the UN to operate in what it traditionally considered its sphere of influence. Moreover, both states approved the creation of ONUVEN, ONUCA and ONUSAL in the Security Council. U.S. flexibility allowed countries with a long peacekeeping tradition like Ireland, India, Sweden and especially Canada to become involved in the region. Moreover, it is important to emphasise that Pérez de Cuéllar's

Latin American ties and his personal interest in a satisfactory solution to the Central American crisis provided the peace process with added impetus. The UN officials involved in the process also proved flexible and pragmatic enough to keep the peace negotiations from stalling permanently, providing face-saving compromises to rabid enemies trapped by their own rhetoric.

Clearly, there are flaws in the peace process. The land reform and the job training programs in both Nicaragua and El Salvador have stalled. Political murders have continued, albeit at a much reduced level. In both countries, the armed forces, despite dramatic cuts in personnel, are not completely under the control of the civilian authorities. Finally, some insurgents have grown dissatisfied with the process and turned to banditry or returned to guerilla action. While the real protagonists of the peace process were the leaders of both the governments and the insurgencies, who agreed to compromise in their struggle, peace would not have been achieved without the atmosphere of trust, the technical expertise, the funds and, when necessary, the pressure of the United Nations and the cooperation of the United States and the Soviet Union.

PART THREE

Analytical Issues

9

UN Peacekeeping: A Participant's Point of View

Gerald Hensley

The Changing Nature of Peacekeeping

The new world suddenly unveiled by the collapse of the Cold War took the peacekeepers—contributors as well as the international organisations—by surprise. Peacekeeping as a concept was a daughter of the United Nations Charter. Over the forty or so years of the Cold War there were a significant number of peacekeeping operations, more than enough to make the blue berets and helmets of UN forces a familiar sight around the world. But almost all of these operations were to support agreed ceasefires or to assure stability during a change of regime. Often they operated under what amounted to an indefinite mandate to provide reassurance, and some deterrence against a resumption of hostilities. All were based firmly on consent. In all cases there was clear agreement among the contending parties on the desirability of a UN or other international presence. The duties to be carried out by this presence were clearly understood (though less often the duration). Security problems were usually local and isolated. The international force was therefore lightly armed: its main weapons were tact, mediation and publicity.

This order of things collapsed with its most memorable symbol, the Berlin Wall. The end of the superpower confrontation has increased the risk—and the actuality—of nationalist, religious and linguistic conflicts. Many of these are internal, within the boundaries of a recognised state. A UN report tells us that of the last 81 conflicts involving over a thousand deaths, 79 were internal. We have had to acknowledge a new international category, the failed state. But it takes time for the international community to evolve strategies and techniques for dealing with a new international issue. At present we are still groping for a workable approach to internal conflicts. The UN Charter dismissed the problem, ruling out intervention in the domestic affairs of member-states. This flat prohibition broke down over the issue of apartheid in South Africa and has been weakened further by concerns over failing states. Neighbouring states, threatened by instability, economic dislocation, huge refugee flows or environmental damage, may demand international action. But the international community is increasingly accepting the burden of being its brother's keeper. The main reason is the spread of global television, the "CNN factor." Pictures of death and human suffering have a hugely greater impact on public opinion than newspaper reports. Televised coverage of a disaster leads to public demands for action.

Peacekeeping follows the cameras. There are some important consequences. Remoteness no longer matters. The distance of a country, whether geographical or in terms of interests, is much less important than the impact of the pictures of what is happening there. Conversely, a disturbance which is not within reach of the cameras or does not catch their interest becomes diplomatically invisible. Coverage of the Rwandan disaster produced a demand for urgent international action; the fighting in Tajikistan or in Liberia is soundless. The television cameras and media are increasingly setting foreign policy agendas for Western states. Human nature being what it is, this opens up possibilities for manipulation of these agendas. One's cause can be advanced depending on success in getting an issue on to the world's television screens, or in keeping it off. And the very nature of public demand brings an immediacy and emotionalism to the problem. Careful thought about the limits of successful action and the best preparation for it may be swept away, as perhaps happened in Somalia, by the urgent cry that "something must be done."

It is the United Nations that is expected to answer this cry. In the post-Cold War world the wider role assumed by the UN, and its potential for an even wider one, is a commonplace of every editorial writer. A major transformation has occurred. It is no longer desirable, it seems, for even the most powerful country to use force without obtaining the prior approval of the United Nations. This is as much so in a clear case of aggression, such as the invasion of Kuwait, as it is in the tangled affairs of Bosnia. The United States felt it expedient to obtain advance approval for its intervention in Haiti, though it did not ten years earlier for Grenada.

The difficulty is that the performance of the UN—its organisational and practical arrangements—has not kept up with the potential. Most importantly, the international community has not yet evolved clear strategies to help decide when to intervene, how to intervene and when to get out. Peacekeeping operations tend to be seen as a spectrum, ranging from robust retaliation as in Somalia to supporting negotiations as in Bougainville. In fact they fall into two quite separate categories: *peacekeeping* which requires the consent of the parties involved, and *enforcement* which means the use of force to impose a settlement. Choosing which path to follow means weighing up the costs, accepting the limits of what is possible, and as a consequence drawing up a clear mandate. Inexperience and the clamour for quick action can lead to less than adequate thought being given to these issues. Worse, it can lead to a confusion of aims between the traditional peacekeeping, which requires consent, and enforcement, which means conflict.

Contributors to peacekeeping operations—traditionally these have numbered scarcely twenty—have some practical issues to think about also. Countries like New Zealand have been anxious to see better and less bureaucratic organisation at UN headquarters. The dramatic increase in the workload has caught the support structure by surprise. Security Council resolutions do not by themselves create a peacekeeping force. A great deal of work is entailed in assembling the force, deciding the command and control arrangements and the rules of engagement, transporting, supplying and rotating it. With the help of secondments from many of the contributors, the New York organisation is gradually catching up.

At home the contributors have to think about the effects on their own force structures. Less than five percent of New Zealand's defence force is currently deployed on peacekeeping duties, but this has a disproportionate effect on the training and capabilities of the rest. Over the longer term there will be questions about whether to modify training and equipment to better reflect the demands of peacekeeping. If the present level of demand is maintained there will undoubtedly be some cumulative impact on force structures. But for all contributors, the key issue will be good judgments about the limits of peacekeeping and mandates that are "doable." Countries contribute to peacekeeping as good international citizens. Still to be tested, though, is the reaction of those who see their sons and daughters lost "along the burning fuse of someone else's war." The shadow of the UN operation in the Congo (1960–64) still hangs over us and the future growth of peacekeeping is not assured. One ill-judged operation ending in disaster could overturn the encouraging progress of the past six years.

The Tempo of Peacekeeping

The figures speak for themselves. The UN has launched more peacekeeping operations in the past five years than in the previous forty. There were thirteen from 1946–87 and fifteen from 1988–93. The tasks too have greatly expanded. Traditional operations were usually organised to interpose forces between combatants who had agreed to negotiate, or to monitor a ceasefire. In addition to this, UN forces may now be tasked with preventive deployment, demobilisation of troops, humanitarian relief and the control of population movements. The environment in which these tasks are carried out may be uncertain and volatile. To a much greater degree than in past operations, contributing states must now consider the degree of risk and the likelihood of any proposed operation achieving its goals.

Two quite distinct types of operation now have to be considered. The long-familiar peacekeeping operation assumed, indeed depended on, the prior consent of all the parties to the conflict. Because the UN was there with *consent*, it was required to act with *impartiality*. Force might be used, but only to deal with local and isolated acts of lawlessness. Peace enforcement, a slightly Orwellian term, means ensuring compliance with the UN's demands through the use of the requisite degree of force. Impartiality is not possible in these circumstances, for the UN is in effect party to an armed conflict.

There cannot therefore be any smooth progression between peacekeeping assignments under chapter VI of the Charter and enforcement under chapter VII. Without impartiality, the UN cannot mediate or carry out the traditional supervisory duties. It has joined the conflict. And, once relinquished, impartiality cannot easily be regained. Peacekeeping operations thus cannot move back and forth between chapters VI and VII. A choice has to be made, and moving to chapter VII enforcement operations carries significantly greater risks and costs.[1] Careful consideration may show them to be necessary, but it is important that the euphemisms do not blur the distinction. "Peace enforcement" is synonymous with armed conflict and war.

Along with these tasks the international community has widened its ambitions for peacekeeping. The definition of success for peacekeeping used to be "conflict containment, completion of the military task and withdrawal"—even if the last of these sometimes had to be postponed indefinitely. But wider duties have brought larger hopes, for peace and reconstruction rather than ceasefires.[2] The risks of failure, or of limited success, are greater.

In Somalia the aims of UN intervention broadened as time went on. There was a confusion between peacekeeping and enforcement, between operations under chapter VI of the Charter and the more demanding

---

1. The concept of "wider peacekeeping" has been promulgated as British peacekeeping doctrine in the Army Field Manual *Wider Peacekeeping*. See also Charles Dobbie, "A Concept for Post-Cold War Peacekeeping," *Survival* 36 (Autumn 1994), pp. 121–48.

2. This approach was emphasised by Gareth Evans in *Cooperating for Peace: The Global Agenda for the 1990s and Beyond* (Sydney: Allen & Unwin, 1993).

requirements of chapter VII. The tragedy of famine—the original reason for international intervention—was ended but it has not been possible to achieve a political settlement. Indeed, the military intervention in Somalia may have made matters worse by upsetting old balances and methods of power-broking. In the world any more than at home, good intentions do not guarantee good results.

By contrast, the results of the UNTAC effort in Cambodia have led to cautious optimism about future stability. Building on the 1991 peace accords, the UN set about reconstructing a viable state in Cambodia. The UNTAC operation supervised the work of government and organised elections, supervised the partial disarming and demobilisation of rival forces, helped repatriate and rehabilitate refugees, kept an eye on human rights and organised the removal of a large number of mines. There is a long way to go, but the UN Secretary-General, Boutros Boutros-Ghali, has saluted UNTAC as "the flagship for this UN-led voyage to the future."[3]

Internal Conflict and Failed States

As Somalia shows, however, navigation can be a problem. The kind of aggression most familiar to the drafters of the UN Charter was that between sovereign states. In recent years conflicts within a state, where a state's authority is challenged on the grounds of nationalism, language or religion have become more frequent. Such conflicts can produce great suffering, refugee flows and large-scale violations of human rights. They also bring active lobbying by the parties for international recognition of their case.

There are no international rules for dealing with this. The UN Charter, reflecting orthodox international law at the time, specifically excluded intervention in a member-state's internal affairs. This was eroded by the arguments over decolonisation and by the long international campaign against apartheid. Any member-state attempting to invoke it now would be suspect. In 1992 the Secretary-General stated that the "principle of non-interference with the essential domestic jurisdiction of states cannot be regarded as a protective barrier behind which human rights could be massively violated."[4] A view is emerging, at least among the liberal demo-cracies, that states have the right to intervene in other states where there is a humanitarian need to do so.

This is understandable—the alternative is to tell a public aroused by scenes of human suffering that legal requirements prevent anything being

---

3. "Singapore: UN seeks to draw peacekeeping lesson from Cambodia," Reuters News Service, 2 August 1994.

4. Phillip McCarthy, "Australia : A mission to Somalia that could set a pattern," *Age* (Melbourne), Reuters Textline, 16 December 1992.

done. However, it gives no guidance as to how to go about such intervention in internal conflict. The lack of such guidelines is perhaps the largest single challenge which the UN has faced since the Charter was drafted. Is each situation to be treated as a special case and examined on its merits? What weighting is to be given to the practicability of intervening as against the horror of standing by? Experience will gradually evolve answers to the dilemmas of internal conflicts, but experience is a notoriously expensive teacher. For the present all we can do is to try to match the impulse to act with the clearest possible views of what is possible, recognising the fact that intervention is not in itself an easy answer.

The problem has emerged in its sharpest form in this decade with the concept of the "failed state." The failed state has been described as "incapable of sustaining itself as a member of the international community... states descend into violence and anarchy—imperilling their own citizens and threatening their neighbours through refugee flows, political instability, and random warfare."[5] These symptoms have led to international intervention in countries as diverse as Cambodia, Rwanda, Haiti, the former Yugoslavia, Somalia, Angola and Mozambique.

Internal conflict in such states affects civilians much more than those prosecuting the conflict, in the form of terror, deaths, displacement and destruction of food supplies. The proportion of war-related civilian deaths has increased from 73 percent in the 1970s to close to 90 percent in the 1990s.[6] Combatants have found it advantageous to rely more on "dirty war" tactics, seeking gains not through the battlefield but through terror. "Civilians, rather than soldiers, are the tactical targets, and fear, brutality and murder are the foundation on which control is constructed."[7] In the six years of internal conflict on the island of Bougainville, for example, there have been an estimated 300 combatant deaths and over 900 civilian deaths. The use of landmines has multiplied worldwide. There are something between 65m and 115m mines scattered through 62 countries, two million of them laid in the former Yugoslavia.[8] In Cambodia alone there are 30 000 amputees. This has led to a new branch of peacekeeping and New Zealand among others has provided personnel for mine clearance programmes in

5. Gerald B. Helman and Steven R. Ratner, "Saving Failed States," *Foreign Policy* No. 89 (Winter 1992–93), pp. 3–20.

6. *SIPRI Yearbook* (Stockholm Peace Research Institute, annual, various publishers).

7. C. Nordstrom, "The Backyard Front," in C. Nordstrom and J. Martin, eds., *The Paths to Domination, Resistance and Terror* (Berkeley: University of California Press, 1992), p. 261; cited in A. B. Fetherston, "Putting the Peace Back Into Peacekeeping," *International Peacekeeping* 1(Spring 1994), p. 6.

8. *Hidden Killers: The Global Problem with Uncleared Landmines* (Washington, DC: U.S. Department of State, 1983); *The Scourge of Land Mines* (New York: United Nations, 1993).

Afghanistan, Cambodia and most recently Mozambique.

Humanitarian Focus

Peacekeeping in failed states has first and foremost a humanitarian aim. But humanitarian operations conducted in the midst of a war zone raise complex issues of whom to protect and how to manage that protection. Judgments have to be made about whether force should be used to ensure the delivery of humanitarian assistance, or whether the presence of troops jeopardises the aid mission to the extent of endangering the lives of relief workers. Such tensions are unavoidable and, despite the contradiction inherent in armed humanitarian intervention, some successes have been achieved. Starvation has been averted in Bosnia and Somalia, and the scale of disaster lessened in Rwanda.

It is clear, though, that more work has to be put into better communication and cooperation between peacekeeping troops and relief workers. Friction may be endemic but the repeated complaints in the course of the UN Operation in Somalia suggest that poor civil–military relations may have affected that operation. Before Somalia, relief agencies had not usually sought military protection, relying on the International Committee of the Red Cross for safety. Certainly the presence of armed soldiers when relief is being distributed strikes a discordant note. The agencies' impartiality may come into question and they risk being used or seen as participants in the conflict. The members of some agencies see such a presence as in itself a threat to aid principles. Yet the reality is that the agencies are increasingly dependent, in the world of the "dirty war," on protection by peacekeeping troops. Whether in Somalia or in Rwanda, the orderly distribution of relief is not possible without a military safeguard.

The relief agencies have worked together many times before and a degree of understanding exists among them, just as many military forces are accustomed to working together in a multinational force. Now there needs to be a similar degree of interoperability between the civilians of the UN and the non-governmental agencies and the military elements of a peacekeeping operation. The UN Department of Humanitarian Affairs was set up in 1991 to coordinate all UN relief agencies. Together with the UN's peacekeeping arm it could perhaps draw up a general code of conduct and provide more specific guidelines as part of the orientation and training at the start of each peacekeeping mission.

Media Coverage

Awareness by the international community is the key to mobilising the political will to mount a peacekeeping operation. Through vivid and instantaneous coverage the conflict becomes part of our own personal world, and as a result we feel a degree of moral responsibility for what is happening. It is this simple fact rather than any vision of a new world order which has driven the recent expansion of peacekeeping. The public of a small and geographically isolated country like New Zealand calls for a contribution to the international effort in Somalia or Rwanda, not because of any national interest at stake but because of simple human outrage.

There are of course drawbacks. The camera has a narrow focus; it deals in sharp, simple images devoid of context. Thus its message can be manipulated. If one of the combatants can gain international airtime for a "documentary" setting out its point of view, pressure can build on a number of governments to adjust their foreign policies accordingly. In Australia and New Zealand public concern and human rights campaigns were sparked by television programmes on Cambodia and East Timor which had a clear purpose of advocacy.

The range of the television team is limited. Coverage of Bosnia and the other areas of current international concern serves as a prompt to our conscience. But shaped as they are by television, our consciences go unprompted by the internal conflicts suffered by Liberia, Sudan, the former Soviet republics of Central Asia, or the troubles in Myanmar or Sri Lanka. Perhaps, given the limitations on the UN's resources, hard choices have to be made. But it is as well to be aware that these choices are often made for us by the practicalities of television coverage, and that there are many other painful and destabilising conflicts that are invisible to the viewer.

The media are shaping national decision-making in other ways. Democratic governments are vulnerable in military operations to any significant level of casualties. A political consensus in New Zealand firmly supports taking part in peacekeeping. The great test for New Zealand and for others, though, has yet to be faced. Casualties have been accepted in the past where a vital national interest has been seen to be at stake. No one knows how parents and voters will react to the loss of their young people in someone else's war, in some obscure and far-distant land.

We know enough to be cautious. In October 1993 a U.S. Ranger company was caught in an ambush in Mogadishu and took heavy casualties. Some of the dead then suffered inhuman and televised indignities. The spectacle of a dead American soldier being dragged through the streets caused outrage in the United States and understandable concern that risks should be taken in Somalia in the face of such ingratitude.[9] Support for the operation

---

9. Edward Pilkington, "Somalia—Shots That Shook the World—Reuters Television," *Guardian*, Reuter Australasian Briefing, 11 October 1993.

shrank and the administration announced a withdrawal deadline. The scaling down of the UNOSOM operation, following the American casualties, was mirrored by the April 1994 withdrawal of most UN personnel from Rwanda following the killing of eleven Belgian soldiers. Images of dead peacekeepers sink into the public consciousness, making it harder to build support for future risky actions. The combatants know this too, and know that a well-aimed bomb may cripple a peacekeeping operation and free their hands.

Implications for the International Community

The UN was founded as a vision for the achievement of global security. It was equipped with a range of instruments to keep the peace and to suppress conflict. The vision was realistic: it foresaw the need for military forces, set out the framework for employing them and established a Military Staff Committee to advise the Security Council. Within a short time the concepts of truce supervision and peacekeeping had begun to evolve and, most notably in the Middle East and Korea, the image of the blue helmets began to be accepted. There were some notable successes but the UN overreached itself in the ambitious Congo operation. This, together with the constraints of the veto in the Security Council, meant that the potential envisaged in the Charter was never realised and some of the supporting machinery was left to rust.

With the rapid expansion of peacekeeping in the early 1990s, it became clear that the existing UN systems could not cope. There was a need for more professional methods of operation in the Security Council, long used to rhetoric rather than action, and for more detailed and more realistic mandates to be given to commanders in the field. More effective mechanisms for consultation among the UN Secretariat, the Security Council and prospective troop-contributors were required. Broader consultation also became desirable, such as summitry between political leaders, discussions with regional bodies and coordination of effort with humanitarian agencies. Better management of the UN's own efforts, in New York and in the field, was needed. And more funds and prompter payment was required from the UN's membership.

Like other regular contributors of troops, New Zealand has argued strongly for a more integrated administrative structure for peacekeeping. The Secretary-General amalgamated the two departments in the Secretariat previously concerned with peacekeeping into a single Department of Peacekeeping Operations (DPKO) and strengthened the planning staff. A body of professional military staff, funded from regular UN contributions, is highly desirable but for some time yet the Secretary-General will need specialist staff seconded from member-states. New Zealand, like Canada, Australia and others, provides such staff officers on a regular basis. It may be possible for the UN to contract for the supply of some specialist people, equipment and services.[10]

In the middle of 1992, the UN's New York headquarters still operated on a nine-to-five basis, with only a handful of military staff. A Canadian commander in Bosnia became famously frustrated at being unable to get guidance outside these hours. There is now a twenty-four hour Situation Centre with a military hierarchy of staff officers and a capability to plan. By March 1994, 26 officers were serving in the Centre, 19 on loan from their governments and seven on UN contract. The Situation Centre, which initially provided headquarters support for the UNPROFOR mission in the former Yugoslavia, now handles all UN peacekeeping operations.

There has been a marked improvement in efficiency with the establishment of the DPKO, bringing the Secretariat's responsibilities under one roof and ending the confusions and turf battles of earlier years. The DPKO comprises:

a. The Office of the Under Secretary-General for Peacekeeping, including the Executive Office, the Military Adviser's Office, the Policy and Analysis Unit, and the Situation Centre;

b. The Office of Operations, including the Africa, the Asia and Middle East, and the Europe and Latin America Divisions; and

c. The Office of Planning and Support, including the Planning Division (a Mission Planning Service, Civilian Police Unit, Demining Unit and a Training Unit) and the Field Administration and Logistics Division (the Finance Management and Support Service, the Logistics and Communication Service, and the Personnel Management and Support Service).

The mid-1994 staffing level of the department was 267, of whom 128 were professional officers and 139 general service staff. There were in addition 80 military officers assigned by their governments at no cost to the UN. Plans by the Under-Secretary-General, Kofi Annan, to further rationalise the structure by dividing the department's work into "Planning and Support" and "Operations" and increasing the staff levels to 459 have yet to find favour with the UN's budgeting committee.

The organisational challenge to the UN, however, is much more

---

10. *Improving the Capacity of the UN for Peacekeeping.* Report of the Secretary-General, Addendum, Replies Received from Member-States: New Zealand (Document A/48/403/Add.2, S/26450/Add.2), 1 December 1993.

fundamental than staffing levels. The crises of famine, internal conflicts and refugee flows arise faster than the present international machinery of consultation and voluntary contributions can deal with them. All too often the UN peacekeepers arrive after the massacres.

Considerable thought has been given to ways of speeding up the world's response. In 1992 the Secretary-General tabled his *Agenda for Peace* which among other ideas suggested the establishment of a UN standing army to be used as a rapid reaction force. This attracted little backing from member-states. Handing over command of national forces to an international committee, and accepting without any say deployments and possible casualties in far-distant places, did not appeal to any government. Smaller countries could not guarantee the availability of particular units and capabilities: New Zealand, for example, has contributed from a wide range of units over the past few years and has rarely been asked for the same capability twice. The cost was also seen to be prohibitive, particularly by developing countries which were concerned that peacekeeping could drain resources away from development. The Australian Foreign Minister has recently proposed by way of modification that the UN should recruit a small ready reaction force of its own,[11] but as long as the UN's funding remains so straitened this too will be out of reach.

The Secretary-General has therefore fallen back on the concept of standby forces—forces and units notified by member-states to the UN as being available for peacekeeping duties, subject to authorisation in each case. In January 1993 he appointed Colonel Gerard Gambiez of France to lead a UN Standby Force Planning Team, tasked with gathering as many pledges of support as possible from member-states.

These arrangements should lead to some improvement in response times once a peacekeeping operation is approved. An up-to-date database of available forces and specialties should shorten the consultation period. Each potential contributor, and the UN planners themselves, will be better placed to begin contingency planning for a possible deployment ahead of the formal decision to establish a new operation. By declaring units under the standby system, member-states are making no commitment but simply signalling the kinds of support they have available. Any actual contribution remains to be decided on a case-by-case basis, as the requirement arises.

In June 1994 the Secretary-General published a *Report on Stand-By Arrangements for Peacekeeping*. Along with a description of their purpose and a listing of the personnel and equipment which were most needed, he set out the commitments declared by 21 countries for possible peacekeeping deployments and noted that a further 27 states (including New Zealand)

---

11. Reuters News Service, 2 August 1994.

were expected to make offers. If all do so, the number available for a faster response would rise from 30 000 to 70 000.

This in itself will not guarantee a rapid reaction to a particular crisis. There are inherent limits on international action which may simply have to be accepted. Even within a national force there is a minimum time for warning out a unit and preparing it for movement. If to this are added the time required for international consultation, gathering the information on local conditions which will define the mandate, and national decision-making on whether or not to make a contribution—then it is prudent to assume that the despatch of a peacekeeping force will take weeks if not months. Cutting corners will not necessarily save time. The UNAMIR mission to Rwanda could not meet the milestones set for it: personnel despatched ahead of their equipment proved to be a liability and had to be withdrawn.

There are other ways to encourage troop-contributors. The Security Council has at present no formal mechanism for gathering the views of potential contributors when deliberating on current or proposed peacekeeping operations. Many of the contributors will not be members of the Council but their concerns will play an important part in shaping the outcome. Restricting information and consultation to Council members has therefore caused some resentment. During its membership of the Council in 1993–94, New Zealand pushed for an improvement in the triangular relationship between the Secretariat, Security Council and troop-contributors. During its April 1994 presidency, New Zealand broke with protocol to hold meetings with all troop-contributors to Rwanda and incorporated the results in its presidential statements. It would be useful if an informal convention could develop along these lines to ensure that potential troop-contributors were involved at the earliest practicable stage.

With a rising rate of casualties, the safety of personnel on peacekeeping duty has also become important for contributors. Fifty-one peacekeepers were killed in 1992, and 201 in 1993. Risks have to be accepted in the disorder which surrounds some missions but, whether for soldiers or civilians, losing lives in other peoples' quarrels must affect public support for peacekeeping operations. To fill a gap in international law, and to provide for some deterrence and perhaps punishment, New Zealand has tabled draft conventions for the safety of UN personnel and establishing criminal responsibility for individual attacks on them, and these are now working their way through the UN system.

Most important of all is placing the UN's peacekeeping finances on a more reliable basis. In 1994 member-states owed a total of US $1.5bn in UN dues and contributions to peacekeeping operations. Adequate financial underpinning is essential to a robust system of peacekeeping. Without it the

Secretariat cannot plan an efficient operation and must endure unnecessary delays. Without it, troop-contributors cannot be sure of repayment and in a time of generally declining defence budgets difficulties over the prompt reimbursement of costs may affect some countries' willingness to contribute. But above all, reluctance to pay constrains the possibilities for peacekeeping. More ambitious schemes to deal with conflict will be idle if member-states do not have enough confidence or interest in the present commitments to pay their dues in full and on time.

Implications for a Small Contributor

The rapid expansion of peacekeeping and the likelihood that its demands will not diminish in the foreseeable future raise a number of issues for the traditional contributors. New Zealand's defence policy rests on a triad consisting of national tasks, contributing to regional security and being a good international citizen in supporting the UN. It has taken part in 60 percent of all UN peacekeeping operations. It is a founding member of the UN and a commitment to collective security is part of its fundamental foreign policy framework. But most peacekeeping commitments over the past decades required it to supply only a few observers or small teams of specialists. Now an eightfold increase in deployments, and the expectation that this will continue, means that New Zealand like other contributors is having to think about some wider questions.

Balancing Demand and Supply

The number of preliminary soundings and tentative requests from the UN Secretariat now considerably exceed the ability of New Zealand's small, general-purpose forces (about 10 000 in uniform) to supply. It is not simply a problem of numbers. Those most often needed are the experienced, middle level officers—precisely those who are essential to enable the New Zealand Defence Force (NZDF) to fulfil its other tasks at home and to maintain its training schedules. The drain has been such that the Chief of the Defence Force has stated a preference where possible for sending formed units.

This has led to the development of a set of policy criteria to help sift through the requests and provide government decision-makers with a firmer basis for selection (Appendix 10.1). The criteria, adopted in 1993, cover national interests and also the acceptability and achievability of the proposed peacekeeping operation. They are not a rigid set of requirements but rather a comprehensive checklist of points of concern to be considered in the course of reaching a decision. Each decision will be based on an individual balance of considerations.

Effects on Force Structure

Peacekeeping will be the most likely reason for deployments by the NZDF and similar forces over the next few years. The question has therefore been raised whether such forces should be more closely tailored for their peacekeeping role.

There are two difficulties here. The first is that there is no single and well-defined peacekeeping role. Different units and different specialities have been required for each operation in recent years. The only common factor has been the need for self-protection for which general combat training is the only source. New Zealand has supplied engineers, signallers, demining teams, river patrols, air transport, logistic teams, helicopter pilots and medical teams within the past few years. It is not possible to specialise when the same capability is almost never asked for twice.

Secondly, to do so would divert effort from the NZDF's national defence tasks. Peacekeeping is essentially a foreign policy matter. It means playing a part in upholding international order rather than any direct contribution to national security. That is a separate need and in New Zealand's case the claims of regional stability and national protection must have at least equal attention. Fortunately, the maintenance of highly-professional, general-purpose combat forces covers both requirements. UN experience has confirmed the desirability of combat-trained troops for peacekeeping operations, even where there is little likelihood of combat. The confidence and discipline of such training is the best preparation for difficult and stressful situations.

Some specific training is still required. Some of this—familiarity with the local climate, customs and laws—can be provided in predeployment training. So can some knowledge of the most likely challenges of the mission. Techniques of communication, negotiation and dealing with local populations, knowledge of international law, the more complex rules of engagement needed in peacekeeping and an understanding of the intricacies of civil–military relations are likely to figure more largely in staff colleges.

Levels of Readiness

Over time a continued high level of peacekeeping duties will have some blurring effect on force structures. The procurement of new equipment will inevitably be influenced by its most frequent use, as will the size of some units. No army could consist simply of sappers, medics and logistics experts—the three specialties most frequently sought by the UN—but those armies most often called on for peacekeeping duties could well increase the size of such capabilities beyond their strict defence requirements.

There is already a trend towards increasing the levels of readiness of those forces which might be expected to deploy. Reserves are of little use except for protracted operations. Quick reaction is the essence of peacekeeping missions; it takes time to move even regular troops at a high state of readiness. Such readiness is expensive but the UN's need will figure more and more in defence planning for readiness levels. The strategic doctrine of New Zealand, which is in the fortunate geographical position of being able to assume that it will always have to deploy to meet a threat, already stresses the need for readiness. A country with small forces gets maximum advantage from being able to move them quickly.

Interoperability

Countries which wish to make any worthwhile contribution to collective security must maintain an adequate level of interoperability. This means having training, equipment, standards and doctrine that are compatible with one's likely partners. Without it, contributions to the more demanding peacekeeping missions will not be effective, and probably they will not be welcome. As New Zealand's Defence Minister said in 1993:

> The military skills required for UN peacekeeping operations around the world are not developed in isolation. They're the product of continuing military exercises with our main alliance partners.... It is those exercises that provide the common doctrines and operating procedures so vital to effective teamwork in UN operations. The European and Canadian forces deployed in the Balkans conflict, for example, are using doctrines and methods developed by NATO. Our people are able to contribute to peacekeeping operations in Sarajevo because they are competent in those same doctrines and techniques.[12]

This kind of interoperability enabled NZDF forces to serve alongside the Australians in Cambodia, to work with American aircrew in Rwanda and to attach an infantry company to a British battalion in Bosnia.

Training for Peacekeeping

The NZDF aims to provide most of the training necessary for a UN peacekeeping assignment as part of its general training programme. In the predeployment period a contingent is given briefings on UN procedures, specialist training and language instruction. Military observer candidates receive additional training in vehicle skills, weapons system recognition, medical training, mine awareness, stress management, physical fitness and the UN Guidelines for Standard Operating Procedures.[13]

---

12. Warren Cooper, "Kiwi troops overseas—giving peace a chance," *Evening Post* (Wellington), 3 March 1993, p. 7.
13. *Training for Peacekeeping.* UN General Assembly, 48th Session, A/48/708, Agenda

Returning personnel are debriefed within 30 days of the end of their posting. The debriefing procedure includes psychological and medical tests, and follow-up action taken to assist readjustment, especially if the assignment has been difficult. The first cycle of returnees offers the possibility of more focused training of replacement personnel and some are brought back early on rotation to provide this.

The Australian Defence Force (ADF) has taken a more structured approach. The ADF Peacekeeping Centre was established in January 1993 to develop and manage peacekeeping doctrine and training. It is intended to provide a memory bank for Australian peacekeeping experience and to monitor international peacekeeping issues and to help in the training for peacekeeping missions.[14] New Zealand's needs do not warrant a national training facility, but it makes use of the Australian Centre's resources and will contribute staff to help with the training.

A Closer Relationship with the United Nations

The most critical factors for any peacekeeping operation, though, are its organisation and its mandate. All regular troop-contributors have learnt to work as closely as possible with the UN Secretariat. In addition to its diplomatic establishment (increased for the 1993–94 term of Security Council membership), the NZDF has three officers serving in New York: a Defence Adviser at the New Zealand Permanent Mission, an officer in the Situation Centre, and a logistics specialist in the DPKO. Additional personnel from New Zealand have also been provided from time to time to assist with special tasks. The Defence Adviser, at colonel level, is able to discuss possible New Zealand contributions with the Secretariat at an early stage, and to forewarn defence and foreign policymakers at home of likely UN requests.

The Security Council itself has perhaps absorbed some lessons about the scope, and the limits, of UN action. Members have learnt to try for a more precise drafting of mandates and instructions to a peacekeeping force, knowing that better mandates will enlarge the number of contributors—and the chances of success. There will always be compromises and some vagueness to cover differing standpoints. A peacekeeping resolution in the heat of a crisis cannot be a detailed rulebook. But the earlier exasperation of some UN commanders has been muted as the military requirements of the

item 87, 14 December 1993.
14. *ADF Peacekeeping Centre Briefing Package* (Williamtown: ADF Peacekeeping Centre, 1993).

more complex peacekeeping operations are better understood and brought into the drafting process.

The unprecedented expansion of peacekeeping is now coming up against the limits of the practicable. In the enthusiasm which followed the end of the Cold War exciting visions danced before editorialists and some statesmen of a UN able at will to suppress conflict and violence wherever it broke out. The Security Council, freed of its chains, could fulfil the hope of its founders and become the world's policeman.

Such a vision is that of a world government, and we are a long way from that. The veto still exists in the Security Council and it would be unwise to assume that the five veto powers will always enjoy the degree of unanimity that they did over Kuwait. More than that, the realities of funding, of differing national interests and perceptions, the "friction" in the Clausewitzian sense involved in creating multinational forces and managing them in the confused and fluid situations which more often than not characterise peacekeeping—all these have put a framework of reality around our hopes. Progress along such a difficult road will be gradual and some-times stumbling. Not all the peacekeeping operations that seem desirable will be possible—or in the end successful. But the framework of reality today is much larger than it was even five years ago. That is a remarkable international achievement, and a point worth keeping in mind when the inevitable frustrations occur.

Appendix 9.1: Criteria for the Assessment of Proposed Contributions of New Zealand Personnel to Peacekeeping, Peacemaking and Peace-Enforcement Operations

National Considerations

Does the operation:
Enhance security in a region of strategic or economic interest to New Zealand?
Support humanitarian objectives; and enhance New Zealand's multilateral or bilateral relationships?
Offer a distinctive role for New Zealand?

Achievability

Does the political framework of the mandate suggest a reasonable chance of success; and does that mandate establish achievable objectives, while allowing an opportunity for any changes required by developing conditions?

Is the operation based on a sound plan and does the operational concept offer a reasonable chance of success?

Is there effective direction and control of military operations by appropriate authorities, including provision for suitable in-place civilian components?

Are there adequate provisions for humanitarian assistance; and is there sufficient international support and commitment to both mount and sustain the operation?

Acceptability

Would the proposed New Zealand contribution be nationally identifiable and fulfil a useful role, be acceptable to the protagonists, and be able to operate effectively with other elements of the force?

Be of a nature and size that is consistent with and appropriate for the benefits and costs?

Demonstrate a willingness to accept a fair share of risk; and be likely to result in benefits which are acceptable in the light of the risks to NZDF personnel?

Be able to be mounted and sustained without serious degradation of NZDF capabilities raised for other Defence tasks?

Is there public support for participation and is the support sustainable should New Zealand suffer or inflict casualties?

Is the commitment finite and are there adequate provisions to review and terminate participation if conditions change to the extent that costs and risks outweigh the benefits?

Do the resultant limitations to New Zealand's ability to respond to other situations represent an acceptable risk?

Would an early offer provide a better chance of securing agreement to New Zealand's preferred contribution, and would an early offer permit New Zealand's objectives to be met with a smaller-sized contribution than otherwise would be the case?

10

Reforming the UN's Organisational Capacity for Peacekeeping

Mats R. Berdal

There is no shortage of prescriptive literature on how to reform the UN's organisational capacity in order to improve both the effectiveness of peace-keeping forces in the field and the "higher management" of operations from its headquarters in New York.[1] Indeed the resurgence of academic interest in the United Nations and the dramatic increase in UN field operations since 1989 have been accompanied by a steady stream of practical proposals, schemes and government papers about how best to strengthen the organ-isation.[2] Very few of the proposals that have been advanced, however, have been genuinely novel. In fact, the much-quoted report by the Secretary-General, entitled *An Agenda for Peace* and presented to the Security Council in June 1992, is little more than a codification of ideas, most of which were first discussed in the wake of the Congo operation in the mid-1960s.[3]

More importantly, and indeed worryingly, few of the reforms that have

---

1. This chapter is based on a paper presented to a Research Seminar at the London School of Economics in June 1994. I am grateful for research assistance provided by Simon Hildrey.

2. See, for example, Erskine Childers and Brian Urquhart, *Towards a More Effective United Nations* (Uppsala: Dag Hammarskjold Foundation, 1992); John M. Lee, Robert von Pagenhardt and Timothy W. Stanley, *To Unite Our Strength: Enhancing the United Nations Peace and Security System* (New York: University Press of America, 1992); and Gareth Evans, *Cooperating for Peace* (Sydney: Allen & Unwin, 1993).

3. See, for example, the collection of essays in Per Frydenberg, ed., *Peacekeeping Experience and Evaluation: The Oslo Papers* (Oslo: The Norwegian Institute of International Affairs, 1964); and the study by D. W. Bowett, *United Nations Forces: A Legal Study of the United Nations Practice* (London: Stevens & Sons, 1964), pp. 403–06. The latter work is a particularly thorough study of the problems associated with multinational operations under UN auspices.

been introduced since the Security Council summit in January 1992 have significantly enhanced the management of peacekeeping functions in the Secretariat. While it is true that important progress has been made in certain areas (most notably within individual departments, such as the Department of Peacekeeping Operations or DPKO), the positive effects of such developments have been largely negated by countervailing tendencies. As will be argued in this chapter, reforms introduced by Boutros Boutros-Ghali since February 1992 have not addressed the root cause of the peacekeeping management problems: the growing decentralisation of peacekeeping functions in the Secretariat and the consequent diffusion of authority in the management of operations. Indeed, as will be argued below, recent developments within the Secretariat appear rather ominously to have reinforced a general process of fragmenting decision-making power. As during the Cold War, the management of UN field operations continues to rely on improvisation, *ad hoc* arrangements and "close working relationships" among members of the Secretariat and between officers and civilian personnel in the field.

If there is no shortage of ideas about how to strengthen the organisational capacities of the UN for peacekeeping, why has progress been so limited? This is the central question that this chapter will attempt to answer. In doing so, it will focus on the Secretariat and the Secretary-General's own efforts to improve the capacities of the organisation in recent years. This is not to suggest that political support from member-states is not a crucial factor in ensuring that proposals for reform are actually implemented. Indeed in some cases (most obviously, perhaps, over the question of a permanent UN army) the lack of political will has meant that proposals, which in the abstract may merit further attention, have little chance of survival beyond the General Assembly working group stage. Still, there has been a distinct tendency, not surprisingly, for UN officials to hide the limited achievements of the past two years behind the broader issue of insufficient political support. The fact is, however, that even if political will would be forthcoming, this in itself is no guarantee of effective reform. Moreover, political will is not immutable; it must be generated and cultivated. If the United Nations is not able to put its own house in order, securing the necessary political support will pose an even more arduous challenge.

This chapter, then, will look at what the UN itself has or has not done to cope more effectively with the challenges posed by large-scale contemporary peacekeeping operations. It will do so by looking both at the "higher management" of operations in New York and the organisation and activities of forces in the field. It will also briefly consider the mounting crisis of UN finances which increasingly threatens to undermine the future of all UN field operations.

UN Headquarters in New York

There are two aspects to any discussion of how the machinery for peacekeeping in New York can be strengthened in support of peacekeeping. The first of these concerns the processes of *vertical integration:* that is, the attempts that have been made to enhance resources and streamline procedures and decision-making within individual departments. The key department in this context is, of course, the DPKO, which maintains primary responsibility for the "day-to-day management of peacekeeping operations."[4] The second aspect concerns the process of *horizontal integration:* that is, those measures aimed at improving overall coordination among the various departments, offices and divisions involved in UN field operations, such as the DPKO, the Department of Political Affairs (DPA), the Department of Humanitarian Affairs (DHA), the Department of Administration and Management (DAM), the Office of Legal Affairs, and the Office of the Security Coordinator, as well as specialist agencies such as the UN Development Programme (UNDP) and the UN High Commissioner for Refugees (UNHCR). Each of these aspects need to be examined in turn.

Vertical Integration: Strengthening the DPKO Since 1993

Since March 1993 a number of initiatives aimed at upgrading the DPKO (formerly the Office of Special Political Affairs) in New York has produced significant results by UN standards.[5] The initiatives include, above all, a major expansion of staffing levels, including both contract and seconded personnel with specialist officers given responsibility for training, demining and civilian police matters. As of mid-April 1994, the staffing complement of the DPKO was 267, with proposals being drawn up to increase the total number of staff to 459.[6] More specifically, a Planning Division has been established under a newly-created Office of Planning and Support, to be headed eventually by an Assistant Secretary-General (ASG) who will "serve as the principal source of advice to the Secretary-General on all matters relating to the planning and support of field missions, including staffing, finance, logistics and procurement."[7] This new ASG for Planning and

---

4. "Improving the Capacity of the United Nations for Peacekeeping," Report of the Secretary-General, S/26450, 14 March 1994, para. 32.

5. On 3 March 1993 Kofi Annan replaced Marrack Goulding as Under-Secretary-General (USG) for Peacekeeping Operations. Goulding, who became USG for Political Affairs, was until then widely regarded as conservative and cautious about any expansion of the DPKO. He has maintained his scepticism about strengthening the military component of the DPKO.

6. "DPKO: Proposed Staffing and Organisation," 13 April 1994, pp. 2–3.

7. The DPKO will consist, then, of two major offices—Planning and Support and Operations—each of them headed by an ASG. Mr S. Iqbal Riza is presently the ASG for Operations and is responsible for the "day-to-day direction of all peacekeeping operations."

Support will also oversee the work of the Field Operations Division (FOD) (renamed Field Administration and Logistics Division), which has finally, and after much bureaucratic resistance, been incorporated into the DPKO, having previously been located within the Department of Management. The incorporation of the FOD should help to remedy the old problem of dual lines of reporting between the administrative and logistic aspects of an operation and the military.

It should be stressed that the addition of a planning element and the consolidation of FOD's traditional activities into the DPKO represent, arguably, one of the most significant of recent developments. This is because, as the 1978 edition of the *Peacekeeper's Handbook* pointed out: "pre-planning or advanced preparation has never been part of the United Nations policy with regard to international peacekeeping."[8] The sheer scale of contemporary operations has made this traditional approach utterly untenable. The acknowledgment that systematic predeployment planning is actually needed represents a major stride forward.

The creation in April 1993 of a Situation Centre within the DPKO has received rather more public attention. It was originally set up with a view to monitoring the U.S.–UN humanitarian-peacekeeping operations in Somalia, but has since been significantly upgraded and now operates in accordance with proper and regularised staff procedures. Steps have also been taken to enhance the flow of information into the UN headquarters from member-states through the installation of an intelligence processing system in the DPKO. The system, known as the Joint Deployable Intelligence Support System (JDISS), was donated by the U.S. government and enables the UN to receive low-grade, finished intelligence (including satellite imagery) on a regular basis. Although some concern has been expressed about the political significance of relying too heavily on the U.S. for information, there is now a general acceptance among member-states of the need to improve the UN's "information" gathering and processing capability. Thus the value of the Situation Centre is now widely recognised and accepted (by member-states, officials in the field and at UN HQ), though its capacities for collection and dissemination of information remain underdeveloped.

Another development that merits special attention is the establishment of a Stand-By Forces Planning Team. In the course of 1993, a Stand-By Forces Planning Group, consisting of seven middle-ranking officers, was charged by the Security Council with developing a system by which forces assigned in advance of any operation would be constituted for UN duties when

---

The ASG for Planning and Support has yet to be appointed. *Ibid.*
  8. *Peacekeeper's Handbook* (New York: International Peace Academy, 1978), Ch. 3, p. 8.

required. In theory, standby forces would be available for deployment "as a whole or in parts, within an agreed response time at the Secretary-General's request as mandated by the Security Council." While the concept is a sound one (and far more politically realistic than the idea of a permanent UN army), the response from member-states has not been as positive as might have been expected. This, however, as discussed above, is a question of political will, and the DPKO Stand-By Planning Group cannot be faulted for their work over the past two years.

The major initiatives described above are all steps in the right direction and the DPKO should be encouraged to further improve its ability to engage in mission support, force generation and planning. The department (and indeed UN HQ more generally) should not, however, aspire to become an "operational headquarters" in the strict military sense. The exercise of command functions—"the authority to assign force elements to tasks and direct their actions on a day-to-day basis"—should not come from New York, but instead should be delegated to the Special Representative and Force Commander in the field. The reasons for this are both practical and political. From the practical point of view, the ability of New York to direct nearly twenty separate operations is bound to be fragmentary and selective. More crucially, few governments, and certainly not the permanent five, wish to see the UN HQ given responsibilities for "Mission command" as opposed to "Mission support."[9]

The Failure of Horizontal Integration

While measures of vertical integration have undoubtedly enhanced the ability of the DPKO to coordinate activities in the field, the problem of horizontal integration persists. Put more plainly, the various actors involved in some aspect of peacekeeping management within the Secretariat find it very difficult to coordinate their activities and delineate responsibilities. The root cause of the problem is perhaps best illustrated in the long-awaited report of the Secretary-General on "Improving the Capacity of the United Nations for Peace-Keeping," requested by the Security Council in May 1993 and released by the Secretariat in March 1994.

In an attempt to clarify reporting channels and delineate the respective roles of key departments (DPA, DPKO, DHA, DAM), the Secretary-General's report embodies a formula that reflects bureaucratic interests as much as any desire to rationalise decision-making procedures. Under this "new order," the DPA is described as the "political arm" of the Secretary-

---

9. These terms are used by David Ramsbotham, "UN Operations: The Art of the Possible," *RUSI Journal* 138 (December 1993).

General, the DPKO his "operational arm...for the day-to-day management of peacekeeping operations," while the DHA is responsible for "coordination and humanitarian operations." Peacekeeping operations, however, by their very nature, encompass overlapping political, military and humanitarian components, and it is simply not possible to separate the "political" and "operational" aspects of a mission from each other. This has been shown repeatedly in contemporary operations. Within a bureaucratic structure such as the United Nations, this contrived allocation of functional responsibilities makes effective decision-making contingent on close working relationships between departmental heads, directors and officers further down the hierarchy. While relations at the USG level have been relatively smooth over the past two years, current arrangements ensure that the potential for future conflict is built into the system. More worryingly, it also means that unity of reporting and, therefore, unity of strategic instructions from UN HQ to the field remains deficient.

There have been several attempts to rectify this state of affairs and to reduce, as far as possible, redundancy and duplication among departments. Most prominently, as the "primary instrument of coordination among departments," a Task Force on UN Operations was established in 1993 at the USG level. Although it meets on a weekly basis, it acts, however, more as a forum for information-sharing than policy-formulation and integrated decision-making. While the Task Force has proved useful for its limited purpose, it does not ensure that integration is effective further down the hierarchy. Contacts and exchanges of information at the working level between departments are poorly developed. For example, DPA officers have avoided and shown no interest in using the assets of the Situation Centre; indeed, many DPA officials are still unsure of its physical location within the Secretariat. Similarly, a weekly meeting of DPKO, DHA and DPA representatives was "cancelled until further notice" in the summer of 1994.

Another telling example of the lack of effective coordination among departments can be found in a "Note" on DHA–DPKO cooperation.[10] The document stressed that DHA and DPKO planning and desk officers should "interact continuously"; that the DPKO should be "invited to contribute towards the planning of humanitarian assistance operations"; and that the DPA should also be invited to participate in the process. The concrete steps proposed included "exchanges of information" and "staff consultations." That these kinds of recommendations should be circulated in August 1994— after the experience of Somalia, Cambodia and a whole string of other complex missions—is eloquent testimony to the limited progress that has

---

10. "Note on DHA/DPKO Cooperation in UN Humanitarian and Peace-keeping Operations," (New York: UN DHA, 15 August 1994).

been made.

As indicated above, there is a further development that since 1992 has complicated the management of operations in New York and has contributed to the state of affairs outlined above. This is the increasingly important role of the Secretary-General's immediate circle of advisers, reflected in the expansion of the Executive Office of the Secretary-General (EOSG), with both geographical and functional responsibilities accorded to his immediate advisers (the geographical distribution of responsibilities took effect from mid-January 1994).[11] This has resulted in a top-heavy structure in New York and has, in effect, created another layer between the Secretary-General and the substantive departments of the Secretariat. At the very least, this development increases the potential for policy differences in New York to slow down decision-making. This may in turn create critical delays in making decisions of urgent concern to Special Representatives of the Secretary-General and Force Commanders in the field.

The aforementioned survey of the "higher management" of UN peace-keeping points to a continuing fragmentation of decision-making power within the Secretariat and a consequent diffusion of authority in the central management of operations. This trend has intensified with the emergence of large-scale multicomponent missions in recent years. The vast number of departments, offices and divisions involved in UN field operations has undermined unity of command within the Secretariat. This has weakened the lines of authority and reporting between Chiefs of Mission and HQ in New York. The management style of the present Secretary-General has often further complicated this situation. The unfortunate upshot of these developments has been a general loss of responsiveness to rapid changes on the ground and a concomitant weakening of operational efficiency.

Continuing Problems in the Field

The dramatic increase in UN field operations since 1988 has been accompanied by a growing number of tasks assigned to the military units involved. These now include, *inter alia,* assisting in the delivery of humanitarian aid to beleaguered populations, such as in Bosnia–Herzegovina and Somalia; human rights monitoring, as in El Salvador and Cambodia; the

---

11. Under the new arrangement, Chinmaya Gharekhan was given responsibility for Africa (north of the Equator), Europe (excluding the CIS countries east of the Urals) and the Middle East; Ismat Kittani was given responsibility for Africa south of the Equator, Asia, CIS countries east of the Urals, Australia and the Pacific; Alvaro de Soto was given responsibility for North and South America, including the Caribbean. In addition to this, each of them have been given functional responsibilities on behalf of the Secretary-General (for example, Gharekhan deals with Security Council Affairs).

disarmament, cantonment and demobilisation of armed factions as envisaged in the peace plans for Angola, Mozambique and Cambodia; and the preventive deployment of forces as in Macedonia. At the same time, the context of UN peacekeeping has also changed markedly, with a far greater number of missions deployed in conditions of intra-state conflict or, in some cases, outright civil war. Such conflicts, involving intense hatreds, countless armed factions and the ready supply of weapons and ammunition, present peacekeeping forces with a highly dangerous operational environment.[12]

These developments have placed severe strains on traditional UN practices for initiating and supporting field operations. While the problems of "higher management" were outlined above, the situation in the field also merits continuing attention. Indeed, recent and on-going operations have shown that many of the self-imposed restraints that have come to characterise UN peacekeeping—improvised mounting procedures, the lack of pre-deployment planning, a complex procurement system and restrictions on the collection and use of intelligence material—are undermining the ability of multinational forces to carry out their missions. While differing markedly in size and the nature of their mandates, missions launched since 1992 all point to certain basic weaknesses that have been accentuated by the need to operate in the context of actual or latent civil war with only sporadic consent from the parties on the ground. Four areas merit specific attention.[13]

First, the limited logistic capabilities available to the United Nations and the absence hitherto of an effective planning agency to coordinate and direct logistics support continue to bedevil operations.[14] The creation of a Mission Planning Service within the DPKO and its absorption of the FOD should at least begin to address this problem. A critical challenge, however, still lies in the area of civil–military integration and cooperation in the field. As recent missions show, integration of civilian and military operations must be encouraged at all levels; missions must be viewed, and perceive themselves, as one indivisible operation. As General John Sanderson has pointed out, many of the practical problems encountered in Cambodia stemmed directly from the fact that "there was never any strategic planning within the UNTAC mission."[15] "Integration" in this sense involves a process of

---

12. See the chapter by Paul Diehl in this volume.

13. I have addressed these and other problems in much greater detail in *Whither UN Peacekeeping?* (London: International Institute for Strategic Studies, Adelphi Paper No. 281, 1993). I have singled out these four areas in this paper as they appear particularly important in terms of improving future operations.

14. For a discussion of UN logistics problems, see *ibid.*, pp. 32–39.

15. Lieutenant General J. M. Sanderson, "UNTAC: Successes and Failures," in Hugh Smith, ed., *International Peacekeeping: Building on the Cambodian Experience* (Canberra: Australian Defence Studies Centre, Australian Defence Force Academy, 1994), p. 22.

psychological adjustment as much as it requires concrete steps to facilitate cooperation. Integration, in the words of Lt. Gen. Lars-Eric Wahlgren, former Commander of UNPROFOR (the UN Protection Force in ex-Yugoslavia), is essential for promoting "unity of purpose" within missions.

Second, the failure to establish an efficient command and control system in the field and to provide commanders with political and military intelligence have plagued all missions. The command and control issue, however, is not merely a "UN problem." In the first place, effective communications are notoriously difficult to establish within any multinational coalition, owing to differences in staff procedures, training, language barriers and equipment incompatibilities among participating forces. These problems are magnified in the UN context by the very broad geographical spread of contingents involved in peacekeeping. Second, the tendency for national governments to intervene directly in the chain of command of a peace-keeping mission has also become a growing obstacle to command, control and coordination by the United Nations. This tendency has increased in proportion to the perception of danger to soldiers involved in operations, and has been facilitated by the ease with which contingent commanders can now communicate confidentially with national authorities. As a result, the formal command status of contingents (technically under the Operational Control of the Force Commander) has often been more apparent than real and the "United Nations-ness" of operations has been called into question. This problem has been particularly acute in the former Yugoslavia and Somalia, and needs to be looked at again while acknowledging that political and technical constraints will persist.

Third, peacekeeping operations also continue to suffer from inadequate training of many participating contingents and, especially, from the acute shortage of specialised units and personnel in three areas: logistics, communications and engineering. A recurring deficiency has been the lack of specialised personnel to carry out early movement and control functions. This is important considering the frequency of troop rotations (generally every six months) and the very large number of different contingents involved in UN operations. Traditionally, overall movement control functions have been exercised from New York. Recent experience, including that of the UN in Cambodia, has demonstrated that excessive centralisation generates supply dislocations and that any logistical systems must be responsive to input from field staff. For the efficient flow of supplies—that is, the movement of supplies at the appropriate time and place and in sufficient quantities—planning cells must drive the process locally. The inability of the UN to coordinate in-theatre movement control and airfield management units (indeed, in some cases of establishing such units) has been a major factor delaying, especially, the forward movement of forces to final deployment areas.

Fourth, lack of tactical mobility (especially air assets) to support operations and outdated procurement regulations continue to create major complications on the ground, as recent events in Mozambique illustrate. In late February 1994, for example, the grounding of eight MI-8 heavy transport helicopters after contracts expired threatened to derail the entire demobilisation schedule in the country. Although UN HQ knew about the problem for some time, procurement regulations prevented a rapid resolution of the problem. When the UN did eventually hire some more helicopters, these turned out to be unsuitable (because there were too few crews per helicopter; they did not have night-flying capability; and their range and loading capacity was too limited for operations in Mozambique).

The Financial Crisis

Although the UN's financial difficulties have long been a subject of concern, the present state of affairs is arguably more critical than it has ever been, and short-term remedial solutions (such as borrowing from one peacekeeping account or from the regular budget to pay for the costs of starting a new mission) may no longer be sufficient to stave off a "financing disaster."[16] Increasingly, the financial situation is impacting directly on operational activities. Thus a recent Task Force report on the future role of the Department of Humanitarian Affairs stressed the "precarious financial situation the Department is facing and the likelihood that existing resources could finance current operations only up to the end of September 1994." What is perhaps most worrying is that in spite of the comparatively modest sums involved, arrears continue to accumulate while very few of the measures proposed (by member-states and advisory bodies) to improve the situation have been acted upon.[17]

As far as peacekeeping operations are concerned, one of the most urgent problems relates to the effective financing of the preliminary logistics surveys and the start-up phase of an operation. This phase is critical as it

16. Anthony McDermott, *United Nations Financing Problems and the New Generation of Peacekeeping and Peace Enforcement* (Providence, RI: Brown University, Thomas J. Watson Institute for International Studies, Occasional Paper No. 16, 1994), p. 1. For a review of the UN's system of financing its activities, see also *Financing an Effective United Nations: A Report of the Independent Advisory Group on UN Financing* (New York: Ford Foundation, April 1993).

17. As of 30 June 1994, the total amount of outstanding assessed contributions for all peacekeeping operations was $2.1bn. It has been estimated that the total costs of UN peacekeeping between 1948 and 1992 (in 1990 dollars) was $8.3bn; McDermott, *United Nations Financing*, p. 4.

involves the deployment of the initial logistic, engineer and communications elements. The problems of financing this early phase stem from the nature of the UN budgetary process, which remains slow and resistant to modification. As long as the Advisory Committee on Administrative and Budgetary Questions of the General Assembly (ACABQ) reviews the initial budget prepared by the Secretariat, the expenditure may not exceed a $3m annual limit on the Secretary-General's "unforeseen and extraordinary" spending authority. Once the budget has been approved by the ACABQ, the UN is legally permitted to contract services and equipment for up to $10m while still awaiting formal approval of the mission budget by the Fifth Committee (Budget) of the General Assembly and, finally, by the General Assembly itself. It is this limited initial spending authority, combined with a complex procurement system and high freight costs, which has created major delays in places such as Cambodia, Angola and Mozambique.[18] Since the initial phase of any UN field operation is usually the most expensive one, this system of budgeting can cripple new missions. To remedy this deficiency, a Peacekeeping Reserve Fund of $150m was created in December 1992. This fund, however, has already been depleted while a satisfactory mechanism for reimbursing troop-contributing countries has yet to be agreed.

Although the Special Committee on Peacekeeping Operations has discussed the problem of resources and finances,[19] the General Assembly is most reluctant to relinquish its prerogatives in the area of finance. In its reviews of UN peacekeeping operations, the Fifth Committee of the General Assembly routinely reaffirms the "importance of the role of the ACABQ as an advisory body to the General Assembly in the budget process."[20] It was this tendency on the part of the "General Assembly to micro-manage each department, office, division, unit, etc. through control of staffing tables and expenditures" which Dick Thornburgh so deplored in his notorious report on the organisation's management practices that was submitted to the Secretary-General in March 1993.[21]

---

18. Report of the Secretary-General on the United Nations Angola Verification Mission II (UNAVEM II), S/23191, 31 October 1991, para. 20.

19. One suggestion, for example, has been that the Secretary-General should be allowed to obligate as much as 20 percent of the "initial estimated cost of a peace-keeping operation once it is approved by the Security Council, but while the budget of the operations is still being considered by the ACABQ and the General Assembly." See, "Comprehensive Review of the Whole Question of Peace-keeping Operations in all their Aspects," A/AC.121/41, 16 March 1994, 2(a).

20. Financing the UN Protection Force, Report of the Fifth Committee, A/48/819/Add.2, 21 March 1994, para. 7.

21. Report to the Secretary-General of the UN by Dick Thornburgh, USG DAM, 1 March 1993, reprinted in "Hearing before the Sub-committee on International Security, International Organisations and Human Rights of the Committee of Foreign Affairs; House of

Conclusion

In its essential characteristics, the UN system for planning, organising and supporting peacekeeping operations in the field remains largely unchanged since the end of the Cold War. For its effective functioning, it continues to rely heavily on improvisation, *ad hoc* procedures and arrangements. Although a series of changes to the Secretariat structure have been ordered by the Secretary-General since January 1992, these have not addressed the chief problem in the management of peacekeeping operations. Designed, in the words of the Secretary-General, to "eliminate duplication, redundancy and excessive layering of offices and duties at the headquarters," changes have not reversed the growing decentralisation of peacekeeping functions in the Secretariat. The result has been a continuing diffusion of authority in the management of operations.

The picture which emerges from this overview of UN peacekeeping practices points to the need for centralisation (or, at least, genuine coordination) of management functions within the Secretariat on the one hand, and greater delegation of operational, financial and administrative responsibility to the field on the other. Such delegation to the field should not be thought of as implying that the UN HQ's overall political and strategic control of operations will be lost; such control must remain firmly with the Secretary-General under the authority of the Security Council. The delegation of operational, administrative and financial authority is bound, however, to increase the operational efficiency of peacekeeping forces. It should be high on the list of priorities in any future discussion about how best to improve the organisational capacities of the UN for peacekeeping.

Representatives, 103rd Session of Congress, 5 March" (Washington D.C.: U.S. Government Printing Office, 1993.

11

Peacekeeping Operations: Problems of Command and Control

Andrei Raevsky

Among the many issues which have come to the forefront of the debate surrounding peacekeeping operations is the command and control of these operations (Actually, it might be preferable to speak of command, control communications and intelligence or "C3I."[1]) In particular, two recent and most testing peacekeeping operations, one in Somalia and the other in Bosnia, have triggered a sometimes heated debate on the problems of command and control: how were U.S. and UN actions in Somalia co-ordinated and did U.S. and UN actions support each other or not; who should have the authority to order air strikes in Bosnia; if strikes are executed by NATO forces, should UN commanders have the authority to order them, or should the decision be taken in Zagreb by the UN Secretary-General's Personal Envoy, the UN in New York or NATO in Brussels? There are also other less well publicised controversies, such as the issue of intelligence-gathering and intelligence-sharing for a peacekeeping operation.

Many of these problems have a common cause: the peacekeeping mission is one, but the number of actors is multiple. Furthermore, the actors involved have very different capabilities, different agendas and, often, different understandings of both the context and the goal of the peace-keeping operation. Sometimes, these actors are even competing against each other for political influence or dissimilar goals.

---

1. Although a fourth C has been added to the expression for "computers" (making it "command, control, communications, computers and intelligence" or C4I), this new term is more suited to AirLand Battle types of operational environments than to peacekeeping operations.

The operation in Bosnia is a good example of such contradictions. Here is an operation which is under UN control, but which is executed while a number of other organisations or groups are directly influencing or even shaping the negotiations between the parties in conflict: the European Union (EU), the Western European Union (WEU), the Contact Group, etc. Furthermore, it is generally accepted that the United Nations itself is far from having the means to conduct the operations in Bosnia. The large UN contingent in Bosnia is composed of troops, observers and police officers drawn from 35 different countries. However, even this rather large contingent is dependent on NATO for its firepower and even more so for its intelligence capability. In turn, NATO is itself very dependent on U.S. fighting and intelligence capabilities. Nevertheless, the United States has been unwilling to commit ground forces to the UN Protection Force in former Yugoslovia (UNPROFOR) and is strongly opposed to complete intelligence-sharing with most of the 35 countries which have committed forces to UNPROFOR or with the UN itself. Obviously, among equals some are more equals than others: the U.S. does, under specific circumstances, share intelligence with one or several countries. Such a decision is taken on a basis of a bilateral agreement or understanding and does not imply a U.S. commitment or obligation to extend it to all other allied forces.

Clearly, the parallel political competence and mandates of different organisations, and the discrepancy between their political authority and their military means, are a major source of tensions. Furthermore, the various and dissimilar peacekeeping doctrines developed by the many actors involved in peacekeeping operations (international organisations or individual nations) are compounding these problems.

Finally, it can be argued that the C3I arrangements of most peacekeeping operations are shaped with prevailing political rather than military considerations. This is, in fact, almost inevitable because most UN peacekeeping operations are highly political in their nature and, thus, the military forces involved are operating in an environment in which military considerations are secondary to political priorities. This situation is well illustrated in the complex chain of authorisations usually needed by UN peacekeeping forces to use military force or even simply to return fire.

Unfortunately, as the operations in Somalia and Bosnia have shown, peacekeeping operations are becoming increasingly complex and even dangerous: as of 24 May 1994, the UNPROFOR and UNOSOM II operations had already cost the lives of 200 peacekeepers.[2] There is, therefore, an urgent need to evaluate carefully the problems associated with

---

2. *United Nations Peace-keeping* (New York: UN Document PS/DPI/6/Rev.5, May 1994), pp. 55 and 98.

the C3I aspects of peacekeeping operations.

Command Problems

Unity of command, however, is a necessary condition for the operational effectiveness, especially in these difficult missions. If an operation fails to function as an integrated whole, both the mission's ability to reach its objective and the safety of its personnel are jeopardised.[3]

Command and control, while often used together, are different concepts. In NATO terminology, for example, *command* refers to "the authority vested in an individual of the armed forces for the direction, coordination and control of military forces." *Control* refers to "that authority exercised by a commander over part of the activities of subordinate organisations or other organisations not normally under his command, which encompasses the responsibility for implementing orders or directives. All or part of this authority may be transferred or delegated."[4] Next to these official definitions, it might be preferable to differentiate command and control by stating that command is "who is in charge of the military" while control is "how the military know what their own people are doing and how they tell them what to do."[5] As we shall see, peacekeeping operations are plagued with difficulties on both levels.

States usually define "who is in charge of the military" by means of official documents such as military doctrines (NATO or Russia) or presidential directives (U.S.). Furthermore, most armies have field manuals of some sort which also make reference to command issues. Three of the key issues which are addressed in such doctrinal statements are:

1. When is the commitment of peacekeeping forces warranted?
2. Who should be in charge of the C3I of the operation?
3. When and how is the use of military force warranted in a peacekeeping operation?

Many aspects of the C3I component of a peacekeeping operation are dependent upon the answers to these questions. The command level is particularly affected, because these considerations underline the entire "philosophy" behind the peacekeeping operation. It is thus interesting to

---

3. Boutros Boutros-Ghali, *Report of the Secretary-General on the Work of the Organisation,* 2 September 1994, p. 56.

4. Patricia Chilton, Otfried Nassauer, Dan Plesch and Jamie Patten (Whitaker), *NATO, Peacekeeping, and the United Nations* (London: British American Security Information Council, September 1994), p. 33.

5. *Ibid.*

compare the answers to these questions provided by the United States, NATO, the UK and Russia.

In recent years, in particular under the Clinton administration, the United States has issued a number of official documents and statements on participation in and conduct of peacekeeping operations.[6] Some key characteristics of U.S. views on peacekeeping can be inferred from these documents:

a. The commitment of U.S. forces is warranted only if the execution of the mission serves U.S. national interests.

b. The degree of U.S. control of the peacekeeping operation is proportional to the importance of U.S. participation. The U.S. might agree to support an operation controlled by, for example, the UN, but the execution of this support would remain wholly under U.S. authority. Control over U.S. military personnel is never given to non-U.S. commanders.

c. The U.S. has a reluctance to use force. Force should be used only in the last resort during a traditional peacekeeping operation, and should be used with restraint during a peace-enforcement operation which in U.S. terminology implies a coercive enforcement of peace without the need for consent from all parties to the conflict. If force has to be used, then (according to *FM 100-23*) the degree of force used has to be "no greater than that reasonably necessary under the circumstances." However, the U.S. conventional military doctrine supports the idea that "massive force and maximum firepower should be used to achieve a limited objective."[7] The reason for this is the ever-present U.S. fear of taking casualties.

NATO has developed the term "peace support operations" to describe a wide range of operations ranging from conflict-prevention to peace-enforcement.[8] Such operations can be conducted in support of UN or CSCE (Conference on Security and Cooperation in Europe) activities. NATO holds the view that:

a. NATO forces can be committed within NATO's area of responsibility (i.e. those of the member-states) and in out-of-area peacekeeping operations in support of UN or CSCE operations. It

6. See *U.S. Army Field Manual 100-23 (Peacekeeping)* Draft version 6 (Fort Monroe, VA: HQ TRADOC); the U.S. *PPD Presidential Decision Directive 25;* and the U.S. *PRD Presidential Review Directive 13.*

7. Dennis J. Quinn, ed., *Peace Support Operations and the U.S. Military* (Washington DC: National Defense University Press, 1994), p. 163.

8. See *NATO Doctrine for Peace Support Operations* (Mons: SHAPE, 1994); and *MC 327 NATO Planning Principles and Guidelines for Combined Peacekeeping Operations* (Mons: SHAPE, 1994).

should be noted that this policy has never been submitted to the legislatures of the NATO member-states.

b. If NATO forces are committed, then the unity of command should be preserved at all levels. In other words, while NATO member-states might choose to subordinate certain units of their armed forces to the authority of, for example, the UN, forces engaged within a NATO action would remain under NATO control only.

c. Force should be used only very carefully during peace-support operations, but decisively during a peace-enforcement operation. The goal is then to achieve, rapidly and decisively, a military objective with minimum collateral damage.

The UK has rapidly adopted a new version of its semi-official doctrine on peacekeeping. The key concept of this document is that peacekeeping and peace-enforcement are completely different in their nature and that no middle ground between them exists. In the words of its author,

> The idea, therefore, that post Cold War there is a new middle ground of military operations lying on a linear spectrum somewhere between peacekeeping and peace enforcement seems not only unfounded historically, but impractical and dangerously destabilising doctrinally.[9]

Clearly, the UK believes that it should be unambiguous and clear *before* a peacekeeping operation is initiated as to whether it is conceived as a wider peacekeeping operation or a peace-enforcement operation. A wider peace-keeping operation should only be initiated when the following consensual principles can be upheld throughout the operation: impartiality, minimum force, legitimacy, credibility, mutual respect and transparency. A peace-enforcement mission implies a "crossing of a Rubicon" without a way back to wider peacekeeping.[10] In this context, it appears that Britain will commit and subordinate its forces to UN (or possibly CSCE) operations so long as the risk of uncontrolled escalation is avoided. When escalation is foreseen, the UK is likely either to withdraw its forces unilaterally, or to reinforce them to a level required by what is likely to become a fullscale war.

As has been shown in Bosnia, the UK is willing to put British soldiers on the ground and under UN command. However, it is also obvious that the UK commitment is contingent upon the nature of the proposed peacekeeping mission: the UK will be an effective but prudent participant in future peace-keeping operations.

Regarding the issue of use of force, the British believe that "activities that

---

9. Lt. Col. Charles Dobbie, *Army Field Manual "Wider Peacekeeping"* (Third Draft), (UK Doctrine and Training HQ, Trenchard Lines, Wilts: UK Army, no date), p. 2-15.

10. *Ibid.*

breach the consent differential should not be undertaken in a wider peacekeeping campaign."[11] In light of these statements, the engagement of British Harrier attack aircraft against Bosnian Serb positions in the area of Gorazde appears to be in clear contradiction of British military doctrine: "The long term effects of force may prove substantially different from the short term ones—a tactical success resulting from the use of force may lead to a long term strategic failure."[12] It could be noted that the U.S. position (whose A-10s also participated in the strike, albeit unsuccessfully) is no more consistent than the British one since the U.S. *FM 100-23* contains exactly the same language:

> Armed action will almost certainly prejudice the acceptability of the troops carrying it out and could have far-reaching international political consequences.... The long term effect of force may prove substantially different from the short term ones—a tactical success resulting from the use of force may lead to a long term strategic failure.[13]

This inconsistency can be explained by the fact that documents such as *Wider Peacekeeping* or the *FM 100-23 (Peacekeeping)* reflect the views of the military, whereas specific military actions can be ordered by the political leadership for political considerations rather than for their military consistency. These sometimes contradictory priorities are a source of very real tensions between civil and military authorities in many countries.

Two rather different approaches seem to have been taken by Russia for peacekeeping operations: one for international peacekeeping operations under UN or CSCE mandates, and another for operations under CIS (Commonwealth of Independent States) mandates or within Russia. In the first case, Russia will commit and subordinate forces to international authorities (as is the case in Croatia and Bosnia); in the second, Russia will retain an overwhelming control of the operation (as in Tajikistan).

Three official documents have been recently adopted in Russia which constitute the legal framework for Russian armed forces, the *Fundamental Provisions of the Russian Military Doctrine,* the *Military Security Concepts of the States Participating in the Commonwealth of Independent States* and the *Tashkent Protocol of May 1992 "Temporary Procedures of the Formation and Function of Military Observers and Collective Peacekeeping Forces."* These documents specifically refer to the participation in peacekeeping operations of the UN, CSCE or CIS by both the Russian armed forces and/or the CIS Joint Armed Forces.

The Russian use of force policy is also different according to cases: in

---

11. *Ibid.*, p. 2-17.
12. *Ibid.*, p. 4-4.
13. *FM 100-23,* pp. 1-15 and 4-2.

UN operations, the decision to use force is left to UN authorities, while for operations within the CIS the approach to the use of force is similar to the U.S. one: to use force only in the last resort but, if force is needed, then overwhelming force should be used (including the use of fixed and rotary wing aircraft, multiple rocket launchers and helicopter gunships).[14]

The key operational concepts for U.S., NATO, UK and Russian command for peacekeeping operations are summarised in Table 11.1. These principles illustrate the complexity of the problems affecting many UN peacekeeping operations. Not only are the most powerful prospective participants unwilling or unable to subordinate their forces to a UN command, but they have different philosophies on the use of force issue, and finally, the priorities of their political leadership might put them at odds with their own military doctrines. This reality is made even more intricate by the large number of frameworks under which peacekeeping operations could be initiated; in Europe alone, peacekeeping operations could be initiated under the Partnership for Peace proposal, under CSCE auspices, by the WEU through NATO's Combined Joint Task Forces initiative which allows alliance assets to be used for joint or combined task forces, and by the UN. While there are many views and preferred options among European countries, it remains true that NATO support seems to be indispensable for anything besides a smallscale (and low-risk) operation: no other body can commit enough forces and means.

Table 11.1: Differing Operational Concepts of Command of Peacekeeping Operations

Actor	Commitment	C3I	Force
USA	Only if compatible with national interest	U.S. only	If necessary then massive
NATO	Peace support	NATO only	Decisive
UK	UN or CSCE	Operational sub-ordination to UN possible	Preferably none*
Russia	UN, CSCE, CIS or Russian	UN or Russian (within CIS)	If necessary then massive

* Unless a peace-enforcement operation is decided on.

14. Andrei Raevsky and I. N. Vorob'ev, *Russian Approaches to Peacekeeping Operations* (New York and Geneva: UN Institute for Disarmament Research, 1994), pp. 52–74.

Control Problems

Contrary to the concept of command, control depends upon *means*. In military terms, means include intelligence, planning, communications, logistics, firepower, mobility, etc. In this sense, the United Nations, not having a "UN Army," has almost no means of its own; neither does the CSCE; while the WEU's capabilities are only in the development stage. The Eurocorps will represent a real force (albeit still largely dependent on external C3I means) but it will not be suited for peacekeeping operations; only individual countries and military alliances have comprehensive military means. (Peacekeeping sections, departments, staffs etc, do not qualify as "military means.") The question then becomes: where can these international organisations find the means to conduct a peacekeeping operation? The answer is again obvious: short of developing their own permanent militaries (which implies huge financial and organisational headaches), international organisations simply must rely on assets belonging to individual nations and military alliances.

It can be argued that the availability of military means in itself yields political power: the power to veto an action through the denial of means. For example, the no fly zone over Bosnia could be maintained only with great difficulty if NATO and France refused to detach their AWACS planes for this purpose. Unfortunately, any such help has its price: by becoming dependent upon the means of external entities, the UN becomes susceptible to political pressure. This danger is illustrated by recent NATO attempts to impose rules of engagement (ROE) for NATO tactical airpower over Bosnia that are different from those of the UN. Since a change in the ROE could have a major impact upon the situation on the ground, there is the very real risk of the UN becoming the instrument of one or several military powers. Conversely, the same can be said of CIS peacekeeping operations and their dependence on Russian support.

After the breakup of the Soviet Union, Russia lost some of the best military assets of the Soviet army to the armies of newly-independent states, including many transport aircraft, elite divisions (such as the 103 Guards Airborne Division of Vitebsk, Belarus), and military production capabilities (such as a number of Antonov or Tupolev factories). However, Russia also took control of the main military intelligence assets such as the Main Intelligence Directorate of the General Staff (the GRU), all space-based intelligence means, airborne intelligence-collection means such as AWACS aircraft and other reconnaissance aircraft (MiG-25RBV, SU-24MR or M-17), signals intelligence means which have now been largely incorporated into Russia's Federal Agency for Government Communications and Information (the Russian analogue of the U.S. National Security Agency), etc.

The same is true for firepower. Russia retained the most capable means and forces (including 4 airborne divisions, 8 special designation brigades, 8 air assault brigades, most Interior Troops units, etc). The other states of the CIS currently only have the means and expertise to conduct smallscale operations with little intelligence-collection assets. Furthermore, Russia is also the most powerful CIS country in economic and political terms. As a result, all current CIS peacekeeping operations are Russian-controlled.[15]

Much has been written about the lack of "UN teeth" (that is, firepower). It is often forgotten, however, that besides being short on "teeth," the UN has no "eyes" and no "ears": no independent intelligence capability. This often overlooked issue is arguably even more important than firepower. While firepower can be needed in certain circumstances for a peacekeeping operation, intelligence is always crucial at all stages of a peacekeeping operation from the very beginning to its termination. Without accurate, timely and comprehensive intelligence, how can peacekeepers know how to assess the situation, how to build consensus, how to negotiate and with whom, what the warring factions are doing, etc?

In the Bosnian case, a number of absolutely crucial questions need to be answered before any decision regarding peacekeeping operations is made: who are the key people (if any) who on all three sides have most power, what exactly are the links between factions warring inside Bosnia and outside powers; to what type of arguments and/or pressures are the three parties susceptible? Besides these obvious questions, other, more specific items of information can be central to very far-reaching decisions: how effective is the trade embargo against Yugoslavia; how effective is the arms embargo; who organised the massacres of civilians inside Sarajevo; do the Bosnian Serbs have Scud missiles and could they launch them at Austria or Italy in case of intervention; could a Serb defeat in Bosnia trigger an uprising in Kosovo; how stable is the government of Slobodan Milosevic? Such examples can be listed almost endlessly.

The reality is that the United Nations is completely dependent upon NATO for most of its information. Of course, there are UN military observers in Bosnia. But while they can indeed observe troop movements or gather intelligence from conversations, they can hardly locate and monitor scrambled radio conversations or track helicopter flights. NATO could, of course, share some intelligence with the UN at different levels, as was the case in the operation in Somalia. The multinational intelligence flow architecture used by the U.S. during UNOSOM II comprised two levels of

---

15. James M. Greene, "The Peacekeeping Doctrines of the CIS," *Jane's Intelligence Review* (April 1993), pp. 156–59; Michael Orr, "Peacekeeping—A New Task for Russian Military Doctrine," *Jane's Intelligence Review* (July 1994), pp. 307–09.

information: level 1 (intelligence which is shown to but not retained by coalition or UN personnel), and level 2 (intelligence which has been cleared for release for coalition or UN personnel). Next to this official architecture, "informal" intelligence-sharing also takes place randomly. For example, according to the British-American Security Information Council:

> ...the international mediators in former Yugoslavia were not in receipt of NATO intelligence. Nevertheless, as individuals, each had informal access to national channels of information, through low level diplomatic traffic from their own national governments. Thus their level of private knowledge was quite high. UN Commanders in the field fared similarly, relying on their unofficial access to national intelligence. *Only the UN in New York was not informed at all.*[16]

This is very troublesome: first because such informal information is "sanitised" at best and subject to outright manipulation at worst; and second because fundamental decisions are taken precisely in New York.

Actually, the same problem is already present within NATO itself. It is little known that NATO is very dependent on U.S. C3I capabilities, particularly for the intelligence aspect.[17] Within NATO, however, the intelligence flow is not completely free either, and different degrees of classification and sanitation also exist. Hence the problem for the United Nations appears even more overwhelming: how can the UN operate if it relies on NATO (which is willing to release only sanitised information) for most of its information, while NATO is dependent upon the intelligence capabilities of the U.S. (which also carefully checks which information is passed on to NATO member-states). Keeping in mind that the U.S. has repeatedly stated that its single most important priority is the promotion of U.S. national interests (which is perfectly legitimate), what then is left of the UN requirements of impartiality, transparency and independence from any one single country?

This problem is unlikely to find a solution in the near future. If, for example, the U.S. National Security Agency had intercepted a telephone conversation between Bosnian Serb Army Commander General Ratko Mladic and the Chief of the Yugoslav Air Force in Belgrade during which different retaliatory options in case of a NATO air strike against the city of Pale had been discussed, how likely is it that this information would have been made available to the UN Security Council? In fact, who even within NATO would receive this information? And what would happen in the case of even more sensitive information (such as a hypothetical Security Council

---

16. *NATO, Peacekeeping, and the United Nations,* p. 53 (emphasis added).

17. See the chapter on "Command, Control, Communications and Intelligence," in Simon Duke, *United States Military Forces and Installations in Europe* (Oxford: Oxford University Press for SIPRI, 1989), pp. 324–50; Paul Stares and John Pike, "The Contribution of U.S. C3I to the Defence of NATO," in Jane M. O. Sharp, ed., *Europe After an American Withdrawal: Economic and Military Issues* (Oxford: Oxford University Press for SIPRI, 1990), pp. 400–28.

member-country covertly violating the arms embargo)? It is most likely that such information would simply not be released. This is a problem not just for the UN in New York, but also for UN commanders in the field.

Canadian General Lewis Mackenzie, former UN Commander in Bosnia, once said that UNPROFOR "had *absolutely no intelligence*" and that he "hoped that General [Sir Michael] Rose now had satellite imagery and signals intelligence from the international community to do his job."[18] While medium quality satellite imagery can be obtained from the private market at rather high cost, signal intelligence is impossible to find outside national militaries as they require not only expensive radio-electric equipment, but also specialised operators, translators, analysts, etc. In the case of Bosnia, other means (such as remotely controlled drones, high-altitude reconnaissance aircraft, AWACS aircraft, special operations reconnaissance teams, etc) have been used by the U.S. but their intelligence was not made available to the UN commanders on the ground.

The result of all this is a paradox: in a typically intelligence-intensive environment (such as most peacekeeping operations), the people who know the least are the political decision-makers in New York and the UN field commanders. One could always argue that if, for example, Britain, France Russia and the U.S. did have access to crucial information through their respective national intelligence-collection means, they would be able to make well-informed decisions at the Security Council. This is quite true, but it should be made clear that in this case, it would be a U.S.–UK–French–Russian decision *through* the Security Council and not a decision *of* the Council. If the UN in New York is not informed at all and if UNPROFOR has absolutely no intelligence, then what is left of the autonomy of the UN Security Council? Under such conditions, can the Security Council take independent decisions?

Unfortunately, there are few reasons to hope that this issue will be dealt with in the foreseeable future. For example, in his 1994 report about the work of the organisation, Secretary-General Boutros Boutros-Ghali wrote that although many member-states have made offers of personnel and resources, these offers had not yet covered deficiencies in the areas of "communications, health services, supply, engineers and transportation."[19] The issue of intelligence is conspicuously absent from this paper.

New technological advances, such as the U.S. *JSTARS* airborne ground mapping and surveillance system or the Russian *Zoopark* 3D phased-array artillery location radar, have made it possible to develop new means which

---

18. In a BBC Radio interview on 11 February 1994, quoted in *NATO, Peacekeeping and the United Nations*, pp. 51–52 (emphasis added).

19. Boutros-Ghali, *Report of the Secretary-General* (1994), p. 57.

could be extremely useful in peacekeeping operations. However, due to many reasons (costs, secrecy, etc) these systems are unlikely to be made available to the UN itself. In terms of human intelligence, the UN cannot develop its own intelligence agency either. It might be possible therefore to conclude that (1) the United Nations will continue to rely upon information obtained from individual states to make its decisions and (2) no real independent, transparent and unbiased debate will take place because some Security Council members will be better informed than others.

Conclusions and Recommendations

Actually, the reality is not necessarily quite as bleak as it seems. Indeed, the worst of the problems outlined above are primarily related to peace-enforcement options and are far less acute if looked at in the context of non-coercive or consensual peacekeeping.[20] This is true for a number of reasons.

First, if a consensual peacekeeping operation is taking place with the consent of all parties to the conflict, the risks of escalation are reduced. If one party was to hinder the operations of the peacekeeping force, the "sanction" against this party would be diplomatic condemnation (for formally agreeing to a peacekeeping mission and then undermining it) and a withdrawal of the peacekeeping force. Under such circumstances, the United States and other countries would be more willing to contribute forces because an escalation would be precluded from the outset. It is true that a withdrawal triggered by hostile actions could be perceived as a "retreat" and an admission of failure. However, if from the outset of the operation the possibility of such a withdrawal is openly announced, then it might appear more as a planned sanction than a reaction due to fear or panic. Besides, the worst option is to withdraw under fire after having failed in a peace-enforcement attempt and to leave the opposing force in control of the operation area.

Second, in a consensual peacekeeping operation, no firepower is needed

---

20. By non-coercive or consensual peacekeeping I mean those operations which provide a service to the parties of a conflict, such as the delivery of humanitarian aid (but not protection of aid convoys from anything larger than small bandits or plundering), the storage of weapons or monitoring of ceasefires (but not the enforcement of "safe areas"), or mediation among warring factions (but not the generation or imposition of peace plans). Such non-coercive or consensual peacekeeping actions would not require more firepower than small arms for the immediate self-protection of the peacekeeping force from criminal elements; and little more intelligence than that available from open sources or provided by the parties benefiting from the operation (which by assumption are all the parties to the conflict, since the operation is defined as consensual). If the consensus is lost, the operation would have to be terminated immediately and the forces withdrawn.

beyond the immediate self-protection of the peacekeepers. Actually, even this is far from certain: delegates of the International Red Cross have for many years operated in environments far more dangerous than UN peace-keepers without ever having any self-protection capability. In the case of the civil war in Rwanda, while the UN withdrew its personnel, the Red Cross actually sharply increased its presence in Kigali, even though it knew very well that a bloodbath was taking place and that its personnel in the country would have no protection whatsoever.

Third, C3I difficulties for a consensual peacekeeping operation are far less problematic than in the case of a peace-enforcement operation because it is precisely peace-enforcement operations which require the most sophis-ticated means (AWACS aircraft, signal intelligence, etc). The consensual peacekeeping environment is far less intelligence-intensive than one where combat actions might begin at any time, simply because far less contin-gencies have to planned for. The type of intelligence most needed for con-sensual peacekeeping operations can be obtained from open sources. There is a source of often very high-quality information and analysis of conflict areas which has been neglected both by nations and international organ-isations: humanitarian non-governmental organisations (NGOs) such as the Red Cross or Médecins Sans Frontières. It is often overlooked that while military or intelligence people might have a certain degree of expertise in any given area, only Red Cross delegates stake their lives solely on their under-standing of and contact with all factions involved in a conflict. Due to their obligation to remain neutral and impartial *(devoir de reserve),* Red Cross delegates are obviously not going to assist any force by providing it with operational intelligence, particularly not for peace-enforcement operations. However, they could be helpful in providing peacekeeping forces with an understanding of the local customs and culture. For example, if the Red Cross area specialists had been consulted about the situation in Somalia, a somewhat more sophisticated approach could have been used in dealing with General Mohamed Farah Aideed than bombing his head-quarters and putting out a bounty for his capture.

Fourth, consensual peacekeeping operation could be implemented without the great military powers. Many smaller nations with less military power have a vast and rich experience in UN peacekeeping missions, for example Canada, Egypt, Malaysia and Nepal. Obviously, such smaller nations do not have the firepower of the major military powers. It is precisely for this reason that they might devote much more effort to a negotiated solution than other nations which might be inclined to bomb their way out of the intricacies of a complex culture, history and conflict. Depending on the region, the creation of a purely regional peacekeeping force could be desirable. In such a case, richer countries could contribute primarily financially rather than by directly participating in the mission.

Furthermore, a UN peacekeeping military doctrine which would outline exactly possible peacekeeping missions, mandates, possible C3I variants, responsibility for ROEs, etc should be discussed and adopted by all states willing to participate in UN peacekeeping operations. Also, there should be a defined procedure by which peacekeeping operations would be decided upon. Obviously, meetings of the Security Council are not enough to ensure that all aspects of a crisis are assessed before decisions are taken.

Particular attention should be paid to the source of the information provided to the Security Council and to whether this information can be independently corroborated. Sources which have proven to be erroneous in the past should be accordingly rated and appraised. If an item of information has passed through numerous channels, every single one should be evaluated separately and the quality of the information judged by the quality of the least reliable one. Hence, a formal system of information evaluation should be adopted and made accessible to all governments. For information is at the core of C3I, and C3I is central to successful command and control of peacekeeping operations.

12

Regional Organisations and UN Peacekeeping

Amitav Acharya

Can regional organisations[1] make an important contribution to the peacekeeping operations of the United Nations? Answering this question is problematic for two reasons. First, since the very inception of the UN system, there have been doubts as to whether regional organisations complement or compete with the UN peace and security framework. The dual role of regionalism was clearly anticipated during the drafting of the UN's Charter at the San Francisco conference.[2] At this time, the so-called "universalists" viewed regional arrangements as a potential impediment to the realisation of a universal collective security system. The regionalists on the other hand argued that investing exclusive authority for settlement of international disputes in the Security Council would amount to "denying

---

1. Some of the better known multipurpose regional organisations today are: the Organisation of American States (OAS), the Arab League, the Organisation of African Unity (OAU), the North Atlantic Treaty Organisation (NATO), the Conference on Security and Cooperation in Europe (CSCE), the European Union (EU), the Western European Union (WEU), the Association of Southeast Asian Nations (ASEAN), the Gulf Cooperation Council (GCC), the South Asian Association of Regional Cooperation (SAARC), the South Pacific Forum, the Economic Community of West African States (ECOWAS), the Southern African Development Community (SADC), and the Organisation of Eastern Caribbean States (OECS).

2. For analyses of the universalist and regionalist positions, see: Francis W. Wilcox, "Regionalism and the United Nations," *International Organization* 19 (1965), pp. 789–811; Ernst Haas, "Regionalism, Functionalism and Universal Organization," *World Politics* 8 (January 1956), pp. 238–63; Inis Claude, *Swords into Plowshares* (New York: Random House, 1964), ch. 6; Norman J. Padelford, "Regional Organizations and the United Nations," *International Organization* 8 (1954), pp. 203–16; Lynn H. Miller, "The Prospect for Order Through Regional Security," in Richard A. Falk and Saul H. Mendlovitz, eds., *Regional Politics and World Order* (San Francisco: W. H. Freeman and Company, 1973).

permission to small states in regional groupings the chief responsibility for their own security."[3] The outcome of this debate was a compromise in which regional organisations were allowed a role in managing peace and security issues, albeit subject to the overall authority and jurisdiction of the UN. Thus the UN Charter listed mediation by regional agencies as one of the techniques of international conflict control (Article 33.1), while UN members were encouraged to "make every effort to achieve pacific settlement of local disputes through such regional arrangements" before taking the matter to the Security Council (Article 52.2).

Concerns that the peace and security role of regional organisations would undermine the UN's authority persisted over subsequent decades.[4] The emergence of regional alliances such as NATO and the Warsaw Pact (which qualified as regional agencies under the broad definition allowed by the UN Charter) was a direct response to the breakdown of the UN's peace and security role caused by the US–Soviet rivalry.[5] Even general-purpose regional groupings such as the OAS were found to be challenging the UN's authority in regional conflicts. As a later study by Haas concluded, throughout the Cold War period the relationship between the UN and regional groups was largely a competitive one. Haas concluded that in general, the effectiveness of the OAS declined sharply after the Dominican Republic crisis of 1965, coinciding with the emergence of the Soviet–Cuban alliance and the declining hegemony of the U.S. within the OAS; the Arab League's decline could be traced to the Camp David Accords in 1979; while for the OAU, a creditable performance during the 1966–75 period was followed by a poor record during the 1976–84 period.[6]

A second problem in assessing the role of regional organisations in peacekeeping is that their past involvement in such operations has been neither frequent nor, in most cases, successful. Almost by definition, peacekeeping remains a somewhat exclusive preserve of the UN. After all, peacekeeping, is "the deployment of a United Nations presence in the field...normally involving United Nations military and/or police personnel...."[7] Regional organisations that have been active in the area of peace and security have tended to focus broadly on the pacific settlement of

---

3. Miller, "Prospects for Peace Through Regional Security," p. 52.
4. Minerva M. Etzioni, *The Majority of One: Towards a Theory of Regional Compatibility* (Beverley Hills: Sage, 1970).
5. Ernst Haas, *Tangles of Hope: American Commitments and World Order* (Englewood Cliffs, NJ: Prentice Hall, 19), p. 93.
6. Ernst B. Haas, *Why We Still Need the United Nations* (Berkeley: Institute of International Studies, University of California, 1986), pp. 29–34.
7. Boutros Boutros-Ghali, *An Agenda for Peace: Preventive Diplomacy, Peacemaking and Peace-Keeping* (New York: UN, 1992).

disputes through mediation and conciliation, rather than on the more specific area of peacekeeping.[8] This is reflected not only in the limited number of peacekeeping missions undertaken exclusively by regional organisations to date, but also in their failure to develop capabilities and mechanisms required for peacekeeping. For example the charters of the OAU and the Arab League contain no specific provision for establishing peacekeeping operations. In general, peacekeeping operations by regional organisations are likely to suffer as much from their lack of resources and experience and inadequate institutional mechanisms as from the more obvious problems in overcoming intra-regional political differences in perspective and approach, the ever-present threat of external meddling and the problems of coordination between the UN and regional organisations.

These constraints were clearly highlighted in the case of the OAU's peacekeeping force in Chad.[9] The reasons behind the failure of this operation, which aimed at promoting national reconciliation in the civil war in Chad, was succinctly highlighted in a statement made to a UN meeting in Africa by Mamadou Bah, Director of the Political Department of the OAU:

1. The inexperience of the OAU in this field...there was no technical provision in the Charter of the OAU in that regard. The operation undertaken for Chad was simply promoted by United Nations examples, but without having the financial or technical resources...

2. Political differences of all kinds and interference by all and sundry.

(a) The role of the Force, although clearly defined, was not perceived in the same way

---

8. There is a vast literature on the role of regional organisations in the pacific settlement of disputes. See: Joseph S. Nye, *Peace in Parts: Integration and Conflict in Regional Organization* (Boston: Little, Brown, 1971), Ch. 5; Ernst Haas, Robert L. Butterworth and Joseph S. Nye, *Conflict Management by International Organization* (Morristown, NJ: General Learning Press, 1972); Ernst B. Haas, "Regime Decay: Conflict Management and International Organizations," *International Organization* 37 (Spring 1983), pp. 189–256; Mark W. Zacher, *International Conflicts and Collective Security, 1946–1977* (New York: Praeger, 1979); Leslie H. Brown, "Regional Collaboration in Resolving Third-World Conflicts," *Survival* 28 (May/June 1986), pp. 208–20; Boutros Boutros-Ghali, "The League of Arab States and the Organization of African Unity," in Yassin El-Ayouty, ed., *The Organization of African Unity After Ten Years: Comparative Perspectives* (New York: Praeger, 1975); Lau Teik Soon, *Conflict Resolution in ASEAN: The Sabah Issue* (Singapore: Department of Political Science, National University of Singapore, no date); S. O. Oshunbiyi, "The Role of ECOWAS in the Peaceful Settlement of Disputes," *Disarmament* 12 (Winter 1988/1989), pp. 67–72.

9. The OAU peacekeeping mission, sanctioned under the Lagos Agreement on national reconciliation in Chad of August 1979, was a multinational operation with troop contributions from Nigeria, Senegal, Kenya, Zaire, Benin, Congo and Guinea. For details of this operation see Amadu Sesay, "The OAU Peacekeeping Force in Chad: What Are the Lessons for the Future?" paper presented to the 30th Annual Convention of the International Studies Association, London, England, 28 March–1 April, 1989.

by the Heads of State of Chad at the time and by the OAU authorities.

(b) The Agreements were broken by various factions, either in bad faith or because of uncontrolled passion.

(c) African and non-African Powers, variously involved in the conflict, threw matters out of kilter and further complicated a situation, which was already extremely complex.

3. Pitiful dearth of financial and logistical resources.

(a) The OAU relied on voluntary contributions by its Member states; it was only able to find $400 000 out of a budget estimated at $162 298 500.

(b) The OAU turned to the United Nations. Unfortunately, for obvious political reasons, the OAU wished to retain sponsorship of the operation, whereas the Security Council refused to finance an operation which it did not control.[10]

Unlike the OAU members, those of the Arab League are not short of financial or military resources. But the League's peacekeeping operations during the Cold War period,[11] while successful in the 1961 Kuwaiti crisis, were marred in Lebanon by political conflicts between its member-states as well as lack of clear procedures for the settlement of regional disputes. The OAS, while possessing a well-developed institutional structure for peace-observation and peacekeeping operations, was perceived as an instrument of its dominant member, the U.S. Its most significant role in regional peace-keeping, in the Dominican Republic in 1965, was criticised as a legitimising cover for U.S. military intervention in that country.[12] In fact this episode, and the U.S. attempt to place a peacekeeping force in the last days of the Somoza regime in Nicaragua in 1979, led to such a deep mistrust of regional peacekeeping among the Latin American nations that in subsequent regional peace efforts the peacekeeping element had to be downplayed and redefined to highlight only the verification and technical aspects.[13]

In the final stages of the Cold War, as the UN's involvement in peace-keeping grew rapidly as a result of superpower cooperation in resolving regional conflicts, regional organisations played a marginal role in both the conflict resolution process and the resulting peacekeeping operations. The UN's success in ending several protracted conflicts (Afghanistan, the Iran–

---

10. Mamadou Bah, "Statement on the Maintenance of Regional Peace in Africa," UN Regional Disarmament Workshop for Africa, Lagos, Nigeria, 3–7 April 1989.

11. The Arab League has undertaken three major peacekeeping operations, first during the Kuwaiti crisis of 1961, and twice during the 1975–76 period in the Lebanese Civil War.

12. Paul F. Diehl, "Institutional Alternatives to Traditional U.N. Peacekeeping: An Assessment of Regional and Multinational Options," *Armed Forces and Society* 19 (Winter 1993), p. 211.

13. Jack Child, *The Central American Peace Process, 1983–1991* (Boulder: Lynne Rienner, 1992), p. 150.

Iraq War, Angola, Namibia, and Cambodia) contrasts sharply with the virtual irrelevance of the OAS in the Nicaragua–El Salvador conflict; the failure of the Arab League to deal with the Lebanese conflict, the Iran–Iraq War and the Iraqi invasion of Kuwait; and the OAU's lack of effectiveness in the Morocco–Polisario conflict. The only major exceptions to this trend are ECOWAS' peacekeeping operation in Liberia and the role of the Contadora and Esquipulas groups in promoting a resolution of the Central American conflict.

Regional Peacekeeping in the Post-Cold War Era

With the end of the Cold War, the outlook for regional peacekeeping operations seems brighter now than at any other point of time in the history of the UN system. A key contributing factor is the need for greater de-centralisation of the UN's peace and security functions. In recent years, UN peacekeeping operations have become more numerous, broader in scope and increasingly complex in functions. This, especially with the advent of electoral, rehabilitation and post-conflict peace-building activities, has imposed severe resources constraints on the organisation. The consequent political, financial and logistical problems encountered in several recent UN peacekeeping operations have created the rationale for a greater decentral-isation and delegation of UN peace and security operations with the involvement of regional organisations.

Another factor fuelling demand for regional peacekeeping concerns the democratisation of the UN's role in global peace and security. While the end of the Cold War might have given the UN a new lease of life, it continues to be seen by many countries as being dominated by a handful of Western powers. The developing countries in particular want an expansion of the permanent membership of the Security Council to include some from their own ranks. As the resistance of the major industrial powers makes this a remote possibility, developing countries see regional arrangements as the kind of fora in which they may be able to exercise greater control over multilateral peace and security operations, including peacekeeping and conflict resolution.

In addition, peacekeeping by regional organisations offers several advantages in compensating for the existing deficiencies of the UN mech-anism. Many recent UN peacekeeping operations have suffered from a lack of familiarity with the particular conflict situation. Regional organisations could provide a better understanding of conflicts in their respective areas. Similarly, with a smaller and more homogeneous membership with simi-larities in history, culture, language, level of development and, in some cases, political outlook, regional organisations are perhaps in a better position to reach a consensus on peacekeeping operations within their jurisdiction. Similarly, regional peacekeeping might receive greater local support, since states and peoples are generally wary of intervention by "outsiders," including the UN, in local conflicts. Last but not least, regional organisations are better able to provide early-warning, information-gathering and fact-finding, all of which are critical to the success of any peacekeeping operation.

The UN authorities no longer see regional arrangements as a threat to the authority of the UN system. Instead, their potential to contribute to UN peacekeeping and other functions has been given explicit recognition by the UN Secretary General in his *Agenda for Peace:*

> In the past, regional arrangements often were created because of the absence of a universal system for collective security; thus their activities could on occasion work at cross-purposes with the sense of solidarity required for the effectiveness of the world Organization. But in this new era of opportunity, regional arrangements or agencies can render great service if their activities are undertaken in a manner consistent with the Purposes and Principles of the Charter...
>
> What is clear...is that regional arrangements and agencies in many cases possess a potential that should be utilized in serving the functions [of]...preventive diplomacy, peace-keeping, peacemaking and post-conflict peace-building. Under the Charter, the Security Council has and will continue to have primary responsibility for maintaining international peace and security, but regional action as a matter of decentralization, delegation and cooperation with United Nations efforts could not only lighten the burden of the Council but also contribute to a deeper sense of participation, consensus and democratization in international affairs.[14]

A particularly striking example of regional peacekeeping in the post-Cold War era is the ECOWAS role in the Liberian civil war, an operation which was initiated at a time when the UN was preoccupied with the Iraqi invasion of Kuwait. In August 1990, an ECOWAS monitoring group (ECOMOG), with troops drawn from Gambia, Ghana, Nigeria and Sierra Leone, was sent to Liberia with a mandate to bring about a ceasefire between rival factions, restore public order and establish an interim government pending elections. Although the 4000-strong force (later raised to 8000 and then to 11 000), failed to prevent the capture and killing of Liberian President Samuel Doe in September 1990, it was able to arrange a temporary ceasefire and install an interim President. A new ceasefire agreement was signed in February 1991, followed by the establishment of a temporary government by a national conference organised by ECOWAS. While the ECOWAS force was unable to pacify the whole country (much of the territory remains in rebel hands), the ECOWAS operation has been far more successful than the

---

14. Boutros-Ghali, *An Agenda for Peace*, paras. 63–64.

ill-fated OAU peacekeeping operation in Chad.[15]

The ECOWAS mission may also be a major turning point in African regionalism. The conflict control mechanisms of the OAU Charter, such as its Commission of Mediation, Conciliation and Arbitration, were designed almost exclusively with inter-state disputes in mind. The ECOWAS mission in Liberia, on the other hand, "represented a new experiment in which an African regional organisation crossed that hitherto sacred boundary between internal affairs of states and matters more permissible for collaborative action."[16] In June 1993 an OAU summit in Cairo agreed to create a mechanism for preventing, managing and resolving African conflicts.[17] Among other things, this mechanism is intended to organise African peacekeeping operations in close cooperation with the UN. In 1991, the OAU Council of Ministers approved, for the first time, a budget for use in functions related to conflict resolution. In March 1992, the OAU set up a new division of "conflict management" within its secretariat to prepare for peacekeeping missions.[18] The OAU Secretary-General, in a report on "Proposals for Resolving Conflicts in Africa," submitted to the OAU Summit in Dakar in July 1992, called for the institutionalisation of the Bureau of the Assembly of Heads of State and Government so that it can authorise peacekeeping operations.[19]

Interest in peacekeeping is also evident on the part of other regional groups. In the Middle East the Arab League, which was dealt a severe blow by its inability to prevent the Iraqi invasion of Kuwait and the subsequent US-led attack on Iraq, has nonetheless established a committee to examine the possibility of establishing a peacekeeping force within the League.[20]

In Europe the CSCE, under the provisions of the Helsinki Document of 1992, is authorised to call upon the military resources of other European regional groups, such as NATO, the EU and the WEU, for regional peacekeeping operations. But the CSCE's peacekeeping provisions are somewhat more restrictive than those of the UN. Under the 1992 Rome Council provisions, the CSCE provides institutional legitimacy and monitoring and

15. "Economic Community of West African States," *Europa Yearbook: Africa: South of Sahara, 1992* (London, Europa, 1992), p. 185; "Liberia: Imposing Peace," *Economist* (London), 18 August 1990, pp. 35–36; "Liberians Sign Truce, A First Step," *International Herald Tribune*, 30 November 1990, p. 2; "Liberia's Cowboys," *Economist*, 13 October 1990, p. 51; Gerald Bourke, "In Nigeria, the Talks Get Serious," *International Herald Tribune*, 4 July 1991, p. 6.

16. Oluyemi Adenji, "Regionalism in Africa," *Security Dialogue* 24 (June 1993), p. 215.

17. Gareth Evans, *Cooperating for Peace* (Sydney: Allen and Unwin, 1993), p. 31.

18. "Africa's Peace-Force Project," *Economist Foreign Report*, 4 March 1993, p. 7.

19. Adenji, "Regionalism in Africa," p. 218.

20. "Arab League Secretary-General Calls for Formation of Arab Peace-Keeping Force," BBC, *Summary of World Broadcasts*, ME/1694/A, 21 May 1993, Part 4.

operating principles, but does not have an independent peacekeeping capability.[21] The primary responsibility for supporting UN peacekeeping operations in the Balkans has therefore fallen on the hands of NATO, the one regional organisation with the most developed capacity and resources for peacekeeping. In June 1992 members of the North Atlantic Council stated their willingness "to support, on a case by case basis in accordance with their own procedures, peacekeeping activities under [CSCE] responsibility."

NATO has made a similar declaration of support for peacekeeping operations undertaken by the UN Security Council.[22] To make good its pledge, NATO has provided support to the UN's operation in the Balkans in a variety of ways, such as deploying a naval force in the Mediterranean to enforce UN economic sanctions in the region and monitoring the no fly zone over Bosnia–Herzegovina. It has also advised the UN on the provision of humanitarian assistance, the monitoring of heavy weapons, the establishment of relief zones and the prevention of a spillover of the Bosnian conflict.[23] While many of these operations fall under the category of enforcement, rather than peacekeeping *per se,* they provide valuable support to the UN's overall peacekeeping mission in the area. NATO has also adopted a number of measures to enhance its peacekeeping capability in such areas as command and control, logistic support, infrastructure, training and exercises. In recognition of the importance of peacekeeping to NATO's future role, the North Atlantic Cooperation Council (NACC) has established an Ad Hoc Group on Cooperation in Peacekeeping with the aim of advancing "discussion and consensus on general principles, political and conceptual issues, and practical measures for cooperation" in peacekeeping.[24]

Eastern Europe has seen a different kind of regional peacekeeping effort, undertaken by the Commonwealth of Independent States (CIS). In March 1992 the CIS member-states signed an agreement entitled "Groups of Military Observers and Collective Peacekeeping Forces in the CIS" which authorised peacekeeping operations "for the purpose of providing each other assistance...in settling and preventing conflicts on the territory of any member of the Commonwealth."[25] A CIS peacekeeping force of 1500, consisting of Russian, Georgian and Ossetian troops was dispatched to

21. Janie Leatherman, *A Contingency Model of Third Party Institutional Interventions: Assessing the Effectiveness of the CSCE as a Regional Organization,* Working Paper Series (Notre Dame, Indiana: Joan B. Kroc Institute for International Peace Studies, University of Notre Dame, 1994), p. 19.

22. *NATO's Role in Crisis Management and Peacekeeping* (Brussels: NATO Office of Information and Press, July 1993).

23. *NATO and Peacekeeping* (Brussels: NATO Headquarters, undated).

24. *NATO's Role in Crisis Management and Peacekeeping,* p. 4.

25. Kevin A. O'Brien, "Russian Peacekeeping in the Near Abroad," *Peacekeeping and International Relations* (July–August 1994), pp. 14–16.

South Ossetia in July 1992, while another CIS force from Russia, Moldova, Romania and Ukraine was deployed in Trans-Dniester in 1992. Russian peacekeepers have been also been deployed to Tajikistan to provide protection to the civilian protection.[26]

Problems and Difficulties

Despite the growing interest in regional peacekeeping in the post-Cold War era, several difficult challenges remain. First, few regional organisations have the necessary military and institutional structures required for peacekeeping. As noted, NATO and, to a lesser extent, the OAS, are important exceptions to this. The Arab League's institutional structure contains a Joint Defence Council and a Permanent Military Commission, but no standing force.[27] The OAU Charter provides for a Defence Commission, but this has never been activated. Proposals for an African High Command for collective defence and peacekeeping have never been seriously pursued.[28] The GCC has developed a "rapid deployment force"[29] which could be used for peacekeeping operations. But political rivalry between Saudi Arabia and the smaller GCC members might preclude this. The OECS members are part of a "Regional Security System" based in Barbados, which coordinates measures to improve the internal and external security of its members.[30] But this force by itself is inadequate to meet the challenge of

26. Roger Hill, "Preventive Diplomacy, Peace-Making and Peace-Keeping," in *SIPRI Yearbook 1993* (New York: Oxford University Press, 1993), p. 58.

27. The limitations of the League's Treaty for Joint Defence and Economic Cooperation, adopted in 1950, are summarised by one scholar in the following terms: "In spite of the theoretical significance of this treaty, it amounts in practice to very little. First, the treaty is not considered a part of the charter [of the League], and membership of it was left optional. Second, it failed to grant the League an independent armed force under its command. In fact, the goals of the treaty were thus aborted even at the moment of its signing since it shared with all the League's decisions the lack of effective means of implementation, other than the free will of member states. The same fate afflicted a series of decisions made by the summit conferences since 1964 which established a joint command of Arab Armed Forces. While this command exists in theory, it does not possess any independent power." Mohammed El Sayed Said, "The Arab League: Between Regime Security and National Liberation," in Mohammed Ayoob, ed., *Regional Security in the Third World* (London: Croom Helm, 1986), p. 259.

28. T. A. Imobighe, "An African High Command: the Search for a Feasible Strategy of Continental Defence," *African Affairs* 79 (April 1980), pp. 241–54; B. David Meyers, "An Analysis of the OAU's Effectiveness at Regional Collective Defense," in Yassin El-Ayouty, ed., *The Organization of African Unity After Ten Years: Comparative Perspectives* (New York: Praeger, 1975), pp. 118–32.

29. Laura Guazzone, "Gulf Cooperation Council: The Security Policies," *Survival* 30 (1988), pp. 134–48; Amitav Acharya, *The Gulf Cooperation Council and Security: Dilemmas of Dependence, 1981–88*, Contemporary Strategic Issues in the Arab Gulf No.1 (London: Gulf Centre for Strategic Studies, 1989).

30. David A. Simmons, "Militarization of the Caribbean: Concerns for National and

peacekeeping and has had to rely on the superior resources of a large power, such as the U.S., as evident in Grenada and Haiti.

ASEAN, despite a creditable record in political cooperation, has traditionally shied away from any collective defence structure. Its members prefer to keep intra-regional military cooperation informal and mostly bilateral.[31] Thus it was not surprising that ASEAN members did not find it necessary to deploy a joint peacekeeping force to support the UN Transitional Authority in Cambodia, one of the largest UN peacekeeping operations ever. But recently ASEAN has shown an interest in increasing cooperation with the UN in areas of preventive diplomacy and peacekeeping. Among the more specific proposals in this regard is the idea of a regional peacekeeping centre. Such a centre could be used to train ASEAN and other regional personnel for UN peacekeeping missions worldwide. It could also serve as a vehicle for multilateral military exchanges and cooperation within ASEAN itself, although this aspect has proven to be controversial.[32]

The South Pacific has seen its first peacekeeping venture stalled. When Sir Julius Chan was prime minister of Papua New Guinea (PNG) in 1980, he had floated the idea of a regional peacekeeping force to be organised by the South Pacific Forum. Although the idea proved stillborn then, Sir Julius was able to return to it when he became prime minister for a second time in August 1994. One of his first acts was to sign a ceasefire with the Bougainville Revolutionary Army (BRA) which had been fighting a secessionist war over Bougainville for six years. The ceasefire was signed in Honiara, Solomon Islands on 8 September and went into effect the next day. As part of the accord, a 400-strong South Pacific peacekeeping force, comprising troops from Fiji, Tonga and Vanuatu under Australian command, was organised and deployed to Bougainville in October. A peace conference opened in Arawa, Bougainville on 10 October amidst tension caused by the shooting of three PNG soldiers and the retaliatory shooting of a BRA rebel on the previous day. As the talks broke down under the weight of mutual distrust and suspicion, a secessionist spokesman Moses Havini warned that

---

Regional Security," *International Journal* 40 (Spring 1985), pp. 348–76; Gary P. Lewis, "Prospects for a Regional Security System in the Eastern Caribbean," *Millennium: Journal of International Studies* 15 (Spring 1986), pp. 167–83.

31. Amitav Acharya, *A Survey of Military Cooperation Among the ASEAN States: Bilateralism or Alliance?* Occasional Paper No.14 (Toronto: Centre for International and Strategic Studies, York University, April 1990); J. N. Mak, *Directions for Greater Defence Cooperation* (Kuala Lumpur: Institute for International and Strategic Studies, 1986).

32. Jusuf Wanandi, "Regional Peacekeeping: ASEAN's Role and Contribution," paper presented to the Third Workshop on ASEAN–UN Cooperation in Peace and Preventive Diplomacy, Bangkok, 17–18 February 1994.

the peacekeepers could be in danger.[33]

In general, regional organisations face a number of obstacles in developing collective military structures for peacekeeping operations. These include differing levels of military capabilities, variations in weapon systems, doctrines and procedures, divergent threat perceptions, and incongruent political and security interests among their members.[34] In the absence of a collective institutional capacity, peacekeeping operations by regional organisations have to rely heavily on the resources of their largest or most powerful member-state. This has the potential to make peacekeeping a highly divisive issue within a regional grouping, especially if the dominant regional partner is seen to be using peacekeeping as a pretext for advancing its own interests and influence. This problem is highlighted in the ECOWAS operation in Liberia which is dominated by Nigerian troops and financial support. (ECOWAS as an organisation was able to provide only $3m out of the total $50m operation, with the remainder coming mostly from Nigeria.) Nigerian dominance is resented by most of ECOMOG's French-speaking members as well as Ghana.[35] Similarly, the peacekeeping operations undertaken by the CIS in South Ossetia, eastern Moldova and Tajikistan are dominated by Russian troops, with only token contributions by other CIS members. They have been plagued by accusations that they protect the interests of the Russian minority in the area at the expense of other segments of the local population.[36]

Partly because of their perceived lack of impartiality, regional peacekeeping efforts have a special problem in dealing with internal conflicts.[37] Small states within regional groupings are especially unwilling to abandon the time-honoured doctrine of non-interference in internal affairs so as to permit regional peacekeeping efforts in such conflicts.[38] But these are precisely the kind of conflicts that are, and will remain, the focus of peacekeeping efforts in the post-Cold War period. The number of peacekeeping operations in internal conflicts has risen dramatically, with 21 out of

---

33. This paragraph has been inserted by Ramesh Thakur, one of the editors, after the completion of the chapter by the author. It is based on accounts in the *Pacific Islands Monthly* (October 1994), p. 11 and the *Otago Daily Times* (Dunedin), 14 and 17 October 1994.

34. Amitav Acharya, "Regional Military–Security Cooperation in the Third World: A Conceptual Analysis of the Association of Southeast Asian Nations," *Journal of Peace Research* 29 (February 1992), pp. 7–21.

35. "Ganging up on Nigeria," *Economist Foreign Report*, 18 July 1991, pp. 6–7.

36. Mats R. Berdal, *Whither UN Peacekeeping* (London: International Institute for Strategic Studies, Adelphi Paper No. 281, 1991), p. 68.

37. Linda B. Miller, "Regional Organization and the Regulation of Internal Conflict," *World Politics* 19 (July 1967), pp. 582–600.

38. S. Neil MacFarlane and Thomas G. Weiss, "Regional Organizations and Regional Security," *Security Studies* 2 (Autumn 1992), p. 31.

23 UN peacekeeping missions established between January 1992 and mid-1993 dealing with an internal conflict.[39] While regional organisations may claim a greater familiarity with peace and security issues in their respective areas, their ability to control internal conflicts is far from impressive.[40] This situation is unlikely to change and could prove to be the single most important impediment to regional peacekeeping efforts in the post-Cold War period.

Peacekeeping and Preventive Diplomacy

Given the constraints on peacekeeping operations by regional organisations, in what other ways could they contribute to the UN's peace and security role? The answer may lie in the notion of preventive diplomacy.[41] The UN Secretary-General defines preventive diplomacy as "action to prevent disputes from arising between parties, to prevent existing disputes from escalating into conflicts and to limit the spread of the latter when they occur."[42] His notion of preventive diplomacy is specifically distinguished from other types of UN action, such as "peacemaking," "peace-keeping" and "peace-building."[43] Regional organisations are considered to be suitable agents for preventive diplomacy. *An Agenda for Peace* specifically notes that preventive diplomacy may "be performed by the Secretary-General personally or through senior staff or specialized agencies and programmes, by the Security Council or the General Assembly, *and by regional organizations in cooperation with*" the UN (emphasis added).[44]

The exercise of preventive diplomacy involves a broad range of measures such as:[45]

• Confidence-building;

---

39. Alan James, "Internal Peacekeeping: A Dead End for the UN?" *Security Dialogue* 24 (December 1993), p. 359.
40. See Nye, *Peace in Parts*, Ch. 5.
41. Victor Issraelyan, "Preventive Diplomacy and Maintenance of Peace," in John P. Renniger, ed., *The Future of the United Nations in an Interdependent World* (Boston: Martinus Nijhoff, 1989).
42. Boutros-Ghali, *An Agenda for Peace*, para. 20.
43. *An Agenda for Peace* defines "peacemaking" as "action to bring hostile parties to agreement," while "peace-keeping" involves "the deployment of a United Nations presence in the field, hitherto with the consent of all the parties concerned, normally involving United Nations military and/or police personnel and frequently civilians as well." "Peace-building," a major innovation of *An Agenda for Peace*, is "action to identify and support structures which will tend to strengthen and solidify peace in order to avoid a relapse into conflict." *Ibid.*
44. *Ibid.*, para. 23.
45. Amitav Acharya, "Preventive Diplomacy: Issues and Institutions in the Asia Pacific Region," paper presented to the Eighth Asia-Pacific Roundtable, Kuala Lumpur, 6–8 June 1994.

- Early-warning (monitoring of developments in political, military and other areas);
- Preventive humanitarian action (preventing and managing the humanitarian costs of political conflicts as well as the political and humanitarian consequences of naturally-occurring phenomena);
- Fact-finding (the collection and analysis of timely and reliable information on conflict situations);
- Dispatch of good offices and goodwill missions (undertaken before or at the onset of a crisis and involving the dispatch of senior officials); and
- Crisis-management (action in reducing the immediate possibility of violent action in a conflict situation which may require measures such as reconciliation, mediation and arbitration).

These are precisely the kinds of measures which regional organisations might have a "comparative advantage" in undertaking. Indeed, regional organisations may be better able to mobilise the resources required for a preventive diplomacy role than for peacekeeping operations:

> The logical approach [for regional organisations] is to concentrate on fulfilling their roles in areas in which they have comparative advantage. These areas are early warning, information gathering and preventive diplomacy. As neighbors with deep interests in preserving regional peace and stability, regional states would be better informed on incipient conflicts and be able to provide continuous information to the United Nations on developments and dangerous trends.[46]

It is worth noting that in contrast to their poor record in peacekeeping, regional organisations have in the past been far more active and successful at preventive diplomacy. Examples of successful preventive action by the three major general-purpose regional organisations (the OAS, the OAU and the Arab League) include:

- The Arab League's mediation in the Iraq–Kuwait dispute over the former's claim to the latter;
- The OAU's role in disputes between Algeria and Morocco (1963), Ethiopia and Somalia (1964) and Rwanda and Burundi (1967); and
- The OAS' mediation in conflicts between Costa Rica and Nicaragua (1948 and again in 1955), Honduras and Nicaragua (1957), Panama and Cuba (1959), Venezuela and the Dominican Republic (1960)

---

46. Mark Hong, "The Role of Regional Groupings and Bodies in Cooperation with the United Nations," paper prepared for the Second Workshop on ASEAN–UN Cooperation for Peace and Preventive Diplomacy, Singapore, 6–7 July 1993, p. 4.

and Haiti and the Dominican Republic (1963).[47]

The end of the Cold War has prompted many regional organisations to enhance their role in preventive diplomacy in close cooperation with the UN. In Europe, for example, the CSCE has declared itself as a regional arrangement within the scope of chapter VIII of the UN Charter. In May 1993, it signed an agreement with the UN providing for mutual cooperation and coordination on peace and security issues. The CSCE and the UN have already cooperated in sending observer and mediation missions to trouble-spots in the former Soviet republics. Indeed, the UN Secretary-General has identified the UN–CSCE cooperation in the post-Cold War era as an example of "a new division of labour with regional organisations."[48]

In Africa, in 1990 ECOWAS created a Standing Mediation Committee to facilitate pacific settlement of disputes among its members.[49] Another notable African regional initiative is the 1991 Kampala Declaration for the Creation of a Conference on Security, Stability, Development and Co-operation in Africa (CSSDCA), jointly sponsored by the OAU, the UN Economic Commission for Africa and the African Leadership Forum.[50]

In Latin America, the efforts of the OAS in promoting respect for human rights and democracy, as evident in the "the Santiago Commitment to Democracy and the Renewal of the Inter-American System," are aimed at preventing future domestic and regional instability.[51] Among other things, the OAS and the UN organised a joint effort to send a special envoy and an international human rights commission to Haiti.

In Southeast Asia, ASEAN has taken the lead in creating a forum for dialogue on regional security issues among the principal Asian–Pacific nations. The 18-member ASEAN Regional Forum (ARF), which held its first meeting in July 1994, seeks to reduce regional tensions by initiating transparency and confidence-building measures and promoting a regional

---

47. Haas, *Why We Still Need the United Nations*, p. 31.

48. Boutros Boutros-Ghali, "UN Peacekeeping in a New Era: A New Chance for Peace," *The World Today* 49 (April 1993), p. 68.

49. See Igezundia Abutudu, "Regime Change, Political Instability and Economic Integration in West Africa: The Experience of ECOWAS," *Nigerian Journal of International Affairs* 16:1 (1990), pp. 90–107. See also the series of articles under the section on "Conflict Resolution, Crisis Prevention and Management and Confidence-Building in West Africa," *Disarmament: A Periodic Review by the United Nations* 12 (Winter 1988/1989).

50. Adenji, "Regionalism in Africa," pp. 211–20.

51. The OAS foreign ministers, in a joint declaration at Santiago in June 1991, stressed their "uncompromising commitment to the defense of democracy" and to the renewal of the OAS as "the political forum for dialogue, understanding, and cooperation among all countries in the hemisphere"; Robert B. Andersen, "Inter-IGO Dynamics in the Post-Cold War Era: The OAS and the UN," paper prepared for the 1994 Annual Convention of the International Studies Association, Washington, DC, 28 March–1 April 1994, p. 2.

"code of conduct" based on the 1976 Treaty of Amity and Cooperation in Southeast Asia.[52] ASEAN has also completed a series of high-level workshops, entitled "ASEAN-UN Cooperation in Peace and Preventive Diplomacy," which have enhanced its members' knowledge of the role of the UN system in regional security and generated valuable ideas and proposals concerning peacekeeping, preventive diplomacy and multilateralism.[53]

To be sure, regional efforts at preventive diplomacy are yet to prove effective in the post-Cold War milieu. In Somalia (and subsequently in Rwanda), the relevant regional organisation, the OAU, not only failed to alert the international community to the impending tragedy, but was also "largely irrelevant" in responding to the humanitarian needs, national reconciliation processes and peacekeeping efforts.[54] The disappointing role of regional organisations in undertaking preventive action in Somalia and Haiti seems to have dampened the UN Secretary-General's initial enthusiasm for regional peace and security efforts. In an interview with the *Washington Times,* he noted:

> In Somalia, I constantly invited in representatives of the Arab League, the Muslim Conference, the European Union. I said, "Please help us." In Haiti, I welcomed the Organization of American States to do something about the problem. This is decentralization. But something new is happening in the world that they do not want to do it—or they don't believe in regional or subregional arrangements.[55]

The Task Ahead

Clearly, more needs to be done to increase the level of interaction and cooperation between regional organisations and the United Nations to enhance the capacity of both in preventive diplomacy and peacekeeping. A number of practical measures might be suggested. These include:

1. Securing observer status for regional organisations in the UN;
2. Establishing formal links between regional organisations and the UN

---

52. Peter Ho Hak Ean, "The ASEAN Regional Forum: The Way Forward," paper presented to the Third Workshop on ASEAN–UN Cooperation in Peace and Preventive Diplomacy, Bangkok, 17–18 February 1994.

53. Amitav Acharya, "ASEAN–UN Cooperation in Peace and Preventive Diplomacy: Its Contribution to Regional Security," Report prepared for the Co-Chairmen of the Workshop Series on ASEAN–UN Cooperation in Peace and Preventive Diplomacy, March 1994.

54. Jeffrey Clark, "Debacle in Somalia," *Foreign Affairs* 72 (America and the World 1992–93), p. 116; Samuel M. Makinda, *Seeking Peace From Chaos: Humanitarian Intervention in Somalia,* Occasional Paper Series, International Peace Academy (Boulder: Lynne Rienner for the International Peace Academy, 1993), p. 84.

55. "The World as Viewed from the U.N. Helm," *Washington Times,* 3 April 1994, p. B4.

Secretariat;

3. Inviting the UN Secretary-General to attend important meetings of regional organisations;

4. Conducting regular meetings between representatives of regional organisations and the members of the UN Security Council and the Secretariat;

5. Action by the UN Secretary-General in sending periodic fact-finding missions to the headquarters and member-state capitals of regional organisations;

6. Promoting closer cooperation between multipurpose regional organisations and the UN Regional Commissions;

7. Developing early-warning centres within regional organisations which will bring to the attention of the UN any developments affecting regional peace and security; and

8. Increasing cooperation between regional organisations and the UN in providing information on preventive diplomacy and peacekeeping to both the general public and policymakers in the region.[56]

Implementation of these measures will not remove all the constraints on regional peacekeeping efforts, but it will help the realisation of hopes for a meaningful post-Cold War division of labour between the UN and the regional organisations. Such a division of labour might be the best case scenario for regional organisations as they struggle to define their role in the post-Cold War international security order. Because of the range of political, legal, institutional and resource constraints discussed above, regional organisations cannot pursue a unilateral role in peacekeeping. But they can make an important contribution to regional security by concentrating on preventive diplomacy, where they might have a comparative advantage, and which, if successfully undertaken, will do much to reduce the need for UN peacekeeping operations.

---

56. Many of these ideas were discussed at the ASEAN–UN workshops and can be found in Nitya Pibulsonggram, "ASEAN–UN Cooperation in Peace and Preventive Diplomacy: Linkage with the United Nations," paper presented to the Third Workshop on ASEAN–UN Cooperation in Peace and Preventive Diplomacy, Bangkok, 17–18 February 1994.

13

Peacekeeping in Civil Wars

Paul F. Diehl

The end of the Cold War and the much-heralded emergence of a new world order has moderated the threats to international security imposed by the superpower rivalry. But it has also altered the scope and types of roles that the United Nations is asked to assume. The most prominent among these, for the purposes of this chapter, is the shift in threats to global peace from those that have historically been interstate to ones that involve a primary or significant civil or internal component. In this chapter, the unique problems associated with UN peacekeeping in civil conflicts are explored, with the goal of identifying potential pitfalls as well as guidelines for future success in the challenges of this new era. For although there may be agreement that the United Nations will play a more central role in the 1990s and beyond, this is no guarantee that it will always be successful.

Of the fifteen UN peacekeeping and observation missions launched before 1989 (often considered the symbolic date for the end of the Cold War), only six might be considered as having had to deal with significant civil conflict as part of their mandates. By contrast, since 1989, twelve of the thirteen UN peacekeeping and observation missions have involved civil war-related issues.[1] Beyond the increase in concentration on civil wars, UN peacekeeping has had to adapt to the challenges and roles occasioned by that shift. When intervening in civil wars, in addition to simply mitigating the armed violence, the United Nations must attempt a redefinition of national sovereignty[2] as well as confront peacemaking concerns. Furthermore,

---

1. For the latest survey of UN peacekeeping operations, see United Nations, *United Nations Peace-Keeping* (New York: United Nations Department of Public Information, 1993).

2. Michael Barnett, "The New UN Politics of Peace: From Juridical Sovereignty to Empirical Sovereignty," *Global Governance* 1 (Winter 1995), forthcoming.

peacekeeping in civil conflicts requires an expansion of roles beyond tradi-tional operations of the past. Traditional peacekeeping operations involved the stationing of lightly-armed troops as an interposition force separating combatants following a ceasefire. So-called "second generation" peace-keeping operations[3] have expanded the roles of peacekeeping to include, among others, humanitarian assistance and election supervision. These new missions pose problems not commonly found with traditional peacekeeping operations and may require a rethinking of the basic premises underlying UN peacekeeping.

To understand the challenges for UN peacekeeping posed by civil wars, this chapter first identifies the key factors associated with peacekeeping success and failure. Then these factors are examined in light of the contex-tual variables related to civil wars. Discussion centres on concerns inherent in all civil conflicts as well as those specific to certain UN peacekeeping roles (e.g., humanitarian assistance). In the concluding section, some policy relevant suggestions are offered for understanding how best to use UN peacekeeping operations in civil conflicts.

Success and Failure in Peacekeeping Operations

The success of a peacekeeping operation is largely a function of its ability to limit armed conflict during its deployment and promote the conditions for long-term stability after the peacekeeping force leaves. In achieving these goals, there are a range of factors associated with that success, or its absence, and these include conditions related to the deployment as well as local conditions. Here, I review some of the most important factors—neutrality, geography, third-party cooperation and peacemaking—and relate them to a UN peacekeeping force in the context of a civil conflict.

Neutrality

Among the fundamental principles of UN peacekeeping forces is that they maintain their neutrality and perform their missions in an impartial manner. Neutrality of the troops is an essential ingredient of peacekeeping success for several reasons. Neutral troops are more likely to be accepted by the parties involved and thereby give them greater confidence in the peacekeeping operation. It is hard to imagine a disputant accepting or supporting a peacekeeping operation composed of troops that might be viewed as hostile to its interests. Furthermore, neutral troops are less likely

---

3. John Mackinlay and Jarat Chopra, "Second Generation Multinational Operations," *Washington Quarterly* 15 (Summer 1992), pp. 113–34.

to stir controversy during the course of their deployment. Disputants will be less likely to attribute the actions of the peacekeeping force to the interests of the nations that supplied the troops. Even if the troops behave in a neutral fashion, that behaviour has to be perceived as such by the disputants for the troops to complete their mission. Neutral composition removes one source of blame that can be used to justify hostile actions against, or non-support of, a peacekeeping force. By virtue of prior agreement with the host states, peacekeeping personnel are generally only subject to their home states' jurisdictions for criminal offences; this is further reason for peacekeeping troops to have the trust of the host state. If a peacekeeping force is composed of interested parties and those troops openly favour one side or the other in the conflict, then there is bound to be an escalation in violence and casualties.

Civil wars may complicate the ability of UN peacekeeping forces to maintain their neutrality. Some of this is inherent in the context that civil war presents. Peacekeeping always favours the *status quo* at the time of the deployment, but this is particularly important in civil conflict. A ceasefire and the insertion of peacekeeping forces relieves some pressure on the challenged government; the government may also gain some political capital with the populace, who may long for stability in the country. In the eyes of the rebel groups, however, peace means continued domination of the government by the *status quo* elites.

This is not to say that some groups may not support peacekeeping forces. Yet civil conflict poses two distinctive problems. Not all groups may find it in their interest to have a ceasefire. Paradoxically, a ceasefire in Bosnia in 1993 may have been objectionable both to Serbs and Muslims. The Serbs preferred to expand territorial gains, and the Muslims rejected a peace plan that would have stopped the fighting but resulted in a significant loss of territory. Even those that do agree with the peacekeeping deployment may only support the ceasefire and the peacekeeping forces for a short period of time. The threat of violence is their principal mechanism to force concessions from an opponent. Long-term deployment of peacekeeping forces and the limitation of armed conflict without political change is inimical to the interests of some groups. By contrast, participants in an interstate dispute may be more willing to tolerate a freezing of the *status quo* over a longer time frame. In those circumstances, the government elites at least retain their domestic power and do not have to make genuine concessions to their foreign enemies.

There may be particular problems when UN peacekeeping forces attempt to distribute humanitarian aid in a civil conflict. What may seem to the global community to be neutral, purely humanitarian aid may be regarded as otherwise by parties to the conflict. Those opposing the government, especially terrorist groups, will have maximum incentive to disrupt the operation of everyday life in the country. Their strategy is that the resulting chaos will be blamed on the government, making it more vulnerable to a takeover or collapse. Preventing food and medicine shipments to government-held areas may force the ruling group to devote more of its own resources to humanitarian rather than military efforts. Rebel groups also do not want to see food supplies and assistance go to those who support the government. Part of their strategy is to demoralise the population and persuade them that a viable alternative to government authority and inefficiency exists. Thus, it is conceivable that some groups will oppose the establishment of a peacekeeping operation.

Even the *status quo* group may have reason to oppose the distribution of food and medicine to its population. The government may want to punish people who live in areas controlled by rebels (and are thereby assumed to support the opposition). To the extent that the civil war mirrors ethnic, tribal or other divisions, there may be little feeling of obligation on the part of the government to feed some of its citizens. The government may also resent what could be viewed as a violation of its sovereignty. Many governments insist on being involved in the distribution of supplies in their territory and that opens up the possibility of diverting those supplies to military purposes.

The difficulty of preserving neutrality is also complicated when the peacekeeping force is assigned the duties of maintaining law and order. This is an important component of peacekeeping operations that intervene in the absence of strong government authority (as in Somalia) or as a prelude to election supervision (as in Cambodia). In Somalia, UNOSOM II ran into great difficulties when part of its mission became the capture and punishment of General Mohamed Farah Aideed. This unsuccessful effort clearly favoured the interests of other Somali factions vying for political power and undermined the credibility of the UN troops in the eyes of Aideed supporters. This helped increase the number of attacks on UN personnel and the general level of violence in the Somali capital. It is probably no coincidence that the level of violence and UN casualties have declined since the organisation abandoned its policy of targeting General Aideed.

In sum, a peacekeeping force may be viewed (regardless of its composition or mandate) as inherently biased in a civil conflict by groups who are disadvantaged by the *status quo* or do not benefit proportionately from its actions. The risk to the UN is that such groups will act to disrupt the operation, escalate violence and perhaps even attack the peacekeeping personnel.

Geography

Peacekeeping operations cannot dictate the location of tension or ceasefire lines. Neither can they move the disputants to another part of the globe that has the ideal geographic conditions for an interposition force. Yet the locus of deployment is not entirely fixed by the situation. The size of the buffer zone, the area for patrol, the number of observation sites and other aspects of the operation can be influenced by the requests of the authorising agency or the field commander. Thus it may be possible to set up a peacekeeping operation in such a way as to improve its chances of success. The major concern is in ensuring that detection of ceasefire and other violations is easy. Being able to detect violations allows the peacekeeping operation to head off problems that could escalate to war. More importantly, good detection is a deterrent to either protagonist's plans for a surprise attack. The fear of getting caught and the loss of a preemptive advantage from surprise may be enough to prevent disputants from taking hostile actions.

Generally, the larger the area of deployment, the more difficult it will be for the peacekeeping force to achieve its mission.[4] Peacekeeping forces usually only number a few thousand and it is impossible for them to maintain constant vigilance over thousands of miles. There is clearly more opportunity for violations to remain undetected. The disadvantage of a large area to patrol is partially offset, however, by other characteristics of the deployment zone. The terrain of the area can also affect the operation. An open area with little vegetation or few buildings provides an easy line of sight to detect hostile activity. By contrast, natural barriers such as mountains and hills, or man-made obstructions such as factories and houses, decrease the ability of peacekeeping forces to supervise the area of deployment.

Problems with a large area can be offset to some extent by a low population density.[5] If there are few people in a desert area, for example, then almost any movement is a portent of trouble. By contrast, an urban area of deployment means that thousands of people are constantly moving about and it may be next to impossible to stop all of them at checkpoints to detect smuggling of weapons or explosives. Thus, peacekeeping forces are likely to be most effective when they are the only group in the area and hostile movements will be most obvious.

Beyond a concern for detecting violations, peacekeeping troops must be adequately positioned to act as an interposition force. This means first that

---

4. Kjell Skjelsbaek, "UN Peacekeeping: Expectations, Limitations and Results—Forty Years of Mixed Experience," in Indar Jit Rikhye and Kjell Skjelsbaek, eds., *The United Nations and Peacekeeping* (New York: St. Martin's Press, 1991), pp. 52–67.

5. *Ibid.*

the disputants must be separated at an adequate distance.[6] If engagement, accidental or otherwise, is too easy, violent incidents will tend to occur and escalate. Just as a peacekeeping deployment area can be too large, it can also be too small if it does not properly separate the combatants. One difficulty is preventing attacks from the air. Peacekeeping forces usually have only helicopter reconnaissance and cannot prevent disputants from clashing in the airspace over or beyond the deployment zone.

The peacekeeping force must also be deployed so as to protect itself. If the force is in an area where it is easily subject to attack or infiltration, then fatalities involving the force are likely. Although a peacekeeping force is not a military one in the traditional sense, it still needs to adopt defensive positions that are the most invulnerable to attack while providing the locus necessary for achieving its goals.

UN peacekeeping operations with traditional interposition mandates in civil wars could experience great difficulties. Civil instability may mean that several groups are operating in different parts of the country. This could necessitate that the peacekeeping operation cover a broader territory, opening up the possibility of more incidents. Furthermore, unlike an identifiable international border or ceasefire line, it may be impossible to demarcate a line or area that separates the many sides in the conflict. Being from the same state and often not wearing military uniforms (indeed, sometimes not being traditional military or paramilitary units at all), participants in a civil conflict are hard to identify, much less to separate when they occupy the same geographic area. Interstate disputants can more easily be identified and separated across internationally recognised borders or militarily defined ceasefire lines.

Less traditional missions in civil conflicts are even more problematic. There are logistical problems associated with providing humanitarian assistance. The peacekeeping force increases its vulnerability by not being deployed at fixed positions in a neutral area. In the air and on the ground, the peacekeeping force will be frequently in motion and cannot secure the areas in which it travels. Again, this necessitates the cooperation of the combatants and perhaps some changes in the normal procedures of UN peacekeeping. Indeed, one analyst argues that NATO, a traditional military group, is a better institution than a UN peacekeeping operation for these kinds of missions.[7] This is quite evident by the inability of UN convoys to

---

6. *Ibid.*
7. John Mackinlay, "The Role of Military Forces in a Humanitarian Crisis," in Leon Gordenker and Thomas Weiss, eds., *Soldiers, Peacekeepers, and Disasters* (New York: St. Martin's Press, 1992), pp. 13–32.

deliver food to Sarajevo and other besieged cities in Bosnia.

In election supervision, geography may dictate that the size of the peacekeeping force be dramatically increased. Traditionally, peacekeeping forces have ranged from a few thousand to ten or fifteen thousand. Election supervision necessitates that troops be deployed throughout a country to monitor activities, as well as at all or most polling sites on election day. This requires the force size to be much larger than in traditional operations. (The exact size will vary according to the size of the area, the number of people in the territory and the potential severity of the conflict). This means that election supervision cannot be handled by the modal number of troops, and the United Nations will need to solicit more contributions to meet those increased requirements. The UN Transition Assistance Group (UNTAG) in Namibia was supposed to number 7500, but financial haggling in the United Nations delayed its deployment and the number eventually put in the field was only 4000.[8] This was not sufficient to monitor the actions of 1.5m Namibians, not to mention South African security forces in the country.

Traditional peacekeeping missions in interstate conflicts are deployed in narrow geographic areas, often at a few fixed points. For example, the UN Force in Cyprus (UNFICYP) is concentrated along the line separating the Greek and Turkish communities. Potentially, a peacekeeping force might have to supervise elections and disengagement activities in an area that is hundreds of thousands of square miles. This may make it impossible to detect violations even after an expansion in the size of the force. The enormous area that UNTAG had to cover proved problematical. UNTAG was often unable to verify that South African forces had been confined to their bases, relinquished their weapons or released political prisoners. In some cases, the South African forces moved troops, weapons and prisoners from location to location several steps ahead of the peacekeeping force which could not monitor the whole country. The UN Transitional Authority in Cambodia (UNTAC) also had similar difficulties in monitoring the military activities of the Khmer Rouge. Thus, the problems with geography experienced by traditional peacekeeping forces are likely to be magnified when they are given the task of supervising an election.

Overall, the geographic requirements for a peacekeeping force in a civil conflict magnify several potential problems that even traditional missions face. In civil conflicts peacekeepers will have greater difficulty in separating combatants and monitoring ceasefire violations as well as being more vulnerable themselves to attack.

---

8. "UN Council Agrees to Cut Namibian Peace Force," *New York Times,* 17 January 1989.

Third-Party Cooperation

When a UN peacekeeping force is deployed, it is usually with the permission of the host country. Nevertheless, the behaviour of third-party actors can have a tremendous impact on the success of the mission. For our purposes, we focus on two of those categories of third parties; states in the immediate area and subnational groups.

Third-party states can influence the success of a peacekeeping operation in several ways.[9] Most obviously, they can directly intervene militarily in the conflict, causing a renewal of the fighting or jeopardising the safety and mission of the peacekeeping operation. More subtly, they might supply arms and other assistance to one of the disputants (or to a subnational actor: see below) that serves to undermine the peacekeeping force's ability to limit violence. They might also bring diplomatic pressure to bear on one of the actors, such that the actor is more or less disposed to support the peacekeeping presence.

Third-party states might also have an indirect influence on the peacekeeping operation by virtue of their relationship to the primary disputants in other contexts. Conflict between a third-party state and one of the disputants, over issues related or unrelated to the conflict in question, can heighten tension in the area. The new conflict could spill over and poison the ceasefire between the primary disputants. Most dangerous would be a situation in which a primary disputant is aligned with a third-party state that becomes involved in a militarised dispute or war with the other primary disputant. In that case, the primary disputants are often dragged into renewed conflict by virtue of competing alignment patterns.

Third parties have the potential to play either a positive or negative role in the performance of peacekeeping operations. Yet, there are potentially more ways to complicate a peacekeeping operation than to assist it. Furthermore, a third-party state that supports a peacekeeping operation will likely stay out of the conflict, whereas in opposition it will tend to take a more active role.

Just as third-party states might influence peacekeeping operations, so too might subnational groups in the host or surrounding states.[10] The behaviour of these groups could be especially important when peacekeeping forces are thrust into areas of internal instability. In some cases, subnational actors

9. Brian Urquhart, "Peacekeeping: A View from the Operational Center," in Henry Wiseman, ed., *Peacekeeping: Appraisals and Proposals* (New York: Pergamon Press, 1983), pp. 161–74 and Alan James, "International Peacekeeping: The Disputants' View," *Political Studies* 38 (June 1990), pp. 215–30.

10. Augustus Richard Norton, "The Shiites and the MNF," in Anthony McDermott and Kjell Skjelsbaek, eds., *The Multinational Force in Beirut, 1982–1984* (Miami: Florida International University Press, 1991), pp. 226–36.

may actually control larger geographic areas than the recognised government. Furthermore, there has been a trend towards such groups gaining more resources and autonomy over time, often at the expense of state power.[11]

As noted above, peacekeeping may be viewed as hostile to the interests of subnational groups that wish to undermine the extant government. Unlike third-party states, however, subnational actors affect peacekeeping operations primarily by direct actions of support or opposition. Their cooperation could be crucial in fostering a minimum level of violence in the area of deployment.

Third-party support for peacekeeping operations can be especially difficult in civil wars. Civil conflicts often involve more than two identifiable groups in conflict; Lebanon's conflict alone involved more than half a dozen indigenous political factions, each with its own militia. This does not even consider the presence of terrorist groups, the Palestine Liberation Organisation (PLO), Israel, or Syria. In contrast, interstate disputes have been overwhelmingly dyadic.[12] It is much more difficult to aggregate the preferences of more than two actors such that all parties are satisfied with the outcome; indeed, "Arrow's paradox" shows that it may be impossible under certain circumstances.[13] Thus, as the number of actors in the dispute increases so does the likelihood that one or more of them will object to the ceasefire and the provisions for the deployment of the peacekeeping forces; they may take military action against other actors or the peacekeeping forces. A dyadic interstate dispute is much easier to control. Presumably both sides have agreed to the ceasefire, indicating that they support the peacekeeping operation (at least initially).

Beyond the sheer number of actors, a peacekeeping operation may be jeopardised by third-party support of groups opposed to a ceasefire or peace settlement. The most obvious recent case is in Bosnia. The Serbian government of the former Yugoslavia consistently supported efforts by Bosnian Serbs to "ethnically cleanse" and seize territories formerly occupied by the Muslims. The actions of the Croatian government also complicated the activities of the UN Protection Force (UNPROFOR) there. In contrast, the strong backing given to UNTAC by China, Russia, Japan and the United States was responsible, in part, for the ability of that operation to certify free and fair elections in Cambodia.

---

11. James N. Rosenau, *Turbulence in World Politics* (Princeton: Princeton University Press, 1990).

12. Over three-fourths of militarised interstate disputes involve only two parties; Charles Gochman and Zeev Maoz, "Militarized Interstate Disputes, 1816–1976: Procedures, Patterns, and Insights," *Journal of Conflict Resolution* 28 (December 1984), pp. 585–616.

13. Kenneth Arrow, *Social Choice and Individual Values* (New York: Wiley, 1951).

Peacemaking

Among traditional peacekeeping operations, the most problematic aspect has been their inability to promote conflict resolution following intervention. Symptomatic of this is the UNIFCYP operation which has been keeping the peace in Cyprus since 1964, a testament to its effectiveness in preventing war between the Greek and Turkish communities, but also to its ineptness at setting the conditions that would facilitate stability and its ultimate withdrawal.

There are several reasons why peacekeeping forces have been ineffective at peacemaking.[14] In some cases, peacekeeping operations could not achieve conflict resolution if they were unable to stop the violence; some missions were preoccupied with short-term problems with keeping the peace [e.g., the UN Interim Force in Lebanon (UNIFIL)] and therefore did not devote much attention to long-term resolution efforts. Nevertheless, even those operations that did limit violence had difficulties in peacemaking. A second explanation centres on the connection (or lack thereof) between the peacekeeping efforts and the diplomatic efforts to resolve the dispute. Yet failure has occurred in a variety of peacekeeping scenarios; it seems not to matter whether a peacekeeping operation has extensive diplomatic initiatives or no mechanisms at all for finding a peaceful settlement to the dispute. A third explanation is that peacekeeping actually inhibits negotiations by removing some of the urgency from the situation. This has some validity, although one could not offer this as a general explanation for why peacekeeping operations fail.

The final explanation, the inappropriateness of peacekeeping operations for conflict resolution, while not negating the utility that parts of other explanations may have, may be the one that is able to account for all operations' experiences. Consistently, regardless of the circumstances of the peacekeeping operation (type of conflict, the actors involved and other elements of context), the end result is often still failure at conflict resolution. It may be true that no diplomatic efforts can resolve two or more fundamentally incompatible positions. Yet it appears that peacekeeping is not the mechanism to achieve satisfactory diplomatic outcomes.

Thus, peacekeeping tends to work best when it follows peacemaking, rather than precedes it. The implementation of the peace accords in Namibia and Cambodia demonstrate that United Nations peacekeeping is better as an implementing mechanism than it is a means to facilitate the diplomatic process. When UN peacekeeping is put in place after a ceasefire, but prior to a

---

14. Paul F. Diehl, *International Peacekeeping* (Baltimore: Johns Hopkins University Press, 1993).

peace agreement, the force tends to just "sit there." The end result is that it either is unable to quell violence in the area (as is the case with UNIFIL) or it faces the prospect of indefinite deployment (as with UNIFCYP).

The use of UN peacekeeping forces in civil conflict offers both hope and warning with respect to peacemaking. On the one hand, using peacekeeping forces in election supervision indicates that some agreement has been reached among warring parties, such that a free election will allow the creation of a legitimate government to rule the country. Election supervision also entails a definitive time frame, including an endpoint, for UN peace-keeping involvement. Of course, there is no guarantee that all factions in a given country will support the peace agreement, but consensus is usually broad enough to suggest that the United Nations will have fewer problems than if it merely was deployed after a temporary ceasefire.

On the other hand, many uses of the peacekeeping forces in civil conflicts will not occur after a peace settlement, and indeed perhaps not even before a ceasefire. UN peacekeepers supervising humanitarian assistance distribution or seeking to preserve law and order in the absence of government authority (as in Rwanda) will have to contend with sporadic or persistent violence. Unfortunately, a traditional peacekeeping force will be small in number and lightly armed. This is hardly the type of military force that may be necessary to defend itself, much less achieve the mission for which it was authorised. Here the absence of peacemaking is particularly dangerous to UN peace-keeping personnel.

Beyond the danger involved, the absence of a peace settlement is more troubling in a civil conflict than in an interstate one. In the latter, the UN may be forced into a long standing stalemate, but at least its responsibilities are clearly defined and can be routinised. If a ceasefire is achieved in a civil conflict, one has to assess what the next step is for the United Nations. If a viable government is non-existent and/or if the UN is assigned some law and order functions, the UN may find itself in a quandary about its future courses of action. The organisation may be placed in the unenviable position of governing the country until a negotiated settlement is achieved. The alternative may be to tolerate various forms of anarchy that would result in the loss of lives and possible a renewal of fullscale warfare. This is a role that the United Nations has been heretofore reluctant to assume. Never-theless, its diplomatic capacity to force a settlement among the disputants is suspect, especially in light of the many failed attempts to do so in Somalia. The risk of indefinite deployment is much greater and has more profound implications for national sovereignty and other issues when the United Nations intervenes in a civil conflict.

Guidelines for UN Peacekeeping in Civil Wars

The above analysis suggests that the use of UN peacekeeping troops in civil wars is prone to failure, and indeed the historical record lends some credence to this belief.[15] Yet this does not mean that such operations are inherently doomed. The UNTAG and UNTAC efforts, to mention two, can generally be considered successful in stabilising Namibia and Cambodia respectively in preparation for free and fair elections. Rather, what is needed is the appropriate application of the peacekeeping strategy instead of its adoption as a panacea for every threat to international peace and security whether interstate or intrastate. Below are some guidelines for increasing the prospects for success of UN intervention in civil conflicts.

The first guideline is that UN peacekeeping forces should only be used when they have the support of all or most of the relevant parties and there is a ceasefire in place. A neutral, lightly-armed force is poorly suited to intervene in a civil war in which the combatants are heavily armed and there is a strong possibility that the peacekeepers will come under fire. This most likely involves situations in which the peacekeeping troops would be assigned interposition or humanitarian assistance functions while a civil war is in progress. In the face of thousands of starving refugees, it may seem to be a cruel prescription to refrain from sending peacekeeping troops. Nevertheless, it is often forgotten that the deployment of peacekeeping forces is only one in an array of options available to the United Nations and the global community. In cases in which war is ongoing, it may be that a military enforcement option is the preferred one. A military force may be necessary to secure stability in a given area or offer a credible deterrent (or defence) against attacks on food convoys and the like. The experience of Pakistani peacekeepers (prior to U.S. military intervention) in Somalia and of UN forces in Bosnia suggest that peacekeeping forces will have serious problems achieving their missions in the face of ongoing war. The absence of the necessary consensus or political will in the United Nations to authorise a more coercive option does not obviate the inadequacies of peacekeepers for these tasks.

It might be suggested that traditional peacekeeping forces adopt some elements of enforcement when faced with the situations described above. However, the inclusion of any enforcement functions in a peacekeeping operation's mandate has serious and detrimental consequences. First, it clouds the international perspective on what peacekeeping is and how it operates. This may undermine support for the strategy, as people and governments object to various enforcement actions taken by the peace-

---

15. *Ibid.*

keeping troops. Furthermore, it may make disputants less likely to accept even a traditional peacekeeping force, perhaps fearing that the troops might take actions against their interests and in violation of their sovereignty.[16] Years of precedent in establishing the neutrality of the force may be lost when enforcement actions are undertaken. The stature of peacekeeping, and therefore the likelihood that it will be adopted by international and other organisations, will be diminished by the likely failures that accompany the expansion of peacekeeping roles to include enforcement.

Second, and equally important, enforcement actions by the peacekeeping force may complicate its ability to perform monitoring duties. Will training or participation in enforcement duties contaminate the ability of the force to exercise restraint in other contexts? Will troops know when to draw the line between offensive and defensive use of military force? Will peacekeeping forces have to be armed with more sophisticated and more deadly weapons? Will the protagonists be more likely to attack the peacekeeping force because of fear of those weapons and the relaxed limits on the use of force? These are significant risks that cannot be tolerated within the peacekeeping framework. If enforcement actions are to be taken and justified, they are best done by a different force under UN authorisation, rather than by mixing those incompatible functions with those of peacekeeping. The alternative is not likely to be successful and the result could jeopardise the positive benefits yielded by traditional peacekeeping.

A second guideline is that the United Nations (or some collectivity of major or regional powers) must lay the groundwork for peacemaking as a prelude to UN peacekeeping deployment. There is some value to deploying peacekeeping forces to stabilise the situation after a ceasefire; stopping the bloodshed alone may be justification for the deployment. Yet, this must be followed up by intense diplomatic efforts to secure a more lasting resolution to the conflict. The deployment of the UN forces should be temporary and their withdrawal should signify that the chances of renewed armed conflict are low. Unfortunately, there is a risk that the global community will turn its attention away from the situation once it is stabilised and the United Nations will be left to monitor a protracted and increasingly dangerous stalemate. The optimal use of UN peacekeeping forces in civil conflict is with regard to election supervision. In that instance, a peace agreement precedes the deployment of troops. If such agreements can be achieved early, and the mechanism of holding democratic elections to resolve internal struggles for power is becoming more common, then UN forces can be an important and effective implementing mechanism.

---

16. Alan James, "Peacekeeping and Keeping the Peace," *Review of International Studies* 15 (1989), pp. 371–78.

Once peacekeeping forces are placed in the appropriate situations, there are some steps that can be taken to ensure greater effectiveness. One of these is the third guideline: UN forces must continue to maintain neutral troops in its operations. There has been a trend since the end of the Cold War for UN peacekeeping operations to include troops from major powers and often not disinterested states (e.g., U.S. troops in Somalia, French troops in Bosnia). This heightens the risk that UN forces will be viewed as biased tools of the contributing state. This has already been a problem in Somalia where the UN has been accused of being a U.S. pawn. Russia has even requested, and had rejected by Secretary-General Boutros Boutros-Ghali, to have its peacekeepers sent to Bosnia. UN operations will have difficulty enough with issues of neutrality during a civil conflict without the complicating factor of having troops that are inherently perceived as biased because of their national origin. This is not to say that such troops cannot behave in an impartial fashion or that there is a guarantee that other states will provide the necessary forces. Yet, it would seem wise to revert to the old UN standard for troop contribution by relying on personnel from smaller and disinterested states, if only to eliminate the perception of bias by the disputants.

Fourth and finally, UN peacekeeping operations in civil conflicts will need many more personnel than traditional operations. Peacekeeping in civil conflict necessitates monitoring a broader geographic area. This alone will require many more troops deployed in various strategic positions. Furthermore, UN peacekeepers in civil conflicts often assume functions beyond the traditional interposition and monitoring role, such as election supervision, law-and-order maintenance and distribution of food and medical supplies. These will require more personnel and perhaps supplemental assistance from the UN in the form of civilian police and civilian technical experts. The UNTAC operation was the largest in UN history, numbering almost thirty thousand strong; this size was essential given the area and terrain of the country and the range of government duties assigned to the United Nations during the transition.

The end of the Cold War has rekindled nationalist and ethnic tensions around the world and the major threats to international peace and security now addressed by the United Nations will disproportionately involve civil conflict. The analysis here suggests that UN peacekeeping force will encounter serious problems and risks in dealing with these threats. Although one cannot provide a guarantee of success in an uncertain and often turbulent world, the proper application of the UN peacekeeping strategy and appropriate planning can lessen the prospects for failure that have plagued some UN operations in the recent past.

14

Peacekeeping and Peacemaking

William Maley

The post-Cold War world is frequently characterised in terms which emphasise the emergence of turbulence and the erosion of state sovereignty.[1] While one can argue about the precise scale of such turbulence or the extent of such erosion, it is marked when compared to the tendency towards bipolarity in the Cold War world of antagonistic superpowers with their own spheres of influence. While simmering ethnic conflicts in many parts of the globe predated the end of the Cold War,[2] the disintegration of Soviet and American spheres of influence has exposed the UN to heightened demands that it play a role in the substantive settlement of intractable regional or even internal disputes, not merely by interposing peacekeepers between hostile forces as a confidence-building measure, but by contributing to the development of new political institutions for traumatised societies. These demands have stretched the human and material resources of the UN system and created expectations of the UN which it is not presently equipped to meet. There is a real danger that the result will be deepening disillusionment with the UN and a rush by at least some major powers to fill the vacuum created by the UN's inadequacies. Since the major powers most likely to act are those with interests to protect in the country at risk, the result may not be an outbreak of peace but an upsurge of war. For

---

1. See Robert H. Jackson, *Quasi-States: Sovereignty, International Relations, and the Third World* (Cambridge: Cambridge University Press, 1990); James N. Rosenau, *Turbulence in World Politics: A Theory of Change and Continuity* (Princeton: Princeton University Press, 1990); Joseph A. Camilleri and Jim Falk, *The End of Sovereignty?: The Politics of a Shrinking and Fragmenting World* (Aldershot: Edward Elgar, 1992); and Zbigniew Brzezinski, *Out of Control: Global Turmoil on the Eve of the 21st Century* (New York: Scribner's, 1993).

2. Ted Gurr and Barbara Harff, *Ethnic Conflict in World Politics* (Boulder: Westview, 1994), pp. 10–11.

this reason, the ability of the UN to discharge a "peacemaking" as well as "peacekeeping" function is a matter of considerable importance.

The aim of this chapter is to highlight some of the dilemmas which the UN faces as a consequence of the emergence of "peacemaking" as one of its tasks. It is divided into four sections. The first addresses the meaning of "peacemaking" and the way in which it surfaced in the complicated vocabulary of peacekeeping. I argue that it is based on a somewhat different conception of "peace" from that which underpins classical ideas of peacekeeping, and one which is intrinsically more difficult to realise in a practical political context. The second section examines some of the dilemmas faced by the UN in undertaking the task of peacemaking. The third examines the limitations on what can be achieved through international and internal peacemaking. The fourth offers some conclusions.

The Substance of Peacemaking

From ancient times—when Isaiah proposed the beating of swords into ploughshares—peacemaking has been a recognised activity. However, the emergence of international organisations such as the UN has changed the constellation of actors in world politics and altered the forms which peacemaking may take. While the role of a neutral broker is not unprecedented, as shown by the Pope's adjudication of claims to the New World by European Catholic powers, the institutionalisation of the role through the so-called "Good Offices" of the UN Secretary-General is. With the shift to condominium in the Security Council, that role has come into sharper focus than at any time since the death of Secretary-General Dag Hammarskjöld in 1961.

The canonical text of the new era of "peacemaking" is Secretary-General Boutros Boutros-Ghali's 1992 report *An Agenda for Peace,* according to which peacemaking "is action to bring hostile parties to agreement, essentially through such peaceful means as those foreseen in Chapter VI of the Charter of the United Nations."[3] Three main problems, he argued, hinder the use of these peaceful means: first, "the lack of political will of parties to seek a solution to their differences" through these means; second, "the lack of leverage at the disposal of a third party"; and third, the "indifference of the international community to a problem, or the marginalization of it."[4] To address these problems, he recommended increased resort to the International Court of Justice, improved mobilisation of resources to ameliorate circumstances contributing to conflict, assistance to innocent parties dis-

---

3. Boutros Boutros-Ghali, *An Agenda for Peace: Preventive Diplomacy, Peacemaking and Peace-keeping* (New York: United Nations, 1992), para. 20.

4. *Ibid.,* para. 34.

advantaged by the application of a sanctions regime, and steps to make armed forces available on call to the Security Council should military action to maintain international peace or security pursuant to Article 42 of the Charter be required. While these remedies relate largely to peacemaking in international conflicts, it is notable, although not particularly surprising, that the main focus of peacemaking efforts on which Boutros-Ghali reported one year after *An Agenda for Peace* was released related to what are substantially *internal* conflicts.[5]

It is possible also to distinguish different stages of peacemaking. It is above all concerned with dealing with conflicts which are in progress, in contrast to other forms of activity such as preventive diplomacy which may serve to avert the outbreak of hostilities in the first place, or peace-building which seeks to buttress peace which has been attained. The aim of peacemaking, Australian Foreign Minister Gareth Evans has recently argued, "is to reduce conflict intensity, separate belligerents, halt bloodshed, put the parties back on a path to peaceful resolution and ultimately to arrive at a durable solution."[6] In his view

> Initial (or "Stage I") peace making efforts will usually be aimed at the immediate goals of cessation of hostilities, and stabilisation of the situation on the ground; subsequent (or "Stage II") efforts—which might continue in parallel with the deployment of a peace keeping mission—might be aimed rather at securing a durable political settlement.[7]

The type of "peace" at which peacemaking activities are directed differs somewhat from that with which peacekeeping is concerned. Peacekeeping operations are intended as temporary measures to "stop or contain hostilities" or to "supervise the implementation of an interim or final settlement which has been negotiated by the peace-makers."[8] They advance what Michael Howard has called

> ...the bedrock meaning of "peace" which men have known and used ever since they were literate: the simple *absence of violence,* especially random or endemic violence, from the society in which we live: the absence of armies traversing and re-traversing the land, burning, raping, plundering, killing, whether those armies are official or unofficial, organised and uniformed or mere robber bands; whether they inflict destruction with knives or from a safe distance with bombs.[9]

---

5. Boutros Boutros-Ghali, "An Agenda for Peace: One Year Later," *Orbis* 37 (Summer 1993), p. 326.

6. Gareth Evans, *Cooperating for Peace: The Global Agenda for the 1990s and Beyond* (Sydney: Allen & Unwin, 1993), p. 89.

7. *Ibid.,* p. 11.

8. *The Blue Helmets: A Review of United Nations Peace-keeping* (New York: United Nations, 1990), p. 8.

9. Michael Howard, "The Concept of Peace," *Encounter* 61 (December 1983), p. 18. For a

Peacemaking aims to secure peace in this sense, but it aims for more as well: for a peace *which will survive the withdrawal of the peacekeepers.* War, Thomas Hobbes noted, consists not solely in actual fighting, but in the "known disposition thereto:"[10] it is in addressing such dispositions amongst antagonists that peacemaking faces its great challenge. To eliminate the disposition to armed conflict, as well as armed conflict itself, involves not simply the physical separation of combatants, but some reconciliation of their interests. To attain the latter may prove extraordinarily difficult, especially if much blood has already been shed.[11]

Dilemmas of UN Peacemaking

The UN faces a range of dilemmas in exercising peacemaking functions, but five are particularly important. These relate to the timing of peace-making, the attitude of the great powers to peacemaking, the nature of the parties to a conflict, the demands of the parties, and the institutional adequacy of the UN system to perform the task of peacemaking. In practice these factors can impinge upon each other in significant ways, but for analytical purposes it is useful to discuss them distinctly.

The timing of peacemaking endeavours is extremely important. Some conflicts are simply not amenable to resolution by peacemaking at the moment when international interest in them is at its height. A messianic movement of rage may see violence, à la Sorel, as a necessary means of purifying a society of decadence and corruption: to abandon violence would be to abandon the cause itself. A resistance movement may seek to expunge a regime rather than become part of it: few French *maquisards* aspired to become partners of the Vichy administration. Those who expect a low-cost total victory are unlikely to welcome a "settlement" that denies it to them. Indeed, in some cases, the complete victory of one party may provide the best guarantee of lasting peace. The circumstances for peacemaking become propitious when contending elites wish to escape from a situation where *all* have suffered heavy enough losses to make an alternative approach seem worthwhile.[12] At this point, once the interests of the parties begin to

---

more detailed discussion of this and other concepts of peace, see William Maley, "Peace, Needs and Utopia," *Political Studies* 33 (December 1985), pp. 578–91.

10. Thomas Hobbes, *Leviathan* (Glasgow: Collins/Fontana, 1962), p. 143.

11. For a classic account of the problems faced by leaders in agreeing to end hostilities, see Fred C. Iklé, *Every War Must End* (New York: Columbia University Press, 1991).

12. Michael G. Burton and John Higley, "Elite Settlements," *American Sociological Review* 52 (June 1987), pp. 295–307; Richard K. Betts, "The Delusion of Impartial Intervention," *Foreign Affairs* 73 (November/December 1994), pp. 20–33.

converge, peacemaking can smooth the negotiating process: the Norwegian role in bringing Israel and the PLO to the point of agreement is a recent example.

The attitude of the great powers to peacemaking is also a problematical matter for the UN, in three ways. First, peacemaking efforts, especially of the kind found in so-called "Second Generation" peacekeeping, can be extremely expensive and only the goodwill of major powers guarantees that they will receive sufficient funding to get off the ground. Proposals that economic giants such as Germany and Japan be given permanent membership of the Security Council surely reflect in part a desire to tap their resources to fund operations to which they would be committed by Security Council resolutions with which they had directly concurred. Second, great powers have multiple linkages in the international system and the UN is only one of a number of agencies which can be drafted to play a peacemaking role. Powers in broad alliance, but with somewhat different agendas in respect of particular conflicts, may opt to pursue those agendas through the agency which seems most congenial. One can plausibly argue that the involvement of the UN, NATO, *and* the European Union in efforts to manage the crisis spawned by the collapse of the former Yugoslavia has diminished the credibility of all three and done little to ensure long-term stability in the Balkans. Third, if the deployment of UN peacekeepers is to be part of a peacemaking exercise, the agreement of the five permanent members of the Security Council to an enabling Security Council resolution will be required. If the theatre of conflict is one which a permanent member regards as falling within its sphere, then UN peacemaking efforts may face additional obstacles. For example, in Tajikistan, the support of the Russian Federation for the feeble Rakhmanov regime and Moscow's desire to see its military forces re-flagged as UN peacekeepers[13] have undermined the peacemaking efforts of successive representatives of the Secretary-General, although divisions in Russia over the approach to take to the conflict mean that the obstacles are not insuperable.[14] In the Western hemisphere, the

13. On Russian forces in the "Near Abroad" as "peacekeepers", see Suzanne Crow, "The Theory and Practice of Peacekeeping in the Former USSR," *RFE/RL Research Report* 1 (18 September 1992), pp. 31–36.

14. See Sanobar Shermatova, "Suppression or Conciliation?" *Moscow News,* 25–31 March 1994, p. 4. For further discussion of the conflict in Tajikistan, see Helsinki Watch, *Human Rights in Tajikistan in the Wake of Civil War* (New York: Human Rights Watch, 1993); Barnett R. Rubin, "The Fragmentation of Tajikistan," *Survival* 35 (Winter 1993–94), pp. 71–91; Anthony Richter, "Springtime in Tajikistan," *World Policy Journal* 11 (Summer 1994), pp. 81–86; Barnett R. Rubin, "Tajikistan: From Soviet Republic to Russian-Uzbek Protectorate," in Michael Mandelbaum, ed., *Central Asia and the World* (New York: Council on Foreign Relations Press, 1994), pp. 207–24; and Amin Saikal, "Russia and Central Asia," in Amin Saikal and William Maley, eds., *Russia in Search of Its Future* (Cambridge: Cambridge

resignation of the Secretary-General's envoy to Haiti in protest at the UN's exclusion from bargaining between the Haitian junta and the Carter delegation in September 1994 illustrates the same tension.

With conflicts increasingly internal rather than international, it is now commonly the case that parties who are not UN members find themselves in conflict with parties who are. This can have significant implications for the peacemaking efforts of the UN system.[15] The ability to dispatch a delegation to the UN and have its credentials accepted is a useful buttress to a regime's legitimacy, and UN dealings with its opponents are unlikely to be welcomed. On occasion a "puppet" regime's credentials have not been accepted (for example, those of the Kádár regime in the seven years following the Soviet invasion of Hungary[16]) but on other occasions, where caution might have been advisable, they have (for example, those of the Karmal regime following the Soviet invasion of Afghanistan[17]). It is a matter of individual discretion for a Secretary-General as to how far he will allow his "Good Offices" to be constrained when internal conflicts pose a threat to international peace and security. During the Congo crisis Hammarskjöld found himself in conflict, at different times, with both President Joseph Kasavubu and Prime Minister Patrice Lumumba, not to mention the USA, the Soviet Union and Belgium.[18] On the other hand, Javier Pérez de Cuéllar, doubtless with the USSR's status as a permanent member of the Security Council firmly in mind, took a very narrow view of his freedom of action in responding to the Soviet invasion of Afghanistan: it would be "against our philosophy," he argued, "to be in touch with the enemies of governments."[19] This effectively allowed the Karmal regime a veto over direct UN contact with the popular armed opposition and, by prompting opposition distrust of the impartiality of the UN, contributed to

University Press, 1994), pp. 142–57.

15. See Alan James, "Problems of Internal Peacekeeping," *Diplomacy & Statecraft* 5 (March 1994), pp. 21–46.

16. See Alan James, *Sovereign Statehood: The Basis of International Society* (London: Allen & Unwin, 1986), pp. 140–42.

17. See William Maley, "The Geneva Accords of April 1988," in Amin Saikal and William Maley, eds., *The Soviet Withdrawal from Afghanistan* (Cambridge: Cambridge University Press, 1989), pp. 12–28.

18. See William J. Durch, "The UN Operation in the Congo: 1960–1964," in William J. Durch, ed., *The Evolution of UN Peacekeeping: Case Studies and Comparative Analysis* (London: Macmillan, 1994), pp. 315–52.

19. Quoted in Thomas M. Franck and Georg Nolte, "The Good Offices Function of the UN Secretary-General," in Adam Roberts and Benedict Kingsbury, eds., *United Nations, Divided World: The UN's Roles in International Relations* (Oxford: Oxford University Press, 1993), p. 150.

the subsequent failure of UN peacemaking: the April 1988 Geneva Accords on Afghanistan provided cover for the withdrawal of armed forces which the Soviet leadership had decided to make in November 1986.[20] It also ignored Robert Randle's shrewd warning that a "political settlement will be inadequate if the peace negotiators have not reached all the issues and leave unresolved some of the disputes that were the basis for the war."[21]

Once the problem of access to parties is overcome, there is a further problem: choosing with whom to deal. On the one hand, to exclude a popular or powerful group invites the prompt failure of a peacemaking exercise. On the other hand, by dealing—perhaps at the instigation of regional or great powers—with a group which lacks these characteristics, the UN may accord it a status which neither its popular support nor its military capacity would justify. To demand as an axiom of peacemaking that all groups be part of a peace process may simply empower marginal intransigents. For this reason, peacemaking should never be considered a "learning process" for its practitioners, as "threshold" decisions made by "learners" might rebound to their disadvantage at later stages. A thorough understanding of the relative importance of different parties, as well as of their objectives, organisational attributes and cognitive processes, is essential. The peacemaker also needs to be extraordinarily sensitive to how dealings with one party to a conflict are perceived by others. The Secretary-General's 1991 plan for a political settlement in Afghanistan collapsed in part because in the eyes of significant elements of the Afghan resistance, his Personal Representative had been too close to the communist President Najibullah to function as a credible peacemaker.[22] Those who sup with the Devil should use a long spoon.

The demands of the parties may also create difficulties for the peacemaker. On the one hand, as Chester A. Crocker, one of the most successful peacemakers of recent years, points out in a somewhat different context, "it

---

20. See "Sekretnye dokumenty iz osobykh papok: Afganistan," *Voprosy istorii* 3 (1993), pp. 3–32.

21. Robert F. Randle, *The Origins of Peace: A Study of Peacemaking and the Structure of Peace Settlements* (New York: The Free Press, 1973), p. 487.

22. On the failure of this exercise in peacemaking, see William Maley and Fazel Haq Saikal, *Political Order in Post-Communist Afghanistan* (Boulder: Lynne Rienner, 1992), pp. 23–29; Barnett R. Rubin, "Post-Cold War State Disintegration: The Failure of International Conflict Resolution in Afghanistan," *Journal of International Affairs* 46 (Winter 1993), pp. 469–92; and William Maley, "Peacemaking Diplomacy: United Nations Good Offices in Afghanistan," in Kevin Clements and Robin Ward, eds., *Building International Community: Cooperating for Peace* (Sydney: Allen & Unwin, 1994), pp. 250–54. To the embarrassment of the UN, as of late 1994, Najibullah remained in the UN compound in Kabul, a fugitive from justice rather than persecution.

is *their* settlement."[23] However, that the parties may agree to something is no guarantee that it is realistic. What they are prepared to accept may be unmanageably expensive. More seriously, the parties may be insensitive to the logistical problems entailed in their proposals. For example it is by now reasonably clear that without the services of a well-organised peacekeeping force, it is impossible for the UN to conduct free and fair elections in a deeply traumatised society.[24] Yet a generally measured and realistic July 1994 report from a UN peacemaking mission to Afghanistan, while concluding that free and fair elections "would be the best way to ensure that all segments of Afghan society participate in determining the future of the country,"[25] at the same time noted that most Afghans "opposed a non-Afghan armed military presence, including United Nations peace-keeping troops."[26] Since only the UN is in a position to organise free and fair elections in Afghanistan, the idea of an Afghan settlement involving the holding of free and fair elections, but *without* the presence of UN peacekeepers, is nonsensical.

The institutional failings of the UN system could occupy a whole book, and the following remarks touch only on those which impinge most directly on peacemaking. First, it is absolutely vital that once peacemaking has produced an agreement between contending parties for the deployment of peacekeepers, the deployment proceed without undue delay. Any failure promptly to deploy can provide a pretext—or even a reasonable justification—for a party to withdraw from the settlement. Almost as seriously, it can fuel suspicions about the UN's impartiality which rebound to the UN's disadvantage at a later point: this certainly happened in Cambodia, where the Khmer Rouge regarded the slow UN deployment as playing into the hands of the Phnom Penh regime.[27] Problems will continue to plague both peacekeeping and peacemaking as long as the organisational culture of significant parts of the UN system is mechanistic and process-oriented rather than organic and outcome-oriented.

Second, from top to bottom, the UN needs to improve its matching of tasks with expertise. While the UN has some superbly able staff, the

23. Chester A. Crocker, *High Noon in Southern Africa: Making Peace in a Rough Neighborhood* (New York: W. W. Norton, 1992), p. 482.

24. Michael Maley, "Reflections on the Electoral Process in Cambodia," in Hugh Smith, ed., *Peacekeeping: Challenges for the Future* (Canberra: Australian Defence Studies Centre, 1993), pp. 87–99.

25. *Progress Report of the Special Mission to Afghanistan* (New York: United Nations, A/49/208, S/1994/766, 1 July 1994), para. 40 (d).

26. *Ibid.*, para. 23 (h).

27. William Shawcross, *Cambodia's New Deal* (Washington DC: Carnegie Endowment for International Peace, Contemporary Issues Paper No.1, 1994), pp. 13–14.

politicisation of UN staffing means that it has some abominably incompetent staff as well. To an extent it has addressed this problem in recent "Second Generation" peacekeeping operations by drawing on professionals (experts rather than retired politicians) from member-states, but it could extend this more rigorously to its peacemaking activities as well. It is not impossible to marry expertise and seniority: Dr Gunnar Jarring of Sweden (in the Middle East) and Martti Ahtisaari, now President of Finland (in Namibia) are prime examples of Special Representatives who did just that. But to appoint "peacemaking" Special or Personal Representatives of the Secretary-General because they happen to have the right level of seniority in the UN system rather than because they have any knowledge of the situation they are charged to handle is no favour to the appointee, and even less to the citizens of the country or region in point.

Third, for an organisation of its importance the UN has surprisingly low levels of institutional memory, and many missions spend their early months reinventing the wheel. The UN should be prepared more systematically to assess the strengths and weaknesses of its performance in particular operations, and to disseminate such assessments through the UN system. Much went wrong in the operation of the UN Transitional Authority in Cambodia (UNTAC) prior to the holding of the May 1993 Cambodian elections, but few in the UN showed much subsequent interest in exploring exactly what. Organisational solidarity is valuable up to a point, but runs the danger of producing sclerosis. Some would argue that it already has.[28]

While peacemaking has its dilemmas, it also has its triumphs. The most compelling example is Namibia, which through the painstaking efforts of UN staff was brought successfully to independence through a complex process involving both peacemaking and peacekeeping. This investment of time and effort has been rewarded by political stability in the period since the UN Transition Assistance Group (UNTAG) concluded its mandate.[29] However, it sometimes seems that for every UNTAG, there is a MINURSO (the UN Mission for the Referendum in Western Sahara): the latter provides an excellent example of a peacemaking exercise which came badly unstuck.[30] It is not enough for the UN to succeed only where no one could fail: the international community is entitled to expect more.

---

28. For an acerbic discussion of this problem, see Shirley Hazzard, *Countenance of Truth: The United Nations and the Waldheim Case* (London: Chatto & Windus, 1991).

29. For a general discussion of the Namibian case, see Robert S. Jaster, *The 1988 Peace Accords and the Future of South-western Africa* (London: International Institute of Strategic Studies, Adelphi Papers no. 253, 1990); and Lionel Cliffe, *et al.*, *The Transition to Independence in Namibia* (Boulder: Lynne Rienner, 1994).

30. See William J. Durch, "Building on Sand: UN Peacekeeping in the Western Sahara," *International Security* 17 (Spring 1993), pp. 151–71.

The Limitations of Peacemaking

A full-scale peacemaking and peacekeeping operation may be extremely expensive and certainly absorbs scarce resources with alternative uses. Money wasted on a poorly-conceived peacemaking exercise might have been used for a range of admirable purposes: to feed the hungry, heal the sick and shelter the homeless. It is useful, therefore, to establish the limitations of peacemaking exercises so that hard choices about the allocation of resources can be made realistically.

The Cambodian operation, unquestionably the largest combined peacemaking and peacekeeping operation ever undertaken, provides a useful starting point for this discussion. At the heart of the exercise, as mandated by the 1991 Paris Accords on Cambodia and by Security Council Resolutions 717 and 718, was the organisation and conduct by UNTAC of a "free and fair"[31] election in which the people of Cambodia, survivors of a period of the most acute and traumatic suffering,[32] would have the chance to elect a Constituent Assembly and in the process choose between the different groups which claimed to enjoy their loyalty. The UN had a long history of involvement in election monitoring and observation,[33] but the Cambodian exercise was on a scale never before attempted by the organisation. To that extent, the successful holding of the elections—as marked by the high turnout and the technical efficiency with which they were conducted—was rightly hailed as a triumph. However, as some of the literature on "democratic crafting" clearly warns,[34] and as most diplomats are fully aware, there is much more to stable pluralism than the mere holding of elections. In particular, it is important never to forget four major problems

---

31. On this elusive notion, see *Enhancing the Effectiveness of the Principle of Periodic and Genuine Elections.* Report of the Secretary-General (New York: United Nations, A/46/609, 19 November 1991).

32. On the background to the involvement of the UN in Cambodia, see William Maley, "Regional Conflicts: Afghanistan and Cambodia," in Ramesh Thakur and Carlyle A. Thayer, eds., *Reshaping Regional Relations: Asia–Pacific and the Former Soviet Union* (Boulder: Westview Press, 1993), pp. 183–200.

33. For discussion of this involvement, see Lawrence T. Farley, *Plebiscites and Sovereignty: The Crisis of Political Illegitimacy* (Boulder: Westview, 1986); Sally Morphet, "UN Peacekeeping and Election-Monitoring," in Roberts and Kingsbury, eds., *United Nations, Divided World,* pp. 183–239; Yves Beigbeder, *International Monitoring of Plebiscites, Referenda and National Elections: Self-Determination and Transition to Democracy* (Dordrecht: Martinus Nijhoff, 1994).

34. Important works in this literature include Guillermo O'Donnell and Philippe C. Schmitter, *Transitions from Authoritarian Rule: Tentative Conclusions about Uncertain Democracies* (Baltimore: Johns Hopkins University Press, 1986); Guiseppe Di Palma, *To Craft Democracies: An Essay on Democratic Transitions* (Berkeley: University of California Press, 1990); Samuel P. Huntington, *The Third Wave: Democratization in the Late Twentieth Century* (Norman: University of Oklahoma Press, 1991).

which peacemaking cannot address on its own, and which have surfaced in Cambodia since the elections.

The first relates to political culture. The character of a country's politics is significantly affected by the prevailing values and attitudes in a society.[35] These in turn shape norms and traditions, which provide reasons for action beyond those provided by considerations of interest. Some political cultures are inimical to stable democracy. In traditionally martial or adversarial societies, marked by powerful norms of honour and revenge, politics even after a "founding election" may have a zero-sum character which thwarts the best intention of the peacemakers. Clan or ethnic tensions can be cynically fuelled by aspirants to leadership status. A "democratic" political culture, one which recognises the importance of tolerance and compromise, cannot be built overnight. Political cultures are not immutable: there is no doubt that the experience of occupation by the U.S., Britain and France significantly altered the political cultures of Japan and those Länder which made up the Federal Republic of Germany before reunification. However, a UN peace-keeping force is not an occupation force. Its aim is to quit the theatre as soon as possible. In Cambodia, through Radio UNTAC, through electoral education activities more generally, and through the direct recruitment of around 50 000 Cambodian staff to undertake the tasks of voter registration and management of actual polling, some UNTAC staff did almost as much as humanly possible to inject democratic values into a political culture with sadly limited previous acquaintance with them. They were not helped, however, by the deference shown at high levels to the whims of the notoriously eccentric and narcissistic Prince Norodom Sihanouk, which gave the imprimatur of the UN to a traditional power structure which arguably had much to do with Cambodia's descent into barbarism in the first place. It is perhaps no surprise that Cambodia's new rulers, from King Sihanouk down, have continued to behave as if their mandate came from Heaven rather than Earth.[36]

The second relates to leadership. It is virtually impossible to ensure that a peace-making process delivers a consensually-unified elite of statesmen rather than a disunified elite of self-serving politicians. The former can on occasion emerge: one of the most remarkable features of the transition to majority rule in South Africa was the statesmanship of both African National Congress leader Nelson Mandela and State President F. W. De Klerk, who proved able during the election period to rise above narrow party interests

---

35. Seymour Martin Lipset, "The Social Requisites of Democracy Revisited," *American Sociological Review* 59 (February 1994), pp. 1–22.

36. See Shawcross, *Cambodia's New Deal*, pp. 89–103.

for the good of the transition process as a whole.[37] Cambodia was not so fortunate. The voters had an unimpressive list of candidates from which to make their choices and the post-election machinations of the various political factions, aggravated by Sihanouk's resort almost as second nature to divide-and-rule politics, displayed a lamentable lack of *gravitas*—especially when compared to the courage and sense of occasion which the voters had shown in going to the polls even in the face of credible threats from the Khmer Rouge. The devastation of civil society which frequently creates the need for peacemaking is at the heart of this problem. The political parties which contest a "peacemaking" election are prone to be based on either the clientelist networks of traditional notables or military leaders, or on ethnic, religious, sectarian or regional groupings. Neither provides a notably sound basis for stable democracy.[38]

The third relates to institutional design. In Namibia and Cambodia, the objective of the electoral process was to elect a constituent assembly which in turn would draw up constitutional rules to govern the practice of politics thereafter. While the assemblies were constrained by the requirement that a two-thirds "super majority" be mustered before a new constitution could take effect, their discretion in choosing institutions of government was otherwise wide-ranging. There was no guarantee that this discretion would be used wisely, and one can argue that in Cambodia it was not. There is an emerging consensus amongst students of institutional design that active-monarchical or presidential systems may not be the best guarantors of political stability: in multi-ethnic societies, only one ethnic group can occupy the apex of such systems, and dissatisfaction may take the form of assassinations or coups rather than votes of no-confidence.[39] The Cambodian assembly may have had the precedent of Thailand's constitutional monarchy in mind when it voted to restore the Cambodian monarchy, but by choosing Sihanouk to occupy the throne it ensured that the Cambodian monarchy would be anything but constitutional. In the design of institutions, especially for war-ravaged societies, there is much to be said for structures which encourage ordinary people to rule well, rather than those

37. For detailed discussion of the South African transition, see Andrew Reynolds, ed., *Election '94 South Africa* (New York: St Martin's Press, 1994).
38. On the importance of parties which do not fully mirror a country's social cleavages, see Myron Weiner, "Empirical Democratic Theory," in Myron Weiner and Ergun Özbudun, eds., *Competitive Elections in Developing Countries* (Durham: Duke University Press, 1987), p. 32.
39. See Juan Linz, "The Perils of Presidentialism," *Journal of Democracy* 1 (Winter 1990), pp. 51–69; Fred W. Riggs, "Fragility of the Third World's Regimes," *International Social Science Journal* 136 (May 1993), pp. 199–243. For an overview of different institutional options, see Matthew Soberg Shugart and John M. Carey, *Presidents and Assemblies: Constitutional Design and Electoral Dynamics* (Cambridge: Cambridge University Press, 1992).

which work only if extraordinary talent is available.

The fourth relates to institutionalisation, the process by which institutions acquire legitimacy and become the accepted venue for political activity.[40] Even well designed institutions may not take root. They may be subverted by the ambitions of political actors or by the scale of problems which a society faces. There is not much that the individual peacemaker can do about this, but the UN and its member-states can. The process of postwar reconstruction can be assisted by agencies such as the UN Development Programme, the UN High Commissioner for Refugees, the World Food Programme and the UN International Children's Emergency Fund, whose activities may reduce the scale of the problems which a new regime faces as it tries to find its feet. If problems are truly acute, rulers may be tempted simply to loot the polity before it collapses completely. There are already worrying signs of this happening in Cambodia, in a fashion hauntingly reminiscent of the last few years of the Lon Nol regime.[41] To provide untied aid in such circumstances is pointless, but assistance with mine clearing, rural development, primary health care and education is vital. To make assistance conditional on the complete restoration of stability and on the development of a fully institutionalised polity is a good recipe for ensuring that neither will come about.

Conclusions

The preceding pages have focused more on peacemaking than peacekeeping, the reason being that many of the problems of peacekeeping in complex peacemaking operations are the same as in classic peacekeeping. It is important, however, to note two differences. First, in complex operations the range of tasks which fall to the military may be much more diverse than the well-defined activities of classic peacekeeping, and an ability to undertake these tasks is essential. Second, peacekeepers must be able to interact not simply with the military forces of enemies whom they physically separate but also with local civilians and with different elements of the UN system. The behaviour of peacekeepers towards the locals is a matter of enormous sensitivity, because popular confidence in the UN may be essential if the peacemaking exercise is to stay on course. Their behaviour towards a mixed bag of UN field staff is equally important, because dis-

---

40. See Samuel P. Huntington, *Political Order in Changing Societies* (New Haven: Yale University Press, 1968).

41. See Shawcross, *Cambodia's New Deal*, p. 89. On politics under Lon Nol, see William Shawcross, *Sideshow: Kissinger, Nixon and the Destruction of Cambodia* (London: Hogarth Press, 1991).

organisation too can blow a peacemaking exercise off course.

In recent years, UN peacemaking has gone beyond low-level mediation between states in conflict, and now involves a more thoroughgoing commitment to address the basic problems of political organisation within member-states. This is in principle an admirable commitment but, as the preceding pages show, it is a difficult one to fulfil. While Secretary-General Boutros-Ghali's elaboration of the problems facing peacemaking is persuasive, his proposed remedies hardly come to terms with the complexity of the problems. These problems, nonetheless, do not justify the abandonment of a commitment to peacemaking, for three reasons.

First, some peacemaking efforts succeed on their own terms. While the Namibia settlement is the most obvious example, similar arguments might be made about the El Salvador Accords, the British "Lancaster House" Agreement which brought independence to Zimbabwe and, (with somewhat more reservations) the elaborate negotiations which led to the December 1988 agreements on military disengagement in Southern Africa. A successful peacemaking exercise, while aiming at more than transient peace, does not and cannot ensure perpetual peace. That is ultimately in the hands of the former combatants.

Second, those that fail to achieve all their goals may nevertheless leave a country better placed than otherwise would have been the case. In Southern Africa, while Angola remains a venue for costly conflict, Mozambique is now better placed than when RENAMO plundered and massacred almost at will. In Cambodia, the UN provided a veil behind which the Chinese could abandon their support for the Khmer Rouge without suffering loss of face, and may yet be seen to have provided a crucial opportunity for the Cambodian people to break with their tragic past.

Third, the UN may be the last hope for the ordinary people in a traumatised country. When states fail, it is people who suffer. The 1994 UN report on Afghanistan poignantly recorded that "the Afghans often implored the United Nations not to abandon or fail them and to be involved at every stage of the political process,"[42] and when the UN mission moved to suspend its activities for a month in September 1994, even the Afghan government requested it to continue. Peacemaking is a laborious, frustrating and often fruitless endeavour, and wasteful if it fails. But the costs of war to ordinary people are almost beyond measure.

---

42. *Progress Report of the Special Mission to Afghanistan* (New York: United Nations, A/49/208, S/1994/766, 1 July 1994), para. 23 (g).

15

Peacekeeping or Peace-Enforcement?

Kenneth Christie

The United Nations has undergone a large-scale transformation in the wake of the end of the Cold War. Not only has there been a change in the style of conflict management, there have been fundamental changes in its very nature and role. We have a new historical context in which superpower rivalry and the "rules of the game" appear significantly less important and ethnic conflict and humanitarian concerns pose enormous challenges to the world body. In other words with the changes in the global security environment after the Cold War we find that there have been significant changes in the style of UN conflict management.

Peacekeeping operations too have undergone similar transformations. They are large and complex missions: Cambodia, the Balkans, Somalia and Rwanda were and are among the most pressing trouble spots and clearly ones that reflect different agendas, problems and operating styles. Japan and Germany are increasingly being pressed to contribute more manpower and the UN appears to be experiencing severe financial disarray as to how to finance these ventures, with little help from recession-afflicted countries in the West. In the wake of a recent coup and fierce tribal fighting in October 1993 in Burundi, the request for peacekeepers was turned down by the United Nations which appeared to have overextended itself.

UN peacekeepers have played an important role in defusing, stabilising and containing conflicts in many parts of the globe since 1945. Peace-keeping missions should not be viewed simply in terms of their success or failure to achieve mandates created by politicians, diplomats and officials, because their operations often have to adapt to complex socioeconomic, cultural and political realities unforseen at the higher levels. In order to carry out their roles peacekeepers have to be able to cope with changing on-the-ground realities, which influence the ways they interpret their mandate and perceive their functions.

The expansion of UN peacekeeping activity in the post-Cold War period has in turn led to an increased academic interest in the UN role in third-party intervention as an important aspect of conflict management. In the first part of the chapter I will be examining some of the changes in the UN's style of conflict management in the post Cold War period, the shifting ideas of peacekeeping and some of the conditions for its success. In the second section, the case studies of the recent operations in Cambodia and Somalia will be assessed in the light of peacekeeping versus peace-enforcement.

The End of the Cold War: A Shift in Managing Conflict?

Perhaps the major problem for the UN during the Cold War era was that its effectiveness was constrained by superpower rivalry. History showed that the organisation was more successful in managing conflict when the conflict did not involve the Cold War superpowers and was between middle and small states with modest military capabilities. It also helped if the superpowers were implacably opposed to such conflicts. In fact most if not all cases of peacekeeping during the Cold War were conflicts which did not really involve the superpowers. With the emergence of a "multipolar" rather than "bipolar" or even "unipolar" world, will the UN have a large role? Or will there be a reversal to the role of regional security mechanisms in managing conflict such as the North Atlantic Treaty Organisation (NATO) and the Association of Southeast Asian Nations (ASEAN) for instance?[1] The answer on both accounts appears to be yes and no.

The UN is already enjoying a larger role in the wake of the Cold War with large missions in Cambodia and the Balkans; in addition Japan and Germany have joined the ranks of peacekeepers for the first time. On the other hand whereas the UN previously appeared susceptible to influence from the two superpowers *vis-à-vis* the power of veto, now it appears susceptible to the whims of the so-called Cold War victor, the U.S. In short the UN is in a period of transition and ambiguity as it operates in a world characterised more by disorder than order.

Second, some may have surmised that regional organisations would have

---

1. Describing ASEAN as a regional security mechanism in the same light as NATO has to be qualified. ASEAN members clearly have diverse economies and political systems. Nevertheless, they have managed to coordinate their political and diplomatic activities fairly successfully, including a distinctive role in the Cambodian problem. They might be better analysed as being in the process of developing security mechanisms which are designed to safeguard, among other aspects, the idea of "economic security." See the chapter above by Amitav Acharya.

been regenerated and invigorated by the end of the Cold War. This is not the case. Security and its meaning has rapidly changed and many of these organisations such as NATO for instance have not yet found a real role in the midst of confusion. There is a wide gap between the various international security organisations that emerged in the post-1945 period and the new issues and agendas that have emerged in the wake of the Cold War. In this sense while more stress is put on such groups to show initiative, in the same breath their inability to define clear threats and goals leaves them in a security quandary. This is complicated further by the fact that many of these regional organisations fell under the security umbrella of Cold War antagonists and are still in the process of adjusting to new independent roles. This may lead of course to more and more competition between regions and organisations like the UN in the management of conflict. Or it may be that regional organisations will seek to alleviate the deficiencies of the global system.

The end of superpower rivalry has simultaneously put an end to the idea that peacekeeping was used merely as a ploy to prevent the Cold War expanding into other areas. Global geopolitics is more complex because we are no longer in a world dominated by Cold War thinking which tended to "strip regions of their characteristics, yielding an invariant foreign policy and an isotropic plain of strategic commitments."[2]

There is an increasing possibility of conflict management being applied to problems of self-determination within existing states and to situations of resurgent ethnonationalism where ethnic boundaries do not correspond to political boundaries (such as in the territory of the old Yugoslavia). Furthermore, following the 1991 Gulf War, the international community is at least theoretically in a stronger position to intervene in the internal affairs of states if it considers there have been gross violations of human rights (such as the case of the Iraqi Kurds). The scope for an extension of international and regional conflict management mechanisms is enormous, but so are the potential dangers. Ironically, the post-Cold War world may witness an increase in localised conflicts. As Lucienne Beuls noted, "regional conflicts are now decoupled from the earlier linkage with superpower rivalry. Regional conflicts may now be globally less critical but they may be freer to escalate to higher levels of violence."[3]

---

2. See John O'Loughlin and H. Heske, "From 'Geopolitik' to 'Geopolitique': Converting a Discipline for War to a Discipline for Peace," in N. Kliot and S. Waterman, eds., *The Political Geography of Conflict and Peace* (London: Belhaven Press, 1991).

3. Lucienne Beuls, "UN Peacekeeping in the Post Cold War Era: The Case of Cambodia," paper presented at the ECPR–Pan European Conference, Heidelberg, Germany, 16–20 September 1992.

Management of Internal Conflict by the United Nations

Inter-state peacekeeping often involves peacekeepers in clear-cut tasks such as placing troops into UN-monitored demilitarised or buffer zones, or the observation and maintenance of ceasefires along recognised boundaries or *de facto* borders. "Internal" missions frequently involve a more complex set of duties: civil administration; supervision of elections; maintenance of civil law and order; repatriation and resettlement of refugees (usually in conjunction with the UN High Commission for Refugees (UNHCR); and infrastructural improvements, to name a few. Most of the recent UN operations are of the "internal" type (e.g., Angola, El Salvador, Western Sahara, Croatia and Bosnia–Herzegovina, Somalia and Cambodia). Yet these recent operations are not entirely new ground for the UN, and past peacekeeping missions can provide lessons which inform current ones.[4]

In discussing the basic features of the UN-style conflict management, it is helpful to distinguish between two key terms—peacemaking and peacekeeping. Evans and Newnham have suggested that peacemaking may be regarded as the function of conflict settlement and resolution rather than of management.[5] Whereas Burton says that mediation (a peacemaking activity) is actually management of conflict that will hopefully lead towards some kind of negotiated political settlement, although not necessarily an end to conflict.[6] More often than not the final outcome is more likely to be a partial settlement with some of the underlying sources of conflict left unresolved. In UN usage, arbitrators and mediators often accompany the lower-level activities of civilian and military peacekeepers.

Mediation efforts include "multilateral diplomatic efforts within the framework of the Security Council, bilateral efforts of Member States, or through the good offices of the Secretary-General." Peacekeeping on the other hand often has modest aims, as Miall points out: "Peacekeeping by the UN or the international community usually means reaching a cease fire and bringing the parties to the negotiating table. It does not necessarily include settling the underlying conflict."[7] Although peacekeeping operations have become a common means of trying to defuse and stabilise violent conflicts, the word peacekeeping appears nowhere in the UN Charter. In effect peacekeeping arrangements have been made on an *ad hoc* basis. Increasing

4. See Alan James, "Internal peacekeeping," paper presented at the 6th Annual Conflict Studies Conference, Peacekeeping and the Challenge of Civil Conflict Resolution, Centre for Conflict Studies, University of New Brunswick, Fredericton, Canada.
5. G. Evans and J. Newnham, *The Dictionary of World Politics* (London: Harvester Wheatsheaf, 1992), p. 53.
6. J. Burton, *Conflict: Resolution and Prevention* (London: Macmillan, 1990), p. 129.
7. H. Miall, *The Peacemakers* (Basingstoke: Macmillan, 1992), p. 4.

demand in the post-Cold War period has encouraged more academic debate on the subject.

Peacekeeping forces are often deployed in areas of potential or actual conflict where the major powers have no real strategic or national interest at stake and they are typically made up of lightly armed infantry units.[8] It is an attempt in some ways to place or interpose forces between conflicting parties. Thus, peacekeeping and peacemaking are distinct but often inseparable activities, the former creating the on-the-ground conditions for the latter to continue. In this way they can both be viewed as part of the process of conflict management. And in the case of Cambodia, the peacekeeping operation actually incorporates elements of peacemaking.

The words "peaceful third party intervention" are particularly apt for peacekeeping under UN auspices. Unlike military enforcement campaigns where soldiers often fire first and ask questions later, the blue-helmeted soldiers have to show restraint, patience and tact, and are required to use friendly but firm persuasion without the use of bullets. This sometimes places peacekeepers in dangerous situations when up against militia and guerrillas who only respect force of arms. At least three conditions are necessary to establish a successful peacekeeping operation: consent, impartiality and non-enforcement.[9] Consent is regarded as one of the basic requirements, particularly in light of the principle of sovereignty. If consent is not provided by the host state to the presence of peacekeepers, then this can be claimed as interference in the domestic affairs of the state. Peacekeeping is a secondary activity "that is dependent, in respect of both its origins and its success, on the wishes and policies of others. In appropriate circumstances peacekeeping can make a valuable contribution to peace—but only if, and to the extent to which, disputants choose to take advantage of it."[10]

In the case of Cambodia, UNTAC never had the cooperation of one of the key actors in the dispute—the Khmer Rouge, and has had only partial cooperation from other key parties. Impartiality and non-enforcement are also prerequisites for a successful peacekeeping operation. The ability not to take sides is a crucial element in the success of these types of operation.[11] If the UN wants to continue its claim to intervene in its members' civil wars, it may be necessary to ensure that it is neutral and unbiased in its protection of

---

8. See United Nations, *The Blue Helmets: A Review of United Nations Peace-keeping* (New York: UN Department of Public Information, 2nd ed., 1990).

9. See Secretary-General Dag Hammarskjöld's list of six principles for peacekeeping as quoted in Charles C. Moskos Jr., *Peace Soldiers: The Sociology of a UN Military Force* (Chicago: University of Chicago Press, 1976), p. 13.

10. Alan James, *Peacekeeping in International Relations* (London: Macmillan, 1990), p. 5.

11. See Indar Jit Rikhye *et al., The Thin Blue Line: International Peacekeeping and the Future* (London: Yale University Press, 1974).

human rights. In that sense the UN must not have the same objectives as governments pursuing self-serving own national interests. In addition the subject of non-enforcement is also a very controversial and delicate aspect of this larger process, for there is "no viable half-way house between peace-keeping and enforcement."[12] And it appears quite clear that once peace-keepers have crossed the line into peace-enforcement there is very little hope of retracting their steps.

Cambodia

On 28 February 1992 the UN Security Council unanimously approved the "biggest, most expensive, and most ambitious peacekeeping operation in UN history."[13] The UN Transitional Authority in Cambodia (UNTAC) was an internal peacekeeping operation with a specific mandate to achieve "a comprehensive political settlement of the Cambodian conflict." Those goals however were not as comprehensive as the rhetoric and included elements such as the restoration of human rights, developing a civil administration, the maintenance of law and order through a civilian police component; the repatriation and resettlement of over 370 000 Cambodian refugees on the Thai side of the Thai–Cambodian border; disarming and demobilising the four factional armies, controlling the ceasefire agreement, verifying the withdrawal of foreign forces and organising and supervising the general elections held during 23–27 May 1993. In effect, UNTAC was given unprecedented powers for a UN operation which allowed "the world body to assume control of all important state functions...designed to prevent partisan manipulation ahead of the 1993 elections." [14]

UNTAC faced criticisms from all political factions, and it was unable to prevent widespread political intimidation, corruption and killings. Prince Norodom Sihanouk, who has acted as the "neutral chairman" of the Supreme National Council (SNC), which the UN set up as Cambodia's interim authority until the May 1993 elections, suggested that he would cooperate with UNTAC only as the quickest way of "getting rid" of it from Cambodia.

The State of Cambodia under Hun Sen had been equally critical of the UN. Their ceasefire violations were described as defensive acts to protect the rice harvest, regain hold over productive lands and help to provide some semblance of security in the country prior to the elections. But they also had

---

12. James, *Peacekeeping in International Politics,* p. 368.

13. A. Peang Meth, "The United Nations Peace Plan, the Cambodian Conflict, and the Future of Cambodia," *Contemporary Southeast Asia* 14 (June 1992), p. 33.

14. Nate Thayer, "Unsettled Land," *Far Eastern Economic Review,* 27 February 1992, p. 22.

a political purpose, to show that only the government army was able to take effective military action against the Khmer Rouge. In February, Hun Sen invited UNTAC to act as a buffer force between the government and rebel troops as a condition for the withdrawal of the Phnom Penh forces from various contested zones.

Cambodia has had a long history of violent conflict even prior to the infamous period of Democratic Kampuchea (the so-called "Pol Pot regime" of April 1975–January 1979). The greatest obstacle to the peace plan was the Khmer Rouge. In fact, throughout the "transitional" period the Khmer Rouge have resisted the implementation of the Paris Agreement, and they have continually made life difficult for UNTAC, which they regard as a "colonialist force." In early April four Bulgarian peacekeepers were killed by the Khmer Rouge. A Japanese electoral worker and his Cambodian interpreter were also killed.

The issue of territorial control highlights a fundamental problem, not only for UNTAC, but for the other UN peacekeeping missions. The UN interpretation of peacekeeping is that it should as far as possible be an impartial act in which force of arms is only resorted to for purposes of self-defence. This often places UN "blue helmets" in extremely delicate and dangerous situations, especially so when they are dealing with various internal factions, militia groups and bandits, as in the case of Cambodia. Without the cooperation of these armed groups peacekeepers are limited in their ability to manage conflicts. For instance, had UNTAC agreed to form buffer zones between the government and rebel forces, it would have placed lightly-armed blue helmets in front-line positions at the request of one faction but without the consent of the other. This would have immediately jeopardised the fragile impartiality of the UN mission, but more than this, it would have exposed UNTAC personnel to possible attacks from the Khmer Rouge on the pretext that the UN was acting on behalf of the government forces.

The question of how to deal with Khmer Rouge intransigence was a central dilemma for UNTAC. In July 1992, French Brigadier General Jean-Michel Loridon, who had headed the military component of the UN Advance Mission (UNAMIC), was dismissed from UNTAC due to "irreconcilable differences with his civilian and military chiefs." Loridon favoured a more forceful UNTAC response against the Khmer Rouge: "...it is possible ...at some point they will try to block the UN move by force. If it comes to that one may lose 200 men—and that could include myself—but the Khmer Rouge problem would be solved for good."[15]

These views are clearly more in line with peace-enforcement but the

---

15. Quoted in Nayan Chanda, "UN Divisions," *Far Eastern Economic Review*, 23 July 1992, p. 9.

higher chain of UN command appears reluctant to push for peace-enforcement and there appears to be conflict between the military commanders at the scene and the UN politicians behind the scenes.

In early April 1993, one of the Khmer Rouge leadership, Khieu Samphan, warned of more attacks on Vietnamese settlers. He also argued that UNTAC would meet with "complete failure" in its mission. Despite the condemnation of the violent attacks by the Khmer Rouge the official UN line has been to keep the doors open for the possible re-entry of the faction into the peace process. On the ground, UNTAC faced criticism that it was unable to provide the security needed to conduct free and fair elections. Just as the UN Protection Force (UNPROFOR) has faced criticisms from Bosnian Muslims that it has allowed Bosnian Serbs to seize more territory, UNTAC faced similar charges from different factions in Cambodia.

UNTAC Achievements

UNTAC represents a package of conflict management roles—civilian, police and military; economic, social and political. The cost is likely to run into several billions of U.S. dollars. As Segal and Berdal commented: "even enormous UN operations cannot rebuild countries…. There is clearly a need to lower expectations and to objectively reassess precisely what kind of role the UN can have when the real problem is one of nation-building."[16]

UNTAC tried but was obstructed in its efforts to extend the registration of voters and the political process throughout the territory of Cambodia. The Khmer Rouge have been the most obstructive opponents to UN efforts on the ground. Despite this obstruction the UN was credited with preparing the electoral roll and holding the election. Because of this Cambodia stands out as a post-Cold War success story in terms of UN management. More than 90 percent of the eligible electorate turned out to vote in difficult conditions.

An examination of the processes for and against nation-building in post-1993 election Cambodia is clearly an area for in-depth research. The important point here is that elections do not in themselves produce peaceful settlements, particularly if one or more of the factions involved in the conflict find that their political aspirations are not met or are even undermined by the election results. At the operational level UNTAC faced a fundamental dilemma common to other UN operations. The intransigence of the Khmer Rouge continues to have the effect of making UNTAC appear to be an impotent force. UNTAC was quite modest in size in comparison to the numbers of soldiers belonging to the main factions in the conflict. UNTAC

---

16. G. Segal and M. Berdal, "Failure in Cambodia would hurt the effectiveness of UNTAC," *Straits Times* (Singapore), 13 January 1993.

established its own military sectors with various regional headquarters for each of the main contingents. But its presence in the Cambodian countryside was selective and it was largely dependent upon mobile patrols for wider monitoring and visibility. UNTAC was unable to prevent sporadic incidents of violence. This does not mean the blue helmets are ineffective. Rather, it is a reflection of the realities that the Paris peace agreements did not persuade all armed factions to put down their weapons; that UNTAC was a big peace-keeping operation but still a small force given its responsibilities and the size of Cambodia; and that UNTAC could not use conventional military means to deter aggression.

The last point is a particularly sensitive one in conflict management. The fact is that once enforcement is used by peacekeepers they lose the semblance of impartiality. As Urquhart argues, violation of the principle of non-violence "almost invariably leads to peacekeepers becoming part of the conflict and therefore part of the problem."[17] The dangers of this should be clear in the Cambodian context—an internal situation where a high degree of violence is ongoing and there are still thousands of well-armed soldiers and militiamen despite UNTAC's efforts at demobilisation and disarmament.

Imperfect as it may be, UNTAC's role was to try to stabilise the situation and prevent further violent conflict by peaceful means, and certainly not to become an externally imposed enforcement operation. Nevertheless, when one or more factions continue to violate ceasefire arrangements and gain stronger *de facto* positions despite UN mediation, there is justification in questioning the UN mandate.

Another key difficulty in the conflict management process is that the diplomats, bureaucrats and politicians who are responsible for framing peace plans or mandates for UN operations often fail to appreciate the dynamic changes that have taken place over time. Different and new situational factors, socialisation experiences and interactions with adversaries are just some of the elements that caution us against assuming that the preferences of actors involved in conflict can be taken for granted or are static.

Related to the above is the fact that UN peace plans are formulated in what Lizée has called "the Western tradition of conflict management" involving the intersection of two fundamental dynamics: the state system, based on the localisation of the control of the means of violence in the state structure, and the capitalist system, based for its part on the logic of the accumulation of capital.[18] He argues that this is at odds with the Cambodian

17. Sir Brian Urquhart, "Foreword," in F. T. Liu, *United Nations Peacekeeping and the Non-Use of Force* (Boulder: Lynne Reiner, 1992), p. 7.

18. Pierre Lizée, "Prospects for Effective Conflict Resolution in Cambodia," paper presented at the 6th Annual Conflict Studies Conference, Peacekeeping and the Challenge of

tradition of conflict. In the analysis presented here I have not examined the local sociological and cultural context of the Cambodian conflict, which would help in developing a better understanding of its internal dynamics. As other research on peacekeeping operations has shown, misunderstandings and misinterpretations of actions can occur because third-party managers may not fully appreciate local culture, customs and traditions.

Somalia

The case of Somalia is a vastly different one. It serves to highlight some of the consequences involved in overstepping the line from peacekeeping to peace-enforcement. It is the Somalia case that appears as the best-known case of humanitarian intervention in the post-Cold War period in terms of the changing "rules" of the game and represented the first time that a force provided military backup for humanitarian operations. In this sense the Somali case provides a precedent. Clearly any ideas of territorial integrity or state sovereignty were sidelined in this case; one in which the humanitarian aid could not have been delivered to the people without enforcement measures. The notion that the government of a state should provide its consent to such action and that military involvement in a state's internal affairs was out of the question was abandoned in the desperate Somali circumstances. Principles of self-determination enshrined in the UN Charter were put on hold in East Africa in this period.

In the initial operation in Somalia, the government did actually provide consent, despite the fact that one could dispute whether Somalia actually had a government at the time. By late 1992 however the relief efforts had reached stagnation due to the protracted faction fighting amongst the Somali Warlords. As Robert Oakley argued:

> The UN had not originally calculated the political situation very well and its humanitarian efforts were not moving rapidly. This is a perennial problem that has been recognised and efforts are underway to improve it. When the UN got Mohamed Sahnoun there, who seemed to understand the political situation, he didn't have enough support for humanitarian efforts.[19]

The initial UN operation was regarded as a failure and served to highlight the inadequacy of peacekeeping forces operating in a state of near anarchy. Initially the UNOSOM mandate had extended to no more than monitoring a

---

Civil Conflict Resolution, Centre for Conflict Studies, University of New Brunswick, Fredericton, Canada.
19. "US Special Envoy to Somalia Recounts Mission," *US Institute of Peace Journal*, 6 (June 1993).

ceasefire in Mogadishu and providing escorts for food supplies being sent to the various distribution centres in and around the city. The breakdown of law and order, central authority and finally civil society finally left the UN with little other choice than to pursue enforcement measures *vis-à-vis* the deployment of U.S. forces.[20] The Security Council therefore decided to act under chapter VII. What was at stake in Somalia was clearly not international or regional peace or security *per se;* the vicious in-fighting posed no real threat to other states. However, the scale of the human tragedy which may have occurred was invoked to ensure the safe delivery of the aid. It was in effect a resolution based on a scenario of international conscience. This was different also from the situation in Northern Iraq in April 1991, when a U.S.-led coalition intervened to deliver relief supplies to Kurdish refugees who were under attack from the Iraqi armed forces. In this case Security Council Resolution 688 carried no real "enforcement" terms in the same way as a chapter VII motion.

The mandate in Somalia was in a state of expansion; chapter VII provided for the disarming of the various Somali factions invoked after the deaths of 24 Pakistani peacekeepers who were killed by supporters of General Mohammed Farah Aideed, the Somali warlord. Following this, the operation clearly became a military offensive. Its collapse signalled the difficulty of placing lightly armed soldiers into hostile and volatile situations. Somalia after all was a state of virtual anarchy. Consent and the non-enforcement rules were a major obstacle to peacekeepers.

In the case of Somalia, the UN found itself in a catch-22 situation. When engaged in peacekeeping operations with no real chance of success it was criticised for not taking enforcement action; on the other hand when it changed strategy it was accused of endangering the relief supplies. Similarly the ambiguity over the UN and U.S. roles in the operation raised the question of how effective such a response could be: major powers may be ill-equipped for peacekeeping particularly, in highly volatile and vulnerable situations.

Conclusion

Peacekeeping and peace-enforcement have undergone a transformation in the post-Cold War period; in both of the cases that have been examined in this chapter, the mandates were expanded beyond the traditional parameters of UN peacekeeping forces. Humanitarian intervention in one form or another has come to play a far larger role than previously thought possible or was politically acceptable.

---

20. See the chapter on Somalia by Robert Patman earlier in this volume.

While the UN-sponsored Agreements on a Comprehensive Political Settlement of the Cambodian Conflict represent over a decade of negotiations, the unanimity of the permanent five of the Security Council would have been impossible under Cold War conditions. Important global and regional geopolitical changes helped foster conditions for compromise between the four main factions involved in the internal conflict. Improved Chinese–Vietnamese relations, the backing of China for the UN peace plan, and ASEAN support for the plan, including the sending of personnel (from Indonesia, Malaysia and Singapore) to serve with UNTAC, have all helped to internalise the Cambodian conflict. And as we have seen the actual peace process within Cambodia and Somalia has not had the support of all the protagonists and actors involved.

A key argument based on studies of other peacekeeping missions is that those responsible for drafting high-level peace agreements should not expect the sudden injection of a large foreign peacekeeping force into a complex internal conflict to be able to create all the necessary conditions for a national political reconciliation. Part of the problem lies in the jargon used, with everything from peace-enforcement to peacemaking, peace-building and "humanitarian intervention" among others. Without clearcut definitions of these terms the confusion continues. The elasticity of these terms also leads to problems of application; just when do you use which strategy in which instance? It has been argued that peacekeeping in Bosnia in this light was a failure where peace-enforcement may have succeeded. In Somalia, however, as we have seen, this new term and practice of enforcement has had difficult results.

Classical concepts of "peacekeeping," while relevant to the Cold War, have undergone transformation in the 1990s. Humanitarian intervention, whether in the form of delivering relief supplies to starving populations or preventing the widespread abuse of human rights in some states, will become more acceptable over time. Necessarily many of the measures involved will entail a degree of force. Whether they will prove more successful in resolving or ending conflicts remains to be seen.

16

Peacekeeping, Peace-Enforcement and National Sovereignty

Alan James

Sovereignty is often thought to have something to do with freedom of behaviour. On that premise, the recently-extended ambit of the UN's peace-support activity could perhaps have had an adverse bearing on the sovereignty of those on whose territory the activity takes place. Such a development could also betoken—as the other side of the coin—a qualitative change in the UN's role in international relations. It does seem frequently to be supposed that both such things have occurred, or are in the process of occurring. But the exact nature of what has taken or is taking place remains less than clear. In part this reflects the accepted difficulty of seeing contemporary events in full perspective. There are, however, other factors which contribute to this result. The concept of sovereignty is notoriously elusive, which tends to afflict discourse on the subject with a measure of cloudiness. The splendid rhetorical resonance which attaches to the term "sovereignty" sometimes encourages those using it to seek after effect rather than clarity. And the goodwill which the concept of the UN can engender seems occasionally to stand in the way of a clear-eyed analysis of its political role.

In the examination of the relationship between state sovereignty and the UN's peace-support operations (that is, both peacekeeping and peace-enforcement) in this chapter, distinctions will be drawn between three ways in which, in this connection, the term sovereignty may be used. The first of them is to refer to a state's jurisdictional sovereignty—the state's legal freedom within its territorial domain. Secondly, the term is used to connote the state's political sovereignty—its freedom actually to pursue particular courses of action, both internally and in relation to other states. Finally, sovereignty is used to mean the state's international sovereignty—its status as a formally independent entity which is thereby eligible to participate in its own right in the processes of international relations.[1]

So far as the other aspects of the chapter's title are concerned, the word "peacekeeping" will be used to refer to the kind of activity which, since the 1950s, has been associated with that term, and more particularly with UN operations which have been so described: the deployment, in the cause of peace and with the consent of the host state, of impartial and non-threatening military personnel (with whom civilians may be associated). However, and in reflection of the developments of the last few years, a distinction will be introduced between peacekeeping of the traditional kind and peacekeeping which has a prickly aspect.

The prickliness of such a force (sometimes also described as muscular or assertive) may be evident in one or both of two ways. First, the UN Security Council may have departed from usual peacekeeping practice by dealing somewhat ambiguously with, or even directly denying, the principle that the host state must consent to the presence of the force and has the right to require its departure. Secondly, the mission's mandate and equipment may be more imposing than is usual for peacekeepers, signalling that the force has the right, the ability and, if necessary, the intention to engage in defensive measures of a significantly painful kind; and that some breaches by the parties of their undertakings or obligations may elicit a tough peace-restoring response. Some emphasis should be placed on the word "response." Such a force is not meant to take coercive initiatives nor has it been assigned a specific target state or group—which is why it has not been equipped for fullscale battle. It has been mounted to *assist* the disputants to live in peace, not to compel them to do so, and is even-handed in its approach to all of them. In consequence of its overall character and intent being impartial and non-threatening it may, notwithstanding its prickly elements, be categorised as in the peacekeeping mode.

Peace-enforcement, by contrast, refers to military activity which is both partial and threatening, and for which the consent of the target state or group is certainly not deemed necessary. In principle, therefore, it is clearly distinguishable from peacekeeping. Of course, real life may not always fit neatly into the analyst's categories. Thus it is possible that the circumstances of a particular case may result in some blurring of the division between prickly peacekeeping and peace enforcement. However, it is thought that the division is one which has a sound empirical base. As the commander of a UN force with prickly aspects has recently said, one does not go to war in

---

1. For an examination of these concepts, see Alan James, *Sovereign Statehood: The Basis of International Society* (London: Allen & Unwin, 1986), Chs. 9, 7, and 2 respectively.

white-painted vehicles![2]

In the ensuing discussion a distinction will periodically be drawn between the two typical locales in, or in relation to, which peace-support operations occur. They may be mounted at or with reference to a point of international demarcation, such as an established frontier or a ceasefire line —border operations. Alternatively, they may take place throughout part or all of the territory which lies within the jurisdiction of a single state, and with reference to a problem of internal origin—internal operations. Almost all the relatively numerous UN peacekeeping missions established during the first half of the 1990s are of this last type.

Jurisdictional Sovereignty

To the extent to which a state is under no specific or general international obligations regarding its internal behaviour, it is free to conduct itself as it sees fit. It may, to that extent, exercise its jurisdiction within its domain unrestricted by international legal requirements. It is, in this sense of the term, sovereign.

However, this particular concept is not an absolute. It is not something which a territorial entity either has immutably, or not at all. Rather, sovereignty in the sense of a state's domestic jurisdiction is relative in nature, a matter of degree. It is like a bundle of separable rights. Thus the bundle remains in existence notwithstanding the renunciation or involuntary loss of some of the individual items of which, collectively, it is composed. It also remains in existence even if the state is in some political disarray. The state continues to be sovereign—in the sense of having jurisdictional rights— over those areas of its affairs which are not subject to the obligations of international law.

Traditional Peacekeeping

Any peacekeeping mission inevitably involves restrictions on the host state's internal legal freedom—and thus diminishes its jurisdictional sovereignty. This is because such multinational bodies require rights both of a general organisational kind (organisational rights) and ones which enable them to carry out their specific tasks (functional rights). The granting of these rights is, in effect, a condition of the peacekeepers' presence.

It will probably take a little while for agreement to be reached between the host and the UN regarding the exact extent of the rights which are to be exercised by the peacekeeping mission. It could even be that a formal

---

2. The remark was made in the writer's hearing but in a non-attributable context.

agreement is never secured. Thus the UN Disengagement Observer Force (UNDOF) has operated in Syria since its establishment in 1974 without the benefit of a status-of-forces agreement. But informal understandings will undoubtedly come into existence with the arrival of a peacekeeping operation and, in the absence of a formal agreement, will be developed as necessary on an *ad hoc* basis.

Typically, a mission's organisational rights will involve the exclusion of the peacekeepers, civilian as well as military, from the criminal jurisdiction of the host and from some aspects of its civil jurisdiction. The premises of the mission will almost certainly be a no-go area for local officials; the mission is likely to have the right to control its own communications, and its members to be exempt from local taxation; and the mission will probably be entitled to import goods duty-free for its own use (including resale to its members). To facilitate the work of a peacekeeping force (as distinct from an observer group), the host can be expected to agree that the force may operate its own military police, and that as they go about their official duties the members of the force may bear arms for the purpose of self-defence. All peacekeepers are customarily granted the right of freedom of movement for the purpose of executing their tasks.

So far as a mission's functional rights are concerned, in the case of a border force it is likely to be agreed that an exclusive operational area be established for the force, to which the host state will not send its own military personnel. Furthermore, if this area has no settled population it may be placed under the full control of the peacekeeping force. The UN's Second Emergency Force (UNEF II) was given this responsibility in respect of the buffer zones between Egyptian and Israeli forces which were established by the Disengagement Agreements of 1974 and 1975.[3]

The functional rights given to internal peacekeeping missions, in reflection of the nature and extent of their tasks, are likely to be more intrusive than the ones granted to a border mission. Multifaceted internal missions are likely to have responsibility for the oversight and maybe the conduct of elections; the investigation of alleged breaches of human rights; political education; the shadowing of the local police; the repatriation and resettlement of refugees; assisting in the disarmament of formerly warring groups; watching over ceasefires; and even supervising government ministries. Such roles take the peacekeepers virtually to the centre of the domestic political stage, involving them in activity which is widely seen as characteristically governmental. Concomitantly, the jurisdictional sov-

---

3. See Ensio Siilasvuo, *In the Service of Peace in the Middle East, 1967–1979* (London: C. Hurst, 1992), p. 247. His comment refers to the first agreement, but is equally applicable to the second.

ereignty of the host state suffers a relatively severe limitation.

Two bodies which exercised more or less the full range of the above-mentioned responsibilities were the UN Transition Assistance Group (UNTAG) in Namibia (1989–90), which watched over the departure of South Africa from that territory and Namibia's consequential emergence as an independent state; and the UN Transitional Authority in Cambodia (UNTAC, 1992–93), which fostered the process of national reconciliation in that war-torn country.

Whether the host state has the right to require a traditional peacekeeping body to leave will probably not be spelt out, leaving the law on the issue somewhat uncertain. It is, of course, possible for the host specifically to agree not to make such a demand unilaterally,[4] but undertakings of that nature are most unusual. In the absence of any indications which suggest that the host has qualified or abandoned its rights in this respect, it is arguable that as a matter of law the host is entitled to withdraw its consent to the continued operation of a peacekeeping mission, and that this removes the legal basis for its presence.

Be that as it may, a traditional peacekeeping mission entails some not insignificant limitations on the host state's jurisdictional sovereignty. It is not entitled to subject the peacekeepers to the normal requirements of its law regarding aliens; and its own civil servants, police, and armed forces will, in varying degree, be less legally free than before. To that extent, the host's right to exercise jurisdiction domestically has been restricted. Of course, these restrictions flow from the state's initial consent to the presence of the peacekeepers. But as jurisdictional sovereignty consists of the extent of a state's legal freedom within its own territory, it is the mere fact of the curtailment of that freedom which represents a diminution of its sovereignty. The source of the curtailment is immaterial.

Prickly Peacekeeping

This type of peacekeeping will involve additional limitations on the host's sovereignty (in the sense now being discussed), and will do so in areas which tend to be particularly sensitive. One respect in which this may be so concerns the circumstances relating to the arrival and eventual departure of a peacekeeping body. For it is open to the UN Security Council, basing itself on chapter VII of the UN Charter, to determine that a particular state or pair

---

4. It was intended that this should be the position with regard to the UN Force which was to operate under the Egypt–Israel Peace Treaty of 1979. In the event the plan for such a force was stillborn. But such an undertaking was entered into with regard to the non-UN force which took its place, the Multinational Force and Observers; see Mala Tabory, *The Multinational Force and Observers in the Sinai* (Boulder: Westview, 1986), Ch. 8.

of states must accept a peacekeeping body and that it is up to the Council, not the host(s), to decide when the mission should leave.

The Iraq–Kuwait Observation Mission (UNIKOM) was established on this non-consensual basis in 1991.[5] The two states concerned, being UN members, were in no position to deny the legal propriety or effect of this procedure. Nonetheless, depriving them, in this instance, of their right to say yea or nay to the idea that UN troops should operate on their soil represented a substantial curtailment of their jurisdictional sovereignty.

A possibly comparable case, which engages in both border and internal peacekeeping, is that of the UN Protection Force (UNPROFOR) in Croatia. Here the UN's role is partly to watch over the borders of the Serbian enclaves in Croatia (the so-called UN Protected Areas) and partly to operate within the enclaves. Since early 1993,[6] the Security Council has taken to prefacing its resolutions regarding Croatia, including several which extended the force's mandate, with the declaration that it is "acting under chapter VII" of the Charter. This implies that Croatia must accept those decisions. For its part, however, the host state has gone out of its way to emphasise that it has the right to withdraw its consent to the continued presence of UNPROFOR in Croatia,[7] and at one point said that it would require its departure by a certain date unless the situation improved.[8] The weight of the argument in this legal standoff is probably on the UN's side.

With regard to operational activity (as distinct from matters relating to arrival and departure), it is unlikely that prickly peacekeeping at a border will entail organisational and functional rights of a more extensive kind than those which flow from a mission with a traditional orientation. Internal prickliness, however, will make its mark. For if peacekeepers have, under chapter VII of the UN Charter, been given the right to exercise a measure of assertiveness, this means that the jurisdictional sovereignty of the host state has to that extent been curtailed. The state concerned is now less than exclusively in command of the right to engage in the internal use of armed force. Such an additional abridgement of a state's legal freedom has occurred in respect of Bosnia–Herzegovina. Here, in the overall context of a peacekeeping operation, the Security Council has given its force the right to protect the delivery of humanitarian supplies; banned all military flights in the state's air space; asserted the right to ensure compliance with the ban; established six "safe areas"; authorised certain measures to protect their

5. See para. 5 of Resolution 687 (3 April 1991) and para. 2 of Resolution 689 (9 April 1991).

6. The first instance was Resolution 807 (19 February 1993)

7. See UN Documents, S/25749 (11 May 1993), S/25953 (15 June 1993), S/26300 (13 August 1993), and S/1994/305 (16 March 1994).

8. See UN Document S/26491 (24 September 1993).

civilian inhabitants; and demanded a nationwide ceasefire.[9] Looked at in this way alone, it is as if, in these limited but significant respects, the state has been nudged aside and the UN has taken over some of its central tasks.

Peace-Enforcement

In the case of peace-enforcement, it is not a matter of the state suffering some limited overriding of its prerogatives. Instead, it is treated in a peremptory way in respect of a whole area of its central concerns. Such imperative action by or with the authority of the UN is very likely to result in a substantial curtailment of the sovereignty, in the domestic jurisdiction sense, of the state concerned.

If, for example, the response to cross-border aggression involves action on the soil of the state being disciplined—as in the early 1950s and in 1991 in the cases of North Korea and Iraq respectively—that state will be unable to exercise jurisdiction in the areas temporarily occupied by the peace-enforcing personnel. The specific provisions of the "host's" legal regime can be expected to remain much the same. But it will operate by the leave of those temporarily in charge, and be subject to their overall control. Long-term punitive measures may also be imposed on the aggressor state—as happened in respect of Iraq—placing considerable restrictions on its jurisdictional sovereignty.

The alternative kind of peace-enforcement is where the international community assumes far-reaching rights within a state with a view to the restoration of order or "peace-building." Here, too, at least on the surface of things, the state's relevant jurisdictional rights are being put into suspense. An instance of this sort of activity is the undoing by the UN of the secessionist Congolese Province of Katanga in the early 1960s. Latterly, the UN embarked on a similar role in Somalia, first authorising others to use "all necessary means" in a humanitarian cause, and then relaunching its own operation with the ambitious mandate of creating and maintaining "a secure environment" throughout the country.[10]

Jurisdictional Sovereignty Re-Conceptualised?

The above discussion has proceeded on the premise, thought to be well established, that sovereignty in the domestic jurisdiction sense is to be conceived as a bundle of rights. Alternatively, it is like a sliding scale, the marker on which may go up and down in response to individual additions to

---

9. See Security Council Resolutions 781 (9 October 1992), 816 (31 March 1993), 819 (16 April 1993), 824 (6 May 1993), 836 (4 June 1993), and 913 (22 April 1994).

10. Security Council Resolutions 794 (3 December 1992) and 814 (26 March 1993).

and diminutions of the state's jurisdictional ambit. So envisaged, and for as long as the state itself remains in existence, so does its sovereignty.

However, in recent years there has been a good deal of talk about the possible erosion or altered content of sovereignty, suggesting that the concept needs reformulation. Exactly what in this connection is meant by sovereignty has not always been made clear. But inasmuch as sovereignty is often thought to be legal in character, the issue has relevance to jurisdictional sovereignty. The question may therefore be posed whether at some point along the jurisdictional spectrum a line exists or should exist which demarcates one type of inroad into a state's jurisdictional sovereignty from another—one being seen as an unremarkable and acceptable curtailment of sovereignty while the other in some way undermines that sovereignty. More particularly, in the present context it may be asked whether some of the developments surveyed above suggest a case for the drawing of such a line. The implication is that recent peace-support operations may have broken new empirical ground, and that this should be expressed in a revised concept of the amount of jurisdictional sovereignty which a territorial entity must enjoy for it still to be considered, in this sense, a sovereign state.

It is extremely hard to see how such an approach could be operationalised, or what consequences would flow from a declaration that a state had in this respect fallen short. But quite apart from its impracticality, there are logical grounds for rejecting the line-drawing suggestion, and support for that response comes from history. The logical case is that the suggestion is incompatible with the concept of jurisdictional sovereignty. As this sort of sovereignty is envisaged as a fully-sliding scale, the marker can, by definition, freely move about on the scale. The very nature of domestic jurisdiction, in other words, is such that it has a hugely variable content—which is inconsistent with line drawing. If the state concerned, or a legally entitled outsider, wishes it, quite substantial particularised limits may be placed on the state's exercise of its jurisdictional sovereignty, so enabling an external agency lawfully to perform specified functions within the host state's domain. But so long as the state remains in existence (and that has to do with a different conception of sovereignty from the one now being discussed), it remains a jurisdictional sovereign, and continues to exercise some measure of jurisdiction.

Besides this logical argument, it may be pointed out that there is little basis in history for the implication that the state as a jurisdictional sovereign may be threatened if limitations on the exercise of its domestic jurisdiction reach beyond a certain (difficult-to-specify) point. It is worth remembering that states have long accepted, even as far back as the origin of the international society half a millennium ago—when diplomats were given some immunity from local jurisdictional processes—that as a practical matter they can hardly enjoy complete legal freedom within their borders. Sometimes such inroads have gone deep. It is not uncommon for defeated states to experience this—the peace treaty imposed on Germany in 1919 comes to mind. Weak states have also sometimes found it necessary to accept large limitations on their jurisdictional sovereignty. The reconstruction of Austria's and Hungary's finances in the 1920s was controlled by international committees. But it is not just weak states who grant far-reaching jurisdictional rights to outsiders. During the Cold War a number of weighty Western states allowed the United States to emplace military bases within their metropolitan territory on legal terms which unquestionably had a quite substantial restricting impact on the host's jurisdictional sovereignty. (Such arrangements were, in fact, very like those which attach to peacekeeping missions.)

In short, the play of international politics is such that there is nothing unusual about a state limiting its domestic jurisdiction, even to a considerable degree, or having such limits imposed upon it. Therefore the UN's recent peace-support operations do not call for a reconceptualisation of sovereignty in its domestic jurisdiction sense. Rather, in respect of what they entail for a state's legal arrangements, such operations find a place in a long historical tradition.

Political Sovereignty

The concept of sovereignty often connotes political freedom. As such, like the previously-discussed usage, its nature is necessarily relative. Even a state with huge political assets finds that there are many circumstances in which, as a practical matter, it cannot do what it would like to do. Lesser states are likely to find themselves more circumscribed—although there are also occasions on which, paradoxically, their smaller size may give them a greater immediate freedom. Nonetheless, constraint is the general factor of which participants in the international political game are perhaps most aware. The question now to be considered is whether the UN's peace-support operations place limits on the political sovereignty of the states in relation to which such activity is undertaken, and so subjects their sovereignty, in this second sense, to some diminution.

Border Operations

It could easily be thought that a traditional peacekeeping operation at a border would have little or no political impact of a limiting kind. A small, lightly armed force presents no significant military obstacle to a national army on the march, or even to armed provocations. If the peacekeepers are a tiny observer group, their properties as a physical obstacle are that much less. Moreover, it could be supposed that a state would hardly consent to the presence of an operation which might obstruct its national purposes. Political sovereignty would therefore seem unaffected by border peace-keeping of a traditional kind.

At one level, comments such as these cannot be faulted. If a state is determined to cross a border, the fact that it is patrolled or observed by UN peacekeepers is not going to stand in the state's way. This has been demonstrated on several occasions in the Indo–Pakistani and the Arab–Israeli contexts, most notably in 1982 when the Israeli Army swept through the area in South Lebanon occupied by a relatively sizeable UN force.

But there are many other occasions when political calculations are less stark. In these circumstances a UN border operation, particularly a force which has an exclusive operational area—such as the UN Force in Cyprus since 1974 and UNDOF between Israel and Syria since the same date—can assume something in the nature of an independent deterrent life of its own. The states on either side of it are likely to impress their frontline forces with the need for tight discipline, as they will not wish to have an accusatory finger pointed at them by an impartial body. They will probably think several times before authorising a land raid on the other side, given that this will involve passing through the peacekeepers' lines and hence will have adverse diplomatic repercussions—in relation both to the UN itself and to the states from which the peacekeepers come. Such a move will also in-volve, on the part of the host state, a breach of its agreement with the UN.

Of course, there are still going to be problems between the peacekeepers and the parties, especially when the latter test (as they frequently do) the vigilance and resolve of newly arrived observers and contingents. But generally, and for as long as the disputants are anxious to avoid armed conflict, a peacekeeping body encourages them to take extra care to ensure that their behaviour is not open to unnecessary criticism. In these ways their political freedom, and hence (in this sense) their sovereignty, is additionally constrained by a peacekeeping watch on one of their borders.

This aspect of the situation may well be intensified if such a watch has a prickly aspect. For then any aggressively minded disputant knows that mis-behaviour could have greater costs, possibly much greater ones. This may not be immediately evident from the number and equipment of the troops on the ground. For unless a border is bubbling with tension, it is perhaps unlikely that the peacekeeping body will be physically formidable. But if the mandate invokes chapter VII, and the diplomatic constellation suggests that these words will be backed by deeds, then a state contemplating a hostile move will probably be given sharp pause by the likely repercussions. This must surely be Iraq's calculation as it thinks about what UNIKOM's one thousand or so men represent. Its political sovereignty is in consequence sharply curtailed. And if successful enforcement should take place across a border, as it did across this one in 1991, the limits on the enforcee's political freedom are made abundantly plain and may, through subsequent punitive measures, be extended well into the future.

Internal Peacekeeping

Provided there is cooperation (or sufficient cooperation) from all concerned, the impact of a traditional instance of internal peacekeeping activity on the state's political sovereignty will be comparable to that of peacekeeping at a border. Given that the state in question will be concerned to be seen as playing fair, its freedom will to that extent be limited. However, there are other circumstances in which the state's political freedom may be little influenced by peacekeepers. And yet others where, far from being limited, the state's sovereignty (in the sense now being discussed) will, through peacekeeping help, be restored rather than restricted.

There are two rather different kinds of context in which traditional peacekeeping has little or no bearing on the political freedom of the host state, or on that of any other state which is associated with the peacekeeping agreement. The first of these is where the state concerned decides that to do what has been promised, or to allow the peacekeepers to do it, would have political costs which outweigh the benefits which would accrue from compliance and cooperation. Thus Morocco is at least partly responsible for the inability, so far, of MINURSO (the UN's peacekeeping body) to prepare for and organise a referendum over the future of the ex-Spanish colony of Western Sahara. This was originally scheduled for January 1992. In theory, the issue is still moving forward, and MINURSO maintains a preliminary presence in the area. But Morocco's political sovereignty has not been curtailed in the manner originally envisaged.[11] Likewise, the military authorities in Haiti reneged on a 1993 peacekeeping agreement, resulting in the abrupt departure of the advance elements of the UN's Mission in Haiti (UNMIH).[12] In other words, a state may sometimes simply override the peacekeepers, asserting its political sovereignty in a particularly direct way.

The other context where political sovereignty is unaffected by traditional peacekeeping within a state is where serious armed conflict has broken out.

---

11. See Security Council Resolution 907 (29 March 1994).
12. See UN Document S/26802 (26 November 1993). [This chapter was completed before the U.S. invasion of Haiti. Editors.]

What the peacekeepers face in this sort of situation is not so much the assertion by the state of its political sovereignty as an internal struggle for dominance, in respect of part or all of the state. They find themselves in the midst of a civil war, or even of a more generalised breakdown of governmental authority. Here traditional peacekeeping becomes largely irrelevant. Thus the outbreak in 1994 of serious fighting in Rwanda cut almost all the ground from underneath the UN Assistance Mission for Rwanda (UNAMIR), which had been established in October of the previous year to assist in the implementation of a peace agreement. In April 1994 the Security Council therefore reduced it from 2500 military personnel to 270.[13] In a similar way, the UN Observer Mission in Georgia (UNOMIG) was reduced to single figures following the outbreak of fighting in September 1993 between the Government and the Abkhazian secessionists.[14]

It may, however, be questioned whether in this kind of extreme context there is much meaning, from an internal perspective, to the concept of "the state." From an external point of view the state may still be deemed to exist and to be possessed of legal obligations—including ones relating to its internal behaviour. But seen from inside, and in political terms, the state has, at least for the time being, unravelled into two or more—perhaps many more—parts. It will doubtless still be possible to identify "the government." But that body—formally representing the state—is likely in reality to be just one of the parties to the ongoing civil conflict. It therefore does not make much sense to talk as if political sovereignty was still being exercised by an overarching entity.

This draws attention to the ground for the earlier statement that peacekeeping may sometimes help in the restoration of a state's political sovereignty. A high proportion of recent internal peacekeeping operations have been designed to assist in the implementation of an agreement aiming at national reconciliation. If successful, this process will produce a government which will be seen as genuinely representing the state, and hence as having responsibility for the maintenance of the internal political fabric and for decisions regarding external affairs. Accordingly, what this kind of UN peacekeeping is about is, at bottom, the rehabilitation of the state. It is in the business of helping to reconstruct the state's internal political sovereignty and hence its ability to act effectively in external political matters as a sovereign. The process will involve some restrictions on the political freedom of the leading internal disputants, including the one which happens to hold the seals of government. But the outcome is intended to be the

---

13. See UN Document S/1994/470 (20 April 1994) and Security Council Resolution 912 (21 April 1994).

14. See UN Document, S/26646 (27 October 1993).

restoration of the state as a unified political actor.

This is what, as of August 1994, the UN is trying to do in Angola, El Salvador, Liberia, and Mozambique. It is what it tried to do earlier in the 1990s in Cambodia and among five Central American states. And it was also a large part of its role in the 1960s in the Congo (now Zaire) and the Dominican Republic.[15] However, this list also testifies to the difficulty of the task. In form, Cambodia now enjoys a legitimate government, able to act as the authoritative voice box of the state; but in practice the country is still rent by a major division. In Mozambique reconciling elections are due to be held in October 1994, and the UN plans thereupon to withdraw its peace-keepers posthaste, as it did in respect of Cambodia. But, as in Cambodia, substantial problems persist, as might be expected after more than a decade of bitter civil war. In Angola the UN-supervised elections were followed by a resumption of fighting, still unhappily watched over by peacekeepers. The picture is somewhat brighter in El Salvador, but the country is not yet united. And in Liberia fighting continues, notwithstanding the peace accord. Manifestly, traditional peacekeeping is far from an assured route to the restoration of political sovereignty.

Internal Enforcement

Should a state's lack of unity take the form of part of it having declared independence of the centre, it would be possible for the UN to recreate a single politically sovereign entity by taking armed action against the secessionists. It did so in respect of the Congolese Province of Katanga in 1962–63. But, in respect of one roughly comparable current case—Bosnia–Herzegovina—there is little sign that the UN will advance from its present cautious prickliness to the imposition of its preferred territorial arrangement on the Bosnian Serbs. Until some form of settlement is reached, the state of Bosnia–Herzegovina will remain an established legal unit but, in political terms, one divided against itself—and hence lacking political sovereignty.

In the case of a state which has suffered a more generalised collapse, the UN could try to take it by the scruff of the neck and shake its various parts back into a unified pattern. This is what was ambitiously attempted in Somalia in 1993.[16] It went disastrously wrong,[17] resulting in a scaling down of the mandate to one marked by moderate prickliness.[18] If this experience is regarded as typical, the UN may in future show more caution

---

15. See *United Nations Peacekeeping Operations. Information Notes. 1993: Update No. 2* (New York: UN Department of Public Information, November 1993).

16. For the scheme, see UN Document S/25354 (3 March 1993).

17. For the report of the subsequent enquiry, see UN Document S/1994/653 (1 June 1994).

18. See Security Council Resolution 897 (4 February 1994).

over trying to build up a state's political sovereignty by way of coercion.

When internal peace-enforcement is employed against a state which does not lack order but which is deemed untrustworthy or deserving of punishment, the impact of a successful operation on the state's political sovereignty will be immediate: such action will result in its diminution. Thus, the presence of allied forces in Northern Iraq for a few months after the end of the Gulf War undoubtedly curtailed Iraq's internal freedom. This was not specifically authorised by the UN, but those conducting it claimed, controversially, that authority for it was provided by Security Council Resolution 688 (5 April 1991). The same claim has been made in respect of the allies' ban on Iraqi military flights to the north of the 36th parallel enunciated in 1991, and a similar ban on flights to the south of the 32nd parallel enunciated in 1992. Iraq regularly protests to the UN about the enforcing activity of foreign aeroplanes in these "no fly zones,"[19] which have had a large adverse impact on the state's ability to exercise political sovereignty within its own domain.

What the allied powers would really like is a different government in Iraq but they see no easy way of achieving it. In respect of the much weaker state of Haiti, however, the UN has authorised member-states (meaning, principally, the United States) to use "all necessary means to facilitate the departure"[20] of Haiti's military leaders. Significantly, China and Brazil did not endorse this scheme, and it is reported that only some horse-trading brought Russia into line.[21] It is a direct challenge to the political sovereignty of the Haitian state, as presently run, and as such is likely to be a milestone for the UN. Possibly it may also prove to be something of a millstone!

A Great-Power Directorate?

Despite the difficulties which have been encountered in a number of these cases, there is a question as to whether the Security Council is moving into a more assertive role, either through the direct use of UN-controlled forces or by authorising individual permanent members of the Council to take certain action.[22] If it were, this would convey mixed news for political sovereignty. On the one hand, states at whom the UN's ire was aimed would lose; but on the other hand, states which were rebuilt with the UN's assistance would

---

19. See, for example, UN Document S/1994/925 (3 August 1994).
20. Security Council Resolution 940 (31 July 1994).
21. See the *Times* (London), 1 August 1994.
22. This last type of action has also been taken in respect of the humanitarian needs of Rwanda: see Security Council Resolution 929 (22 June 1994). Mention should also be made of the fact that in recent years the Council has imposed economic sanctions on a number of states and groups.

gain.

Such a development would represent the type of role which was envisaged for the Council when the UN was set up. Now, however, circumstances have changed, notably in respect of the size and composition of the UN's membership. It is a much larger company than in 1945, and many of its constituents, being relatively weak, worry about the emergence of a powerful directorate. Quite clearly there is a concern that the Council might get over-authoritarian, that it might take too close an interest in certain internal matters, and that it has already displayed a disturbing disdain for the UN's non-Council members. Put differently, the Council, through its enhanced role in keeping the peace, is seen as possibly assuming something of the aspect of a sovereignty-threatening spectre.

Perhaps partly in response, in December 1992 the General Assembly passed Resolution 47/130 on the need for "Respect for the principles of national sovereignty and non-interference in the internal affairs of States in their electoral processes." It had quite a lot to say on the subject. Significantly, the resolution was opposed by four of the five permanent members of the Security Council: Britain, France, Russia and the United States. But the votes of 99 of the organisation's members—roughly speaking, the Third World element—carried it through (China being among them). Six months later, when the Council's report for June 1991–June 1992 (tardily presented in June 1993) was debated in the General Assembly, the representatives of states from Africa (both north and south of the Sahara), Asia, Latin America, Australasia and Western Europe all gave issue to a veritable litany of complaints about what were portrayed as the Council's high-handed practices.[23]

It is perhaps no bad thing that the Council, and especially its permanent members, should be reminded that leaders do well to do what is possible to keep their followers happy. Manifestly, many members would be far from happy if the UN's peace-support operations came to look too much like the (maybe sovereignty-undermining) tool of the great. Egalitarianism is a deeply-rooted international concept, however difficult it often is to match it with the practicalities of life. And the UN is commonly seen as exemplifying this principle. If there were a marked move away from this position, keen controversy could easily ensue.

There is, however, little the Assembly can do about its feeling of being left out in the cold, notwithstanding the fact that it holds the organisation's purse strings. Its warning shots across the Council's bows are just about the maximum it can assay: it has no torpedoes in reserve. But it is doubtful if this problem will become markedly more serious. Quite apart from the

---

23. See UN Document, A/47/PV.106 (12 July 1993).

frequent practical problems attendant on tough action, the Council is most unlikely to precipitate a confrontation. From time to time its members need votes in the General Assembly, and the non-permanent members (and China, too) will keep the remaining members in touch with grassroots opinion. Collectively it is well aware that it is not in the position of the great powers of the nineteenth century (who almost exactly one hundred years ago dispatched occupying forces to Crete and Macedonia in the interests of international order). Heady though the atmosphere has recently been, it has not become intoxicating. Political sovereignty is not therefore under any general threat.

International Sovereignty

As well as referring to the extent of a state's domestic jurisdiction or its political freedom, the term sovereignty is also used, in an international context, to connote the enjoyment of a certain status—that which indicates that the territorial entity in question is eligible to play a full part in international relations. Indeed, this concept may be seen as the most fundamental of the three. For it is because a territorial entity enjoys sovereign status internationally that its varying jurisdictional and political freedom may sensibly be spoken of as exemplifications of sovereignty. It is, in other words, internationally sovereign states who possess these last two attributes.

In its international sense, sovereignty consists of constitutional independence—a territory's possession of a constitution which is not subject to a superior constitution. Thus a colony or the constituent state of a federation cannot be sovereign in the way in which the term is here used, no matter how large or powerful it may be. Moreover, and unlike jurisdictional and political sovereignty (which are phenomena of a relative kind), international sovereignty is an absolute concept. Thus a distinct territory is either internationally sovereign or not. Sovereignty, in this usage, is either present or absent. There is no halfway house.

Peacekeeping and Peace-Enforcement

Neither peacekeeping nor peace-enforcement, as so far experienced, has resulted in a state's loss of international sovereignty. All such operations have taken place on the soil of and in relation to internationally sovereign states. Such activity does indeed have a limiting effect on the jurisdictional sovereignty of the host, and it may also curtail the host's political sovereignty—or perhaps, where it has become unravelled, lead to its restoration. But the absolute international sovereignty of host states has been unaffected by the peacekeepers' or peace-enforcers' presence. The states in question have unquestionably retained their international sovereign status.

The UN as an International Sovereign?

However, in principle there is no reason why the UN should not, in the interests of what is judged to be international peace, formally take over a sovereign state on an agreed or a mandatory basis. Thus the world organisation would enjoy jurisdictional and political sovereignty in the territory in question, and could be treated internationally as a sovereign. For a variety of sensitive reasons, it is unlikely that things would be expressed in quite that way. Instead, to use the term which has a place in the UN Charter and has currently been used in this connection, the territory would probably be spoken of as in the UN's trust: it would be an instance of UN trusteeship, implying that it was a temporary arrangement.[24] But for as long as the trusteeship lasted the UN would, internally, be more or less (depending on the exact terms of its mandate) in the position of a sovereign state. Concomitantly, the international sovereignty of the state so taken over would have been put into suspense, rather in the manner in which Newfoundland, arguably then a sovereign state, moved into constitutional and international limbo in 1933 in consequence of its financial problems. (It moved out of this position, becoming a Province of Canada, in 1949.)

As a matter of practice, however, there seems little likelihood of the UN asserting clear *de jure* control over a (previously) sovereign state, however parlous its condition. Such a development would be exceedingly unwelcome to the great majority of UN members, so uneasy are they about moves which might threaten the principle that international sovereignty, once achieved, cannot be taken away. However improbable the sequence, they worry that one instance of this kind could provide some encouragement for another, and then another. More than a few of them have good reason to feel keenly about the undesirability of that kind of precedent. It is hard to imagine the Security Council ignoring these considerations.

No doubt for these reasons the UN has shown great formal solicitude towards states in which it has already come to exercise a measure of *de facto* control. Thus, in the case of South Lebanon, from the establishment of the UN's Interim Force in 1978 up to the early 1990s, the UN always punctiliously sought the agreement of Lebanon for the continued presence of the

---

24. For references to this idea, see UK House of Commons, Session 1992–93, Foreign Affairs Committee, *The Expanding Role of the United Nations and its Implications for United Kingdom Policy. Volume I* (London: HMSO, 1993), pp. xxv–xxvi; see also Dick Leurdijk, "Options for a Civil Authority of the UN: Protectorate, Transitional Authority or Trusteeship, or else?" *Internationale Spectator* 47 (November 1993); and see also Simon Jenkins, "Africa's Fate Is Its Own," *Times*, 17 August 1994.

force on its soil—notwithstanding the blatant fact that during that period the Lebanese government exercised not a whit of authority in the area in question. In Cambodia the UN Transitional Authority (1992–93) was working, in formal terms, in conjunction with the host state's Supreme National Council. In Bosnia–Herzegovina, although the host state is in disarray, it is deemed to be there. Even in respect of Somalia, where the UN went furthest in the direction of *de facto* control, it is notable that care was taken not to overstep the *de facto* limit. Thus the international sovereignty of the Somali state was left intact. Admittedly it was a shell without a coherent body—but the crucial thing was that the UN was working inside it, to give it a unified substance, rather than first coming along from the outside with a hijacking and sovereignty-crunching embrace.

Conclusion

Accordingly, international sovereignty does not seem in the least threatened by UN peacekeeping and peace-enforcement. Such activities will, in respect of the very different concept of jurisdictional sovereignty, necessarily have a limiting effect. This may also be true with regard to political sovereignty—although it is also very possible that the UN's peace-support operations will contribute to the restoration of the host state's political sovereignty.

There is a sense in which this last impact is entirely appropriate. For the United Nations is not in competition with any kind of state sovereignty. On the contrary, the United Nations is in the nature of a professional association of internationally sovereign states. Accordingly, the UN is relied on by them—its policymaking members—to safeguard their interests. Of these, far and away the most fundamental for each state is its continued existence as an internationally sovereign entity. Some of the bigger members may, in the manner of great powers, occasionally adopt a seemingly casual attitude towards the significance of the concept—as it relates, not to themselves, but to some of their weaker brethren! But at bottom their interest in it is no less than that of all the smaller fry. Nothing the United Nations does, therefore, is likely to undermine either the concept of international sovereignty or the sovereign status of any of the individual territorial entities which comprise the organisation. To this general proposition, UN peacekeeping and peace-enforcement do not provide an exception.

17

Reconciling National and International Interests in UN Peacekeeping

Robert C. Johansen

Whenever the United Nations deliberates about authorising peacekeeping or enforcement operations to monitor a ceasefire, resist aggression or halt ethnic cleansing, UN officials and national governments usually face difficulties reconciling the national interests of one or more governments with broader international interests in the maintenance of peace and security. When massacres began to erupt in Rwanda in 1994, for example, the UN *reduced* its peacekeeping personnel in the country because the governments contributing forces did not want their nationals in Rwanda to face hazardous duty, even though a broader humanitarian interest in protecting innocent people seemed to call for expanded international peacekeeping. When President Bill Clinton declared before the UN General Assembly in 1993 that "if the American people are to say yes to UN peacekeeping, the United Nations must know when to say no,"[1] he voiced a desire that the UN should do less peacekeeping because the United States did not want to pay for international peacekeeping that did not serve its national interests, even though other members might believe that UN operations served a larger global interest.

The president's statement illustrates the chronic tension within the United Nations system between serving the good of the whole and the good of the parts. The permanent members' veto power itself is a Charter compromise to reconcile differences between national and global interests, designed to ensure that the Security Council will never attempt to express a global interest that conflicts with the national interest of its permanent members. On

---

1. *New York Times*, 28 September 1993, p. A4.

the one hand, the veto is a reconciling instrument because it prevents the UN Security Council from acting unless all the permanent members agree with the contemplated action. On the other hand, this instrument exacerbates conflicts of interests with other states, since non-permanent members feel the veto compromises their interest in equal rights and their possible desire to have the Security Council act even if not all permanent members agree.

Reconciling national and global interests usually proves difficult for the same classic reasons that an individual's interests may be at odds with the interests of the commonweal, or that a particular will conflicts with the general will. One part of the human species tries to obtain benefits for itself while imposing some of the costs on others. Although the good of one is often advanced at the expense of the many, it is also true that in some cases the good of one cannot be advanced without paying heed to the good of all. That relationship, in which the interests of one are inextricably intertwined with the interests of many, provides the basis for harmonising divergent interests in peacekeeping and enforcement.

The "National Interest"

The discussion in this chapter begins by noting four conceptual problems that often mislead citizens and policymakers in thinking about national interests and UN peace operations (preventive diplomacy, peacekeeping, enforcement, and peace-building). A more direct, precise, and ethically responsible approach, focusing on the values that a nation-state or the world community seeks to implement, is proposed. Discussion then focuses on five guidelines that can be used to reduce conflicts of interests in the realm of peacekeeping and enforcement. These principles emphasise (1) reciprocity as the linchpin in efforts to bring separate interests together in support of peace operations; (2) the need for more equitable representation of all peoples within the UN to expand every nation's sense of ownership in maintaining a peaceful global system; (3) the importance of intense efforts to diffuse conflicts before they erupt into violence that makes subsequent UN enforcement much more difficult; (4) the need to minimise violence when enforcement is required; and (5) the crucial role of raising new revenues to enhance the possibilities for reconciling separate interests and enabling UN forces to have the resources they need to be effective. Before discussing these, we turn first to four conceptual problems in reconciling national and international interests.

The National Interest Is Ambiguous

Although the concept of the national interest is employed frequently by politicians and commentators, its meaning is not self-evident, clear, scientifically determinable or logically deducible in many conflicts. There would be wide agreement that serving national interests includes protecting the territorial integrity and political independence of a state, the economic well-being of its society, and the way of life of its people. But it is seldom clear whether these interests require sending British troops to Bosnia, French forces to Rwanda, U.S. troops to Somalia, Japanese defence forces to the Gulf War or Russian soldiers to Georgia. Even if it were clear that such forces should go to those conflict-ridden areas, it would not be self-evident whether they should go under their own flag or behind the banners of the UN Blue Helmets. And even if such forces have marched to the tune of the UN drummer, it is not clear whether they should fall out of step during field operations in order to obey their own national commanders rather than the UN commanders, as occurred during UN operations in Somalia. Moreover, to step back and look again at the three relatively uncontroversial dimensions of the national interest noted above, even they are far from clear. What does "territorial integrity" mean when some ethnic groups desire separation from an existing territorial unit, or when ethnically antagonistic populations are so intertwined that no one can sort out to whom a piece of land really belongs, or when the land is so resource-rich that others, thousands of miles away, may claim access to those lands, as have U.S. presidents to the oil fields of the Middle East? What does "territorial integrity" mean if the territory is used irresponsibly so that the environment, affecting all people, is irreparably harmed? Does the "integrity" of land belong to the local people who promote a tragedy to the common good, or to all those others who are not local but who want to protect the commons?

Furthermore, consider the meaning of national interests in the realm of economic well-being. Is one country entitled to bolster its economic prosperity at the expense of others or by permitting others to live in poverty, especially if a more equitable sharing of resources today would lead in the longer run to more prosperity for the inhabitants of the one country *and* for the rest of the human species? Finally, in reflecting upon that vague yet politically potent mobilising call to protect the "way of life" of a people, what is that way of life? Is it the right of nearly every U.S. family to own an automobile and every Chinese family to own a bicycle? Does the way of life to be protected include nuclear weapons for the United States and China but not for Pakistan and North Korea? In protecting the "people's way of life," who are the people? In the nuclear-weapons countries, are "the people" the present generation that prepares weapons of mass destruction or the generation only being born that may prefer to avoid nuclear war at all costs?

A thoughtful examination of national interests demonstrates that the

concept of the national interest is superficial at best and positively obfus-
cating and ethically devious at worst. Admittedly, to talk about national
interests does not prevent consideration of any of the questions raised
above, but neither does it encourage rational discourse to explore them, nor
does it openly clarify political priorities and value preferences. The familiar
discourse about national interests incorrectly assumes that those interests are
more clear-cut, more inherent in the nature of things and more scientifically
determinable than they truly are. In examining conflicts between national
interests and global interests in UN peacekeeping, one needs to begin with
an understanding that national interests are vastly more malleable than
commonly assumed—if the vested interests that shape their articulation
would allow or encourage genuinely open conversation about their content.
Because the national interest is so variable and heavily laden with emotional
overtones of patriotism, it is especially problematic as an analytic concept
unless used with great care. In addition to the concept's general ambiguity,
two additional problems illustrate its further deficiencies.

National Interests Are No Longer National

As well as being highly subjective and subject to manipulation by power
elites, the concept of the national interest encourages people to believe that
their interests are genuinely national. In the first place, many people believe
that governmental actions serve all people throughout a national society
when in fact many policies serve the interests of the political and economic
elites who exercise disproportionate power within a society. Even before
looking abroad, therefore, the idea that national policies serve the national
interest, or the interests of all people, may cover up the extent to which
national policies serve some segments of a national society much more
favourably than others. "National interests" in peacekeeping or anything else
usually benefit some nationals more than others.

Secondly, the familiar national interest discourse perpetuates the idea that
national institutions and the nation-state territorial unit are supremely able to
protect and advance citizens' interests. In fact, few if any national governments even control the economic well-being of their own economies,
although of course they can do much to contribute to it. Similarly, no nation
can secure itself by itself against a determined aggressor equipped with
weapons of mass destruction. No national government can protect the
environment. Many services that people expect and require can no longer be
provided by national political units. Many people's interests are shared
between local, national, regional, and global constituencies, even though
admittedly political institutions and educational curricula do not yet reflect
these current realities. Yet to pretend otherwise reflects a self-destructive

mental inertia of a bygone age.[2]

National Interests Are No Longer Short-Term

The ways in which the national interest is frequently employed by political leaders put a disproportionate emphasis on short-term goals. Politicians want to win the next election and are too willing to sacrifice the long-term interests of the nation to do so. For example, five U.S. presidents misperceived U.S. long-term security interests in combating the Vietnamese nationalist political movement headed by Ho Chi Minh. Each thought the national interest dictated a deepening U.S. military involvement in war in Southeast Asia even though the costs of 55 000 U.S. military deaths, hundreds of thousands of Vietnamese deaths, and nearly a trillion dollars (in 1993 dollars) could have been completely saved without sacrificing any U.S. security or well-being.[3] We perceive today that five different administrations gained nothing in return for untold human sacrifice; however, during each day of these administrations, officials chose not to extricate themselves from a useless endeavour because they had been schooled on a concept of national interest—and they taught the same concept to the public in their televised speeches—that emphasised short-term fears of a red flag going up in Saigon rather than long-term, reasoned calculations about how to implement widely accepted values like bringing peace and stability while saving lives and dollars in the process.

International Interests Are Not Cohesively Defined

International interests are also vague and controversial because people have not been accustomed to thinking about them, and few if any institutions seek to synthesise them into a cohesive whole. The United Nations of course is a forum in which national governments articulate their interests, but these are seldom melded into an expression of what would be good for all people. Even the Secretary-General and Secretariat officials often feel they must speak in accord with what the Security Council wants in peacekeeping rather than for what serves the long-term values of human dignity.

---

2. See Lynn Miller, *Global Order: Values and Power in International Politics* (Boulder: Westview, 1994), p. 14.

3. As John Stoessinger put it in his excellent chapter, "A Greek Tragedy in Five Acts: Vietnam": "Essentially, what was achieved in Paris in 1973 [when peace talks finally ended the war] was Vietnam's reversion to its status at the time of the 1954 Geneva Accords [before direct U.S. military involvement]. The United States had come full circle in Vietnam, and the clock was turned back twenty years. There was an Orwellian irony to the situation. Progress was regress: 1954 by 1973." John G. Stoessinger, *Why Nations Go to War* (New York: St. Martin's, 1993), p. 106.

National interests dominate, obscure, and distort UN decisions on peace-keeping and enforcement, often making policies haphazard, piecemeal and incoherent. Frequently the Security Council has passed resolutions express-ing a mandate to move relief convoys along a hazardous road to aid em-battled war victims or to protect a UN-defined safe haven in Bosnia but without supplying commensurate means to carry out the mandate. In another example, the UN established an Observer Mission in Georgia (UNOMIG) but member-states failed to provide the modest total of 100 troops which the Security Council had requested.[4] One might conclude that an articulation of global interests would say: "Stop mass starvation, war, and ethnic cleans-ing;" however, an articulation of national interests seems to say: "Don't ask me or my fellow citizens to feed the hungry, disarm the violent, or stand between the rapist and the victim. No, I can't even pay any more to avert the continuation of such misdeeds."

In Angola, Bosnia, Croatia, Rwanda, Serbia, Somalia, Sudan and else-where over the past two years, the effort to reconcile divergent interests has gone poorly because there has been no coherent synthesis of priorities and strategies, whether articulated from national capitals or from the UN system. Because the international interest in peacekeeping is not cohesively defined and national interests are bound by inertia to emphasise short-term goals and national partisanship, a more coherent expression of peacekeeping needs is required, a short-hand way of referring to concrete value realisation that serves a minimal level of safety and human dignity for all people. A concept of "the human interest" can signify this more fully than the sum of national interests *if* we clearly specify its content, insofar as it is discernible, and suggest processes for its further definition[5] by the preferences of the world's people. It presumably is crystallised and expressed in part in documents like the UN Charter and the Universal Declaration of Human Rights, and to some degree it may be found in a collective reading of voices of UN members in the Security Council and General Assembly. Yet these expressions are themselves not internally consistent nor fully satisfactory.

Harmonising Divergent Interests

To sharpen our understanding of how to harmonise divergent interests that now make peacekeeping and enforcement problematic, it is useful to

---

4. Adam Roberts, "Ethnic Conflict: Threat and Challenge to the UN," in Anthony McDermott, ed., *Ethnic Conflict and International Security* (Oslo: Norsk Utenrikspolitisk Institutt, June 1994), p. 22.

5. This concept was first defined in Robert C. Johansen, *The National Interest and the Human Interest* (Princeton: Princeton University Press, 1980), pp. 19–35.

assess how people at all levels of society, and governments from all national and religious traditions, might articulate the human interest in peace and security. Moving one step further, it is essential to bring different understandings of the human interest together to focus on the development of a single, global strategy of war-prevention or, stated positively, a global strategy of peace. Diverse interests can be mediated more effectively if officials and citizens focus less on their positions and more on how a global strategy of peace can serve common interests of all. It is not sufficient to ask what are a country's interests in Rwanda or Somalia, or even what are the human interests in peacekeeping in those societies. Talk of interests needs to include these questions: What is my global strategy of peace? What are the main elements of this strategy? What interests are served by implementing this strategy of war prevention? How do my interests and strategy differ from or harmonise with your interests and strategy? Although this approach does not ensure agreement between the peoples of the United States and Serbia, it enables reasonable people to move beyond repetition of short-term, parochial national positions to consider the good of all, now and in the future.

By developing a strategy of peace within which to harmonise interests, policymakers and scholars gain the benefit of clarifying specific value priorities and institutionalising preferred values rather than repeating shibboleths about the nation's interests. The norms of peace,[6] which enjoy widespread multilateral support even though their optimal application is seldom clear, provide a better basis for employing effective peacekeeping and enforcement procedures than does a focus on national positions. An emphasis on priorities rather than positions and on international norms rather than national interests helps governments transcend short-term partisan pulls of domestic politics and overcome resistance to making sacrifices for maintaining a peaceful world community. The change of focus itself can help harmonise some conflicting interests.

Institutionalising norms and procedures also aids the process of reconciling divergent interests. UN peacekeeping became far more acceptable and less subject to irreconcilable national interests when its pioneering precedents later became routinised. Using norms as a basis for principled decision-making facilitates people's capacity to transcend political, cultural and religious boundaries.

---

6. I use "norms of peace" to refer collectively to international legal prohibition of crimes against the peace (military aggression), war crimes (violations of the laws governing weapons and warfare), crimes against humanity (acts of genocide), and gross violations of human rights that constitute a threat to the peace or cause scores of civilian deaths (such as ethnic cleansing in Bosnia–Herzegovina or the obstruction of efforts to avert mass starvation in Somalia).

Achieving political feasibility for UN peacekeeping and enforcement can be aided by developing an explicit *global* strategy of war-prevention. If properly launched, this process could enable all actors—individuals, local governments, national governments and of course the Security Council—to focus the debate and articulate their interests. Such a policy-making process is essential to building necessary political support for UN operations because problems arising in UN decision-making have not been limited to straightforward conflicts between national interests and international interests. UN peace operations have also been hampered by conflicts between: one country's national interests and another country's national interests; one vision of the international interest emanating from the UN Secretariat and other visions of the international interest within the Secretariat; different visions of the national interest coming from the defence ministry and the foreign ministry of the same national government; municipal governments and their own national government; and those emphasising short-term interests and others pointing to long-term interests. All of these groups express their own interests that bear on peacekeeping decisions. All should enter the debate on developing a global strategy of peace. The choice at the United Nations is not so much between national and global interests as it is among a complex set of actors advancing different versions of each.

In the remainder of this essay, when referring to the need for reconciling divergent interests, I mean to include not only the equation between a national government's interests and the human interest in peacekeeping. I refer as well to reconciliation of all relevant interests that, if allowed to remain divergent, impede the ability of the Security Council to carry out peacekeeping and enforcement in the human interest. The important point is that UN institutions and separate interests do not in themselves keep the peace. To work well these institutions and member-states need to be animated by a cohesive set of policies within a global strategy of peace.

Reciprocity as the Guiding Principle

Respect for reciprocity is probably the single most helpful guideline for harmonising divergent interests in peacekeeping. It means simply that a government willingly evaluates its own policies by the same standards that it holds for other nations' behaviour. A national government that respects the principle of reciprocity does not insist on a right for itself, nor does it specify a duty for others that it does not accept for itself.[7] Such a govern-

---

7. This principle represents a modest international expression of Immanuel Kant's categorical imperative in which each person should behave in ways that, if everyone else behaved in the same way, would result in his or her own happiness.

ment would not precipitously pull its personnel, serving under UN authorisation, out of Somalia while expecting other countries to carry on. It would not refuse to train and earmark its own nationals for UN duty while expecting others to do precisely that. It would not claim a right to nuclear arsenals or offensive military capabilities that it does not willingly grant to others.

The principle of reciprocity is widely endorsed by people of all nationalities, religions and ideologies. However, there are sharp differences about its application. Nonetheless, it can and should play a central role in devising a new global strategy of peace because it rests on the same foundational pillar that undergirds the Charter's prohibition of the use of force and leads naturally to provisions calling for chapter VII enforcement if the prohibition is violated. The Charter makes clear that no nation is entitled to attack another because each nation is entitled to live in peace and each grants that right reciprocally to all others—whether they are friends or enemies. Since no nation wants to be the target of military aggression, no nation can legitimately act aggressively itself. At the same time, if each nation wants all other nations to uphold its right not to be attacked, then every nation has a reciprocal duty to come to the aid of any victim of aggression by supporting UN peacekeeping and enforcement actions to uphold the norms of peace.

The United States often attempts to provide leadership on UN enforcement actions, yet its role is hampered by problems in harmonising its interests with the human interest because it has been so powerful that it seldom has felt the need to reflect on the principle of reciprocity. Washington has refused to train and earmark any special forces for peacekeeping activity, in part because it is reluctant to strengthen UN enforcement and to place its own nationals under UN commanders. Senate Republican Leader Bob Dole, for example, has introduced legislation to prohibit U.S. troops from serving under "foreign command" in UN operations because "our military personnel should be asked to risk their lives only in support of U.S. interests, in operations led by U.S. commanders."[8] If every country operated with reciprocal expectations and in accord with the conditions that Senator Dole seeks to make legally binding on the United States, there would be no UN peacekeepers and no prospect for addressing the long-term security needs of the United States within the world community.

Those who argue against placing U.S. forces under UN command on the grounds that U.S. forces should serve U.S. interests would, if they honed their sensitivity to reciprocity, become aware of the lack of logic in assuming that U.S. interests are not served by UN operations. They ignore that no UN peacekeeping operations have ever been conducted without explicit

---

8. Bob Dole, "Peacekeepers and Politics," *New York Times*, 24 January, 1994, p. A15.

U.S. endorsement, and that the United States has a long-term interest in UN peace operations and in delegitimising the national use of force throughout the world. Even more serious, in asserting a sharp divergence between U.S. interests and the interests of the UN in peacekeeping and enforcement, with a clear preference for the former, they destroy the symbolic transformation needed to turn a nationally partisan combat situation into a nonpartisan UN enforcement operation.

A thoughtful look at one's own national behaviour in the light of sensitivity to reciprocity helps reconcile divergent interests because that examination provides a guide to understanding others' interests more honestly as well. Consciousness of equal rights and duties draws attention to common ground in peacekeeping and common interests in enforcement. It reminds a government that, because it wants other states to honour the norms of peace and obey customary international law, it should abide by the same norms and enforce the law when it is broken.

One of many possible institutional initiatives suggested by this principle is to expand the role of international legal settlement because it is a peaceful instrument, known in all national societies, for adjusting conflicts of interests and adjudicating competing claims without the use of force by drawing on principles of equity and reciprocity. To institutionalise an expanding role for legal settlement would help reconcile national and global interests because it sets standards for behaviour that transcend separate territories and the temptations of political opportunism at particular moments in time. The Security Council should develop a strong set of political and economic incentives to induce countries to accept without reservation the general compulsory jurisdiction of the International Court of Justice (ICJ) under Article 36 of its Statute. Shridath Ramphal has even suggested that acceptance of compulsory jurisdiction of the ICJ should be a requirement for UN membership.[9] The World Court could play a much larger role, for example, in determining how a dispute should be settled or when a government has violated the norms against aggression. Toward this end, the Security Council, already authorised by the Charter's sweeping but seldom utilised provisions for maintaining peace (Articles 41 and 42), could declare that a state's refusal to submit a dispute to the World Court constitutes a threat to the peace. Any threat to international peace authorises the Council to take whatever legally binding action it chooses to nullify the threat.

Although it may seem difficult to gain agreement on such action, it is far more likely that diverse interests can come together around this non-military idea than on the idea of using chapter VII military enforcement or war to

---

9. Shridath Ramphal, "Global Governance in the Global Neighborhood," *Waging Peace Series* No. 35 (Santa Barbara: Nuclear Age Peace Foundation, June 1994), p. 15.

settle disputes. If a dispute threatens war because of a failure to settle the dispute through legal means, the Council should use the Charter authorisation for drawing upon its legal enforcement powers to ensure compliance with a Court decision (Article 94.2). To activate such a legally binding procedure for non-military dispute settlement, the world's peoples simply need to insist that their governments implement the procedures to which they already have agreed.

A related, under-utilised instrument for harmonising interests behind a strategy of peace is to hold individuals—heads of government, military commanders, ordinary soldiers or civilians—accountable to international law that prohibits war crimes. Although difficult to carry out, practical steps towards that end are essential if the prospects for reconciling divergent interests are to enable effective international enforcement.[10] Since enforcement will seldom involve cases as clear-cut as the UN's action against Iraq's annexation of Kuwait, and because military combat under UN auspices is likely to be highly controversial, it has low utility as an instrument of enforcement. Indeed, the UN can hardly enforce law on an entire society through physical force without incurring excessive costs in violence and moral legitimacy. However, the UN can begin to enforce the norms of peace on law-breaking *individuals* without using massive violence and with moral integrity.

Theodor Meron has demonstrated that multilateral efforts to initiate proceedings for prosecuting war crimes can build consensus on deterring atrocities, even though at first individual convictions may be infrequent because of an inability to apprehend those accused of crimes.[11] Some evidence suggests that the failure to prosecute genocidal killings in Rwanda from 1990 to 1993 encouraged the massive bloodletting in 1994.[12] If the world community seriously prepared to hold both officials and ordinary citizens personally accountable for planning or carrying out war crimes, knowledge of this could deter crimes against the peace, ethnic cleansing and rape.[13] Even the knowledge that persons accused of crimes may be required

---

10. See Robert C. Johansen, "Toward a New Code of International Conduct: War, Peacekeeping, and Global Constitutionalism," in Richard A. Falk, Robert C. Johansen, and Samuel S. Kim, eds., *The Constitutional Foundations of World Peace* (Albany: State University of New York Press, 1993), pp. 48–50.

11. Theodor Meron, "The Case for War Crimes Trials in Yugoslavia," *Foreign Affairs* 72 (Spring 1993), 122–35.

12. Wilson Rutayisire, a Rwandan official, reported that timely convictions are the only way to halt a recurring cycle of violence. "The impunity that the killers enjoyed [in previous years] fueled the genocide more than any ethnic hatred." Quoted by Andrew Jay Cohen, "On the Trail of Genocide," *New York Times*, 7 September 1994, p. A17.

13. The prospect of war crimes trials in the former Yugoslavia had little deterring effect because there had not been sufficient historical precedents of impartial prosecutions by the

to answer embarrassing questions years later would encourage people to put emotionally-driven hostilities in a long-term framework—itself a healthy antidote to violent excess.

The creation of a permanent international criminal court would strengthen the prospects for implementing the human interest in a strategy of war-prevention because it could establish an impartial reputation and context in which war crimes proceedings could occur—essential qualities for upholding reciprocity. One of the most frequent objections to the Nuremburg and Tokyo War Crimes Tribunals and to implementing those precedents today is that these were examples of victors' justice imposed on the vanquished alone. A permanent international criminal court could help overcome that objection by trying indicted people of any nationality before a panel of judges representing all regions of the world. This would help reconcile interests that now seem unsupportive of serious efforts to hold individuals accountable to law. In Rwanda the failure to hold prompt trials was not, as is often the problem, due to the accused being unavailable for trial and shielded by a sympathetic government. Many of the accused were abroad in Zaire, Tanzania and the West.[14] The problem was that governments, lacking a global strategy of peace, have failed to enforce the law even when they could. In Bosnia, a new wave of ethnic cleansing in the summer of 1994 was observed repeatedly by officials of both the United Nations and the International Red Cross, so credible evidence for deterring future crimes has been available[15] but has not been well used. If serious plans were laid now to prosecute war criminals, international consensus could be built to the point that commanders or soldiers in the field in the future would not want to risk being identified or captured in a conflict with UN forces. To strengthen enforcement, people everywhere should ask governments on the Security Council to impose sanctions on any government that refuses to extradite for a fair international trial any of its nationals who have been indicted for war crimes.

A polarising, divisive problem in UN discussions has been controversy over how to employ force in Somalia and Bosnia when UN peacekeepers have been deliberately attacked by hostile forces. These controversies and related battlefield deaths in Somalia led directly to an erosion of U.S.

---

international community; citizens and soldiers were not convinced in advance that their behavior could be on trial. Moreover, many people in Bosnia and even at the United Nations did not believe that UN efforts in this domain would result in convictions.

14. Cohen, "On the Trail of Genocide," p. A17.

15. Chuck Sudetic, "In New Campaign, Bosnian Serbs Oust 2,000 Muslims From Homes," *New York Times*, 30 August 1994, p. A1.

support for all peacekeeping and enforcement. Such divisiveness could be reduced in the future by employing the principle, established at Nuremburg, that defendants accused of war crimes cannot use as a justifiable defence the claim that they were obeying orders from superiors. Extending this logic to the protection of UN operations undertaken to oppose crimes against the peace, any person violently opposing UN forces should be charged with crimes against the peace. The world community should insist upon extradition of government officials, who claim, as have Bosnian Serb leaders, that they reserve "the right to retaliate against United Nations peacekeeping troops...."[16] The Security Council could help reconcile conflicts of interests over authorising future peacekeeping if it clearly established that any violent act against any UN peacekeeper is *prima facie* evidence of a crime against the peace. Although some governmental elites may be unenthusiastic about holding states and individuals accountable to law, it seems likely that wide support would exist for this idea among most people in most societies on earth. Thus a reconciling definition of the human interest should include efforts to increase the role of international law and to prosecute war crimes wherever possible.

In sum, the principle of reciprocity can encourage people to broaden their focus to include other societies as equals in setting priorities in a strategy of peace. It encourages them to respect the norms of peace themselves and to help enforce them when violated. It encourages adjudicating disputes through legal means and holding all accountable to internationally established norms.

Representing All Societies Fairly

Nothing can do more to reconcile those national officials who feel unreconciled to supporting UN enforcement than to ensure that they are fairly represented in political processes that decide peacekeeping and enforcement questions. The greater the measure of congruence between the power exercised by the Security Council and the authority that can be credibly claimed by its representational scheme, the more people everywhere will be inclined to regard the resulting Council action as legitimate. On the other hand, because some countries feel that their interests are not fairly represented in the existing UN system, they do not feel they have a stake in maintaining stability or in contributing to the UN on behalf of international stability. Yet with fair representation such societies could more readily be brought to support a global strategy of peace because the long-term interests

---

16. Roger Cohen, "NATO Planes Bomb Serbians Near Sarajevo," *New York Times*, 23 September, 1994, p. A1.

of most people are served by honouring the norms of peace and conserving resources and lives.

Fair representation in UN decision-making structures would encourage an open focus on the interdependence of interests and peoples. Knowledge of interdependence in turn provides a solid basis for reconciliation of conflicting interests. Every country's legitimate national interests can be served by more effective multilateral peacekeeping institutions because, as Joseph Nye has pointed out, such institutions help share the burdens of global policing, increase the legitimacy of such policing, and constrain negative behaviour while motivating positive policies by other countries.[17]

To reconcile divergent interests on peacekeeping, UN agencies must maintain high legitimacy and wide support. Achieving these conditions requires representative decision-making procedures in major organs like the Security Council as well as in less visible committees and Secretariat structures. Perhaps the most important step that can be taken to increase support for a strategy of peace is to make the Security Council more representative so that its membership reflects current political and economic realities. Otherwise it will be seen as an agent of the great military powers and more particularly of the United States. This will render it increasingly useless as an agency to maximise enforcement strength with a minimum of violence. In reflecting the power of the allies that defeated Germany and Japan in 1945 when the UN was founded, the Council does not adequately represent peoples of the then-colonised Third World nor the Germans and Japanese. In the long run a Council that is not representative will be unable to promote genuine reconciliation of divergent interests as required to nurture a strategy of peace. The democratic defects of the Council can be addressed by slightly expanding the Security Council to reflect current political and economic realities, by reorienting considerations in selecting members and by diminishing the role of the veto power exercised by the permanent members.

Representation aimed at fairness and reconciliation of divergent interests should not be tied to assumptions about a government's willingness to project military power around the world. Japan has been impeded from becoming a permanent member by the widespread belief that it has not been entitled to a such status because, constrained by the anti-militaristic Article 9 of its constitution, it does not aspire to sending military forces to UN enforcement operations. Rather than view these provisions as a problem for Japanese status as a permanent member, they could be seen as an example towards which other governments might aspire. To have the world's largest source of investment capital and second-ranking economic power renounce

---

17. Joseph Nye, "What New World Order?" *Foreign Affairs* 71 (Spring 1992), pp. 83–96.

war forever is an attractive precedent for a new strategy of peace.

An optimal strategy for reconciling divergent interests over peacekeeping and enforcement should not encourage the idea that UN members cannot gain full status or permanent membership on the Council unless they prepare to project their armed forces beyond their shores. Such a suggestion encourages states to compete in developing military muscle as an admission ticket to the Council, for permanent as well as non-permanent membership, and sets a poor example for others.[18] Instead, states not wishing to send military forces beyond their shores can contribute to UN peacekeeping through other means. If the world is to demilitarise, it is wise to integrate fully into the representational scheme those who are themselves less militarised.

As a further representational step towards reconciling divergent interests, the veto power now exercised by permanent members should be qualified so that the geostrategic interests of one member cannot dictate to the rest of the world community. Still, it would be unrealistic to think that the Security Council could perform its functions well against the intense opposition of one of the world's most powerful countries. As a way of beginning to move away from the clearly unacceptable possibility that a permanent member could use its veto power to act as the judge in its own case, it would be wise to aim at requiring two negative votes from permanent members, rather than simply one, to block an action that more than two-thirds of the other Security Council members favour. In the long run, it may even make sense to implement the suggestion that the veto be abolished and enforcement decisions be authorised by a three-fourths vote.[19]

Minimising the Need for Heavy-Handed UN Enforcement

Reconciliation of divergent interests on peacekeeping issues usually becomes more difficult as the hazards of peacekeeping and enforcement increase. As a general rule, the instrument of preventive diplomacy harmonises opposing interests more readily than the instrument of peacekeeping, and peacekeeping harmonises more readily than enforcement. When enforcement must occur, economic sanctions as a coercive instrument more easily attracts common support than military combat. As a half dozen recent cases of UN intervention demonstrate, whenever hazards and

---

18. In addition, to encourage the extension of Japanese military power unnecessarily exacerbates conflicts with the people of most Asian states who have raised strong objections to Japan sending armed forces abroad. See Nayan Chanda, "Why They Worry: Asian Neighbours Fear Military Revival," *Far Eastern Economic Review*, 25 June 1992, p. 18.

19. See Peter Wallensteen, "Representing the World: A Security Council for the 21st Century," *Security Dialogue* 25 (March 1994), pp. 63–75.

destructiveness increase, political support begins to erode and divergent voices become louder and more divisive. The Gulf War against Iraq suggests that the longer collective violence lasts and the more destructive it becomes, the greater the likelihood that the problems of national partisanship will increase. Violence complicates, divides and polarises UN processes, even against a clear-cut aggressor. UN members should be willing to pay a high price to enable peace-building and preventive diplomacy to succeed in order to avoid the dissonance that accompanies the use of combat. Because it is usually easier to defuse conflicts by preventing violence from erupting than to stop it once blood has been shed, an effective, consensus-building strategy of peace should focus on doing all that is possible to eliminate conditions that give rise to violence and to develop a culture of enforcement that will avoid military combat to the greatest possible extent.

Thus to promote a strategy of peace that can harmonise diverse interests, the Security Council should treat preventive diplomacy far more seriously. To enable the Security Council to become an effective world crisis management centre, it and the Secretary-General should strengthen their communication and negotiation capabilities; develop an extensive early-warning system; employ more roving ambassadors to meet with those involved in festering conflicts; establish standing conflict resolution committees in each major region of the world; and establish and utilise a UN institute for mediation and dispute resolution.[20] The UN should also establish an international monitoring agency to integrate diverse monitoring functions and attempt to bring together the weight of the entire world community behind verification efforts to ensure compliance with the norms of peace, World Court decisions and Security Council actions rendered to settle disputes, future arms constraints, environmental standards and other rules as these are established. It also could utilise surveillance by high altitude aircraft, satellites and other means. Such an agency could help resolve questions of fact that divide adversaries and that national intelligence services by themselves are incapable of resolving to the satisfaction of all parties.

Just as intense preventive diplomacy can defuse conflicts before they become violent and more divisive, an extensive peace-building programme can also alleviate many of the conditions that give rise to violence and often polarise the UN community. An engaging strategy of peace should provide economic benefits for governments attempting to lower their military spending and demilitarise their societies, initiate equitable economic integration programmes as conflict-dampening instruments poised against both intra-state and inter-state violence, and nurture democratic institutions because

---

20. See Dietrich Fischer, *Nonmilitary Aspects of Security: A Systems Approach* (Geneva: United Nations Institute for Disarmament Research, 1993), pp. 172–73.

these are less likely to launch aggressive wars against other democracies. Such measures can exert a positive integrative influence on conflicting parties, as demonstrated by the success of the economic cooperation in Europe after World War II that gradually laid to rest long-standing Franco-German bellicosity. All UN agencies and national governments should be encouraged to conduct research, planning, and expenditures that will nurture cross-cultural forms of economic and social integration that undergird a strategy of peace.[21]

Minimising Violence When UN Enforcement Is Needed

When peacekeeping or enforcement operations are authorised by the Security Council, it is important to minimise the violence to be employed in order to maintain as much political support among the UN's constituents as possible. Such a strategy would of course undertake diplomatic and economic sanctions as the first line of coercion. Critics of economic sanctions have noted that they do not produce rapid results and may inflict suffering on innocent people who already have been victimised by their own governments. These valid criticisms of economic sanctions do not, however, warrant the conclusion that their potential has been fully exploited. And their capacity to attract much wider UN support than can military action means that new efforts should be made to increase their effectiveness.

Although they cannot be used successfully in every case, sanctions can be made more effective by focusing their impact on elites rather than on entire populations, applying them more strictly and universally and utilising a longer-term strategy. Rather than assume that economic sanctions should attempt to impose heavy costs quickly on an entire society, they may more effectively influence behaviour if they seriously inconvenience only a relatively small elite, but are capable of doing so over a long time.[22] Such an approach can avoid severely negative consequences for an entire population and the "rally-round-the-flag" reaction that increases rather than decreases domestic support for an outlaw government and produces a backlash against UN operations. UN sanctions against South African apartheid illustrate their capacity to remind people in the targeted country as well as elsewhere that

---

21. For a sketch of a global peacemaking economy, see Lloyd J. Dumas, "Economics and Alternative Security: Toward a Peacekeeping International Economy," in Burns H. Weston, ed., *Alternative Security: Living Without Nuclear Deterrence* (Boulder: Westview, 1990), pp. 137–75.

22. For a discussion of the determinants of success see United States General Accounting Office, *Economic Sanctions: Effectiveness as Tools of Foreign Policy*, Report to the Chairman, U.S. Senate, Committee on Foreign Relations, GAO/NSIAD-92-106, (Washington D.C.: General Accounting Office, 1992).

gross violations of the norms of peace will not be accepted.[23]

To make economic sanctions more effective the Security Council should lay plans to train special UN forces especially for enforcing economic sanctions and establish a UN coastguard and aerial surveillance to help in this process. Moreover, the Security Council should establish advance procedures for bringing economic sanctions, if necessary, against any third parties who may be tempted not to honour UN-mandated sanctions against a target government.

If economic sanctions do not seem applicable and the Security Council deploys the Blue Helmets for peacekeeping or enforcement measures, the world community needs the best prepared, most reliable and clearly impartial forces that it can muster in order to achieve the widest possible political support. To build support among divergent national interests for the more complicated UN operations that will be needed in the future, the Security Council should establish a permanent, individually recruited UN police force.[24] Such a force could help overcome problems such as: (1) delays that occur in forming and deploying *ad hoc* forces, (2) fears of some national governments that *ad hoc* UN forces will not be impartial or effective, (3) difficulties in recruiting and deploying *ad hoc* forces for hazardous duty and (4) failures of command and control that arise when attempting to coordinate nationally diverse contingents under a unified UN command. These problems arise from or exacerbate conflicting expressions of national interests by UN members. In contrast, a permanent force could better harmonise national divergencies.

An individually recruited, permanent force, drawn from volunteers among many countries rather than from contingents sent by diverse national military forces, could be deployed quickly, even at a time when short-term interests made many UN members lukewarm towards sending their own armed forces. Better training could relieve fears of partiality or ineffective-

---

23. Even in the small, poor country of Haiti, economic sanctions were not in the main employed in ways designed to maximise their impact on the elite and minimise their hardship for the general population. As the editors of the *New York Times* put it only four months before the U.S. military forces occupied Haiti, "Real sanctions have never been given a chance"; 9 May 1994, p. A10. Similarly, UN economic sanctions against the Serbs were not strictly enforced, even as debates raged about using air strikes against Serbia.

24. For early discussion of a permanent force see Robert C. Johansen and Saul H. Mendlovitz, "The Role of Enforcement of Law in the Establishment of a New International Order: A Proposal for a Transnational Police Force," *Alternatives: A Journal of World Policy* 6 (1980), pp. 307–38; Robert C. Johansen, *Toward An Alternative Security System: Moving From the Balance of Power to World Security* (New York: World Policy Institute, 1983), pp. 26–46; and Robert C. Johansen, "The Reagan Administration and the UN: The Costs of Unilateralism," *World Policy Journal* 3 (Fall 1986), pp. 630–32. More recently Brian Urquhart has given the idea its first prominent attention in "For a UN Volunteer Military Force," *New York Review of Books* 40 (10 June 1993), pp. 3–4.

ness. Violence might be held to a lower level because more rapid deployment might nip a potential war in the bud and because more abundant peacekeeping forces and more effective command and control could enable the forces to function more like a police force than an army while conducting law enforcement in failed states.[25] Preventive deployments, such as might have helped deter the Iraqi invasion of Kuwait in 1990, could more readily occur. It seems likely that if a permanent UN force had been available when massacres began in Rwanda in April 1994, rapid deployment of such a force could probably have saved tens of thousands of lives by protecting safe havens to which multitudes might have fled until the fighting ceased. Equally important, the Security Council probably would have more readily authorised UN action with such a force in being. A permanent UN force could not only be deployed more readily and rationally, but also with the ability to remain in place until it was no longer needed.

Direct recruitment of UN forces from among individual volunteers drawn from many countries would enable personnel burdens to be shared more fairly than at present and thereby ease some current conflicts of interests over UN peacekeeping. Individual Japanese and German citizens, for example, could serve in UN forces without wrenching political battles at home or revising existing policies. Moreover, those peoples who have suffered from German and Japanese militarism in the past would not fear individuals recruited from those countries if they were integrated into units trained and commanded by the UN. Individual recruitment might also enable U.S. citizens to serve under UN command, a condition that Congress and existing public opinion have been reluctant to allow. U.S. citizens could have volunteered to help defend safe-havens in Bosnia or Rwanda in 1993–94, for example, even though those assignments were considered too dangerous for regular units of the U.S. armed forces to accept as long as the goal was "merely" to protect innocent civilians rather than to serve more narrowly defined U.S. national interests.

To have personnel of many nationalities working effectively side by side, regardless of their homelands' animosities, would dramatically symbolise the ability of the world community to pull together to enforce norms established by the entire community without prejudice to any nationality. This is a profoundly important perception to cultivate in reconciling diverse national

---

25. To illustrate, the UN report on the failures of the United Nations Operation in Somalia (UNOSOM) concluded that the force lacked expertise, training, and "the Force Commander of UNOSOM II was not in effective control of several national contingents which, in varying degrees, persisted in seeking orders from their home authorities before executing orders of the Forces Command." *Report of the Commission of Inquiry Established Pursuant to Security Council Resolution 885 To Investigate Armed Attacks on UNOSOM II Personnel Which Led to Casualties Among Them* (New York: United Nations, 24 February 1994), pp. 38–39.

interests with the human interest, because a UN member's fears that the UN may not fairly serve *its* particular interests probably constitutes the primary reason that members refuse to empower the Security Council to carry out peacekeeping more effectively. To help overcome this fear, an individually recruited, permanent multinational force can be a potent teacher about the possibilities for implementing a strategy of peace.

Because a permanent UN force would be more thoroughly integrated and efficient, more readily available, less subject to charges of unreliability and partisanship, and better able to build useful experience and precedents over time, it is an important next step in domesticating the international system. Such a force would help set the institutional stage for educating people and governments about the possibilities for gradually and reliably curtailing national uses of military power by impartially enforcing key rules against armament and aggression.

Even if and when a transition is underway towards a permanent UN force, contingencies may arise in which the Security Council will feel a need to employ collective security of a more traditional military variety. Because a collective UN response is often more likely to find wide support than national or bloc military actions in such cases, UN members should respond favourably to the Secretary-General's request that governments fulfil the provision of Article 43 calling upon members to conclude special agreements to "make available to the Security Council" armed forces and other forms of assistance to help in maintaining peace and security. In particular, Boutros-Ghali called upon countries to train earmarked units of their armed forces to be on call for UN service within 24 hours.[26] A favourable response by influential members to their request would demonstrate seriousness in reconciling divergent interests behind a strategy of peace.

This guideline emphasises the importance of demilitarising and domesticating world society rather than militarising the UN, not only because that emphasis is ethically desirable but also because it is likely to be politically prudent. To illustrate how this might be done, the Military Staff Committee, which has never functioned effectively, could be revived with an expanded, more representative membership and new mandate.[27] As the Security Council prepares to democratise its membership and increase its enforcement roles, it should establish guidelines to begin a global demilitarising process, to use economic sanctions more pointedly and to employ enforcement personnel in a more principled way. Such guidelines could be

---

26. Boutros Boutros-Ghali, *An Agenda for Peace: Preventive Diplomacy, Peacemaking and Peace-keeping* (New York: United Nations, 1992), paras. 42–45.

27. No Charter revisions would be needed because the Charter allows the Security Council to invite any members whose participation is useful to its purposes.

developed by the Military Staff Committee and would help prevent the abuse of power by national officials pursuing their own goals within a UN operation. In addition, wise guidelines would encourage the broad political support required not only for an initial UN decision to use its forces, but also for their continuing successful operation. The Military Staff Committee could begin by carrying out a Charter-mandated function that the Security Council has never exercised: to make recommendations for "the regulation of armaments, and possible disarmament" (Article 47).

Demonstrating Serious Commitment to a Strategy of Peace

Divergent interests will be more easily reconciled around a strategy of peace if governments begin to sense that other influential governments take the idea seriously. International agendas of the officials who rule the world are set in part by what they think a handful of other influential officials think is important to do. If leaders talk about UN mandates for enforcement but no money is appropriated to make it happen, everyone will know that nothing serious is underway. On the other hand, if finding a new source of financing for all peace operations is taken to be absolutely essential to strengthening UN effectiveness, establishing unquestioned seriousness of long-term purpose and exerting necessary influence with UN members, then the world will change. Leaders would then lay the foundation for the support required for effective peacekeeping and enforcement.

Putting its peace operations on a solid financial footing should be considered one of the first and most important pillars in the Security Council's strategy of peace. A promising method for financing peace operations would be to impose a tax on the $900bn worth of international currency exchanges that occur each day throughout the world.[28] Every transaction is already recorded and a small deduction from each would be easy to collect through the computer systems that now monitor each trade. Unlike other suggestions for international revenue raising, this proposal is based on banks that already are regulated. Equally important, the tax would not be regressive or burdensome for those affected by it. Such a tax would be fair because revenues would be drawn proportionally from the role that each currency plays in the world economy. No centre of trade would enjoy a competitive advantage. A tax of only 0.01 percent would produce approximately $28bn annually to finance UN peacekeeping and enforcement and to assist in preventive diplomacy and peace-building operations.

At a time when the UN is insolvent and yet has been asked to carry

---

28. Martin Walker proposed this idea in "Global Taxation: Paying for Peace," *World Policy Journal* 10 (Summer 1993), pp. 7–12.

additional responsibilities, those countries that do not pay their dues, yet have the ability to do so, promote dissension in the world community and communicate an infectious lack of seriousness about supporting a strategy of peace. They deny reciprocal duties and break the law, because their financial obligations to the UN budget are legally binding. The United States, the biggest offender, and Russia together have accounted for 75 percent of the unpaid regular and peacekeeping dues. Vigorous new leadership from them and other members of the Security Council could transform the climate for UN enforcement.

Conclusion

In summary, a continuation of present policies and attitudes towards UN peacekeeping and enforcement will not provide effective enforcement or minimise collective violence in addressing foreseeable security problems. The present focus on advancing separate national interests in a UN enforcement context will continue to obscure common interests, undermine the norms of peace and cause a deepening sense that the United Nations is failing. On the other hand, working to define the human interest in a single, global strategy of peace can help harmonise divergent interests and probably enable future UN enforcement to save thousands of lives and avert many politically violent conflicts. To move in this direction, the Security Council or a summit meeting of world leaders should discuss and launch a global strategy of war prevention. This process should be informed by five guiding principles. A new and visible respect for reciprocal rights and duties should undergird the effort to harmonise divergent interests of nations and expand the role of law in holding states and individuals accountable. By representing all societies more fairly in UN organs and offices, more countries will feel a deeper sense of commitment to the norms of peace and to efforts to uphold them. A wide circle of deep support for a strategy of peace, including new efforts at preventive diplomacy and peace-building, would minimise the need for heavy-handed UN enforcement. In those remaining cases when coercive enforcement becomes necessary, an agreed-upon strategy of peace can minimise violence during enforcement. For all of this to happen, influential leaders need to put their weight behind a demonstration of serious commitment to developing a strategy of peace by placing peacekeeping on a firm, globally integrating, financial basis. To serve the human interest in implementing a global strategy of peace for today's turbulent world is the highest security calling of all national interests.

About the Book

In this distinctive book, an international cast of contributors combines case studies and analytical approaches to explore—both critically and sympathetically—the landscape of UN peacekeeping efforts in the 1990s. Setting the stage with a discussion of the rapidly changing nature of peacekeeping, the contributors provide a comprehensive group of case studies that examines all UN operations in the 1990s.

Analysing the larger issues thrown up by these case studies, the contributors look at UN peacekeeping from a regular state-participant's point of view and assess the relationship between regional organisations and the United Nations in peacekeeping missions. In addition, they examine organisational problems at UN headquarters in New York and discuss problems of command and control in the field. After exploring the difficulties of peacekeeping in civil wars, the relationship between peacekeeping and peacemaking and the tensions created in moves towards peace-enforcement, the contributors conclude by considering the vexing issues of national sovereignty, national interests, and international interests.

Index